Zeami's Style

Zeami's Style

The Noh Plays of Zeami Motokiyo

Thomas Blenman Hare

Stanford University Press

Stanford, California

STANFORD UNIVERSITY PRESS
Stanford, California

© 1986 by the Board of Trustees of the
Leland Stanford Junior University
Printed in the United States of America

CIP data appear at the end of the book

Original printing 1986
Last figure below indicates year of this printing:
04   03   02   01   00   99   98   97   96   95

Stanford University Press publications are distrib-
uted exclusively by Stanford University Press within
the United States, Canada, Mexico, and Central
America; they are distributed exclusively by
Cambridge University Press throughout
the rest of the world.

For
Linda, Jim, Laurie
and my parents

Acknowledgments

It has been a long-lasting pleasure to research and write this book, and I owe a great debt of gratitude to many individuals and institutions for their encouragement and support. The Japan Foundation, the Joint Committee on Japanese Studies of the Social Science Research Council and the American Council of Learned Societies, and the Horace H. Rackham School of Graduate Studies at the University of Michigan provided generous support for my initial research in Japan and the United States, as well as for the writing of the first version of the manuscript.

I was most fortunate to be able to attend classes at the Tokyo University of Fine Arts in 1978 and 1979 to gain background in the performance practice of noh. Yokomichi Mario's lectures and seminars were indispensable for an understanding of historical performance practice and his hands-on approach to the overall musical structure of noh provided me an exhilarating taste of the complexity and artistry of the classic theater. Fujita Daigorō gave me a patient and careful introduction to the music of the noh flute, and Yasufuku Tatsuo kindly guided me through several introductory pieces for the *ōtsuzumi*. Nomura Shirō of the Kanze school spent many long hours with me, explaining the complexities of noh singing and dancing as well as more abstract concerns in acting. His performances of several of the plays I studied provided irresistible encouragement at times when the pleasures of libraries and texts and typewriters had begun to cloy. Kikkawa Eishi always had a kind word as I proceeded with my work in Japan. The students of the "*Sarugaku dangi o yomu kai*" in Tokyo gave me a warm welcome, some solid advice and instruction, and the delightful opportunity to discuss Zeami with them over beer and *yakitori*.

As I was beginning to work on Zeami, I studied under Robert H. Brower of the University of Michigan. The high standard of his own scholarship and the depth of his knowledge of classical Japanese poetry and poetics have been a constant inspiration. This project would hardly have been started, much less completed, without his guidance. William Malm encouraged me to pursue the actual performance practice of noh, echoing Professor Yokomichi across the Pacific, and his engagement in Nagauta provided me an invaluable model. Shuen-fu Lin and Robert Danly read an early version of the manuscript and gave me numerous valuable suggestions.

Susan Matisoff of Stanford University graciously consented to read an intermediate version of the manuscript, and her many concise and thoughtful comments gave me a new perspective on material that had begun to take on a deceptive familiarity. Karen Brazell of Cornell University had incisive suggestions regarding matters ranging from musical theory to bibliography, and Mae Smethurst looked at part of the manuscript from the viewpoint of comparative drama; her insights were fresh and stimulating. Rick Emmert of Musashino Women's College helped me locate certain important documents. An anonymous reader for Stanford University Press was most generous in evaluating the manuscript and made several new and useful suggestions as well.

J. G. Bell, Helen Tartar, and especially Barbara Mnookin of Stanford University Press have been of great assistance, leading me through the publishing process and suggesting solutions for many of the awkward problems a book like this poses.

I am indebted to the Noh Theater Research Institute, Hōsei University, for providing prints of Zeami's sketches for plays in the Aged, Woman's, and Martial Modes; and to Musashino Women's College for permitting me to use photographs of scenes from *Takasago*, *Izutsu*, and *Tadanori*.

Finally, I would like to express my gratitude to Kathryn Kawakami, who helped me take my first steps in Japanese, and to thank my wife, Anne, for her patience and support.

T.B.H.

Contents

Figures and Tables

xi

Zeami's Style

Introduction

There is a crater on Mercury named after Zeami Motokiyo. It is one of 135 that were named for great artists from all over the world at a 1976 convention of astronomers. Among the other artists so honored are Murasaki Shikibu, Andō Hiroshige, Tawaraya Sōtatsu, Ki no Tsurayuki, Kakinomoto no Hitomaro, and Sei Shōnagon. But this is only the Japanese delegation to a celestial arts conference at which Bach, Beethoven, Homer, Chopin, Renoir, Goya, and many other geniuses are also eternally present. It is delightful that the foremost artist of the noh theater should be recognized in this way, and one imagines Zeami must be at home among the other artists there in the night sky; yet I would be willing to bet that even among the Japanese Chopin and Renoir are better known than he is. In the West, the names of Hiroshige and Murasaki would certainly meet with more nods of recognition than Zeami's.

This should be no surprise. The work of a Renoir or a Hiroshige is almost immediately accessible. And anyone with a record player and a willing ear can come to know the sad eloquence of Chopin's music. Murasaki, though hardly very "accessible" in the original Japanese, met with a fine translator early in this century and had the enthusiastic recommendation of Virginia Woolf to help gain her a readership. But Zeami? Excellent translations of his works have appeared in English and other Western languages, and careful Japanese scholarship has produced a daunting number of studies relating to him. All the same, he remains a fairly obscure figure. We who live in the West have almost no access to performances of noh (especially Zeami's noh), and no matter how fine a translation may be, it can offer only a flat silhouette of the full experience of noh. In Japan, one has countless opportunities to see Zeami's plays performed, but relatively few to see them performed well. Moreover, scholarly interest there has been heavily weighted toward Zeami's theoretical works. Even today, there is no book-length study of Zeami the playwright.

I have hoped, therefore, to take some preliminary steps toward remedying this situation in the present volume. The title I have chosen, *Zea-*

mi's Style, is a bit grandiose, and the reader who expects to find here an exhaustive stylistic analysis of Zeami's plays will be disappointed. I retain the title, nevertheless, in order to focus attention on an issue that has been insufficiently addressed in noh scholarship: what characteristics distinguish Zeami from his fellow playwrights? I contend that the literary and, in so much as it is possible, musical analysis of plays confidently attributable to him can provide us a sense of his artistic identity, his style.

The study is divided into six parts. Chapters One and Two serve as a kind of introduction. I have begun with a biography based on the known documents relating to Zeami's life. Then I have set about examining the documentary evidence for authorship and explaining the various technical aspects of noh. Chapter Three takes as its subject Zeami's use of the role of the old man in noh, with particular attention to his play *Takasago*.* The plays for this role exhibit a kind of formal orthodoxy that makes them indispensable for an understanding of noh structure, so much of the information in this chapter applies to Chapters Four and Five as well. Those chapters examine Zeami's plays about women and warriors, respectively, with primary attention to *Izutsu* (The Well Curb) and *Tadanori*. The book concludes with a general discussion of Zeami's style and the relationship between his dramatic theory and his plays.

Because Zeami prepared his treatises for noh professionals, he spoke to them in a technically specific jargon. This presents modern readers with some daunting linguistic obstacles, for although Zeami's ideas are not murky, his terminology can be a heavy burden. Yet a detailed examination of his noh demands a familiarity with certain terms, just as a serious discussion of opera requires an understanding of "recitative," "aria," and so on. In the paragraphs below, I have tried to provide the minimum needed to follow the analyses in the chapters to come. Even so, it is a lot of material to absorb, and readers will no doubt wish to consult the Glossary on pp. 291-300 from time to time.

First a list of frequently encountered terms with which many readers will already be familiar:

Sarugaku is the original name for noh. It is the word Zeami himself most often used to designate the art.

Shite is the name given to the major role in a noh (for just as in opera, where we may speak of a role such as the romantic tenor quite apart from the specific character portrayed by the tenor, so also in the noh one commonly speaks of the shite of a given play rather than of

* Where no translation is offered for play titles at first mention, it is because the title is a proper name. Takasago happens to be a place name; Tadanori, mentioned below, is a personal name. Table 1 in Chapter Two gives translations of the titles of the plays associated with Zeami.

Character X, Y, or Z). In a similar vein, the subordinate role attached to the shite is called the *tsure*.

Sometimes the prefixes *mae-*, "former," and *nochi-*, "latter," are attached to role names to indicate the part of the play during which a given role is performed. This occasionally changes the pronunciation of shite and tsure to *-jite* and *-zure*. The practice is not entirely consistent.

The *waki* plays a secondary role in a noh; and the *wakitsure* is a subordinate role attached to the waki.

The *kyōgen* or *aikyōgen* is the role played by actors from the normally distinct performing art Kyōgen during the interlude between the two parts of a standard noh.

The *hayashi* is the noh "orchestra," which consists of a flute player and two or three drummers.

For the basic unit on which the noh is based, I use the modern term *shōdan* ("small section," or *dan*), coined by the eminent scholar Yokomichi Mario.[1] Shōdan fall into two broad categories, those that are sung and those that are spoken. In the spoken mode of delivery, a kind of slow, declamatory style called *kotoba* ("words," "speaking"), there is no fixed rhythm or melody, but only a general pattern of inflection in which the first part of a phrase is delivered in a more or less level pitch and the second part in a swelling phrase that jumps sharply at the beginning and returns to the original level at the end. Distinctions are made in the degree of swell and the amount of time it takes to reach its highest pitch according to the type of character being represented. In the example from the play *Hagoromo* shown in Figure 1, for instance, we see that the waki, a fisherman, uses an altogether different inflection from that used by the shite, a heavenly maiden.[2] These patterns are basic to all characters delivering passages in kotoba; all female characters deliver their kotoba lines in a pattern much like that of the heavenly maiden, and all male characters follow the pattern of the fisherman, more or less. Spo-

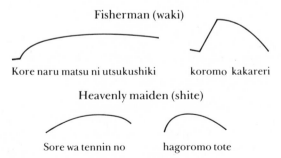

Fig. 1   Speech patterns for male and female characters in the play *Hagoromo*

3

Sashinori

O to me wa ko ro mo o cha ku shi tsu – tsu –

Einori

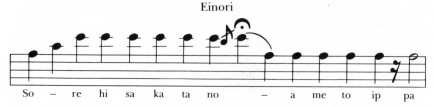

So – re hi sa ka ta no – a me to ip pa

Fig. 2 Sashinori and einori melodic examples from *Hagoromo*

1	2	3	4	5	6	7	8
	so	mo	so	mo	bu	rya	ku
no	ho	ma	re	no	–	mi –	chi
–	• ge	– n	pe	i	to	o	ki

Onori rhythmic pattern

1	2	3	4	5	6	7	8
sa mo	ha na	ya ka	na ru	o n	na ri	sa ma	ni
te su	ga ta mo	ko ko	ro mo	a ra	te n	gu o	– •
• shi	sho o ya	bo o	zu to	• go	sho o	ka n	na

Chūnori rhythmic pattern

1	2	3	4	5	6	7	8
Cho – o	ryo o –	ku	tsu o –	sa	sa	ge	tsu tsu •
n – ma	no u –	e	na ru –	se	ki	ko	o ni •
ha – ka	se ke –	ru	ni zo –	ko	ko	ro	to ke te

Hiranori rhythmic pattern

Fig. 3 The correlation of text and music in the three types of congruent song. The numbers are musical beats; the dashes indicate a continuation of the previous syllable, and the dots indicate rests. The extra syllable in the final line of the hiranori example is a bridge to the next line (uncited). The passage is from the play *Kurama tengu*.

ken shōdan bear various names, depending primarily on their function. For example, a self-introduction in kotoba is called a *nanori*, a narrative is a *katari*, and a dialogue is a *mondō*.

There are two kinds of sung shōdan: those in noncongruent song (*hyōshi awazu*) and those in congruent song (*hyōshi au*).[3] In noncongruent song, as the term suggests, there is no specific one-to-one relationship between the syllables of the text and the beats of the music. Shōdan in noncongruent song that are sung without much inflection in a manner reminiscent of recitative in opera are called *sashinori*. Those that are more highly inflected are called *einori*. Examples of both are shown in Figure 2.[4]

Sashinori and einori shōdan are still further distinguished by function or pitch, or both (and in one important case, by pitch and syllable count). For example, a shōdan in sashinori that rises to the highest pitch in noh singing is called a *kuri*, and a self-introduction in sashinori that rises to this "kuri pitch" is called a *nanoriguri*. Similarly, a shōdan in einori centered on the higher registers is called a *jōnoei*. An *issei* is an einori shōdan that centers on the higher register and has a specific number of syllables. Another einori shōdan, the *waka* shōdan, is so called because its text consists of a poem or part of a poem in the classic 5-7-5/7-7 meter.

Shōdan of the congruent-song category, that is to say, those pieces in which the text and the music *do* correspond, follow three rhythmic patterns called *ōnori*, *chūnori*, and *hiranori*. An example of each is shown in Figure 3.[5] In ōnori one syllable of the text is allotted to each beat in the music (with occasional syncopation), and the text is in the metric pattern 4/4 (a four-syllable line, followed by a second four-syllable line). A shōdan in the ōnori pattern is called a *noriji*. In chūnori (again with occasional syncopation) there are two syllables to each musical beat, and the metric pattern is 8/8. A shōdan in chūnori is called a *chūnoriji*.[6]

Hiranori is not only the most common pattern in congruent song, but also unique to noh. It matches twelve syllables of text to eight beats of music, leaving certain half-beats open.[7] Hiranori shōdan fall into two broad groups, standard and irregular. Standard hiranori shōdan, or *tadautai* ("plain song"), to use their generic name, are composed primarily of 7/5 verse texts, the conventional metrical form of Japanese medieval verse.[8] (Note, however, that not all 7/5 verse texts are set to congruent song; some are set to noncongruent song, and some are even spoken.) Standard hiranori shōdan go by various names, depending on the pitch in which they are sung, their function, or the number of characters who sing them. For example, a tadautai shōdan centered on the higher register is called an *ageuta* (as opposed to a *sageuta*, in the lower register); a *kiri* is used at the end of a play; and a *rongi* is sung by two or more characters or by the chorus and one or more characters.

Some hiranori shōdan contain a large number of irregular verses (i.e., not in 7/5 meter). Since these seem to have come into noh when Zeami's father, Kannami, adapted the medieval dance form known as the Kusemai to his own purposes, they can be called *kusemaiutai* ("kusemai song") to distinguish them from tadautai. Whereas the melody is the central attraction in a tadautai,[9] the musical interest of a kusemaiutai lies in its rhythm, that is to say, in the syncopation of metrically irregular verses matched to regular eight-beat measures.[10] The most common type of kusemaiutai is the *kuse*, which is frequently used to deliver part of a play's central narrative. (The question of structure first comes up in Chapter Two. I have provided a schematic illustration there—Figure 6— that shows these musical distinctions in taxonomic form.)

Wherever possible, I define Japanese words as they appear, but those that are too complex to cover with a brief phrase are left undefined in the text. For these the reader can consult the Glossary on pp. 291-300. In general, I refer to Japanese poetic forms by their transliterated names: *renga*, *chōka*, and so forth. (Note, however, that waka, in roman type, is a poetic form whereas *waka*, in italic, is a shōdan.)

The translations of noh plays, waka, Chinese poems, and historical documents in this study are mine unless otherwise stated. I have attempted to capture some small portion of the poetry of the noh texts by translating them into free verse, generally in iambs, where appropriate.

I have romanized Japanese texts and terms by the system used in Kenkyusha's *New Japanese-English Dictionary*. For Chinese, I have used the Pinyin system. The romanization of names in Japanese reflects the closest approximation of the pronunciation of the name in question during the period studied; thus I romanize the name of Zeami's father as Kannami, not the modern Kan'ami. In romanizing the texts of noh plays, I have adopted the pronunciation of noh actors as they deliver the texts on stage. This is sometimes slightly different from the standard modern Japanese reading of the same characters—for example, *mōshū* ("delusion") becomes *mōshiu*; "the second month" is *jiget'n* instead of *jigetsu* or *nigatsu*; and the common medieval auxiliary verb *sōrō* appears in sentence-final position as *sōro*.

For shōdan names I have relied on Yokomichi Mario and Omote Akira (*Yōkyokushū*, Vols. 1 and 2). When they consider a specific shōdan irregular, I have indicated this by placing an asterisk before the name of the shōdan; thus the *katari of the last act of *Tadanori* is somewhat different from the standard katari. Entirely instrumental shōdan are shown in small caps (e.g., JONOMAI, SHINNOISSEI).

The ages of people in this study are rendered in the traditional Japanese reckoning, which counts the number of years in which a person has lived rather than the number since he was born. Consequently, the ages mentioned are one or two years greater than they would be in the Western way of counting. So far as possible, I have provided people's dates as their names come up. If no dates are given, they are unknown— in other words, I have not resorted to ("?-?") or even ("fl. ca.") in such cases.

Finally, I have attempted to be consistent in using a single name for each person mentioned in this study even though this may at times seem anachronistic. That is to say, though Zeami was known at different times in his life as Fujiwaka, Motokiyo, Kiyomoto, Shiō, Zea, Zeshi, Zeamida-butsu, and so on, I have always referred to him as Zeami. I have retained the Japanese order (surname first, given name last) in introducing all Japanese figures, and then referred to them by the name by which they are commonly known in Japanese scholarship. Thus Zeami Motokiyo is called Zeami, but Nijō Yoshimoto is called Yoshimoto.

CHAPTER 1

A Documentary
Biography

THE PARADOXICAL fabric of documentary history most reveals when most intact and most conceals when fallen into tatters; it leaves Zeami a hidden man, deeply shrouded in the last extant threads of the material of his life. There is no portrait, not even the sort done long after its subject's death by an artist who never saw him. There are a few personal artifacts, a mask he may have worn on stage, some letters, ten playscripts in his hand, three holograph copies of dramatic treatises, even a set of artistic memoirs of a sort, but these pieces are scant in biographical detail. The circumstances of his personal life seem to have occupied him infrequently in his writing. He is concerned, rather, with practical matters—the actor's training, the troupe member's responsibilities, the satisfaction of a fickle patron—or sometimes with dauntingly abstract aesthetic (and perhaps ethical) principles.

We can speculate about the contours of Zeami's life in a general way, assuming that particular experiences lie behind his remarks, but we find little indication of the day-by-day texture of his time. A handful of specific events from his eighty-odd years, a few enticing images, animate the mystery of Zeami's biography. They seem at times to fit together, to delineate a man of yet palpable substance, but as we try to move closer, to regard him in greater detail, the substance dissolves into a shadow, cast by the light of our speculation on the body of Zeami's artistic and intellectual accomplishment.

One can say certain things with confidence:

He wrote some thirty-odd plays.

He met his first major patron in 1374.

He viewed his art as his vocation.

His intellectual environment was eclectic.

He was a formalist: first he chose his topic; then he erected a structure for it; finally he set his lyrics down on the page.

He begat an artistic tradition and fathered several children.

After the death of his favorite son, he sailed in exile to Sado Island.

One can make various judgments about his accomplishments:

He was the foremost playwright of the noh theater.

His tradition represents the classical epitome of noh.

He effected a synthesis of classical poetics with popular song, dance, and drama, thereby revitalizing the classical tradition and broadening its appeal.

He made free and sometimes rather loose use of his intellectual environment.

His treatises on performance represent the first pragmatically centered work on aesthetics in Japanese intellectual history.

One can speculate . . . or fantasize:

He may have turned his back on his own artistic lineage.

He may have been a spy.

He may have owed his earliest successes, in part at least, to the homoerotic interests of his patrons.

He may have been the quintessential "Zen artist."

He may have been a Ji sect priest.

His son may have been murdered, and he himself exiled, for restorationist activities.

In this chapter we will focus primarily on what can be confidently asserted about Zeami's life. At times we will generalize about circumstances that may lie behind the facts. And we will, on occasion, touch on some of the speculation, which is often intriguing if not always well substantiated. Our tools will be the few extant documents of biographical relevance, general remarks from Zeami's treatises, tentative genealogical investigation, and miscellaneous information about the performing arts in Japan in the fourteenth and fifteenth centuries.

We make our beginning in 1374. This is not the year of Zeami's birth, but in respect to the noh theater, it is every bit as significant. By this time, his father, Kannami, had attained broad popularity in the provinces around Kyoto and could count to his credit certain successes in the capital itself as well. Not until 1374 did his troupe play for the first time before the seventeen-year-old shogun, Ashikaga Yoshimitsu (1358-1408). Zeami was twelve.[1] How Yoshimitsu came to attend this performance is unknown, but one of his advisers, a certain Ebina no Naami, seems to have been instrumental in directing the young shogun's attention to Kannami's troupe.[2] In Zeami's words: "The role of Okina used to be played by the oldest member of the troupe, but on the occasion of the Imagumano performance, this custom was changed. Ebina no Naami suggested that the head of the troupe should play the role himself, since this was the first number the shogun would see. Kannami therefore took the part; this was the first time the play was done in such a manner."[3]

This performance is often cited as a turning point in Japanese dramatic history; it not only marks the beginning of shogunal patronage for Kannami's troupe, but also signals a change in the orientation of sarugaku: with this performance, its ostensibly religious purpose was clearly subordinated to that of entertainment.[4] This may not in fact have been the first time such a shift had taken place, but this is the first documented reference to it. The performance is important for yet another reason: it also marks the beginning of a radical transformation in the aesthetic direction of sarugaku. From this point on, aristocratic taste and patronage were to grow increasingly important, and the popular and countrified origins of the art were to exercise their influence from the shadows of the past.[5]

The first documents of direct bearing on Zeami's beginnings—both genealogical and aesthetic—concern the birth of his father, Kannami (1333-84), and the early history of the troupe. Of these, the most interesting—if not most reliable—comes from an inscription on the portrait of Kanze Kojirō Nobumitsu (1435-1516), Kannami's great-grandson:

Hattori had three fine sons. The god Kasuga Myōjin instructed the eldest saying, "Serve me with music." The boy's father would not obey, and the son soon died. A second son also died, so the parents took the youngest son and went into the province of Yamato and there made obeisance to Kannon at the Hase temple. They met a priest on the road and asked him to name their son, and he named him Kanze. Thereupon they made a pilgrimage to the shrine of Kasuga Myōjin and, following the instructions of the god, put their son in his service. So it happened that the son stayed in Yamato and changed his name to Yūzaki and performed at the shrine of the god.[6]

The connection of the name Yūzaki with Kannami is important; the Kanze troupe was originally known as the Yūzaki troupe (from a place name in Yamato) and is often mentioned as such in Zeami's treatises.[7] Although the intriguing story of Kannami's naming cannot be confirmed in other sources, the mention of the Hattori clan coincides with Zeami's own, far drier report of his father's origins:

Yamato sarugaku has been handed down directly from Hata no Kōkatsu. Ōmi sarugaku descends from a certain Ki no Kami and is, therefore, of the Ki clan.
  The Takeda, Deai, and Hōshō troupes of Yamato are all closely interrelated. For generations, the Takeda troupe has possessed the Original Mask [carved by Prince Shōtoku and bestowed on Kōkatsu]. The Deai troupe was originally Yamada sarugaku. A certain Ōta no Naka adopted the son of one Suginoki, a man of Heike descent from Hattori in the province of Iga. The adopted son had a child by his mistress in Kyoto. This child was adopted by Mino Tayū of Yamada, and he in turn sired three sons: the eldest, Hōshō Tayū; the middle, Shōichi; and the youngest, Kanze; all descended from this one man.[8]

The disconnected choppiness of this passage obscures some of the relationships it intends to explain, but certain important assertions are made. Sarugaku, the direct ancestor of noh, is the general topic. The several independent troupes of Yamato sarugaku, Zeami's own tradition, are to be distinguished from Ōmi sarugaku, a rather different kind of sarugaku influential on Zeami later. Among the Yamato troupes mentioned, the Deai seems to have disbanded already by Zeami's time, but the Takeda (or Emai, later Konparu) and Hōshō troupes survive to this day.*

Kannami finds mention as "Kanze," and the interconnectedness of the Yamato troupes is clearly shown by the fact that Kannami's eldest brother was adopted into the Hōshō sarugaku troupe and later assumed its leadership. The other brother, Shōichi, seems to have become the leader of the Deai troupe, following in his father's footsteps. The identity of the rest of those mentioned is uncertain,[9] so we turn to yet a third version of Kannami's origins.

A document known as the Kanze-Fukuda Genealogy, which first came to public attention in 1967, has given birth to some fascinating speculation about Kannami's line and the fate of Zeami and his sons. The document sets out Kannami's family tree as shown in Figure 4.[10] This third account corresponds closely to Zeami's own. Zeami's "Ōta no Naka" can be identified as Nakashige of the Ōta clan. Hōshō Tayū and Shōichi are not mentioned by name, but might well be Iemitsu's two unnamed sons. Kannami's rise to popularity in the capital is recorded as having occurred in 1374, just as we saw above. Most intriguing of all, the genealogy identifies Kannami's mother as the sister of Kusunoki Masashige, a major supporter of the southern court against the Ashikaga shogunate. Though no other extant documents confirm this, the possibility of such a connection is of great interest because of the ultimate sad fate of Zeami and his sons.

Figure 5 sums up Kannami's origins according to all three accounts.

The genealogy and the other documents do not reveal the date of Kannami's birth, but Zeami writes that his father died at the age of fifty-two, and an entry in the death register *Jōrakuki* (Record of Long-Lasting Ease) notes his passing in 1384.[11] Counting backward and making allowances for the traditional way of reckoning age, one arrives at the year 1333.

Little more is known about Zeami's birth than his father's. The actual date has been the subject of some controversy, but it seems fairly certain that he was born in 1363.[12] The Kanze-Fukuda Genealogy identifies him (under the name Motokiyo) as follows:[13] "Childhood name, Kiyomoto. Born in the eighteenth year of Shōhei [1363] at the Kamijima residence

---

* There are five schools of shite acting today. The four Yamato troupes—the Takeda (or Emai, or Enmai), Hōshō, Yūzaki, and Sakato—are the direct ancestors of four of these (the Konparu, Hōshō, Kanze, and Kongō, respectively). The fifth is the Kita school, established in the 17th century.

NAKASHIGE

[Also known as] Naka no Shichirō Yasunobu, later [as] the lay priest Bitchū. Resident of Oda. Originally [called] Murashima Nakashige of the Ōta clan.

IENOBU

The eldest son of the Suginoki house. Adopted by Ōta Shichirō Nakashige.

IEMITSU

After his own family troupe of Yamada *sarugaku* perished, he followed a certain Komino, who was killed by a warrior priest of Tōnomine, Ochi Kaikyō, whereupon Iemitsu succeeded him.

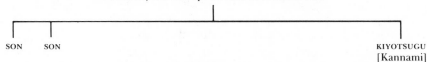

SON   SON   KIYOTSUGU
                                                                                      [Kannami]

First called Kanzemaru Saburō. His actual father, Jirōzaemon Motoshige, was the son of the lay priest Keishin, Kamijima Kagemori, the lord of the fief of Asada in Iga province. [Kiyotsugu was] the third son, born in Suginouchi. He was later adopted by Ichidayū Iemitsu. His religious name was Kannami; his mother [was] the daughter of the lay priest Kusunoki Masatō of the Tamagushi estate of Kawachi Province. Kannami became popular in the capital in Bunchū 3 [1374]. He kept his family line secret from Ashikaga Yoshimitsu and founded a *sarugaku* troupe.

Fig. 4   One account of the family tree of Zeami's father, Kannami. Based on Kubo Fumio, "'Kanze-Fukuda keizu' o meguru shomondai," *Kokugo to kokubungaku*, 434 (May 1960): 57-65.

in Nagaoka. Mother, the daughter of the priest Takehara Daikaku, lord of the fief of Obata. First entrusted to Konparu Yasaburō Katsukiyo, consequently known as Yasaburō Ujikiyo."*

There are no other documents relating directly to Zeami's first years, but we can perhaps see a picture of him in his general comments on the training of a child:

In training at this age [six], there is always something a child does on his own that shows where his talents lie, and he should be allowed to follow such natural inclinations whether they be toward dance (either elegant or vigorous), song, or even the direct display of energy. You should not be too quick to say what is good and what is bad, because if you demand too much, the child will lose interest in noh and weary of it, and make no progress. You should not have the child

* The possibility that Zeami was for some time entrusted to a member of the Konparu troupe is worth noting because it helps to explain his close ties to Konparu Zenchiku later on. Zeami did, on occasion, use the surname Hata, traditionally associated with the Konparu troupe (e.g., the colophon to the first three sections of *Fūshikaden*; FSKD, p. 37).

do things other than song and elegant or vigorous dance, though. Even if he is capable of dramatic imitation, you should not teach him such techniques in any detail, nor should he be allowed to play in the first piece of a formal production. You should let him display his talents in the third or fourth piece, as seems appropriate.[14]

In the 1360's or early 1370's, the popularity of Kannami's troupe began to increase. Father and son performed with great success at Daigoji and gained a substantial following in the capital.[15] Then came the 1374 performance and the attentions of Yoshimitsu mentioned earlier.

The shogun was himself but an adolescent, and the most notable and controversial accomplishments of his reign—his solidification of Ashikaga power, his opening of trade with Ming China under the title King of Japan, his reunification of the northern and southern courts—were all years away in the future. He was already an important patron of the arts, but his interest in Zeami was not, it appears, exclusively aesthetic. His affection for the boy actor was openly apparent and disturbing to certain conservative imperial aristocrats, not because of its homoerotic implications, but because Zeami seemed to come from among the lowest classes in society. One of them, Go-oshikōji Kintada (1324-83), wrote disdainfully in his diary:

The shogun had stands erected at Shijō Tōdōin and watched from there. . . . The child from the Yamato *sarugaku* troupe . . . was called to join him, and he followed the proceedings from the shogun's box. The shogun has shown an extraordinary fondness for him ever since. He sat with the boy and shared drinks with him. *Sarugaku* like this is the occupation of beggars, and such favor for a *sarugaku* player indicates disorder in the nation. Those who give things to this boy find favor with the shogun, so the daimyo all compete with one another in making him presents, and they spend prodigious amounts.[16]

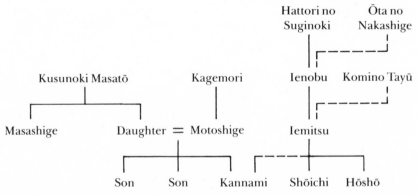

Fig. 5 A summary of Kannami's family tree based on the three existing accounts. A dashed line indicates adoption. The chart shows Kannami as the adopted son of Iemitsu, but by one account he was Iemitsu's natural son.

Kintada probably spoke for countless other aristocrats who had seen their own authority and power decay while the likes of Zeami were enriched by shogunal largesse. The overt patronage of individual actors seems to have been a relatively recent development,[17] and the occasion on which this incident took place, the Gion Festival of 1378, must have been a galling and threatening reminder of Muromachi social change. The festival was a reliable annual event with a five-hundred-year pedigree, but in recent years it had become bigger and brighter and noisier than ever before. Elaborate floats wound about celebrating the city in a lusty and obstreperous parade; the shogun himself watched from stands among the fish markets and pawnshops and sake wholesalers near the intersection of Shijō and Higashi no Tōin avenues. The entire event was a testimony to the displacement of courtly culture and influence by the military class, the rich merchants and burgeoning guilds, and, perhaps worst of all, a band of provincial dramatic players.

This mixing of social classes was vital to the development of Zeami's style in noh, and it was not, in this case at least, so repugnant to all the old aristocrats as to Kintada. In fact, the senior court statesman and renga poet Nijō Yoshimoto himself took an active interest in the boy actor. He seems to have had a profound influence on Zeami's literary style and is credited with much of Zeami's education in the Japanese classics. A letter survives testifying to the extent of his regard for the boy (Zeami is referred to by the name Yoshimoto gave him, Fujiwaka):

Should Fujiwaka have time, please bring him over with you once again. The entire day was wonderful, and I quite lost my heart. A boy like this is rare—why, look at his *renga* and court kickball [*kemari*], not to mention his own particular art! Such a charming manner and such poise! I don't know where such a marvelous boy can have come from.

In *The Tale of Genji*, Lady Murasaki is described as "adorable with her misty, yet-unplucked eyebrows," and this boy is just as entrancing. I should compare him to a profusion of cherry or pear blossoms in the haze of a spring dawn; this is how he captivates, with this blossoming of his appearance.

In praising his waka and *renga*, I refer to his interesting manner of expression and his attention to the elegant beauty of *yūgen*. When he dances, the movements of his limbs and the flutter of his sleeves are, in truth, more graceful than a willow swaying in the gentle breeze of the second month, more beautiful than all the flowers of the seven autumn grasses soaked with the evening dew. . . . It's no surprise that the shogun is so taken with this boy.

They say the most difficult thing to meet with is an opportunity, and to have happened upon this opportunity in spite of such difficulty is indeed a miracle.

"If an excellent horse doesn't meet up with trainer Bo Lo, he won't even be able to line up his hooves. It took three generations for the Bian-he gem to be recognized for its true value." If a person does not find someone capable of appreciating his talents, his true form stays hidden. I think it no trivial matter therefore that this opportunity has presented itself.

Please do arrange to bring the boy here again soon. In spite of myself, I feel as if the flower of the heart still remains somewhere in this fossilized old body of mine.

Throw this note into the fire immediately after you've finished reading it.[18]

Such personal attention, from both Yoshimoto and Yoshimitsu, continues to raise eyebrows today,[19] and to some, the great renga poet may look rather foolish writing a letter like this at nearly sixty years of age. His rhetorical excesses have led at least one scholar to question his motives in writing it, suggesting that the letter is less a sincere expression of admiration for Zeami than an attempt to flatter Yoshimitsu for his own appreciation of the young actor.[20] It would, in any case, be a mistake to assume that Yoshimitsu's and Yoshimoto's appreciation of the Yūzaki troupe was based solely on the sexual allure of one of the actors. The young Zeami seems to have had much precocious dramatic charm in addition to his beauty, and Kannami's genius was widely recognized. There are numerous references to his talent in Zeami's treatises, among them, the following instructive anecdote:

Kannami was a big man, but when playing a woman's role, he would comport himself with slender grace. When he played *Jinen Koji* [a play about a young Buddhist acolyte], he wore a boy's wig, and as he took his seat on the priest's dais, he looked as if he were no more than twelve or thirteen. From the part of the text reading "In the first generation of instruction . . ." he sang with such great variety that the shogun turned to Zeami and quipped, "My boy, you could do your best to fool the audience, but you'd never be able to carry something like this off."[21]

Zeami's talent on stage is mentioned here and there, but no concrete examples of what it was he did so well are given. Again, though, we find hints of what his performance may have offered at this time in his comments on the training of a twelve- or thirteen-year-old boy:

About this time, the child will begin to be able to carry a tune, and he will start to understand a bit about the noh, so he should be taught various sorts of noh. First of all, since he is a child, anything he does will be pretty [*yūgen*]. Furthermore, his childhood voice will be at its peak during this period. With these two advantages, his bad points will disappear and his good ones blossom.

For the most part, you should not have children do too much dramatic imitation. It neither looks good nor increases the child's ability. However, as the child becomes really skillful, he may be permitted to perform almost anything. A pretty little boy with a good voice who is talented besides can hardly go wrong.[22]

Aware though he is of a child's natural advantages on stage, Zeami places little faith in them, and he goes on to say:

Such skill is not true skill. It is merely temporary. . . . Consequently, it does not provide any means by which to judge the boy's potential. At this stage, those things the child can do easily should be made the high points of his performance, and major emphasis should be given to his technique. His movements should be exact and his singing understandable syllable by syllable. His basic gestures in the dance should be strictly correct, and he should be resolute in his training.

These passages point to certain aesthetic goals in the performance of noh. Some have gone so far as to say that the boyish "prettiness" (i.e., yūgen) Zeami speaks of here is the basis for all yūgen in the noh, and whether this is true or not, the importance of dance and song in the young actor's training is obvious from both passages.

Yoshimoto's letter had praised not only Zeami's acting, but also his court kickball and renga. There is no corroboration for the young Zeami's athletic prowess, but we find his skill at renga acclaimed in another source:[23]

Sūkaku told me that the Kanze boy composed some excellent links at a *renga* gathering at Nijō Yoshimoto's residence the other day. When he was called upon to compose . . . his links were not just good, but inspired. The old gentleman praised them extravagantly.

Isao sutsuru wa	One does not leave one's fame behind
Sutenu nochi no yo	Until one leaves the world.

—YOSHIMOTO

Tsumi o shiru	He who knows his sins
Hito wa mukui no	Shall find ahead
Yo mo araji	No world of retribution.

—THE BOY

The first link caused great admiration in the assembly, and Yoshimoto praised the second in the highest terms:

Kiku hito zo	His mind's as empty as the sky,
Kokoro sora naru	The one who listens
Hototogisu	For the nightingale.

—YOSHIMOTO

Shigeru wakaba wa	The flourishing young leaves
Tada matsu no iro	Are just the shade of pine-ing.

—THE BOY

Ijichi Tetsuo, who has made a study of these renga, comments:

[In the first pair of renga], the first link means a person cannot fully cease being attached to his achievements and fame and pay them no attention until he has truly abandoned the world. Zeami has paired this with a link meaning that one who actually comprehends the depth and horror of his own vices will not meet with retribution for them. He has responded to "fame" with "sins," and to "does not leave behind" with "find . . . no . . . retribution." The first link sets "does not leave . . . behind" against "leave the world," using opposites for rhetorical effect, a novel device at the time. The second link says that ordinary men are all tormented with terrible retribution for their sins, while he who understands the true horror of his transgressions is not brought to retribution. Paradox, very popular at the time, is put to use here. Both links deal with Confucian propositions. Usually, following an aphoristic and intellectual generalization of this sort one would compose a vividly descriptive link attesting to the truth of the first link. Whether aware of this practice or not, the sixteen-year-old Zeami instead boldly composed a link of very similar intellectual character. This must have been rather unconventional and consequently interesting. . . .

[In the second pair, the first link describes] the feeling of one who waits for the call of the *hototogisu* [a bird of the cuckoo family with poetic associations rather like those of the nightingale in the West]. This person stares intently into space in anticipation of the call of the bird that will cut across that space. . . .
The second link follows the expectant speaker's line of sight to find the brilliant green of the profuse young needles of a pine (with a pun on "to pine for") floating before him in the air.[24]

Other scholars have found less to praise in these particular renga links, but whatever their literary value, they demonstrate a familiarity with the many and complicated rules and conventions that govern the art. Renga does not come naturally to anyone. It demands conscious dedication to learn, and a teacher is essential. There is little evidence aside from this diary entry to indicate where Zeami acquired his training in the art, but his connection to Yoshimoto is confirmed, and the old gentleman's role in Zeami's education, informal though it may have been, must be acknowledged. Moreover, this diary entry suggests that Zeami owed much credit for his general education (in addition to his knowledge of renga) to highly placed and sophisticated members of the imperial court. Such influence seems everywhere apparent in his plays, so it is encouraging to find external evidence for it. And again, the situation in which we find Zeami, a boy in his mid-teens and a commoner, exchanging poems with one of the ranking statesmen in the land points to a great deal of self-confidence and poise and a strong interest in the arts.

This interest in and sensitivity to the arts is demonstrated time and time again in his treatises. For instance, a full half-century after the event he could still recall a performance by the actor Kiami (a master of the performing art *dengaku*) that he had gone to see in Nara:

When I was twelve years old, I heard about a special costume-donation performance of noh at the Hōon'in in Nara and went to see how it would be. Kiami played the old man's role in a flaxen wig without a mask. When he sang the passage with the line, "Although I was once a dandy in the capital," he did not add any embellishments, but sang in a straightforward and simple manner. The more I thought about it later, the more interesting it became.[25]

Zeami's memory fails him only in the matter of his age. The performance could not have taken place when he was twelve. It was probably in 1375, when he was thirteen.[26] But to be remembered so long at all, it must have made a very strong impression on him.

After this there is again a blank in documentary evidence relating to Zeami's life, and one must turn to his treatises for a glimpse of his training at age seventeen or eighteen:

This period is of such great importance that you must not practice too much. First, since your voice will be changing, you will have lost one of your dramatic charms. Your body will have gotten much taller, and you will have lost the charm of figure you had before. The time when you could, with your pretty voice, perform with effortless flair will have passed, and with this transformation, the essential strategy of performance will have changed, leaving you at a loss. You will find yourself in positions that the audience thinks comical, and you will be embarrassed. With one thing and another, all this can be quite disheartening.

In training at this time, even if people point and laugh, pay them no heed. Practice, instead, in private at a pitch your voice will allow and train hard, using your voice in a manner appropriate to the time of day. Be resolute and realize that this is the turning point; commit yourself to noh for life with complete devotion—no other means of training exists. If you give up at this point, your noh is finished.[27]

The 1380's brought the deaths of Naami (1381), Yoshimoto (1388), and most important, Kannami (1384). "My father passed away on the nineteenth day of the fifth month when he was fifty-two years old," Zeami writes. "On the fourth of that month he had performed before the god of Sengen in the province of Suruga. His noh that day was particularly beautiful and was praised by exalted and humble alike."[28] Zeami appears to have assumed leadership of the troupe immediately, and although this cannot but have been a heavy responsibility for the twenty-two-year-old, it seems he shouldered it with great success. Once again, from the treatises:

About this time a man's artistic potential for his entire life begins to be fixed. Consequently, this is an extremely important time for training. Your voice will have changed already, and your body will have reached maturity. This provides two advantages. . . . Performances worthy of a man in the prime of his youth are possible now. People will begin to take notice and say, "Ah, he's gotten quite good." On occasion you may even win in competitions against famous actors because of the novelty of your dramatic achievement at this particular time.[29]

These are Zeami's comments about the training of the actor at age twenty-four to twenty-five. The change in tone from the comments about an actor at seventeen or eighteen is remarkable, and it seems likely that Zeami himself enjoyed the sort of success he describes. He also realized the dangers of such success. As he goes on to say:

People will be generous with praise, and you may come to think of yourself as a really accomplished actor. This is very dangerous. . . . Your achievement at this time is not true artistic excellence. It is born of youth and the novelty the spectators see in you. Anyone with a discriminating eye will recognize this fact.

Your achievement at this time is a beginner's achievement, and it is a great shame if you mistake it for true artistic excellence and give free rein to your personal eccentricities on stage, thinking yourself a great actor. Even though you are highly praised and win in competition with famous actors, you should realize this is merely temporary achievement born of novelty. You should work at mastering the traditional forms of dramatic imitation and train all the more diligently, inquiring very carefully of truly accomplished actors concerning the fine points. . . . Nearly everyone becomes enthralled with this temporary achievement and fails to realize it will disappear. . . . Ponder this long and hard. If you really have a grasp of your level of achievement at this stage, that achievement will not disappear throughout your life. If you overestimate your level of achievement, even the level once attained will fade away. Think this over carefully.[30]

The actor at thirty-four or thirty-five is the subject of Zeami's next set of comments. Again they provide the most reliable source of information concerning Zeami himself at this age:

[An actor's] noh around this time is at its highest peak. He who fully understands and masters the various articles in this manuscript and attains true expertise in acting will most certainly gain fame and security in his position. He who does not gain sufficient fame and security, no matter how skillful he may be, should realize that he has not yet brought about the full flowering of his art. If you do not achieve this, your noh will decline after age forty. This will become obvious later. . . . Now is the time for you to take full account of what you have learned in the past to be fully aware of your direction in the future.[31]

To repeat, whether we can equate these generally intended comments with Zeami's personal experience is uncertain. But Zeami's fame, at least, is attested by the records of three important performances in which he led the troupe—one in 1394 and two others in 1399.[32]

The first of these came in the midst of the festivities accompanying Yoshimitsu's pilgrimage to the Kasuga shrine in Nara. By this time, the shogun had come into the strongest years of his reign. A nearly sixty-year schism in the imperial court had finally, so it seemed, been healed. The northern and southern courts were reconciled, and the architect of the compromise, Yoshimitsu, now emerged unequivocally superior to the old imperial aristocracy, a feat that the Kamakura shogunate had never clearly accomplished.

On the thirteenth day of the third month of 1394, hard on the heels of this political success, Yoshimitsu set out for Nara to attend a religious festival. He stayed at the Ichijōin, one of two alternating administrative offices for the extremely wealthy and powerful temple, Kōfukuji. For several generations, the *monzeki*, or "princely abbot," at Ichijōin had been an imperial prince of the southern line, so Yoshimitsu's stay there might be seen as symbolic of his recent political triumphs.

Zeami figures in this event in only the smallest way. The record of Yoshimitsu's pilgrimage merely states, "A typical day, nothing particular to mention. But by order of the clerical magistrate, there was a *sarugaku* performance (Kanze Saburō)."[33] Kanze Saburō is Zeami; this is the first reference to any adult performance by him. There is no list of the plays performed, no evaluation of the performance, only the barest acknowledgment that the performance took place at all. But it must, all the same, have been an important performance, given the political significance of the excursion, and it is not surprising that scholars have taken this brief entry as evidence that Zeami had attained some considerable popularity in the dramatic world by this time.

We know little more about the other two performances—only that in the fourth month of 1399, the troupe presented ten plays for Yoshimitsu and other assembled dignitaries at the Sanbōin at Daigoji, and that a month later it held a three-day subscription performance (*kanjinnō*) at Ichijō Takegahana, in Kyoto.[34] Yoshimitsu attended this performance too, along with numerous other dignitaries.

This is scant evidence that Zeami had assured for himself the security he mentions alongside fame in the earlier quotation. Some scholars think, however, that there is support for such an assertion in the fact that in 1400 Zeami found enough time to reflect on his father's teachings and on his own experience to write his first treatise on drama, *Fūshikaden* (The Transmission of the Flower Through [A Mastery of] the Forms).*

Fūshikaden, sometimes called *Kadensho* (Treatise on the Transmission of the Flower), is certainly the most famous of all Zeami's treatises.[35] As the first of his works on drama—indeed, it is the first work of its kind in Japanese history—it provides the earliest formulation of his aesthetic of the theater, but it is more a reminiscence and outline of Kannami's teachings than anything else, and the ideas it contains are sometimes at surprising variance with those of the more mature Zeami. There are seven sections to the whole, and it was composed in several different stages.[36]

The first three sections are of a relatively practical nature. Section 1 deals with the training of the actor at various stages of his life; we have relied on it above for clues about Zeami's youth and young adulthood. Section 2 deals with nine character types that appear in sarugaku. Sec-

---

* For example, Kobayashi, *Zeami*, p. 27. But one might also interpret the composition of *Fūshikaden* in precisely the opposite way: that Zeami was insecure in his position and worried about the proper transmission of the art, and he put his ideas down in concrete form to give them some permanence and set his mind at ease. Indeed, the final entry in section 3 and the beginning of section 5 both contain statements to the effect that some actors were not taking their work seriously enough, and that the very vocation of sarugaku was in serious danger (FSKD, pp. 37, 54). Zeami intended the title to mean the transmission (*den*) of the flower (*ka* or *hana*) from mind to mind by those who have mastered the forms (*fūshi*) of the tradition. *Fūshi* is an imprecise word, but suggests especially the visual form or appearance of a past master's performance. (See Omote's note, in ZZ, pp. 436-37.)

tion 3, written in question-and-answer form, concerns such matters as the proper time to begin a performance, the way to win in dramatic competitions, what makes a proficient actor, and what achieves the greatest dramatic success. In section 4 Zeami discusses various legends about the origins of noh. Section 5 begins with a short explanation of the differences in style between Ōmi sarugaku and Yamato sarugaku, then exhorts the actor to proficiency in all styles. Section 6 deals with the composition of noh and will be discussed in detail later. The final section, 7, is entitled "Confidential Instructions" and is of a slightly different nature from the rest of the work. It is probably the most interesting section for the nonspecialist because it deals with the aesthetic of noh. Thus far throughout the treatise, Zeami has been concerned with what makes a successful performance; this concern remains even here, but in contrast to the earlier sections, where he dealt mainly with technique, he now sets forth ideas about the abstract principles and ideals behind a successful performance.

According to *Fūshikaden*, the noh depends for its existence on the creation of what Zeami terms "the flower" (*hana*). This effect is achieved through technical skill and intellectual understanding. Technical skill requires versatility, breadth in characterization, mastery of the techniques the actor acquires as he matures, and competence in dramatic representation as well as music and dance. Intellectual understanding requires a careful consideration of the psychology of the audience, an ability to gauge the potential of the moment, a feeling for the pace of a work and each of its components, and a respect for the taste of the common people as well as that of the elite. In considering the psychology of the audience, Zeami concludes that people appreciate the novel; therefore, the actor who can show ordinary things in a new light will succeed. For Zeami, the actor's central goal is to gratify the senses (especially sight), and he values highly the physical beauty of the actor himself. Music and dance are important as well,[37] but, as was traditionally the case with Yamato sarugaku, dramatic imitation (*monomane*) is most important of all.

In 1408, Ashikaga Yoshimitsu arranged for himself the unprecedented honor of a visit from the reigning Emperor at his villa in Kitayama. A record of the entertainments offered His Majesty was kept, and among the descriptions of poetry contests, renga gatherings, and *gagaku* (court music) concerts, we find the following item, dated the fifteenth day of the third month:

During the morning it rained, but the evening sky cleared for a period of entrancing spring haze. After night fell, His Majesty's party went to the Sūkenmon'in Palace. The master there [Yoshimitsu] accompanied them and, following an informal concert, *sarugaku* was expressly requested. Since this was an imperial command performance, Dō[ami]'s actors displayed their particular talents to the utmost. It was a truly extraordinary presentation.[38]

Unfortunately, the text identifies only Dōami's sarugaku players. Many have been quick to conclude that Zeami also performed on this occasion, citing as evidence a letter he received from Jūni Gonnokami (1353-1434), a Yamato sarugaku actor, sometime after 1428. The key passage reads: "In years past, when I prevailed upon you for instruction in my performance, you were so good as to oblige, and at Kitayama you taught me most kindly; I still have not forgotten this, and I remain most grateful to this day."[39]

Most scholars have taken the mention of Kitayama as a reference to the occasion of the imperial visit, but as Omote Akira points out, Yoshimitsu moved to Kitayama about 1400, and Jūni Gonnokami could be referring to any of many possible performances there.[40] The fact is, the passage resolves nothing: the clause beginning "In years past" can be taken to refer to general instruction received over a long period of time, whereas the one beginning "and at Kitayama" seems to single out a specific and rather important occasion.

Whether Zeami actually performed for the Emperor at Kitayama, then, remains an open question. In any case, the absence of any mention of Zeami in that connection and the scarcity of other records of his performance suggest that a reexamination of the relationship between Zeami and his supposedly long-term patron, Yoshimitsu, may be in order. We know that Yoshimitsu was fond of the boy Zeami and respected Kannami, and we know that he saw Zeami in performance at Daigoji and Takegahana. But what else can be surmised from extant documents about their relationship?

Zeami's references to Yoshimitsu, as recorded by his son Motoyoshi, suggest that the shogun was a difficult patron who had to be carefully catered to. Consider, for instance, this observation:

The purpose of our profession is to soften the human heart, and unless one is well versed in its workings, one's progress will be hindered at some time. Yoshimitsu's lady, Takayasu-dono (a courtesan from Higashi no Toi), was particularly sensitive to the workings of the heart; Yoshimitsu had a special fondness for her and throughout his life, she never once incurred his displeasure. She could keep him happy.

She knew when to offer him wine and when not to, and because of her sensitivity, she was a success. . . . Zeami, too, was particularly good at this and was praised by everyone.[41]

Perhaps this eagerness to please was merely common sense. Perhaps, on the other hand, we may read between the lines that the relationship between the young Zeami and his patron was not always smooth. An anecdote regarding Zeami's very name is pertinent here. It was apparently

Yoshimitsu who instructed Zeami to voice the first character in his name, saying "Zeami" rather than "Seami," as one would normally expect.[42] The shogun's personal concern over such a matter was an indication of favor for Zeami. But the same anecdote goes on to tell that Yoshimitsu bestowed one of the characters of his own religious name, Dōgi, on the Ōmi sarugaku actor Inuō, calling him "Dōami."

Snatches of information like these seem trivial, but as rare indications of relative position between two acting rivals, they must be given due consideration. These particular details, in fact, call into question a couple of long-standing assumptions about Zeami's success: that Yoshimitsu was a constantly faithful patron, and that Zeami was his favorite throughout the shogun's life. The anecdote reveals a greater favor for Dōami, which in turn sheds some light on the problem of Zeami's reputed performance at Kitayama, for if the records of the imperial command performance at Kitayama fail to mention Zeami, they do not fail to mention Dōami.[43] It seems logical to conclude that however much Yoshimitsu favored Zeami, he favored Dōami more. This is more than a matter of merely historical interest; it seems to have had an important effect on the development of Zeami's style.

In any case, Zeami soon lost his putative benefactor. Yoshimitsu died less than two months after the zenith of his glory, the Emperor's visit to Kitayama in 1408. He fell ill on the twenty-seventh of the following month and expired before evening the next day. He had numerous sons, three of whom are of interest to us: Yoshimochi (1386-1428), Yoshitsugu (1393-1418), and Yoshinori (1394-1441). Yoshimochi, the eldest, had officially succeeded his father while still a boy, becoming shogun in 1394, but remained virtually powerless until Yoshimitsu's death. Thereupon, he gained the support of Shiba Yoshimasa (1350-1410), an important vassal of his father's, thus solidifying his position. His half-brother Yoshitsugu, however, had expectations of his own and was not satisfied to remain in Yoshimochi's shadow. In 1416, he appealed to another powerful lord, Uesugi Zenshū, who was persuaded to take the field against Yoshimochi. Uesugi was defeated in Suruga and killed himself in Kamakura in 1417. Yoshitsugu was taken back to the capital, to be locked away in a temple. Monastic life disagreed with him, and he died by his own hand a year later.

Nonomura Kaizō tries to relate this story to Zeami's life by speculating that since Yoshimitsu had favored Yoshitsugu over Yoshimochi, and since Zeami had been supported by Yoshimitsu and Yoshitsugu, Yoshimochi tended to dislike him.[44] There are no records of specific actions taken against Zeami by Yoshimochi, however, so what Nonomura sees as politically motivated neglect may be nothing more than a matter of taste. Yoshimochi's patronage went instead to the dengaku actor Zōami, and it was very generous patronage indeed, but performance records for Zeami's troupe during Yoshimochi's rule do not show any noticeable loss of popularity or any marked change for the worse from the days of Yoshimitsu's reign. Consider the records of the Kanze troupe's performances during Yoshimochi's rule (1408-28):

Eleventh month, 1412: Zeami performed ten plays for various deities (and, one assumes, the assembled faithful) to effect the cure of the owner of the Tachibana Stores (an event to be discussed later).

Seventh month, 1413: The lord of Bungo issued an official proclamation, calling on Zeami to perform at the Kitano shrine in Kyoto: "Starting on the tenth of this month, the Kanze *tayū* [Zeami] is to perform at Kitano. Whoever wishes to attend, be he rich or poor, young or old, is invited to do so. In consideration of this, all arguments and disputes are to cease./May it be so recorded."[45]

Fourth month, eighteenth day, 1415: "Festival *sarugaku* at the Kiyotaki no miya of Daigoji. Performance by Kanze Shirō."[46]

Fourth month, second day, 1417: "Kanze troupe performance at a Kiyotaki *kō* [devotional lecture] at Daigoji."

Eighth month, twenty-fifth day, 1417: "Competitive *sarugaku* by the four troupes at Kōfukuji. Yoshimochi attended."

Eleventh month, eighteenth day, 1418: "Festival *sarugaku* by four troupes at the Wakamiya of Kasuga shrine."[47]

Fourth month, eighteenth day, 1422: "Festival *sarugaku* at the Kiyotaki no miya of Daigoji by Kanze Gorō and Kanze Saburō. A splendid performance. Lay priest Kanze [Zeami] and lay priest Ushi assisted."[48]

These records show little direct interest in Zeami on the part of Yoshimochi; he is mentioned only once. But then no systematic effort was made to record the regular performances of any troupe in this period; these few records have survived only because most of the performances were given under unusual circumstances (e.g., the first on the list) or in connection with some significant festival or ceremony. Actually, we have more Kanze performance records for this period than we have for the reign of Yoshimitsu.[49] Moreover, in 1424, during Yoshimochi's administration, the tayū (head) of Zeami's troupe was handed an important assignment:

I have appointed the Kanze *tayū* to the musical directorship of the Kiyotaki no miya [a shrine on the grounds of Daigoji], effective this year. The former director committed an offense last year. He was reprimanded and died immediately thereafter. . . . In past years, the Kanze *tayū* has been called in to perform on the recommendation of the former director. Because of his past efforts here, I have given him the position.[50]

The speaker is Mansai (1378-1435), a high cleric of the Shingon sect at Daigoji, who recorded several of the performances referred to earlier in his official diary. The Kanze tayū he mentions may be Zeami, but is more likely to have been his son Motomasa.[51] In any case, the appointment was a great honor for the entire troupe, and although it was not made by Yoshimochi himself, it would probably have been blocked by him had he not approved.

These facts call into question the traditional interpretation of Zeami's position during Yoshimochi's rule. Many have assumed that the downward turn in Zeami's career began with the death of Yoshimitsu. It seems more likely, however, that there was not all that much of a change after Yoshimochi came to power. Yoshimochi certainly preferred dengaku to sarugaku and Zōami to Zeami,[52] but as we saw earlier, Yoshimitsu himself, in his later years, came to prefer Ōmi sarugaku to Yamato sarugaku and Dōami to Zeami.

Moreover, whatever the shogun's attitude may have been, there is good reason to assume that Zeami's position was relatively secure in the 1410's and early 1420's. The Kanze tayū's appointment as musical director of the Kiyotaki shrine alone attests to the troupe's prestige among powerful Buddhist clerics, and the following anecdote hints that Zeami had considerable standing with the urban commercial class as well:

In the eleventh month of 1412 . . . the owner of the Tachibana Stores on Hōjōji Avenue near the Fushimi Inari shrine was involved in an accident, and his condition was very grave. Just as he seemed close to death, the god of the Inari shrine manifested himself by taking possession of one of the serving women. He promised to cure the man on the condition that Kanze [Zeami] was called to perform. The god, speaking through the woman, said, "Ten pieces should be performed, three for the goddess of Ise, three for the god of Kasuga, three for the god of Yawata, and one for me." Zeami performed the ten plays. When he went to call on the family, . . . they made him a present of red silk.*

In short, by all evidence, the middle-aged Zeami was a well-respected public figure with access to varied patrons and diverse opportunities.

There is a blank space of about sixteen years between the last datable parts of *Fūshikaden* and the next work Zeami wrote. Thereafter, he produced something almost every year until 1425: 1418, *Kashū (no uchi nukigaki)* ([Extracts from] Learning the Flower); 1419, *Ongyoku kuden* (Special Instructions Regarding Music); 1420, *Shikadō* (The Way to the Attainment of the Flower); 1421, *Nikyoku santai ningyōzu* (Sketches of the

---

* *Dangi*, pp. 303-4. The Tachibana Stores (Tachibana kura) was probably one of the prosperous moneylending establishments, or pawnshops (*dosō*), of medieval Kyoto. Such establishments were already in evidence in the Kamakura period (1192-1333), and by the 15th century they occupied an important niche in Kyoto's economy. Though most flourished under the protection of court nobles and large temples in this period, the proprietors were commoners, the forerunners of a merchant class that was to become much more prominent in the next century. *Dangi* records a similar incident just after this anecdote. Zeami is called on by the god of Kitano to judge a poetry contest offered to the god to heal a roofer's daughter.

Two Arts and the Three Modes); 1423, *Sandō* (The Three Ways); 1424, *Kakyō* (The Mirror of the Flower).[53]

Kakyō, probably the major work of this period in Zeami's life, concludes with the following postscript:

The various chapters of *Fūshikaden* . . . represent a secret treatise that discusses our art from the point of view of its flower. It is my record of my father's teachings as I mastered them throughout a period of over twenty years. This volume, *Kakyō*, is a summary in six chapters and twelve articles of what I myself have learned about the art now and then, from the time I was about forty until my old age, and I leave it as a record of the art.

1 VI ŌEI 31 [1424]   WRITTEN BY ZEA*

Kakyō, then, by Zeami's own account, is a summary of his personal experience in noh, to be distinguished from *Fūshikaden*, which is as much his father's as his own. He had been compiling notes for it for some time, because he quotes it and mentions it by name in *Nikyoku santai ningyōzu*,[54] and because *Kashū*, the work he brought out in 1418, is actually an early draft of one of its chapters. He does not say whom the work was written for, but almost all of his treatises were written for confidential transmission to specific people, and a note by Zeami's younger son Motoyoshi elsewhere states that *Kakyō* was transmitted to Motomasa.[55] Omote conjectures on this ground that Zeami formally entrusted the work to Motomasa when he retired as tayū in his older son's favor. This would make Motomasa the head of the Kanze troupe by 1424.

The difference between *Fūshikaden* and *Kakyō* can be most immediately seen in a telling change in aesthetic vocabulary. Probably the most important single word in the former work is hana ("flower"). The word appears constantly (Konishi Jin'ichi counts 137 occurrences[56]); even the ka of *Fūshikaden* is a Sino-Japanese reading for the same character. In *Kakyō*, hana is used only once. The concept itself remains important throughout the treatises (the ka in *Kakyō* still means hana, as it does in such other works as *Shūgyoku tokka*, *Shikadō*, and *Kyakuraika*), but the visual beauty of the flower is replaced, or at least augmented, by other types of beauty. In addition to the *Fūshikaden*'s universally perceived beauty, Zeami here treats beauty of sound and beauty beyond both sight and sound, beauty created by the spirit.[57] The demands made on the audience become greater as one proceeds up this ladder of beauty; thus, paradoxically, as the range of effects available to the actor increases, the

---

* *Kakyō*, p. 109. For a translation of the work, with extensive commentary, see Nearman. Zeami does not seem to have called himself Zeami. The closest he came to doing so is this "Zea." (The full form of his name, Zeamidabutsu, is an honorific form and would have been inappropriate for him to use himself.) He also on occasion called himself "Zeshi." The scholar Kanai Kiyomitsu insists that it is wrong to call him Zeami, but I see little reason to concur with his rather eccentric position.

audience at which he directs these effects decreases. This fact accounts for Zeami's increasing concern with the tastes of the elite and what some critics have called a neglect of the masses. Novelty is no longer important for its own sake; it is tied to the striving for a deeper artistic experience, the apprehension of a deeper beauty than was experienced before. This in itself is new, but it is not merely novel.

Much more attention is paid to music and its place in the noh. Where *Fūshikaden* dealt with the voice only in passing, *Kakyō* devotes a number of articles to it. There is a similar, though slightly less obvious concern with dance. Conversely, the concern for dramatic imitation, monomane, lessens significantly. The nine character types of *Fūshikaden* shrink to three modes of representation here.

The most striking new concern is for the spirit or mind (*kokoro*) of the actor. This spirit, not the visible action, imbues a performance with life. The true master can, in fact, totally captivate his audience with spirit alone, without even moving. Furthermore, whereas yūgen (elegant and mysterious beauty) was subordinated to monomane (dramatic representation or imitation) in *Fūshikaden*, here it gains preeminence as an aesthetic ideal.

Various factors explain these differences. The influence of Dōami and Zōami, as suggested before, was very important. Zeami himself singles out Dōami as one of his artistic forefathers, and praises him as an actor of great sophistication and consistent elegance.[58] More telling remarks can be found in *Kabu zuinōki* (Notes on the Essence of Song and Dance), where Zeami's son-in-law Zenchiku (1405-68) discusses Zeami's evaluations of past masters:

Zeami said that Dōami was beautifully elegant and knew nothing whatsoever of the common. He had a whispering sort of radiance, ever so delicate yet enduring. His level of accomplishment might match this poem:

Miwataseba	When I gaze about,
Yanagi sakura o	Willow leaves and cherry blossoms
Kokimazete	Mix in bright profusion.
Miyako zo haru no	The capital, I see,
Nishiki narikeru	Is spring's brocade.[59]

Zōami seems to have been a man of many accomplishments. The renga poet Shinkei calls him a master of the *shakuhachi* (a type of flute), and Zeami corroborates this.[60] He also created a popular type of noh mask that retains his name to this day: *zō onna* ("Zōami's woman").[61] Of greatest concern here, however, is his acting. Zeami says of him:

As for our contemporary Zōami, both his acting and his singing should probably be classed at the rank of the tranquil flower.* The one balances the other

* This is the third of the ranks Zeami outlines in his work *Kyūi shidai* (The System of Nine Ranks; ca. 1428).

30

quite well. . . . At the Tōbokuin in Nara I was moved almost to tears when he turned from east to west and stopped, his dance accompanied by the slight movement of the tip of his fan. If there were no one around to appreciate this, what a lonely profession this would be. . . . In the noh with *shakuhachi* flute, he played a short passage on the instrument, sang something, and in a way all his own, spirited himself off stage. It was chillingly beautiful.[62]

Zeami was a keen observer of both these actors, and given his practical bent of mind and concern for the success of his own troupe, he must have learned whatever he could from their styles. It seems, in fact, that the movement away from monomane toward yūgen in his dramatic theory of the 1420's was in large part a response to Dōami's success with Yoshimitsu and Zōami's with Yoshimochi (a point that I shall come back to in the Conclusion). Some, however, prefer to see the change as a reflection of Zeami's purported interest in Zen.

Zeami's earliest work, *Fūshikaden*, already contains references to a Zen hymn by the patriarch Hui Neng, as well as examples of Zen terminology, but as Kōsai Tsutomu has pointed out, these are used merely for illustration and are not intellectually indispensable.[63] By the time *Kakyō* was finished, however, several terms native to Zen had found their way into prominent positions in Zeami's thought. These words do not always retain their original Zen significance. Zeami, either through unknowing misapplication or purposeful reinterpretation and adjustment to his own needs, uses them in ways completely foreign to their original context. He also coins new words that seem to suggest Zen.[64] Beyond all this, some scholars take certain concepts expressed in *Kakyō* as evidence of Zen influence: that the present moment is the decisive factor in a performance; that emptiness has a positive aesthetic value. But such concepts are not the exclusive property of Zen—they are common to other types of Buddhism as well—and they alone do not suffice to demonstrate a strong Zen influence on Zeami's thought.

There is, however, quite concrete evidence of Zeami's association with certain Zen individuals and institutions. Morisue Yoshiaki, for instance, has unearthed a brief reference to Zeami in a late-fifteenth-century commentary by a Zen priest, Tōgen Zuisen. Zuisen records a bathhouse conversation with another old priest in which the old man recalled occasions at his teacher's place when Zeami would appear and exchange "humorous tales of Zen" with the teacher. The teacher has been identified as the prominent Rinzai Zen priest Kiyō Hōshū (d. 1424). The anecdote attests to Zeami's friendship with the man, if nothing else.* More important is the question of Zeami's connection with Sōtō Zen. The register that records his death some twenty years after he had been given

* Kiyō Hōshū held important positions at Tōfukuji, Nanzenji, and Tenryūji (all Rinzai temples). The anecdote also refers to Zeami as a small man of delicate, disciplined bearing and mentions a discussion of the origins of sarugaku.

the tonsure belongs to a temple of that sect, and barring the highly un-
likely possibility that he was converted to Zen at some point after he be-
came a lay priest, one can assume that the vows he took in 1422 were
Sōtō Zen vows.[65] But registration in Zen temple records and a serious
spiritual commitment to Zen are two different things, and it is important
to keep in mind that Muromachi Japan was dominated by the language
of Zen, just as nineteenth-century Europe was dominated by the lan-
guage of Romanticism, so unless more specific evidence can be adduced,
it seems a bit exaggerated to assume that Zeami's dramatic theories, not
to mention his plays, have some privileged connection to Zen.[66]

The artistic tastes and intellectual currents of Yoshimochi's adminis-
tration wrought several changes in the life and thought of Zeami. One is
tempted, in fact, to see all the changes as a result of Zen and Zōami and
the unsteady course of patronage, but this is to forget the force of time
alone. The Zeami of *Fūshikaden* was thirty-eight, still young, at the height
of his physical potential. The Zeami of *Kakyō* was sixty-two, healthy, it
seems, but aware of the limitations age had imposed on his physical
being. The author of *Fūshikaden* thought a sixty-year-old actor could
serve his own interests best by being as unobtrusive as possible: "From
now on there is nothing to do but do nothing."[67] The author of *Kakyō* re-
peats exactly the same dictum, but he is not talking about being unobtru-
sive. He means that the truly accomplished sixty-year-old actor can *do*
nothing and still captivate his audience absolutely.[68]

Yoshimochi died in 1428. His younger brother had taken the tonsure
and was at the time the official head of the Tendai sect on Mount Hiei,
but he was quick to return to secular life as Yoshinori, the sixth shogun
of the Ashikaga line.[69] It was not a happy change for Zeami. There is no
doubt that he and his sons were poorly treated by Yoshinori; documents
make this abundantly clear. In 1429 Zeami and Motomasa were forbid-
den to appear at the Sentō Imperial Palace.[70] In 1430 the musical direc-
torship at the Kiyotaki shrine was taken away from Motomasa (or Zeami)
and given to Zeami's nephew Onnami.[71] Later that same year Zeami's
second son, Motoyoshi, gave up his career as an actor and retired to the
priesthood.[72] Then, in 1432, Motomasa died—perhaps he was mur-
dered—in Ano no tsu in the province of Ise.[73] Finally, in 1434, at the age
of seventy-two, Zeami was banished to Sado Island.[74] Yoshinori's hand is
clearly seen in the incidents of the Sentō Palace, the Kiyotaki shrine, and
Zeami's exile; he may have played a part in the other events as well. His
motives, however, remain obscure.

Some have clad Zeami and his sons in spies' cloaks, as partisans of the
southern court in the cause of imperial restoration. Kannami's reputed
relationship to Kusunoki Masashige (see Fig. 5) is woven into this argu-

ment, for Masashige was a key agent in the destruction of the Kamakura shogunate and had a concomitantly high position in Emperor GoDaigo's Kemmu Restoration. When GoDaigo rebelled against Ashikaga Takauji (Yoshimitsu's grandfather) in 1335, Masashige died defending him, begetting his own heroic legend. If Kannami was in fact Masashige's nephew, then he had good reason to "[keep] his family line secret from Yoshimitsu," as the Kanze-Fukuda Genealogy states. But these events took place a full century before the great reversals in Zeami's life, and little beyond speculation incites one to assume a direct connection to them.

Then again, circumstantial evidence surrounding Motomasa's retirement and death, four generations later, still pricks the imagination. For a start, Motomasa seems to have retired to Ochi soon after he lost his post at the Kiyotaki shrine in 1430.[75] The lord of Ochi was a partisan of the southern court and was involved in the continued struggle over the imperial succession. Motomasa *may* have chosen to retire to Ochi for political reasons, may even have been forced out of the capital because of ties with the politics of Ochi. Anyway, in 1430, he performed at the Tennokawa shrine near the southern court's traditional stronghold at Yoshino, then made a devotional petition and left the god a mask. One can only guess at the content of his prayer, but the mask can still be seen, and it seems to stare back in tacit acknowledgment of some connection between Motomasa and the southern court.[76] Apart from this, there is his death in suspicious circumstances in Ise, a province that was under the Kitabatake, who often found themselves at odds with the Muromachi *bakufu* (the shogun's administration). Here again, the smell of politics?

Another, wholly different line of conjecture suggests that Zeami, like Ovid, may have been exiled and subjected to all kinds of misfortunes because of his taste—or Yoshinori's lack thereof. This seems at first a rather overblown notion; a ruler does not normally exile a man because he does not like his acting. But Yoshinori was an eccentric and sometimes perverse ruler, and there is evidence to suggest that his animosity for Zeami resulted at least in part from a disagreement about the pleasures proper to the stage.

Long before he became shogun, Yoshinori had shown a taste for simpleminded, colorful noh. As early as 1420, he had supported the Enami tayū, a master of the lion dance, a descendant of which we see today in *Shakkyō* (The Stone Bridge), *Mochizuki* (The Full Moon), and *Uchito mōde* (The Pilgrimage).[77] When Enami died in 1424, Yoshinori turned his attentions to Zeami's nephew Onnami.

Diary entries for the mid-1460's repeatedly mention Onnami's performances in a string of demonic plays.[78] Was he performing the same plays more than thirty years earlier for Yoshinori? There is no way to tell, but one assumes that Onnami liked such plays even then, and Yoshinori, as his ardent patron, probably liked this sort of noh as well. All these plays show an interest in monomane harkening back to the more mimetic drama of Kannami's day. Was it, then, that Yoshinori had no taste for the delicacy and subtlety of yūgen and found the more obvious arts of monomane to his liking?[79] Was it a difference in taste that led to Zeami's exile and the host of misfortunes that preceded it?

This line of conjecture is tempting, but it is not without its weaknesses. The diary entries mentioned earlier do indeed attest to Onnami's interest in monomane and rather lively noh, but they also record his performances of other plays that provide more than sufficient proof that Onnami also had some interest in yūgen.[80] Even assuming Yoshinori did not share Onnami's catholicity of taste, it is still difficult to accept the theory that Zeami was exiled merely for promoting yūgen over monomane.

A third line of conjecture combines political and aesthetic elements. Simply stated, it asserts that Yoshinori took a great liking to Onnami and exacted various penalties from Zeami when Zeami refused to make Onnami the head of the troupe and entrust him with certain treatises. For a fuller understanding of the basis for this conjecture, we need to look more carefully at the relations between nephew and uncle.

Onnami (Kanze Motoshige) was the son of Zeami's younger brother Shirō. Not much is known of Shirō. He may have led his own troupe and played occasionally in the capital,[81] but the troupe cannot have been large, and it is thought that Onnami was frequently given the chance to perform with Zeami's troupe. He may even have been adopted by Zeami for a time. He came to the attention of Yoshinori while the latter was still a Tendai priest, and his name comes to appear more frequently in the extant records after 1428 when Yoshinori became shogun.

On the third day of the fifth month of 1429, the shogunate sponsored a grand sarugaku performance; the Shingon cleric Mansai mentions the performance in his diary:

Both Kanze troupes competed against the Hōshō troupe and Jūnigorō's troupe today on Kasakake Riding Grounds at the shogunal estate. The performance was in the style of Tōnomine: mounted characters actually rode horses and used real armor. The sight was startling to both eyes and ears. The Nijō Regent, abbots of Shōgoin, Nyōiji, Jissōin, Hōchiin, Shōren'in, [and] Daitokuji, and I sat in the same stands. There were fifteen plays, and a donation of ten thousand bolts [of silk] from these stands.[82]

This performance is puzzling in several ways. Most surprising is the style of presentation. The Tōnomine style with its use of horses and actual armor seems far removed from our modern sense of noh, and it must indeed have been an unusual spectacle even in its day. That "both Kanze troupes"—that is to say, Motomasa's (perhaps with Zeami in an advisory

34

capacity) and Onnami's—took part as well as two other troupes indicates the extraordinary nature of the occasion. Then, there is the question of just who performed what and with what degree of success. One suspects that something happened at this performance to displease Yoshinori, for exactly ten days later he took his first overt action against Zeami and Motomasa by ordering their exclusion from the Sentō Imperial Palace. From that time onward, every blow to fall on Zeami and his son seems to have been accompanied by some boon bestowed on Onnami. When Zeami and Motomasa were forbidden to play at the palace of the Retired Emperor, Onnami began to play there. When Motomasa lost the Kiyotaki post, Onnami gained it. When Motomasa died, Onnami became the head of the Kanze troupe. This cannot have made for good relations between Onnami and his uncle and cousin, but there is reason to suspect that in addition to these "family problems," Zeami did not approve of Onnami's acting style.

Onnami seems to have been best at demonic roles, and Yoshinori seems to have enjoyed watching him play such roles. The demon was one of the special roles of Yamato sarugaku in Kannami's time, but Zeami appears to have turned away from this sort of noh under the influence of Dōami and Zōami. By the end of his life, he had come to reject entirely the role of the true demon-hearted demon, and in a very late letter to Konparu Zenchiku, he says as much: "In your letter you inquired about demon noh. This is unknown in our school of noh."[83] The full significance of this statement can be understood only after a more detailed discussion of the evolution of Zeami's aesthetic ideals, and we will return to it in the final chapter. In the context of the present discussion, however, this rejection of the demon in noh might easily be interpreted as a rejection of Onnami's acting and defiance of Yoshinori's taste.

The exclusion from the Sentō Palace and the loss of the Kiyotaki post might have seemed merely temporary setbacks to Zeami. Even Motoyoshi, when he abandoned the noh for the priesthood, was not an irreplaceable loss as long as Motomasa maintained the family tradition and held the position of head of the Kanze troupe. Also, as long as Motomasa was alive, Yoshinori cannot have charged Zeami with unfairness to Onnami. After all, it was only proper that Motomasa retain the hereditary position as long as he remained in secular life; he was Zeami's eldest son. When Motomasa died, however, the position of the head of the Kanze school should logically have gone to Onnami. Eventually it did,[84] but the third line of conjecture holds that in resolutely resisting this move, Zeami so angered Yoshinori that he was exiled.

Documentary evidence clearly shows that Zeami did indeed oppose Onnami's becoming head of the Kanze school. On Motomasa's death, Zeami wrote a short piece entitled *Museki isshi* (A Page on the Remnant of a Dream), in which he stated that with Motomasa's passing, the art of his line had come to an end.[85] He is still more specific in his short treatise *Kyakuraika* (The Flower of Returning):

The deepest mysteries of our vocation, whatever I received from my father or garnered in my own life until this extremity of age—I have entrusted every last one of these to my heir Motomasa and have merely been waiting for the last event of life; but now without warning Motomasa is dead, our vocation thus brought to an end and our troupe already destroyed. Our heir is now but an infant, and so bound am I in aged attachment to this heirless vocation of my father's and mine, that my greatest spiritual aspirations are endangered. Were there anyone, even a stranger, to whom I might entrust my legacy, I would; *but no such artist exists.*[86]

But Onnami, for his part, plainly considered himself to be the artistic successor of Kannami and Zeami. He even took their lead in choosing his name, using the third character of the bodhisattva Kanzeon's name where they had used the first and second. Under the circumstances, it seems quite possible that Yoshinori was deeply angered by Zeami's refusal to recognize his favorite, even angry enough to exile him. An exacerbating factor may have been his equally adamant refusal to surrender the rights to certain Kanze school treatises to Onnami, entrusting them instead to his son-in-law, Konparu Zenchiku.[87] For all these reasons, the third line of conjecture seems fairly strong.

Yet it too has its weak points. No matter how much Zeami resisted, Onnami did eventually become the head of the Kanze school. But Zeami was not exiled until two years later, so the resistance he made to Onnami's assumption of the post cannot have been the immediate cause of his banishment. One might look, then, to his decision to transmit the treatises to Konparu Zenchiku instead of to Onnami. But this practice had begun in 1428, so it cannot have been the immediate cause of banishment either.*

In spite of the unhappy events of his old age (in some cases, one might say because of them), Zeami continued to turn out new works at a prodigious rate. During 1428 he completed both *Rikugi* (Six Genres) and *Shūgyoku tokka* (Pick Up Jewels, Attain the Flower), and by this time or even earlier, he had finished *Kyūi shidai* (often called simply *Kyūi*).[88] These were followed by *Shūdōsho* (On Training in the Way) and *Sarugaku dangi* (Discussions of Sarugaku) in 1430, by *Museki isshi* in 1432, and by

---

* The traditional account of Zeami's banishment states that he was sent to Sado because "he favored Konparu Zenchiku more than his own son." Two lines of misinformation led to this misunderstanding. According to the first, Zeami is said to have ignored Motomasa in favor of Zenchiku. This loses all credence when one reads *Museki isshi* or *Kyakuraika*. The second mistakes Onnami for Zeami's son. If this were true, one might quite rightly say Zeami favored Zenchiku more than his own son. The Kanze-Fukuda Genealogy is one source of this misunderstanding. It lists Onnami as Zeami's eldest son.

Kyakuraika in 1433. *Go ongyoku no jōjō* (Articles Concerning the Five Sounds) was probably written about 1430, *Yūgaku shūdō fūken* (Insights on Training in the Performer's Vocation) probably some time before 1432, and *Go on* (The Five Sounds) probably before 1432, certainly before 1434. Zeami's last work, produced after he was exiled in 1434, is *Kintōsho* (Writings from the Isle of Gold); it dates from the second month of 1436. Finally, to complete the canon of Zeami's expository writings, there are two short letters written to Konparu Zenchiku, one from Kyoto and one from Sado.[89]

Most but not all of these works are treatises on noh. *Museki isshi*, written about a month after Motomasa's death, we have examined; and *Kintōsho* is a collection of songs in the style of noh.[90] *Sarugaku dangi*, though it may be the most valuable work in the entire canon, is not strictly speaking a treatise, but rather a compendium of Zeami's recollections and opinions relating to noh, copied down by his second son, Motoyoshi. *Shūgyoku tokka* is a digest of the theory developed from *Fūshikaden* onward, and was written for transmission to Zenchiku. *Kyūi* is a discussion of levels of artistic achievement marked by an abundant use of metaphor and Zen vocabulary. *Shūdōsho*, unlike the other treatises, was written for the entire Kanze troupe, perhaps to combat the confusion that Yoshinori's patronage of Onnami must have caused. *Go ongyoku no jōjō* and *Go on* are both concerned with the classification of song types and their dramatic effects. The first classifies the singing of noh into five different groups and discusses the characteristics of each group, and the second proceeds to identify particular plays with particular types of singing. *Go on* has proved to be a useful tool for the determination of the authorship of early noh plays and will be discussed more thoroughly in the next chapter.

It is difficult to characterize Zeami's thought in the last years of his life. None of his last works is so comprehensive or so representative of his thought at the time as *Fūshikaden* and *Kakyō* were for his youth and middle years. An increased use of Zen vocabulary is evident, particularly in *Kyūi*, and there seems to be an overall concern with the classification of types: types of artistic skill, types of song. This concern may indicate that Zeami was gaining a critical perspective on the noh as a whole and was more willing to deal with abstract matters than earlier. Yet he did not neglect specific, practical information either, as *Sarugaku dangi* generously demonstrates.[91]

Zeami's last days are less shrouded in mystery than most of the events of his life, for he left us a first-hand record of his exile on Sado in *Kintōsho*. The work is a collection of eight pieces for recitation and singing in the noh style, and though the formal demands of these pieces keep the reader at some distance from Zeami's personal experience on the island, they show a surprisingly fresh and at times even cheerful picture of the old master. It cannot have been easy for him at seventy-two to leave the capital and make the journey north to Wakasa and from there across the sea to the southern coast of Sado, but there is no hint of bitterness, even in the earliest parts of the work, and toward the end, the tone becomes surprisingly like that of a waki noh, auspicious and felicitous. Zeami displays his erudition unassisted by reference works—these he must have left in the capital—and he sees himself in the tradition of others who were exiled to Sado. He specifically mentions the Former Emperor Juntoku (1197-1242) and the poet Kyōgoku Tamekane (1254-1332), and his own experience is shaped in part by what he has learned of theirs.

The final piece in the collection seems to be different from the rest. All the others have titles; it does not. It concerns a noh performed by firelight and mentions several shrines and temples in Kyoto and Yamato, all places that played a part in Zeami's life. This has led to speculation that Zeami may have returned to the mainland of Japan before his death. If so, had he returned already in 1436, the date of the *Kintōsho*, or after 1441, when Yoshinori was assassinated? We have no way of knowing, but there is an old tale that while Zeami was on the island, he composed seven (some versions say ten) plays and sent them to the Zen priest Ikkyū Sōjun (1394-1481) for editing. Ikkyū presented them to the emperor, as the story goes, and His Majesty was so impressed that he had Zeami pardoned.[92] It may be that *Kintōsho* was mistaken for a group of plays, and it is not impossible that Zeami was pardoned by the Emperor himself.[93]

Zeami died on the eighth day of the eighth month of 1443. His death is recorded in a burial-plot registration book from a temple named Fuganji in Yamato; not many pages later a similar entry tells of the death of his wife, known as Juchin by that time.[94] Zeami would have been eighty-one by the traditional Japanese count, about eighty by Western reckoning.

CHAPTER 2

Zeami
the Playwright

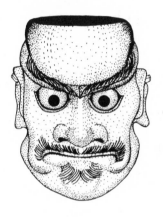

I N 1468, as he wrote his *Hitorigoto* (Talking to Myself), the renga poet Shinkei set down this short passage: "And in *sarugaku*, there was a man named Zeami, outstanding and unequaled in the world; he left behind all sorts of noh plays."[1] It was the second year of the devastating Onin Wars, and the cultural legacy of Kyoto lay in ruins.* Noh itself had fallen on hard times, and the memory of Zeami in the popular imagination faded quickly, to become the exclusive property of certain privileged members of the Kanze and Konparu lines. By Momoyama times (1568–1600), in a new world of prosperity, the noh had again found generous patrons, but the memory of Zeami had grown so dim that a noh primer for the swelling ranks of amateurs could be written with liberal quotations from *Fūshikaden* but hardly any mention of its author.[2]

By the late nineteenth century, Zeami was thought by many to be nothing more than an actor who composed music for plays written by Zen monks from the *gozan* temples of Kyoto.[3] Then his critical writings were rediscovered. In 1908 Yoshida Tōgo presented *Sarugaku dangi* to the public, and in the following year he gained access to fifteen other texts as well, all of which he published as *Zeami jūrokubushū* (Sixteen Works by Zeami).[4] In 1945 Kawase Kazuma augmented this corpus with the publication of seven more texts, though only five have become accepted parts of the canon.[5] Further corrections and augmentations of Zeami's writings continued until 1963—coincidentally, the six hundredth anniversary of his birth. No new texts have been discovered since then.

The rediscovery of Zeami's treatises naturally prompted a new interest in the problem of authorship for the some 200 to 300 plays in the current repertory,[6] and increasing attention was paid to several lists of plays containing attributions that had been compiled over the centuries.[7] Scholars once considered several of these lists fairly reliable, but though they are of some help in establishing the authorship of plays by later playwrights such as Kanze Kojirō Nobumitsu and his son Nagatoshi (1488–1541), they attribute far too many plays to Zeami to be taken at

* During this 11-year-long civil war, a combination of power struggles and succession struggles among the most powerful families in Japan, Kyoto was almost completely leveled.

face value now.[8] Far more reliable information can be found in Zeami's own treatises.

Zeami's most important references to individual plays and their authors are to be found in *Sandō*, *Go on*, and *Sarugaku dangi*. In *Sandō* he names twenty-nine plays that "gained favor with audiences in recent years."[9] No reference to authorship is made, but the list is repeated in *Sarugaku dangi*, where the plays are identified individually as the works of Zeami, Kannami, Seiami (or Iami), and Yokoo Motohisa. *Sarugaku dangi* mentions numerous additional plays in passing, often with comments on authorship, revision, and adaptation.

Go on has proved to be a particularly valuable source because it includes a quotation from each play mentioned and often an explicit attribution as well. Some of these quotations amount to only a few words; others run for twenty to thirty lines. But there are two problems with the attributions. First, the treatise itself is concerned with the musical composition of noh, and the attributions Zeami makes are generally to the composer of the music, who may or may not be the writer of the text as well.[10] Second, in no case does Zeami explicitly say he himself wrote anything on the list. Some works he clearly identifies as the compositions of, for instance, Kannami, Motomasa, or Kiami, but for others he gives no composer's name whatsoever. It is assumed that these pieces are Zeami's, that for modesty's sake he declined to include his own name. Even the strictest of the Japanese scholars who have dealt with this issue accepts such a hypothesis.[11] Nevertheless, the possibility remains that at some point in the recopying of the manuscript—the original in Zeami's hand is no longer extant—a name here or there may accidentally have been left out.

In addition to this evidence from the treatises, ten noh texts in Zeami's hand and one old copy of another such text have survived. We know from the treatises that some of these are not Zeami's own works, but the holograph texts tell us at the very least that he was familiar with all of the plays, and there is good reason to assume that he had a hand in the composition or revision of some.[12]

Finally, there is a list called *Nōhon sanjūgoban mokuroku* (The List of Thirty-Five Noh Plays), which appears to have been the table of contents for a sheaf of playscripts Zeami gave to Konparu Zenchiku (one of the plays may be listed twice). Again, though the appearance of a play's title on this list does not prove Zeami's authorship, we may guess that he had some part in its composition or refinement.

One must begin the identification of Zeami's plays with this body of documentary evidence. Sifting through it, one finds that some ninety-odd independent pieces can be linked in some way to Zeami. Not all of these are complete plays; some are merely songs that may or may not have been part of a play originally. Not all that are full plays are still performed. Only nineteen of the pieces are specifically and unambiguously identified as Zeami's works, but many more can be considered his with little or no hesitation. Some are identified as Zeami's revisions, and several are mentioned in such a way that one is not completely sure, on the basis of external evidence alone, whether they are Zeami's or not. Table 1, following Omote's example, divides the pieces into four groups: works specifically identified as Zeami's; works that can almost certainly be considered his; works that he revised; and works that can be considered his only with some degree of doubt.

This exhausts the documentary evidence mentioning or quoting individual plays, but there is another, perhaps even more telling sort of evidence spread throughout the treatises in the form of various instructions on how to write noh plays. By reviewing these instructions to see what literary and musical features Zeami himself considered the building blocks of noh, and then examining how he put his theories into practice in individual plays, we can come to an understanding of the characteristics that constitute his "style."

Zeami retained an interest in the mechanics of composition throughout his life. His earliest work, *Fūshikaden*, has a section on how to write plays; in his middle years he wrote a full treatise on the subject, *Sandō* (transmitted to Motoyoshi in 1423, when Zeami was sixty-one); and one of his last works, *Sarugaku dangi*, contains three articles entitled "How to Write a Play." *Sandō* is the fullest exposition of his views, and we will look at it in some detail later in this investigation. For now, let us concentrate on the more general comments in the treatises.

Zeami's earliest statement on how to compose noh plays is found in the sixth section of *Fūshikaden*, "Kashu ni iwaku" (On Preparing for the Flower).[13] Here he begins by affirming the importance of the text ("The writing of noh plays is the life of this art"), but quickly goes on to assure the reader that one can write good plays even without a great deal of literary knowledge as long as one is careful about putting them together. Then he becomes more specific, first referring to *waki* noh (plays of a festive, auspicious character presented at the beginning of a program of noh), then moving on to other types:

You should be particularly faithful to your sources when writing *waki* noh, and write in such a way that those sources are immediately recognizable to the audience from the first line of the play. Write in a generally straightforward manner in order to start off the day's performance in a lively and colorful way; you need not exhibit a great deal of dramatic subtlety. When you get to the second or third play for the day, then write subtly, making the fullest use of every turn of phrase and every opportunity for visible expression.

For example, when writing about a famous place or a historical site, one

43

TABLE 1 *Plays and Songs Linked to Zeami*
(as mentioned in his treatises)

Title[a]	Treatise[b]	Alternative title	Remarks
WORKS SPECIFICALLY IDENTIFIED AS ZEAMI'S			
Aridōshi	S	Aritōshi	
Atsumori	S		
Ausaka monogurui (The Madman of Meeting Hill)	S	Ausaka	*Not in current repertory*
Hakozaki	D		*Not in current repertory*
Hase Rokudai (Rokudai at Hase)	G	Rokudai no utai	*Individual song*
Higaki (The Cypress Fence)	S	Higaki no onna	
Hyakuman no kusemai (The Kusemai for Hyakuman)	G		*Individual song*
Kiyotsune	S		
Koi no omoni (The Heavy Burden of Love)	D		
Oimatsu (The Old Pine)	S		
Sanemori	S		
Tadanori	S	Satsuma no kami	
Taisan Pukun (Archdemon Taisan)	S	Taisan moku	
Takasago	S	Aioi	
Tōru	O	Shiogama	
Unoha (Cormorant Feathers)	S		*Not in current repertory*
Yorimasa	S		
Yōrō (Fostering Long Life)	S		
Yumi Yawata (The Bow of Yawata)	S	Yawata	
WORKS THAT CAN BE CONSIDERED ZEAMI'S			
Aishō no kusemai (The Kusemai on Sorrow)	J		*Individual song*
Akoya no matsu (The Pine of Akoya)	–		*1427 holograph; not in current repertory*
Ashibikiyama (The Foot-Dragging Mountains)	O		*Individual song*
Chikata	D		*Only title and a few lines survive*
Fujisan (Mount Fuji)	D	Fuji	
Furu	–		*1428 holograph; not in current repertory*
Fushimi	D	Fushimi no okina utai	*Not in current repertory*

44

TABLE 1 *continued*

Title[a]	Treatise[b]	Alternative title	Remarks
Hanagatami (The Flower Basket)	D		
Hanjo	D		
Hōjōgawa (The River for Setting Things Free)	D	Hōjōe	
Izutsu (The Well Curb)	D		
Kinuta (The Fulling Block)	D		
Kōya monogurui (The Madman of Kōya)	D	Kōya	
Mekurauchi (Beating the Blind)	D		*Only title and a few words survive*
Minazukibarae (The Lustrations of Early Fall)	J	Misogigawa	
Nishikigi (The Brocade Staff)	D		
Nomori (Guardian of the Fields)	G		
Nue (Nightbird)	G		
Saigyōzakura (Saigyō's Cherry Tree)	D		*Title 'Saigyō no utai' used in treatise; probably same play*
Sakuragawa (Cherry River)	D		
Sekidera Komachi (Lady Komachi at Sekidera)	O	Komachi	
Semimaru	D	Sakagami	
Senju	G		*Not the play of the same name in the current repertory*
Shikishima	G		*Individual song*
Shiki shūgen (Auspicious Songs of the Four Seasons)	G		*Individual songs*
Sobu (Su Wu)	G	Sotoba ryū	
Suma Genji (Genji at Suma)	D		
Susanoo no utai (The Song of Susanoo)	D		*Individual song; only title and a few lines survive*
Taema	G		
Tobuhi (Flying Fire)	G		*Individual song*
Tsuchiguruma (The Wheelbarrow)	D		

TABLE 1 *continued*

Title[a]	Treatise[b]	Alternative title	Remarks

Title[a]	Treatise[b]	Alternative title	Remarks
Ukon	D	Ukon no baba	
Yashima	D	Yoshitsune	
Yoroboshi no kusemai (The Kusemai for Yoroboshi)	–		*1429 holograph; individual song*
Yukiyama (The Snowy Mountains)	G		*Individual song*

WORKS REVISED BY ZEAMI

Ashikari (The Reed Cutter)	G	Naniwa	
Funabashi	S	Sano no Funabashi	
Kashiwazaki	D		
Kayoi Komachi (Visiting Komachi)	S	Shii no Shōshō	
Matsukaze (Wind in the Pines)	S	Matsukaze Murasame	
Michimori	S		
Moriya	D		*Not in current repertory*
Shunnei	G		
Tango monogurui (The Madman of Tango)	S	Hashidate	*Not in current repertory*
Ukai (The Cormorant Fisher)	D		
Ukifune (A Boat upon the Waters)	S		
Unrin'in (The Hall in Cloud Forest)	–		*1426 holograph*

WORKS OF UNCERTAIN ATTRIBUTION

Aoi no Ue (Lady Aoi)	D		
Eguchi	–	Eguchi no yūjo	*1424 holograph*
Kagetsu	S		*Only character by this name mentioned*
Kasa sotoba (The Covered Gravepost)	D	Shigehira	*Not in current repertory*
Koremori	N		*Not in current repertory*
Kōya Shōnin (Saint Kōya)	D		
Matakashiwazaki	N		*Only title survives; 'Kashiwazaki' again?*
Matsunoo	N		
Matsura no kagami (The Mirror of Matsura)	–		*1427 holograph; not in current repertory*
Mimosuso	N	Mimosusokawa	

TABLE 1 *continued*

Title[a]	Treatise[b]	Alternative title	Remarks
Murogimi	N		*Title 'Sao no uta' used in list; probably same play*
Naniwa	N		
Obasute (Abandoning the Old)	D		
Sanekata	D		*Not in current repertory*
Seigan Koji	S		*Only character by this name mentioned*
Shirotori	N		*Only title survives*
Sumiyoshi monogurui (The Madman of Sumiyoshi)	N		*Not in current repertory*
Tamamizu (The Crystalline Waters)	D		*Not in current repertory*
Tamura	N		
Tatatsu	–	Kōya no monogurui Tatatsu Saemon	*1424 holograph; not in current repertory*
Tōboku (The Northeastern Hall)	N		*Title 'Nokiba no 'nme' used in list; probably same play*
Tōgan Koji	S		*Not in current repertory; only character by this name mentioned*
Tokusa (The Scouring Rushes)	N		*Title 'Fuseya' used in list; probably same play*
Tomoakira	–		*1427 holograph*
Tomonaga	N		
Tsunemori	D		*Not in current repertory*
Yamanba (The Mountain Hag)	D		
Yoshino Saigyō (Saigyō at Yoshino)	N		*Only title and a few lines survive*
Yūgao (Evening Faces)	S		*Only character by this name mentioned*

NOTE: This four-part categorization is essentially Omote's (*Nogakushi*, pp. 492-93); I have simplified the category names.

[a]Untranslated titles are personal or place names.

[b]Some plays are mentioned in more than one work. The work shown here is the earliest in which the play (song, character, etc.) is mentioned. D = *Sarugaku dangi* (1430); G = *Go on* (1432-34); J = *Go ongyoku no jōjō* (ca. 1430); N = *Nōhon sanjūgoban mokuroku* (n.d.); O = *Ongyoku kuden* (1419); S = *Sandō* (1423).

should use Chinese and Japanese poems about the place—familiar poems—in the more concentrated parts of the play. Do not use key phrases in inconsequential places, even if they are intended as the *shite*'s lines. No matter what, an audience will not pay attention to either the visual or the aural high points in a play unless they are well presented. Indeed, dramatic enchantment occurs when the interesting words of the troupe's star performer come to the forefront of the viewer's mind, and his actions stand out in the viewer's eyes; this is the first rule in writing noh.

Be sure to choose beautiful poetic phrases whose meaning can be immediately understood. When poetry is matched with movement, the character presented will, strangely enough, take on an air of *yūgen* of itself. Stiff language does not usually suit the movements. There are, of course, exceptions to this rule where difficult unfamiliar words may be used; when, for example, such language is appropriate to the character being treated. A distinction should be made according to whether the subject is Chinese or domestic. Vulgar and common language, however, makes for a bad dramatic atmosphere.

So then, the best noh plays are faithful to their original source; are fresh to the eye; have points of concentrated interest; and are elegantly beautiful. Those are second best that proceed in a straightforward manner with points of interest and, although not strikingly original, are not overcomplicated. . . .

A writer should be particularly aware of certain things: plays that are exclusively musical and are written about consistently inactive subjects or, on the other hand, plays that are centered exclusively on dance and movement are easy to write because they are one-sided. There should be plays with movement grounded in the singing of the text; this is very important. These are the plays that really captivate an audience. The language should be easily understood, and individual words should hold interest; the melody should be attractive, and the flow from word to word graceful. Special care should be taken to include points of concentrated interest that can be enacted with strong visual appeal. This is how to write. When all these elements come together at once the entire audience is enchanted.[14]

Three points deserve particular attention. First, a play should be faithful to its source. Zeami's phrase, *honzetsu tadashi*, is open to various interpretations, and "source" need not imply a specific literary work, or even a story per se. By faithfulness he seems to mean not only remaining true to the spirit of a source, but also choosing one that is appropriate for treatment in the noh in the first place. Faithfulness to the source has particular significance in the creation of waki noh, for although it is best to be faithful to one's source elsewhere as well, it is particularly important in these plays of strong religious, ritualistic flavor; the suitability of their thematic material is of great concern. Moreover, since the waki noh is the show-opener, it should be simple, direct, and immediately recognizable in order to settle the audience down and attract its attention.[15]

Second, one of Zeami's most important terms, yūgen, is already mentioned. Here and in other early works, it means elegant beauty, largely visual in character, and it is the second basic aim of the actor's art. The first aim is monomane ("dramatic imitation"). At this stage of Zeami's critical development, yūgen describes the manner in which monomane is to be carried out. It strongly influences the degree to which a specific object can be imitated; the more elegant the object, the greater the representational accuracy.[16]

Finally, music and movement, sight and sound, should ideally complement each other. Noh can be successful with an emphasis on but one of the two, but the combination is, of course, better. Furthermore, the music and movement should be arranged so that there are places with a high concentration of interest (*tsumedokoro*). The poetic phrases chosen to decorate the play are to be put in these places. Such high points are the responsibility of the shite, and it is with them that he succeeds or fails in a given performance.[17]

The ideas Zeami sets forth in this passage are interesting for their concern with form, but they are too abstract to be of direct use in the analysis of the plays or the determination of Zeami's style in anything other than the most general sense. Nevertheless, they provide the earliest view of what he considers important in the construction of noh. Also, despite certain shifts in emphasis, these basic prescriptions retain a central position in his theory in the later, more complete treatise on the creation of noh plays, *Sandō*.

By the time he finished that work, Zeami's experience in his art was some twenty years deeper than it had been when he wrote *Fūshikaden*. The last words of the text reveal his confidence in the achievements of those years: "Having set down the essence of what I have learned from my experience of the past years, I feel that those plays I have written in this Ōei era [i.e., since 1394] will retain a fairly constant value even in ages to come."[18] The relatively broad, abstract suggestions of "Kashu" have now taken on a technically specific, concrete shape, and the composition of a play has become a systematic exercise. Zeami's comments in this treatise range from general observations about all plays to detailed instructions on the creation of plays of particular genres. Three basic modes of performance are identified—the Aged Mode (*rōtai*), the Woman's Mode (*nyotai*), and the Martial Mode (*guntai*)—and Zeami makes certain observations about the range of portrayals these modes allow. His specific instructions on these Three Modes (*santai*) will be discussed when we take each up in detail later. For present purposes, his general observations will serve:

First of all, there are three components to the creation of a noh play, the seed, the structure, and the writing. Understand the seed of the noh; lay out the structure; write down the words and music.

Get a firm grasp on the seed as it appears in the original source, arrange the structure in five sections [*dan*] according to the organizational principles of beginning-development-conclusion [*jo-ha-kyū*]; then write the play, selecting the words and setting the melody.[19]

The source of the play is again Zeami's first consideration. As before, he insists on fidelity to "the original source," but now he voices an additional concern. The source must contain a "seed." That seed is to be a character, not a plot, and it must be a character that can be appropriately treated with music and dance.

What I mean here by the seed is that character who performs the central action in the source upon which the noh is based; be aware that the choice of this seed is of great importance for the dance and song in the play. The bases of this art are dance and song. If the seed is a character who does not sing and dance, there will be no effective way of treating that character in this art no matter what sort of legendary hero or outstanding figure he may be. Be certain you understand this completely.[20]

We observe that whereas in "Kashu" Zeami had made only scant reference to music and dance, he is now absorbed with both arts. When he subsequently cites specific examples of characters to be dealt with in noh, all—aside from characters of unquestionable elegance, and consequently talent (such as Lady Ise, Lady Komachi, Narihira, and Genji)—are characters who have a professional interest in dance and song.[21]

This increasing attention to song and dance reflects a shift away from the mimetic approach of *Fūshikaden* to a more abstract, lyrical ideal of performance. Yūgen is now the central aesthetic goal of noh. (This new emphasis on yūgen is evident in other treatises of roughly the same period as well.)*

Perhaps to compensate for this aesthetic shift, Zeami becomes much more specific than before on the question of structure:

The structure of the play refers to that determination—once one has found the right seed—of what action is to take place where.

First, there are to be five *dan* organized into an introduction [*jo*], a develop-

---

* Consider, for instance, the following passage on the actor's training from *Shikadō* (finished three years before *Sandō*), p. 112: "Though there are many forms of expression [in *sarugaku*], the first steps taken in an actor's training should not depart from the *nikyoku* and the *santai*. *Nikyoku* means the Two Arts of singing and dance; *santai* means the Three Modes of dramatic representation. First, a child should learn music and dance very thoroughly from his teacher. From about age 10 until about age 17 or 18, he should not practice dramatic representation. . . . He should not wear a mask, any mimetic representation should be done in name alone, and his costume should be such as befits a child. The reason for this is to make *yūgen* the basis of his art in the future." Just as an actor is imbued with yūgen by training him in song and dance, so the playwright lays a foundation for yūgen in his plays by choosing characters that can easily be made vehicles for these two arts. Zeami's turn away from monomane may reflect the increasing influence of Inuō Dōami and of Ōmi sarugaku, with its emphasis on yūgen over the original preeminence of monomane in Yamato sarugaku. The change is clearly visible in Zeami's discussion of roles as he proceeds from the nine character types of *Fūshikaden* to the Three Modes of *Kakyō*, *Shikadō*, and *Sandō*. (The matter was touched on in Chap. 1.)

ment [*ha*], and a conclusion [*kyū*]: the introduction consists of one *dan*, the development three, and the conclusion one. In the first *dan*, the *waki* comes on stage to sing his *sashigoe*, *shidai*, and *hitoutai*. The development follows. In the first *dan* of the development, the *shite* appears and sings from the *issei* through his first *hitoutai*. The next *dan* comprises a *mondō* with the *waki*, and a *hitoutai* by the chorus. The last *dan* of the development consists of a musical passage, either a *kusemai* or a piece in *tadautai* style. Then comes the conclusion, a *dan* with a *mai* or a *hataraki*, or *hayabushi* or *kiribyōshi*, and so on.

These are the five *dan* of a noh. Sometimes, depending on the nature of the original source, six *dan* may be necessary, and then again, there may be noh of four *dan*, lacking one *dan* in accordance with the original material. At any rate, the basic pattern has five *dan*.

In setting out these five *dan*, ask yourself how much music should be allotted for the introduction, how much of each of the three types of music is needed for the three *dan* of the development, and how much music is appropriate to the conclusion, thus determining the number of lines in the piece. This construction of the piece is what I intend by the word structure. The musical composition should vary through the introduction, development, and conclusion, according to the type of noh being written and the mood it is to evoke. The length of the play should be measured by the number of lines of music in it.[22]

Zeami presents us here with a highly systematized structural "grammar" of noh—a play made up of (usually) five dan shaped into an introduction, development, and conclusion (jo, ha, kyū). The building blocks of these structural components are, in turn, specific types of songs (shōdan; e.g., shidai, issei).

Zeami has borrowed the terms jo, ha, and kyu from *gagaku* (court music), where they are used to name movements that may or may not form part of any particular piece. In his usage, however, they take on a more abstract meaning that has to do with the temporal configuration of a play (or a day's program of plays, or a song within a play, or, for that matter, any phenomenon occurring through time).[23] Here, in the context of a single play, they prescribe the following dramatic framework:

Jo (introduction)	Appearance of the waki
Ha 1 (development, part 1)	Appearance of the shite
Ha 2 (development, part 2)	Exchange between the shite and the waki
Ha 3 (development, part 3)	Musical performance by the shite
Kyū (conclusion)	Dance by the shite

Zeami calls for particular songs, or shōdan,[24] to be set into this basic framework. Before we see what his requirements are, though, let us pause to review the technical information provided in the Introduction, presented in taxonomic form in Figure 6. (Note, however, that the figure is merely illustrative; there are far too many kinds of shōdan to include in a single chart.)

This taxonomic sorting of the structural components of noh reveals a

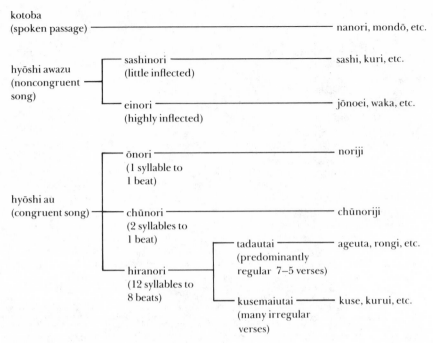

Fig. 6   A taxonomy of shōdan in noh plays

system of remarkable complexity and development, and although some of the names of the songs shown in the figure were not in currency in Zeami's day, their basic formal characteristics have not changed. How early and by what means did this structural differentiation take place, and how conscious of it were Zeami's predecessors? The answers to these questions would greatly clarify Zeami's role in the development of Japanese dramaturgy, but they remain unanswered. In any case, this system underlies the actual structuring of the play in Zeami's process of composition. How do these individual elements come together to make a play?

This question is easily answered by referring back to the passage quoted on pp. 50-51. Table 2 translates Zeami's shōdan names into their modern equivalents.[25] Although this outline, which Zeami presents merely as an introduction to the structure of noh, is too general to compare with the structure of any specific play, it does reveal certain characteristics of Zeami's style. First, there is a careful building of musical (particularly rhythmic) interest from the waki's appearance to the shite's appearance to the dialogue between the two of them, which leads to the first choral piece (the ageuta). So far, all of the drama is either spoken or in noncongruent song or tadautai, which is another way of saying that it

TABLE 2   *The Structure of a Typical Play*

Dan (section)	Function	Shōdan	
		Modern terms	Zeami's terms
1 (jo)	Appearance of the waki	Nanori	Sashigoe
		Shidai	Shidai
		Ageuta	Hitoutai
2 (ha 1)	Appearance of the shite	Issei–ageuta	Same
3 (ha 2)	Exchange between the shite and the waki	Mondō	Mondō
		Ageuta	Hitoutai
4 (ha 3)	Musical performance by the shite	Passage in kusemaiutai (kuri-sashi-kuse) or tadautai	Same
5 (kyū)	Dance by the shite	Mai or hataraki Chūnoriji or noriji	Mai or hataraki Hayabushi or kiribyoshi

NOTE: The correlation of the terms is based on Omote and Katō, zz, 24: 135 (headnote), 462-63 nn. 69-70.

is rhythmically unobtrusive. Then comes the kusemai, followed by the dance and the change to chūnori or ōnori. Rhythmic interest is the central concern of the kusemai, and it is joined to visual interest in the dance of the kyū.[26]

No clear picture of the literary structure of the play is given, but certain inferences can be made. First, the waki plays a primary role only during the first dan. His nanori is a self-introduction to the audience, and his ageuta is often a *michiyuki*, or travel song. This provides an opportunity for a passage filled with evocative poetic place names. The shite's appearance in the second dan (the beginning of the development) leads one to suspect that the waki has arrived at a spot where he can watch the shite. Then, in dan 3, with the mondō, comes an opportunity for more dramatic writing, that is, writing centered on the interaction of two (or more) characters. The rest of the noh is devoted to the shite; the waki no longer plays an important part. This means that the remainder is more likely to be of a narrative, or lyrical, than a dramatic nature. The central role of the dance in the conclusion implies that there will be some difference in literary construction between this dan and the last dan of the ha. Further comments on the literary and musical structure of noh are best postponed until we can turn to Zeami's detailed comments on the Three Modes in the next several chapters.

We return, then, to Zeami's introductory remarks in *Sandō* on the actual writing of a play:

In writing, you should get a firm grasp on the sort of character you are dealing with, from the very beginning all the way through, asking yourself, "With a character such as this, what kind of language is most appropriate?" Make use of phrases from poetry expressive of congratulations, elegance, love, complaint, or despair, according to the type of character being depicted.

In a play there should be a place where the original source is pointed out. If it is a famous place or a historical site, then you should take lines from well-known poems about the place, in Chinese or Japanese, and write them into concentrated points in the three *dan* of the *ha*. These become important places for action. In addition to this, you should work distinguished sayings and well-known expressions into the shite's language.[27]

The concern for appropriate diction that first appeared in "Kashu" carries through here. Again, poetic language is an important component of the text. Five particular kinds of poetic expression are mentioned: "congratulations" (*shūgen*), "elegance" (*yūgen*), "love" (*koi*), "complaint" (*shukkai*), and "despair" (*bōoku*).[28] This classification of emotions has been borrowed from the poetics of waka and renga, with the exception of bōoku, which seems to be Zeami's coinage. Why he narrowed his selection to these five categories is unclear, but they can be seen as a step on the way to his theories about the five types of music (the *go on*, or Five Sounds) of later treatises.[29]

At any rate, poetic expressions of these five sorts should be used to fill out the shite's part. Furthermore, famous lines about well-known places can be woven into the text at this stage. One important point to note, however, is that such lines are to appear in the ha of the play. They do not belong to the waki (this follows the "Kashu" dictum about not putting key phrases in inconsequential places). Nor are they to be put in the kyū. This supports an earlier observation that the kyū is reserved primarily for visual and rhythmic interest.

The next section of *Sandō* treats noh in the Aged Mode and will serve as the starting point for the following chapter. One major question remains before we turn to that chapter, however: how much continuity is there between the noh Zeami wrote and performed and the plays that go by the same names today? Over half a millennium has passed since Zeami himself performed his plays, a period in which changes have inevitably taken place. Discussing Zeami's style without taking those changes into consideration would be tantamount to discussing Shakespeare's style using Polanski's *Macbeth*.

One of the greatest attractions of the noh is its artistic comprehensiveness. It is a literary art that counts among its texts some of the greatest poetic works in Japanese literature. (This is, for the most part, the way noh has been viewed by Western scholars.) It is a musical art with very distinctive and highly formalized musical idioms. It is dance of a unique and extremely formal sort. (The music and dance of noh have always been the central concern of most noh actors.) The dance has been called living sculpture, and this view of it hints at another of noh's facets: it is a visual art as well as a performing art. The masks that the shite generally wears (some of which represent the finest extant examples of Muromachi and Momoyama sculpture) and the costumes that all the characters wear (again, some of these are masterpieces of weaving and dyeing) are both set into a highly systematized body of conventions governing specific plays.

A good performance of noh today, then, is an alloy of numerous arts and can be appreciated from several different aesthetic perspectives. But to what extent is this an accurate reflection of Zeami's noh, and therefore legitimate evidence about his style? How much, on the contrary, is due to the refinements and transformations of later ages?

The most reliable tangible evidence available for an investigation of noh in Zeami's day is found in the ten noh libretti mentioned earlier. These are the texts of *Naniwa, Morihisa, Tatatsu, Eguchi, Unrin'in, Tomoakira, Matsura, Akoya no matsu, Furu,* and *Kashiwazaki.* To these may be added the text of *Yoroboshi,* a 1711 copy of an original in Zeami's hand.[30] Unfortunately, most of these plays are not Zeami's compositions, and none of the others can be proved to be his.[31] But that fact does not diminish their value for a general view of the noh in his day, particularly since all but four (*Tatatsu, Matsura, Furu,* and *Akoya no matsu*) are still performed, giving us modern texts by which to measure, at least in a general way, the extent to which the noh has changed over the centuries.[32]

A detailed and comprehensive examination of all the texts is impossible here, but a brief look at two of them, *Eguchi* and *Unrin'in,* may provide some idea of what kinds of changes have taken place. First of all, compare the waki's nanori, or self-introduction, from Zeami's manuscript of *Eguchi* with the modern Kanze version (Taiseiban edition):[33]

ZEAMI TEXT

Kore wa Hokurokudō yori idetaru shamon nite sōro. Ware kono hodo Miyako ni sōraitsuru ga nao nao shokoku ikken no nozomi sōro. Mazu mazu Kinai no reibutsu reisha sankei no kokorozashi sōraite, dōban no sō nisannin tomonaite, konnichi haya tabidachi sōro. (I am a priest come out of the north. I have been in the capital for some while now, but still have a longing to travel far and wide. First of all, I intend to make my pilgrimage to the miraculous shrines and temples in the home provinces, and already today, I set off with two or three fellow priests.)

MODERN KANZE TEXT (Taiseiban)

Kore wa shokoku ikken no sō nite sōro. Ware imada Tsu no kuni Tennōji ni mairazu sōrō hodo ni, kono tabi omoitachi, Tennōji ni mairabaya to omoisōro. (I am a priest traveling far and wide. I have yet to visit Tennōji in the province of Tsu so this time I have made up my mind, and think I shall set off for Tennōji.)

The modern version, which can be traced back without significant change to the 1620's,[34] is less distinctive and more formulaic than the original, and varies only slightly from the nanori of any number of other plays. But changes of this magnitude are common only in spoken passages and some sashinori passages. In the waki's shidai and ageuta adjacent to this nanori, one finds only minor differences between the Zeami text and the modern version. The waki's spoken passages are in prose and are not of great importance to the play's content, especially at so early a stage. It matters little in this instance where the waki is going eventually or where he is coming from (two things often stated in a nanori).* Such passages are therefore highly susceptible to change. Sung passages, especially passages in congruent song, are more difficult to change since the meter becomes a consideration. Furthermore, the waki's sung passages are often critical to the action. For instance, in the spoken nanori in *Eguchi* it is not the waki's ultimate destination that is important, but the fact that he is on a journey. The ageuta that follows, on the other hand, reveals the waki's specific destination for the duration of the play. It sets the stage for what is to come and is difficult to change without disrupting the story line.

The shite's part in *Eguchi* reveals the same pattern. Spoken passages in prose are more susceptible to change than sung passages in verse. In this case, however, even the changes in the prose passages are relatively minor. There are no revisions in the modern texts that are significantly altered.[35] What changes have occurred are generally on the order of the following: in the mondō, where the original text reads *eijitamaisōrō so* ("recite"), the modern schools have substituted *eijitamō zo* (Kita and Konparu), *eijisasetamō zo* (Kongō), *kuchizusamitamō* (Hōshō), or *kuchizusamitamaisōro* (Kanze). The first two changes make almost no difference whatever in meaning, and even the *kuchizusami . . .* of the last two only changes the meaning of the original's "recite" to something like "intone."

There is one characteristic change here, though, that does affect the play's performance. Many prose passages in the original are now sung prose passages (in sashinori), and vice versa. The passage following the mondō, for instance, was originally spoken but now is sung: "Sate wa inishie no Eguchi no kimi no ato narikeri. Sono mi wa dochū ni uzumoredomo, na wa todomarite ima made mo" ("This, then, is the place where once long ago Eguchi lived. Although her body lies buried in the ground, her name remains, even to this day").[36] Similarly, the first line of

---

* This is particularly true for *mugen* noh (plays about supernatural beings) in which the shite remains at the center of the drama. In *genzai* noh (plays about living human beings) the waki sometimes has a larger part.

the nanori quoted earlier was originally sung but is now spoken.[37] This kind of change affects not only the intonation of the passages in question, but also the speed with which they are delivered. The pace of performance is known to have slowed considerably over the centuries, and this may be one of the factors that have brought about this change.*

It would be reassuring if all the holograph texts showed as little difference from their modern counterparts as *Eguchi* does, but this is not the case. Judging from Zeami's text, *Unrin'in* once must have been a very different play indeed. In the modern version, Kinmitsu (the waki), a great admirer of *Ise monogatari* (Tales of Ise), is prompted by a curious dream to go to the capital. He arrives at the Unrin'in, a temple fallen into ruin, and is about to break off a branch of blossoming cherry in the courtyard when an old man stops him. The two have an argument full of poetic allusions. Eventually the old man asks Kinmitsu who he is. In his reply, Kinmitsu tells the old man about his dream and two mysterious figures that appeared in it. The old man explains that the two were probably the poet Ariwara no Narihira and Empress Nijō of *Ise monogatari* fame. He urges Kinmitsu to sleep under the cherry tree at the Unrin'in to see what his dreams there might bring; then he disappears. Kinmitsu hears more about Narihira and *Ise monogatari* from a man of the vicinity (the aikyōgen) and then settles down to sleep, acting on the old man's advice. His dream forms the kyū of the play: Narihira appears, sings about *Ise monogatari*, dances a JONOMAI, and with a final tribute to the inexhaustible artistry of the tale, disappears. Kinmitsu awakes.

The first part of the play is essentially the same in both texts.[38] However, in the Zeami text, when Kinmitsu falls asleep, instead of seeing Narihira, he first sees a beautiful woman. She identifies herself as Empress Nijō and proceeds to tell Kinmitsu some of the secret traditional interpretations of the following poem:

Musashino wa	Do not burn
Kyō wa na yaki so	Musashi Plain today,
Wakakusa no	For in the new-grown grass
Tsuma mo komoreri	My lover hides away,
Ware mo komoreri	And I too hide away.[39]

When she recites the poem, a demon appears. He explains that he was once Empress Nijō's brother Mototsune, and then the two of them tell the story behind the poem. Empress Nijō has been having a secret affair with Narihira. As she runs off across Musashi Plain to meet him, Moto-

---

* There are other possible factors operating here. The reverence accorded noh in later ages, from the Tokugawa (1603-1867) period on, may have resulted in a performance style that identified gravity and seriousness with slowness. Furthermore, the kyōgen interludes included in modern performances are reputed to be much longer than their earlier counterparts.

tsune follows. Suddenly she disappears. He sets the plain on fire, and when the grasses are burned away, discovers a mound. He suspects his sister may have hidden in the mound, and when he goes inside to see, he discovers her making love with Narihira. The chorus then breaks into a virtuoso recitation of six waka arranged in a loose narrative sequence. Finally, as the play ends, Kinmitsu awakes from his dream.

The differences between Zeami's version of *Unrin'in* and the modern version are so great that the two could be considered entirely different plays.[40] What confidence in the continuity of the text one gained from examining *Eguchi* completely evaporates here. If such vast differences exist between the two versions of *Unrin'in*, how can it be argued that the modern texts of *Takasago* and *Izutsu* and *Tadanori*, to name only a few, reflect Zeami's original style? There is no holograph copy of any of these plays to compare with the modern versions. The oldest extant texts date from the sixteenth through eighteenth centuries, and our confidence is hardly restored by looking to them since the changes that have so transmogrified *Unrin'in* had already been made by 1600.[41]

Is it possible that Zeami's own plays have undergone such radical transformation? Probably not. For one thing, *Unrin'in* is the only play among the holograph texts to show such drastic change. Also, whoever made all the changes in the play left a number of clues that the original had been tampered with. There is one major inconsistency: Empress Nijō, mentioned in a prominent place in the first half of the play (i.e., before the aikyōgen interlude), is never mentioned in the second. Among the more minor inconsistencies is the needless introduction of an episode from the celebrated *Genji monogatari* (The Tale of Genji) into the sashi and kuse of the second half. The last half of the play is not well written and does not fit naturally with the more interesting first half, even in the rather watered-down modern version.

Unrin'in in fact seems a special case, and unless there is evidence to the contrary, we may reasonably assume that the plays to be dealt with in this study did not undergo such drastic change. At the same time, the *Unrin'in* case provides ample warning about the dangers of using a modern printed text without a careful consideration of the individual manuscript(s) upon which it is based and the textual tradition as a whole. As a general rule, it seems safe to conclude that the shite's parts are more reliable than the waki's, and that the passages in congruent song are more reliable than those in noncongruent song, which are in turn more reliable than spoken passages.

Now, what can be said of the music and the changes it has undergone?[42] Before turning to Zeami's holograph texts to explore this question, we need to take stock of certain overall musical changes that have occurred since the fifteenth century. Comparison of noh texts to certain

Modern *tsuyogin*   Original *yowagin*   Modern *yowagin*

Fig. 7   Basic pitches in the vocal music of noh. (These pitches are not to be taken as absolute; the five-line staff is used merely as a convenient way to show their relationship.) Pitch 1 is called *ge*, 2 *ge no chū*, 3 *chū*, 4 *jō*, and 5 *kuri*. Although pitches 1 and 2 are the same in modern tsuyogin (and 3 the same as 4), they are still identified separately by the old yowagin names.

song texts (*sōga*) from the Muromachi period has led Yokomichi Mario to conclude that the hiranori rhythmic pattern outlined in the Introduction (Fig. 3) was somewhat different in Zeami's time.[43] The standard modern-day pattern of

	1		2		3		4		5		6		7		8	
a	–	a	a	a	–	a	a	a	–	a	a	a	a	a	.

(with "a" representing a syllable of a 7/5 verse text) seems originally to have been performed like this:[44]

	1		2		3		4		5		6		7		8	
a	a	–	a	a	a	–	a	a	a	–	a	a	a	a	.

There have been melodic changes as well. In the modern vocal music of noh, there are two kinds of singing. The basic pitch levels and methods of vocalization and ornamentation are different depending on whether the style is *tsuyogin* ("strong chant") or *yowagin* ("lyric chant"). In Zeami's day, however, there was probably only one basic kind of singing, the original yowagin.[45] Figure 7 shows the relationship between the pitch levels of what is thought to be the original yowagin and the modern yowagin and tsuyogin styles. As we see, modern yowagin pitch levels remain fairly close to the original, but the number of levels in tsuyogin has been reduced (in this case, from five to three, *ge* and *ge no chū* having become the same pitch, and likewise *jō* and *chū*). Fortunately for the historian of noh, a native conservatism in the art form has kept traditional notation alive, so that a distinction between the pitches is still made in the printed text even though it has disappeared in actual performance. This means that basic approximations of the original melodic patterns can be reconstructed from even the most modern texts.

The mention of texts suggests another problem: how much of the modern melodic structure of the vocal music of noh can be traced back to Zeami's day, and how much of it is the contribution of later ages? For the answer, we must again turn to Zeami's handwritten texts. Three of them—*Eguchi, Morihisa,* and *Unrin'in*—make some reference to melodic movement and ornamentation. But many of the terms differ from the modern vocabulary, and even where they are the same, they may refer to different things.[46] Moreover, most of the holograph texts have almost no musical notation, and even the most heavily notated, *Eguchi*, contains only a fraction of the notations of a modern text. Therefore, we cannot assume that any of the melodies in modern noh date from Zeami's day. Nevertheless, the basic contours of modern melodies are sometimes surprisingly similar to the melodies notated in early texts. For example, a reconstruction of the most carefully notated passage in *Eguchi*, the issei, reveals unmistakable similarities to the modern version (Fig. 8).[47] True, the end of the phrase seems to have changed rather radically, but some continuity must all the same be admitted for the first three-quarters of the song.

In any event, we can certainly claim continuity in the more important matter of the musical structure of the noh as a whole, the way in which various shōdan are put together to create an entire play. Again, *Eguchi* provides an interesting comparison. In Table 3, which matches the sequence of shōdan in the holograph text with the modern sequence, we see a quite remarkable consistency, for all the changes in vocabulary. As one would expect, the greatest discrepancy is found in the waki's part, but even there the difference is slight and explainable: what is called a *sashigoto* in the original text is, in content, a nanori; but instead of being

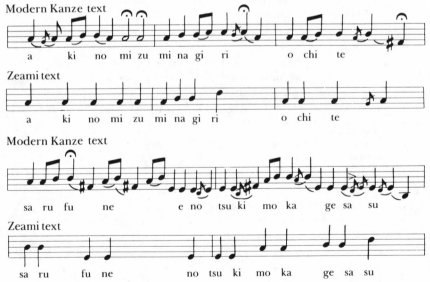

Fig. 8   Musical notation for the issei from the play *Eguchi*, modern and Zeami texts

TABLE 3 *The Structure of Eguchi in the Zeami Holograph and in the Modern Kanze Text (Taiseiban)*

Zeami text	Modern text	Zeami text	Modern text
Shidai	Shidai	Ge, kakaru	Sageuta
Sashigoto	Nanori	Kakaru	Kakeai
Uta	Michiyuki (ageuta)	Sōgabushi	Issei
Mondō[a]	Mondō[b]	Jō	Kuri
Kotoba	Yobikake	Sashigoe	Sashi
Mondō	Mondō	Kuseuta	Kuse
Uta[c]	Ageuta[c]	Waka	*Waka[d]
Rongi	Rongi	Mai	JONOMAI
Mondō[a]	Mondō[b]	Kiribyoshi	Noriji
Uta	Ageuta	Hayabushi	Uta
Utai	Ageuta		

SOURCES: The names of shōdan for the modern text are taken from *Kanzeryu* 1, pp. 529-39, and YK, 1: 50-56. Those for the holograph text can be found in Gotō et al., pp. 102-9, and Kawase, *Zeami jihitsu*, pp. 223-37.

NOTE: Kawase misreads the cursive version of 哥 as a katakana rendering of the syllables *ni-i*, which makes no sense. Gotō and his co-authors compound the confusion by replacing *ni-i* with *ninin* (or *futari*, "two people"). This does not make good sense in this context either. I have transcribed the character throughout as *uta*. A photograph of the original can be seen in *Nō* (1978), p.112.

[a]With "okashi." [b]With kyōgen actor. [c]Sung by chorus. [d]Slightly irregular.

spoken, the first lines of this particular shōdan were sung in sashinori in Zeami's day, so the word sashigoto was used. For the shite's part, Zeami uses broader terminology than that in the modern text, saying kotoba, for instance, against the modern text's more specific *yobikake*, or uta where the modern text specifies ageuta or sageuta. The fact remains that the musical structure of *Eguchi* has stayed intact for the half millennium since Zeami wrote out the text.[48]

The holograph texts do not, unfortunately, provide any idea of the sort of instrumental music used to accompany the noh in Zeami's day.[49] It is certain that the flute, the stick drum (the *taiko*), and at least one form of hand drum were used, but whether the two kinds of drums used today (the *ōtsuzumi* and the *kotsuzumi*) were used then, or even existed as such, is an open question.[50] The actual patterns of accompaniment remain even more of a mystery, and though it seems likely that basic patterns such as *tsuzuke* and *mitsuji* were used in alternation most of the time,[51] there is no proof of this contemporary with Zeami.

Similarly, the holograph texts reveal little about the dance, aside from its placement in the kyū. The fact that it has remained in the same position, however, provides an important clue about the balance between musical and balletic elements in the noh's structure.[52] Fascinating research is just beginning to be done on dance in Zeami's day, but nothing conclusive has appeared as yet.[53]

Still less can be said about the early masks and costumes. Zeami's own notes in *Sarugaku dangi* on mask carvers are not extensive enough to permit fruitful speculation about mid-Muromachi conventions of costuming.[54] There is also the brief reference to the performance on the Kasakake Riding Grounds discussed earlier, with its mention of actors riding live horses and wearing actual armor. Since this performance is specifically said to have been done in the unusual Tōnomine style, it cannot be considered an accurate reflection of standard performance practice. And even though Zeami does make passing comments on costuming here and there in his treatises, they are too casual and brief to provide any systematic understanding of the conventions governing noh costuming in his day.

In sum, useful as the Zeami treatises and holographs are, we must in the end examine the literary texts themselves for clues to Zeami's style. But there is still one subject to address before we turn to that task—the classification of the noh repertory. Many systems of classification are possible. The plays can be divided into two very broad categories: those about living human beings (genzai noh) and those about other beings (mugen noh). Or they can be divided into countless specialized categories, such as plays in which the shite portrays a god of Chinese origin and performs a particular dance wearing a particular kind of mask. Probably the most common system used today is based on the five categories that guide the arrangement of a formal, full-day program: god plays, warrior plays, wig plays, miscellaneous plays, and finale, or demon, plays. This is a useful classification, which gives valuable information about the form and content of the plays in each category, but it was not fully developed until the Tokugawa period, and so is not appropriate for our study. Zeami himself had several classification systems,[55] but the one that seems most suitable is the one mentioned earlier—that of the Three Modes. Zeami introduced this system in *Kakyō*, further developed it in *Shikadō*, *Nikyoku santai ningyōzu*, and *Shūgyoku tokka*, and applied it specifically to the composition of plays in *Sandō*.[56] We shall follow this classification throughout the remainder of this study, taking the Aged Mode (rōtai) as the subject of the next chapter.[57]

CHAPTER 3

Rōtai:
The Aged Mode

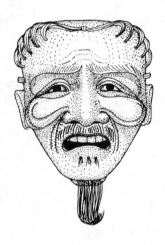

ZEAMI'S pronouncements on the role of the old man provide an intriguing introduction to his plays in the Aged Mode:

An accomplished actor approaches the role of an old man with the same intent as an old amateur decking himself out to dance and perform. . . . Being an old man to begin with, he has no need to imitate an old man, but instead concentrates all his efforts on the particular role he is playing. . . .

The secret in playing an old man, the way to seem old and still bring your performance to full dramatic flowering is as follows. First of all, don't set your mind on the decrepitude of age. It's generally the case that the dances of noh—both elegant and vigorous—are done in time to music; the actor moves his feet, extends and draws back his arms, and performs the appropriate actions in accordance with the beat. But when an old man is dancing, he moves his feet and extends and draws back his arms just a little late, catching the beat slightly behind the *taiko* and song and the cadences of the *tsuzumi*. He does everything just as if he were young, but unavoidably he falls slightly off beat. . . . [His performance] is like blossoms on an ancient tree.[1]

The last line of this brief passage persists in the imagination with the eloquence of paradox and the elevation of classical poetry. Some have compared it to a *kōan*, a "Zen riddle." As a characterization of an actor's performance, it is as charming as it is puzzling. Perhaps the charm is in fact a function of the puzzlement. Perhaps the line is one of those pithy sayings that delight mainly because they are exotic, because they seem so foreign to Western intellectual experience.

The puzzlement is natural, for the old man Zeami speaks of here is worlds removed from the great old men of the Western theatrical heritage. Could a great Lear, or Rigoletto, or Oedipus at Colonus ever remind one of blossoms on an ancient tree? No, there is no hint of tragedy in the character Zeami describes, no sense of the misery that can settle on a man in the hoary twilight of his days. For Zeami an old man in the noh in the Aged Mode is the embodiment of tradition, a testimony to the benevolence of the Emperor and, in a broader sense, an affirmation of the religious, political, and aesthetic values of Zeami's ideal world. The old man is very close to the divine, and more often than not, in fact, turns out to be a god in disguise. It is difficult to trace the origins of this conception, but surely it must reach back into the beginnings of saru-gaku; even today, the most ancient play known to us, *Shikisanban*, or *Okina*, brings just such old men onto the stage. Zeami was well steeped in this tradition when he wrote his theoretical works, and his acknowledgment of it is readily seen in his first remarks on the old man:

The representation of an old man is [one of] the ultimate accomplishments of our art. Since this is a mode in which your level of achievement is immediately apparent to the viewer, it is of the utmost importance. Indeed, many relatively good actors have never mastered the mode. But then, it's really a mistake in critical judgment to assume that someone is accomplished just because he can mimic the actions of an old woodcutter or salt maker. The figure of an old man in formal or informal court dress—*that* can only be done fittingly by an accomplished actor. Without years of practice and lofty achievements, you cannot perform the role suitably. The presentation of an old man bent over at the waist and lame in the knees loses the dramatic flower and looks decrepit, and there is little of interest in that. Don't fidget and fuss; comport yourself with grace. Most important of all is the dance of an old man. Your problem is how to look old and yet retain the dramatic flower—it's just like blossoms on an ancient tree.[2]

Again, "blossoms on an ancient tree." Some of the charm sours to frustration, and the puzzlement is tarnished with exasperation. Zeami still fails to give any palpable notion of an old man on stage. The relatively concrete image of the old man bent over at the waist is dismissed as uninteresting, and for a tangible sense of the role one must, quite literally, grasp at threads: the real test of an actor's experience and achievement is his portrayal of an old man in court dress.[3]

It is difficult to say to what degree this costuming represents a continuous tradition dating from Zeami's day, but there is mention of this old man in court dress elsewhere, which somewhat narrows the focus. One old manuscript of a Zeami text pictures the old man in two endearingly clumsy cartoons (see Fig. 9).[4] In one, he wears only a loincloth—the sketch seems designed to illustrate his posture—and he gazes off expressively into the distance. The artist has drawn a dotted line from his eyes across the page to the Chinese character "see," and a caption beneath this figure contains a dictum from *Kakyō*: "First thoroughly become the object, then thoroughly imitate what it does."[5] Near the top of the page, next to the character "see" is the four-character expression, "a tranquil heart, a distant gaze." In the other cartoon, the old man is pictured in court dress, capering across the page, fan in hand, underneath a branch of plum blossoms.[6] The caption here again mentions the ancient tree in blossom, and ties the dance in a play in the Aged Mode to a tranquil heart. An additional line reads: "The same applies for old nuns and old women. In its various applications, [this mode] produces an air of divinity and utter tranquility."

Fig. 9 Illustrations for plays in the Aged Mode from a 1441 manuscript of Zea-mi's *Nikyoku santai ningyōzu.* "The Aged Mode. A tranquil heart, a distant gaze." *Courtesy of the Noh Theater Research Institute, Hōsei University.*

Even now, little of a concrete nature emerges. The "air of divinity," however, is telling when taken together with Zeami's list of six typical plays in the Aged Mode: *Yawata* (*Yumi Yawata*), *Aioi* (*Takasago*), *Yōrō, Oima-tsu, Shiogama* (*Tōru*), and *Aridōshi*. In all but one of these, the old man is actually a god in disguise; only one of Zeami's "old men" is actually a man.

Another remark, this from the 1423 *Sandō,* further specifies the characteristic play in the Aged Mode. "The play in the Aged Mode," says Zeami, is for the most part "cast in the form of a *waki* noh."[7]

At long last a web of relationships begins to appear. Waki noh are plays that stand at the head of a day's performance, directly after the ritualistic opening with *Shikisanban.* Since waki noh are elsewhere consigned to the musical and emotional category of shūgen, the auspicious, or congratulatory, it follows that most plays about old men—actually gods—appear early in the day's performance and give voice to congratulatory and auspicious sentiments. The mode finally begins to take shape, and an integral component of that shape is structural formalism, necessary because the quasi-ritualistic nature of the waki noh demands structural orthodoxy.

In an earlier discussion of the overall contours of a typical play, we specified the five-dan sequence of appearances, actions, and interactions that inform the dramatic architecture of noh: jo, appearance of the waki; ha 1, appearance of the shite; ha 2, exchange between the shite

TABLE 4 *The Structure of a Noh Play in the Aged Mode*

Dan (section)	Function	Shōdan
Jo	Appearance of the waki	Nanori Shidai ⎫ Ageuta ⎭ 7-8 verses
Ha 1	Appearance of the shite	Issei: 4 verses (5-7-5/7-5/7-5/7-5) Sashi: 10 verses Sageuta ⎫ Ageuta ⎭ 10 verses
Ha 2	Exchange between the shite and the waki	Mondō: 4-5 exchanges Ageuta by chorus: 10 verses in 2 strains
Ha 3	Musical performance by the shite	Kuri: 5 verses Sashi: 1st half, 5 verses Sashi: 2d half, 5-6 verses Kuse: 1st half, 12-13 verses Kuse: 2d half, 12-13 verses Rongi: 2-3 exchanges
Kyū	Dance by the shite	Sashi Issei (chorus sings last verse) Rongi or noriji

SOURCE: *Sandō*, pp. 136-37.
   NOTE: The passage on which the table is based is translated in full in Appendix A with some discussion of the technical terminology. A 12-syllable line broken into 7-5 meter constitutes a "verse." However, the first half of a waka poem (17 syllables: 5-7-5) counts as a single verse.

and the waki; ha 3, musical performance by the shite; and kyū, dance by the shite. This is, of course, the basis on which Zeami builds his typical play in the Aged Mode, but now, in *Sandō*, he goes into considerable detail, often even specifying how many verses (*ku*) there ought to be in certain songs (our modern shōdan). His remarks become extremely technical, but when they are digested—that is, when his terms are translated into their modern counterparts and then integrated into the outline quoted above—a play in the Aged Mode is seen to have the pattern shown in Table 4.

This structure is strikingly similar to that of many plays in the modern repertory, not all of them in the Aged Mode, and not all by Zeami— but more on that later. There are also some striking omissions in the scheme. First of all, there is no mention of instrumental shōdan to allow for the characters' entrances and exits. A lack of evidence on instrumental music in Zeami's day precludes any extensive speculation on this score, but judging from modern practice, and indeed traditional practice in the late sixteenth century,[8] most characters probably did make their entrances and exits to the accompaniment of an instrumental piece. (This is, in fact, so consistently the case in modern practice that the entrance of the shite without accompanying music is used purposely for striking dramatic effect in the play *Hachinoki* [The Trees in Pots].)

Similarly, Zeami fails to say anything about the shite's dance in the kyū other than that there is to be one somewhere in this section. He does, however, provide a clue by remarking that the last line of the nochijite's issei should be sung by the chorus. This happens in a great many modern stagings of the noh, presumably to give the shite a moment to collect himself for the dance. Such plays as *Takasago*, *Hōjōgawa*, *Oimatsu*, and *Tōru* all take this form, and the dance follows immediately on the chorus's completion of the issei. This would suggest that the dance came in such a place in Zeami's day as well.

The third omission from Zeami's schema is the absence of any mention of the aikyōgen's part and the waki's subsequent ageuta. This is puzzling because some sort of break is usually needed between the third part of the ha and the kyū to allow a costume change, and following this, some kind of transition to the nochijite's appearance is expected, usually a shōdan sung by the waki. The holograph text of *Eguchi* provides for both the aikyōgen's part and the waki's ageuta in the appropriate places, so we know that these shōdan were performed in at least some plays in Zeami's day.[9]

We unfortunately have only the vaguest understanding of the instrumental shōdan, the aikyōgen's part, and the shite's dance in Zeami's performance practice, but from the evidence mentioned above, it seems reasonable to assume, at least, that there were instrumental shōdan of some sort to allow for the entrances and exits of major characters, that there was some sort of aikyōgen interlude between the third part of the ha and the kyū in most plays, and that the dance, whatever formal configuration it took, came in roughly the same sequence as in modern performance.

Let us turn, now, to the analysis of one of Zeami's plays in the Aged Mode, *Takasago*. If there is one noh play whose title, at least, is known to every modern Japanese, it is *Takasago*. The singing of "Takasago ya," the ageuta from the second act, is de rigueur even at "Western"-style wedding receptions, and many a go-between has grudgingly memorized the piece. Were merely the auspicious element needed in this situation, any proper waki noh would suffice. *Takasago*'s preeminence, even here, demonstrates that there is more to the play than mere felicitation.

Properly speaking, *Takasago* is not the most structurally orthodox of the six noh Zeami mentions as models for the Aged Mode. That distinction goes to the otherwise rather undistinguished *Yumi Yawata*:

One must learn to write by starting with plays in a straightforward style of a congratulatory sort. The straightforward style is exemplified by *Yumi Yawata*. It contains no particular places of interest and proceeds in a perfectly straightforward manner. It was written for the accession of the present ruler and holds no secrets. The play about the *hōjōe* has a dramatic twist where the fish is set free, so it must be considered a bit idiosyncratic. Even *Aioi* has its fins.[10]

The "play about the *hōjōe*" has been tentatively identified as *Hōjōgawa*, and *Aioi* (Growing Together) is quite certainly the old name for *Takasago*. Both of these plays fall short of *Yumi Yawata*, which has neither "a dramatic twist" nor "fins" to complicate its formal structure.[11]

If *Takasago* is not perfectly orthodox, then why is it more appropriate than *Yumi Yawata* for analysis as a representative play of the Aged Mode? First, whatever eccentricities it may have, it is nonetheless typical of the mode. The very sentence that admits to the "fins" at the same time limits their significance by its use of the word "even." Moreover, remarks in *Sandō* suggest that in spite of its fins, the play serves as an exemplary work in its mode. Zeami probably had *Takasago* in mind when, in setting out his six examples, he made mention of an old couple (*rōfūfu*). There is no old couple in *Yumi Yawata* or *Hōjōgawa*, or indeed any of the other model plays except *Takasago*.

Furthermore, the central image of *Takasago* is the pine tree, and in a section of *Go ongyoku no jōjō* where Zeami compares each musical style to a tree, he chooses the pine for the congratulatory style:

THE PINE TREE
(the congratulatory image):

Yorozu yo o	I celebrate my lord in the aged pine,
Matsu ni zo kimi o	Expecting him to live ten thousand years,
Iwaitsuru	And like the long-lived crane, I draw beneath
Chitose no kage ni	that pine,
Suman to omoeba	There to find protection
	In its thousand-year-long shade.

Among the golden sayings of Prince Shōtoku, it is recorded that "the age of the True Law comes to an end and moves on to *dhyāna*; the common trees wither and the pine alone remains." The pine is from the outset a sacred tree and does not change color according to the times. It is the vision of a thousand autumns, and of itself presents the full spectacle of all-encompassing verdant mountains.[12]

Parts of this passage are rather vague, but all that is of importance at the moment is the connection between the pine and the congratulatory style, shūgen; that connection is clear.

Most important of all, *Takasago* is a long-acknowledged masterpiece. Muromachi and Momoyama performance records show a clear preference for it over *Yumi Yawata*, and this judgment persists to this day.[13]

Takasago opens with the entrance of the waki and the wakitsure. (In modern performance they enter to the accompaniment of an instrumental piece called SHINNOSHIDAI.) Together they sing the following shidai:*

Shidai
1 w/wt Ima o hajime no tabigoromo,
        Ima o hajime no tabigoromo,
        Hi mo yuku sue zo hisashiki.[14]

Shidai
1 w/wt Now we undertake our way in traveling attire,
        Now we undertake our way in traveling attire,
        Journey's end strung far ahead, the sun, too, weaves its course.

As in any standard shidai, the first line is repeated and the meter takes the form 7-5, 7-5, 7-4. The immediacy of the first word of the song, *ima*, "now," is particularly appropriate for the beginning of the play, and is reinforced by the word *hajime*, which can be understood as an objective complement to *ima* for the sense "we take 'now' as beginning." *Hajime* also modifies *tabigoromo*, however, for "our first traveling attire," or simply *tabi*, for "our first trip." The first trip of spring is an appropriately auspicious context for the play. The journey is given concrete form in the image of *tabigoromo*, and this image is linked to the last line through association with the word *himo*, "cords (on a cloak)."† That word, in turn, is hidden by a conventional pun in *hi mo*, "the sun, too," and the sun provides the second image of the song, becoming the traveling companion of the waki and the wakitsure. The last word of the piece, *hisashiki*, "far ahead" (in both time and space), gains emphasis not only because of its position, but also because its four syllables must take up the musical space normally allotted to five.[15] This word looks ahead through the entire length of the play. Modern conventions of performance for waki noh specify that this shidai should be sung three times: first by the waki and wakitsure, then, very softly, omitting the repetition of line 1, by the chorus, and finally once again by the waki and wakitsure, including the repetition.

The waki then proceeds to introduce himself:

* In all transliterations and translations from the plays I use these abbreviations to indicate the speakers (or singers): s = shite, w = waki, k = kyōgen, t = tsure, wt = wakitsure, and c = chorus. When a passage is delivered by more than one speaker, the abbreviations are written with a slash separating them: w/wt = waki and wakitsure. The numbers at the left are line numbers, arbitrarily assigned for the sake of analysis. The punctuation for the transliterated texts reflects the line-by-line and shōdan divisions in Yokomichi and Omote, *Yōkyokushū*: commas reflect line divisions, and periods the separations between shōdan or parts of shōdan.

† The literary device by which two lines or phrases are linked through word association is called an *engo*. Brief definitions of such literary terms can be found in the Glossary. For a full discussion, see Brower and Miner, *Japanese Court Poetry*.

Nanori

4   w   Somosomo kore wa Kiushiu Aso no miya no kannushi Tomonari to
          wa waga koto nari,
        Ware imada miyako o mizu sōrō hodo ni,
        Kono tabi omoitachi miyako ni nobori,
        Michisugara no meisho o ikken sebaya to zonjisōro.[16]

Nanori

4   w   Well, then, I am the priest Tomonari from the Aso shrine in
          Kyushu.
        I have never seen the capital,
        So I have set my mind to journey there,
        And as I go, to see the famous places along the way.

The waki is a Shinto priest who calls himself Tomonari.[17] In all standard waki noh, the waki is an imperial minister or retainer or a Shinto priest. As such, he holds exalted rank and is introduced with elegance and gravity. This accounts for the mixed style of the introduction. Although most prose passages in noh are delivered in the medieval conversational style (characterized by the verbal auxiliary *sōrō*), the first line of this nanori uses the older, more elegant style of the narrative tale (characterized by the copula *nari*) out of respect for the waki's rank.[18]

The nanori is followed by an ageuta, here (as ageuta of this content and position usually are) a michiyuki, or "traveling song":

Ageuta

8   w/wt Tabigoromo,
        Sue harubaru no miyakoji o,
10   Sue harubaru no miyakoji o,
        Kyō omoitatsu ura no nami,
        Funaji nodokeki harukaze no,
        Ikuka kinuran atosue mo.
        Isa shirakumo mo harun'baru to,
15   Sa shi mo omoishi Harimagata,
        Takasago no ura ni tsukinikeri,
        Takasago no ura ni tsukinikeri.

Ageuta

8   w/wt In traveling attire,
        Along the road to the capital as it stretches far away,
10   Along the road to the capital as it stretches far away,
        We set our minds to go today, and ride the coastal waves.
        The ship's course lies across calm seas, and in the spring's soft
          breeze,
        "How many days have we come now, how many days ahead?"
        I wonder. Wandering here beneath the white, far-ranging clouds,
15   Far still, I thought, but here is Harima Bay.
        We have come the long, long way to Takasago Coast.
        We have come the long, long way to Takasago Coast.

This is a standard ageuta: the first five syllables are set to a four-beat musical bar to form a half measure known as a *tori*, and the rest of the song is written in 7-5 meter with few irregularities. A break (after *atosue mo*) divides the ageuta into two parts.[19] The first ends with a question and the second begins with the answer. The rest of the ageuta is then sung through to the end, and, as is generally the case, the last line is repeated.

The image of *tabigoromo*, "traveling attire," carries over from the shidai to this ageuta, and plays itself out in engo throughout the song: *harubaru* contains, in a play on words, *haru*, "stretch (cloth)"; *omoitatsu* contains *tatsu*, "cut (cloth)"; *ura*, "coast," also means "reverse side" (i.e., "lining"); *kinuran* contains both *ki*, "wear," and *kinu*, "clothing," "silk"; and *haru* is repeated in an inflected form in the place name Harima. This wordplay ornaments the narrative content of the song, a description of a spring voyage.

The metrically discrete units of each verse are forged into one continuous chain through various literary devices and syntactic connections: line 10's *miyakoji o*, "along the road to the capital," is the direct object of line 11's *omoitatsu*, "set our minds to go"; line 11's *ura no nami*, "the coastal waves," suggests line 12's *funaji*, "the ship's course," by metonymy; line 12's *harukaze*, "the spring breeze," connects to line 13's *ikuka*, "how many days," with the modifying particle *no* for "how many days in the spring wind"; line 13's *ikuka kinuran*, "how many days have we come now, how many days ahead?," finds an answer in *shira(nu)*, "I wonder" (literally, "I do not know"), contained in line 14's *shirakumo*, "white clouds"); line 14's *harun'baru to*, "far-ranging," ties to line 15's *sa shi mo omoishi*, "I thought . . . just so," adverbially, and finally, line 15's *Harimagata*, "Harima Bay," is set in apposition to line 16's *Takasago no ura*, "the coast of Takasago," in another metonymy. In addition to these links *between* the verses, there are certain devices of note *within* them: *tatsu* in *omoitatsu* means "rise" and associates with both *nami*, "waves," in the same line and *harukaze*, "spring breeze," in the next; and *nodokeki*, "calm," is a *kakekotoba* (pivot-word) modifying both *funaji* and *harukaze*.

This ageuta, because of its sinuous continuity and multiple strands of meaning, creates an illusion of movement through the fluidity of time and space appropriate to such a traveling song. The truncated first line seems to add to this sense of movement, and the repetition of the last line of the song complements the sense of that line musically and metrically, setting the ageuta to rest.[20]

Now let us compare the metrical structure of this dan with the *Sandō* prescriptions (numbers in parentheses indicate a repetition of the preceding verse):

Sandō	*Takasago*
nanori	shidai: 7-5, (7-5), 7-4
shidai ⎫ 7-8 verses	nanori
ageuta ⎭	ageuta: 5-7-5, (7-5), 7-5, 7-5, 7-5,
	7-5, 7-5, 7-5, (7-5)

At first glance, *Takasago* does not seem to conform to the plan shown in Table 4. The shidai and nanori are reversed, and the number of verses seems wrong. The first problem can be explained by historical performance practice. In Muromachi presentations of waki noh, the nanori was customarily delivered first, and the shidai and ageuta sung afterward, thus Zeami's ordering of the shōdan.[21] The second discrepancy is partially explained by the repeated verses in the modern performance. If one drops the repetitions, the number of verses in the modern text totals nine, closer to the *Sandō* suggestion.

In modern practice the ageuta is followed by a *tsukizerifu*, an announcement that the waki and his retinue have arrived at Takasago.[22] After this, the shite makes his entrance preceded by the tsure to the accompaniment of the instrumental piece SHINNOISSEI. The two characters then sing the following shōdan to begin the second dan:

Issei

18	s/т	Takasago no,
		Matsu no harukaze fukikurete,
20		Onoe no kane mo hibiku nari,
	т	Nami wa kasumi no isogakure,
	s/т	Oto koso shio no michihi nare.

Issei

18	s/т	Through the pine of Takasago,
		Spring winds blow the dusk.
20		From the peak of Onoe the evening bell resounds.
	т	Haze along the rocky shore conceals the ocean waves,
	s/т	The crash of tidal surf alone makes known their flux and fall.

After the fluidity of time and space that characterized the first dan, particularly in its final ageuta, this issei brings specificity.[23] Lines 19 and 20 specify the time twice in *fukikurete*, "blow the dusk," and *kane mo hibiku nari*, "the [evening] bell resounds." Lines 21 and 22 do the same for the place with *iso*, "the rocky shore," and *shio no michihi*, "the tidal surf . . . in flux and fall," and this is of course emphasized by the first word of the song, which names the place. In contrast to the primarily visual imagery of the first dan (the traveling clothes, the waves stretched out before the ship, the clouds), aural images become important here. In the darkness that falls and the haze that obscures the coastline, the sounds of the evening bell and the crashing of waves become more apparent. This effect is strengthened by the structure of the song. Lines 19 and 20 are loosely parallel to lines 21 and 22, not only grammatically, but also conceptually: in each pair the first line describes the growing indistinctness of the visual scene, and the second centers on a single aural sensation emerging from that indistinctness. The forms of the copula *nari* that close each of the pairs underline the sense that these phenomena are being perceived by the characters, and might justify the translation: "The evening bell re-sounds and we hear it . . . the crash of surf lets us know of the waves' flux and fall."

The first three lines of this shōdan allude to a waka by Ōe Masafusa (1041-1111):

Takasago no	At Takasago
Onoe no kane mo	From the peak of Onoe,
Oto su nari	I hear the tolling bell.
Akatsuki kakete	Will the nighttime frost remain
Shimo ya okuran	Until the break of day?[24]

This poem, which is central to the play, is to be quoted almost in its en-tirety later on. Here Zeami is content to evoke it by a sort of "allusive variation."[25] Unlike Masafusa's winter poem, it (indeed the whole play) is set in spring.

This issei begins the ha of the play. It functions as a break (the char-acter ha means "break") from the pace established by the jo, with an abrupt slowing of tempo. And then, as we just saw, in the course of the song the primarily visual world of the jo is transformed into a predomi-nantly aural world. The first words, *Takasago no matsu*, "Takasago's pine," also contribute to the break. These or very similar words are to appear again and again in the play, often accenting important structural fea-tures, and, as is the case here, they are often set off by the metrical and musical configurations in which they are found. They are a sort of em-blem of the play.[26]

In the modern staging of *Takasago*, the issei is delivered from the *hashigakari*, the bridge separating the noh stage from the *kagami no ma* (green room) backstage. Then the shite and the tsure move to the stage proper to sing the next song:

Sashi

23	s	Tare o ka mo shiru hito ni sen Takasago no,
		Matsu mo mukashi no tomo narade,
25	s/t	Sugikoshi yoyo wa shirayuki no
		Tsumori tsumorite oi no tsuru no,
		Negura ni nokoru ariake no,
		Haru no shimoyo no okii ni mo,
		Matsukaze o nomi kikinarete,
30		Kokoro o tomo to sugamushiro no,
		Omoi o noburu bakari nari.

Sashi

23	s	Whom, I wonder, do I really know, if Takasago's ancient pine
		Is not my friend from long ago?
25	s/t	The time gone by piles age on age: white snow,
		I do not know how deep,
		But like the hoary crane, keep vigil,

An actor of the Kita school as the maejite in *Takasago*. He wears a typical old man's wig and a mask of the type known as *koujijō*. He has on white trousers (*ōkuchi*) and a starched *mizugoromo* robe over a brocade kimono. He holds a cedar broom. *Photograph by Masuda Shozoh, courtesy of the Noh Research Archives of Musashino Women's College.*

30
> Watching moonlight shine at dawn,
> Cast upon the springtime rime night-shed, and from my bed
> I hear the long familiar pine-blown wind. I take as friend my mind
> And spread before it intertwined the sedge-mat weave of my
> thoughts.

Earlier, darkness and the thickening haze isolated the shite and the tsure from the visual world, and their attention was drawn to sound. Now they proceed to their internal world and express their thoughts.*

The shift from the external world to the thoughts of the shite and tsure pivots on the first three lines of the sashi, which quote a waka by Fujiwara Okikaze, a poet of the mid-Heian period (794-1185):

Tare o ka mo	Whom, I wonder,
Shiru hito ni sen	Do I really know,
Takasago no	For Takasago's ancient pine
Matsu mo mukashi no	Is not my friend
Tomo naranaku ni	From long ago.

Zeami, for metrical reasons (and perhaps other purposes, to be discussed later), changes the last line from *naranaku ni* to *narade*.

The poem recalls "Takasago no" from the issei, of course, and is thus tied to the scene presented there, but it moves into the shite's mind with his query, "Whom, I wonder, do I really know, if Takasago's ancient pine is not my friend from long ago?"[27] An extended series of conceptual and linguistic associations follows: *mukashi*, "long ago," suggests *sugikoshi yoyo*, "time gone by," which in turn leads to *oi*, "aged." The passed time is made visible in *shirayuki*, "white snow," which drifts layer upon layer just as age piles on age; this comparison is made explicit with *tsumori tsumorite*, "piling up, piling up," which refers to both *shirayuki* and *sugikoshi yoyo*. The introduction of snow leads to a series of white images: *oi no tsuru*, "the hoary crane," *ariake [no tsuki]*, "the moon at dawn," and *shimo*, "frost." The aged crane in his nest symbolizes the shite himself, as becomes obvious from the next verses, which describe an old man who wakes just before dawn. From his bed, in complete solitude, he watches the fading moon and listens to the whispers of the wind in the pines, a sound his many years have made familiar. All this ultimately leads to an answer to the question asked earlier: *Kokoro o tomo to su*, "I take as friend my mind."

The mechanics of this song are strongly reminiscent of renga. The

---

* This expression could be called *jukkai*, borrowing a term from Japanese classical poetics. Indeed, the Sino-Japanese word jukkai can be read in a simple, native Japanese fashion as *omoi o noburu*, using words directly from this shōdan. In early waka poetry jukkai usually implied the expression of grievances, but in later waka and renga the term often merely indicated a lament on the passing of time or one's advancing age, or a comment on leaving the vain world for a religious life. The classification of a poem as jukkai was triggered by such words as *mukashi*, "long ago," and *oi*, "age," both of which are found in this shōdan. (See Brower and Miner, *Japanese Court Poetry*, p. 191; Brower, *Fujiwara Teika's Hundred-Poem Sequence*, p. 44; and Konishi, *Sōgi*, p. 254.)

series of associations can be grouped much as one would group topics in
a renga sequence: past days, the passing of time, aging, and expressing
one's thoughts are all topics of the category jukkai; snow and frost are
both *furimono,* "falling phenomena." Nor are traditional literary conceits
such as the kakekotoba and jo neglected: *shirayuki* as a kakekotoba con-
tains *shira(nu),* "I do not know," and relates the falling snow to the pass-
ing years, rhetorically supporting the conceptual relationship mentioned
earlier. *Tsuru no negura,* "the crane's nest," holds *tsuru no ne,* "the crane's
cry," and Yokomichi and Omote suggest that *tsuru no* may be a jo for *ne-
gura.*[28] *Shimoyo no okii ni mo,* "waking in the frosty night," holds *shimo no
ok(u),* "frost falls." *Tomo to su,* "take as friend," links directly to *sugamu-
shiro,* "sedge-weave mat," which, with *noburu,* "spread out," forms the jo
to *omoi o noburu,* "express my thoughts." By resorting to the use of such
techniques from waka and renga, Zeami has put to good use the ambi-
guity and fluidity of classical syntax, compressing abundant meaning
into a few short lines. He describes a scene, or chain of images, at the
same time that he delineates the inner world of the shite, and thereby
gives a more vivid picture of that world than direct statements about age
or solitude might have done.

This sashi is in fact a key to the entire play, in the sense that the shite
here presents himself as a maker of poetry, giving expression to the
thoughts in his mind through the natural phenomena around him,[29] and
hinting that he is actually the spirit of the pine itself. He asks who his
friend is and answers that his friend is his own mind. He explains his
thoughts to his friend, but the only sound heard is the rustle of the wind
in the pines. The pine he hears, then, is the sound of his own voice; in-
deed he is, as becomes explicit later, the spirit of the pine temporarily
disguised as an old man.

All of this argues for a reinterpretation of the poem cited at the be-
ginning of the sashi. Okikaze's waka is a simple statement that Takasago's
pine is not the speaker's friend from long ago. But Zeami's reworking of
it allows an ambiguity. It can be a simple statement—or it can be a rhe-
torical question: "If Takasago's ancient pine is not my friend, who is?"

The shite and the tsure continue:

Sageuta
32 s/t   Otozure wa,
           Matsu ni kototō urakaze no,
           Ochibagoromo no sode soete,
35   Kokage no chiri o kakō yo,
           Kokage no chiri o kakō yo.

Sageuta
32 s/t   The coastal wind comes visiting,
           Conversing with the pine and casting down a cloak of fallen
               needles;
           Sleeve next to sleeve

35   Let's rake away the litter underneath the tree,
            Let's rake away the litter underneath the tree.

This song directs the shite's and the tsure's attention, and of course the audience's, too, back to the pine. The shite and the tsure are first called out of reverie by sound: the wind along the coast is rustling the pine's branches. Personification of the wind in both *otozure*, "visitor" (more literally, "visit"), and *kokotō*, "converse," suggests the presence of divine beings. The wind sends a shower of pine needles down onto the couple's clothes, cloaking them in fallen leaves (or fallen needles; the word *ochiba* means both), and seeing this, they put forth their sleeves (holding a broom and a rake) and set about cleaning up around the base of the tree. The words of this sageuta seem to suggest some movement on stage, but in standard performances of *Takasago*, the two actors merely stand in place to sing. There are variant performances (*kogaki*) in the Kanze, Hōshō, Konparu, and Kongō schools, however, in which the two sweep under a pine tree prop at center stage.[30]

The short sageuta leads to another ageuta:

Ageuta
37   s/t   Tokoro wa Takasago no,
            Tokoro wa Takasago no,
            Onoe no matsu mo toshi furite,
40   Oi no nami mo yorikuru ya,
            Ko no shita kage no ochiba kaku,
            Naru made inochi nagaraete.
            Nao itsu made ka Iki no matsu,
            Sore mo hisashiki meisho kana,
45   Sore mo hisashiki meisho kana.

Ageuta
37   s/t   The place is Takasago,
            The place is Takasago,
            The pine of Onoe grows old;
40   How the waves of age come rippling on!
            Raking plenteous needles from beneath the tree,
            We've grown to such great age.
            How much longer are we still to live? . . . The pine of Iki,
            It too is a famous prodigy of time,
45   It too is a famous prodigy of time.

This ageuta is of somewhat irregular form. The five-syllable introductory line that we see in the waki's ageuta in the first dan (and later as well in the waki's ageuta in the fifth dan) is missing in this case. That, by itself, however, is not particularly exceptional; many ageuta omit that line and simply begin with a full 7-5 line, which is repeated. What is different here is the irregular 4-5 meter of the first line and the repeated line. The four syllables before the caesura create a slightly halting effect—particularly after the metrically regular sageuta—and the missing syllables must be filled in by the drums. The five syllables after the caesura return to standard form, but then, after a short instrumental break (a drum pattern called the *uchikiri* in modern performance), the irregular line is repeated. The rest of the song is metrically regular and relatively straightforward conceptually. The pine is recognized as ancient and eternal; its immortality is made tangible by the inexhaustible supply of fallen needles at its base. The shite and the tsure identify themselves with it, saying, in effect, that their lives are comparable to the life of the pine. (This is not stated directly, but the juxtaposition of lines 41 and 42 suggests as much, and the comparison is strengthened by the use of the kakekotoba *kaku*, "raking," and "such great [age].") The Iki pine, a famous landmark similar to the Takasago pine, is introduced not only for comparison, but also because it fits neatly into a kakekotoba with *nao itsu made ka ik(u)*, "How much longer yet to live."[31] This ageuta is far less complex than the preceding sashi. It is played and sung more quickly, and is also, of course, in congruent song (whereas the sashi is in noncongruent song). This shōdan brings the first section of the ha to a swift, rhythmic conclusion.

The third dan of the play, unlike the previous two, does not begin with an instrumental prelude. Instead the waki simply stands up and begins to question the shite and the tsure:

Mondō

46	w	Satobito o aimatsu tokoro ni,
		Rōjin fūfu kitareri,
		Ika ni kore naru rōjin ni tazunu beki koto no sōro.
	s	Konata no koto nite sōrō ka nanigoto nite sōrō zo,
50	w	Takasago no matsu to wa izure no ki o mōshisōrō zo,
	s	Tadaima kono jō ga kokage o kiyomesōrō koso Takasago no matsu nite sōrae,
	w	Takasago Suminoe no matsu ni aioi no na ari,
		Tōsho to Sumiyoshi to wa kuni o hedatetaru ni,
		Nani tote aioi no matsu to wa mōshisōrō zo,
55	s	Kokin no jo ni iwaku,
		Takasago Suminoe no matsu mo aioi no yō ni oboe to ari,
		Sarinagara kono jō wa ano Tsu no kuni Sumiyoshi no mono,
		Kore naru 'mba koso tōsho no hito nare,
		Shiru koto araba mōsatamae,
60	w	Fushigi ya mireba rōjin no,
		Fūfu issho ni arinagara,
		Tōki Suminoe Takasago no,
		Ura yama kuni o hedatete sumu to,
		Iu wa ikanaru koto yaran,
65	T	Utate no ōse zōrō ya,
		Sansen banri o hedatsuredomo,
		Tagai ni kayō kokorozukai no,
		Imose no michi tōkarazu,
	s	Mazu anjite mo goranze yo,
70	s/T	Takasago Suminoe no,

Matsu wa hijō no mono dani mo,
Aioi no na wa aru zo ka shi,
Mashite ya shō aru hito to shite,
Toshi hisashiku mo Sumiyoshi yori,
75   Kayoinaretaru jō to 'mba wa,
Matsu morotomo ni kono toshi made,
Aioi no fūfu to naru mono o.

Mondō

46	w	As I wait here for a villager to come by,
		An old couple approach.
		You, old man, I want to ask you something.
	s	Are you speaking to me? What would you ask of me?
50	w	Which of these trees is the pine of Takasago?
	s	The very one I am raking under is the Takasago pine.
	w	The pines of Takasago and Suminoe are said to have grown up together,
		But Sumiyoshi is in an altogether different province from this place.
		How is it, then, that they can still be called "the pines that grew up together?"
55	s	In the preface to the *Kokinshū* it says,
		"The pines of Takasago and Suminoe seem just as if they had grown up together."
		I myself am from that very Sumiyoshi in the province of Tsu,
		This old woman is the one from Takasago.
		If you know something about this, tell him.
60	w	This is a surprise. I see the old couple
		Together in one place here,
		But they say they live whole provinces apart,
		In Sumiyoshi and in Takasago, places separated by both land and sea,
		What can they mean by this?
65	T	What foolish things you say!
		"A man and his wife may be separated by mountains and rivers for a full thousand leagues,
		But as long as their thoughts run back and forth,
		They are never far from each other."
	s	Consider this,
70	s/T	These pines of Takasago and Suminoe
		Are nonsentient beings, yet even they are known
		As the pines that grew up together.
		So all the more should we—we who have feelings,
		We, who together have lived through all these years,
75		This old woman and I who am grown accustomed to visit her from far-off Sumiyoshi—
		There's all the more reason that we be known as the couple grown old together,
		Living to this great age with the pines.

Much of this shōdan is spoken, but at key points the actors break into song, and the last eight lines are all sung. For the most part, the meter is irregular, but there is a tendency toward 7-5 meter in the lines that are sung.

The characters begin to develop the play's *honzetsu*, or source, in this passage. First of all, we see a direct reference to the kana preface to *Kokinshū*, Japan's first comment on the purpose and emotional origin of poetry:

In the flowery mornings of spring and the moonlit nights of the fall, the Emperors of ages past used to call their courtiers together to have them compose waka. Some told how they had gone astray while searching for blossoms, others related how they had found themselves lost in the dark, so entranced were they by the moon. The Emperor would then judge which were clever and which foolish. But that was not all, there were those who entertained him by composing poems. Some praised him saying his reign would last as long as it took for pebbles to grow into boulders, or comparing his royal visage to the magnificence of Mount Tsukuba. . . . Some compared their love to the undying smoke that rose from the peak of Mount Fuji, some recalled lost friends on hearing the sad drone of insects, some felt as if the pines of Takasago and Suminoe had grown up together.[32]

In addition to this passage, we may count two waka from *Kokinshū* as part of the honzetsu. One, KKS 909, was seen earlier, in the sashi of the second dan. The second, KKS 905 (also *Ise monogatari*, episode 117), appears in the conclusion. It reads:

Ware mite mo	A long time's gone
Hisashiku narinu	Since first I saw
Suminoe no	This pine on Sumiyoshi shore;
Kishi no himematsu	How many generations
Ikuyo henuran	Has it passed there?

It is obvious from the poems that the pines are to be taken as symbols of longevity. Moreover, the speakers in the poems, like the shite and the tsure in *Takasago*, clearly have some special relationship to the pines. Further explication of the play's honzetsu becomes somewhat problematic, however, and a number of other issues must be addressed in order to understand it fully.

First, we may note that the author of the preface is concerned with the traditional occasions on which poetry was composed and is careful to note its public character. It is in this connection that he mentions the pines of Takasago and Suminoe, and KKS 905 and 909 seem to be among those he is referring to.[33]

Especially relevant is his puzzling phrase "Takasago Suminoe no matsu aioi no yō ni oboe" ("felt as if the pines of Takasago and Suminoe had grown up together"). The meaning of *aioi* is difficult to determine (as the kyōgen actor will later attest), but it seems central to the play's elaboration of the source. *Aioi* means "grow up with" or "be born with," or perhaps "be planted together with"—but with what or whom? Some commentators have assumed it means "grow up together with the speaker," but in neither of the poems is this made explicit (indeed, in KKS

909 the speaker implies that however ancient the pine of Takasago may be, he is himself more ancient). This leaves the alternative that the pines are themselves growing up together. Although this interpretation is not really obvious from the poems either, it seems to be the only logical meaning to follow from the preface, and it is the meaning Zeami understands. This can be confirmed by the comparison that follows the quotation in the mondō: just as the pines of Suminoe and Takasago grew up together, so also have the two old people grown old together. The idea for the comparison and the underlying transformation of aioi 相生, "grow up together," to aioi 相老, "grow old together," is central to the play and seems to be Zeami's contribution to the legend.[34]

It took three days to travel from Takasago to Sumiyoshi when the play was written,[35] so the waki is naturally surprised that the old man and woman can be man and wife even while separated by such a distance. This leads to a digression on the power of love delivered by the tsure. Then the shite and tsure sing together, in fairly regular 7-5 meter, a passage in which the couple's conjugal link is compared to the link between the two pines. The link between the couple is said to be stronger because they are creatures of feeling, whereas the pines are nonsentient trees. Underlying the contrast of tree to man is the Buddhist classification of all existence into ujō and hijō, those entities with feeling (i.e., animals, human beings, and assorted supernatural creatures) and those without (i.e., rocks, trees, and other inanimate objects). The pine tree is hijō, the shite and the tsure ujō.* The distinction is first made explicit in line 71 with the reference to the pines as nonsentient; then, in line 73 the words shō aru add another reminder of it, for although they are written with characters meaning "having life," they suggest as well the words jō aru, "having feeling" (i.e., ujō).

The entire passage is particularly amenable to structural examination in light of Zeami's notion of jo-ha-kyū. The jo seems to run through the shite's remark to the tsure, shiru koto araba mōsatamae, "If you know something about this, tell him" (line 59). This passage is entirely in prose and is spoken. It introduces the honzetsu with an authoritative reference to Kokinshū. The ha of the mondō seems, then, to start with the waki's exclamation, fushigi ya, to run through the tsure's remarks about the nature of love, sung in mostly regular 7-5 meter, and to end with a single spoken but metered line, the shite's only line in the ha. The passage forms a discrete conceptual unit containing the waki's statement and the tsure's reaction; the conceptual unity is supported by the parallel expressions ura yama kuni o hedatete, "whole provinces apart, . . . separated by both land and sea," and sansen banri o hedatsuredomo, "separated by mountains and

---

* Ujō is sometimes limited to beings with consciousness. Although there is some uncertainty in Buddhist sources about whether trees should be considered animate or inanimate, Zeami clearly considers them inanimate in this play.

rivers for a full thousand leagues." The waki's naïve question is cast, appropriately, in native Japanese, and the tsure's aphoristic and therefore authoritative answer is given a contrasting Sinified touch (*sansen banri*). The kyū of the mondō starts with the emblematic word Takasago. It is sung in unison by the shite and the tsure and is written in fairly regular meter. The introduction of the ujō/hijō polarity adds a ring of authority and makes an appeal to logical reasoning.

The jo-ha-kyū progression discussed above applies to the mondō alone. Another progression could be found for the dan as a whole, and indeed there seems even to be a jo-ha-kyū progression for the mondō and the following *kakeai* taken as a pair:[36]

Kakeai

78	w	Iware o kikeba omoshiro ya,
		Sate sate saki ni kikoetsuru,
80		Aioi no matsu no monogatari o,
		Tokoro ni iioku iware wa naki ka,
	s	Mukashi no hito no mōshishi wa,
		Kore wa medetaki yo no tameshi nari,
	T	Takasago to iu wa jōdai no,
85		Mannyōshiu no inishie no gi,
	s	Sumiyoshi to mōsu wa,
		Ima kono miyo ni sumitamō Engi no onkoto,
	T	Matsu to wa tsukinu koto no ha no,
	s	Sakae wa kokin aionaji to,
90	s/T	Miyo o agamuru tatoe nari,
	w	Yoku yoku kikeba arigataya,
		Ima koso fushin haru no hi ni,
	s	Hikari yawaragu nishi no umi no,
	w	Kashiko wa Suminoe
	s	koko wa Takasago
95	w	Matsu mo iro soi
	s	haru mo nodoka ni.

Kakeai

78	w	How interesting, this explanation I just heard!
		But what about my question from before?
80		Is there no local version of
		The story of the pines grown up together?
	s	Someone long ago explained the pines
		As symbols of our auspicious times
	T	Takasago stands for the age
85		Of the poems of the *Man'yōshū*.
	s	What's meant by Sumiyoshi
		Is the karmic link whereby His Majesty lives in this age of the
		Kokinshū.
	T	The pine represents inexhaustible leaves of poetry.
	s	It flourishes regardless of the times
90	s/T	And stands, an illustration of the age.
	w	Careful attention to what you tell me gives great cause for joy.
		Now at last my suspicions clear away;

	s	The spring sun's lambent rays play out upon the Western Sea.
	w	Suminoe over there
	s	and Takasago here,
95	w	The pine's green deepens
	s	in spring's tranquility.

The waki acknowledges the truth in what the shite and the tsure have said in the mondō, and then returns to his original concern, the pines. Scholars have not been able to track down the source of the old couple's explanation that the Takasago pine represents the era of *Man'yōshū*, and the Sumiyoshi pine their own era (the era of *Kokinshū*). In any case, it hinges on the double meaning of three key words in the passage: *Sumiyoshi*, the place name as well as "it is fortunate to live"; *Engi*, the era name, "Extending Happiness," as well as its homophone, "karmic affinity"; and *kokin*, which suggests *Kokinshū* and also means "past and present" (although in this sense the characters are usually pronounced *kokon*[37]). This provides the basis for the links to poetry that have been hinted at before and are to become very important in the kuse: it was during the Engi era that *Kokinshū* was compiled, a fortunate time to be alive.[38] The inexhaustible needles of the pine, which stood for the advanced age of the shite and tsure in the sageuta and ageuta of the previous dan, become the inexhaustible leaves of poetry here, emphasizing the continuity of the waka tradition in this passage.

When all this is explained to the waki, his suspicions are cleared away, and with the use of the kakekotoba *haru*, "clear away," and "spring," the text moves back to the natural scene, which is appropriately sunny and springlike. Line 93 then introduces one of the tenets of syncretic Buddhism that is important to the conceptual background of this and many other waki noh. *Hikari o yawaragu* can be read by the Sino-Japanese pronunciation *wakō*, which suggests the doctrine of *wakō dōjin*. This term comes from a passage in the basic Tendai text, *Mohe zhiguan* (The Great [Treatise] on Concentration and Insight): "wakō dōjin, kechien no hajime" ("Softening their blinding light, they mix with the dust; this is the beginning of their affinity [with the unenlightened]").[39] The "they" referred to are those bodhisattvas who dull the light of their knowledge and virtue and mix with unenlightened souls ("dust") as the first stage in bringing them to enlightenment. In Japan the Shinto gods were considered transformations of these bodhisattvas. The short phrase from this kakeai, then, looks forward to the appearance of the god Sumiyoshi Myōjin at the end of the play, and sets the work in the context of the all-embracing Buddhist cosmos.[40]

This shōdan is in many ways a formal continuation of the preceding mondō. It remains a dialogue between the waki, on the one hand, and the tsure and the shite on the other, and its musical form, metered verse sung in noncongruent rhythm, is a continuation of the last part of the mondō. The shōdan also serves as a carefully measured transition to the ageuta that follows. The kakeai reverts to spoken parts in three places, where the meter then becomes irregular (lines 82-83, 86-87, and 89). All of these spoken passages are given to the shite, and when he finishes each of them, the tsure enters with metered song (joined by the shite, on the third occasion). The effect is to slow the movement of the previous lines, and consequently the first half of the kakeai gives the impression of starting and stopping, starting and stopping. In line 90, however, where the shite and the tsure sing a metrically regular line in unison, the movement in the shōdan seems to accelerate, and it continues to do so through the end of the kakeai. This is accompanied by a succession of exchanges in which the number of syllables allotted each character gradually diminishes, thus:

lines 91-92	w	24 (7-5 + 7-5)	line 95a	w	7
line 93	s	13 (7-6)	line 95b	s	7
line 94a	w	8	(line 96a	c	5
line 94b	s	7	line 96b	c	5)[41]

This movement, as indicated, continues directly into the chorus's ageuta, where the metrical diminution reaches its climax in two five-syllable half-lines. These two half-lines begin the ageuta quickly and crisply and with the added strength of the full chorus of eight voices. Syntactically, too, everything from line 92 through the beginning of the ageuta can be considered a single sinuous unit.

Ageuta
96 c   Shikai nami shizuka nite,
           Kuni mo osamaru toki tsu kaze,
           Eda o narasanu miyo nare ya,
           Ai ni aioi no,
100   Matsu koso medetakarikere.
           Ge ni aogite mo,
           Koto mo oroka ya kakaru yo ni,
           Sumeru tami tote yutaka naru,
           Kimi no megumi zo arigataki,
105   Kimi no megumi zo arigataki.

Ageuta
96 c   Waves upon the four seas still,
           The nation peaceful in propitious winds,
           Not a twig is set to rustle in this happy age,
           Happily encountered it is, too.
100   The pines that grow together show it so.
           No amount of praise
           Does justice to these days.
           The people living in these times find rich prosperity,
           Rejoicing in the grace and magnanimity of our lord,
105   Rejoicing in the grace and magnanimity of our lord.

Formally, this ageuta is rather eccentric in its omission of a repeated line at the beginning; this seems to indicate a purposeful deviation from convention. Is this perhaps because a sense of speed and movement is particularly desirable here? It may seem ironic to call for speed and movement in lines that read, "Waves upon the four seas still, . . . Not a twig is set to rustle," and so on, but the stillness here is not to be understood as torpor or even relaxation. It is instead a dynamic state, that of much energy held in control by the ideal ruler.

The caesura after *medetakarikere* is worthy of note because Zeami, in his instructions for plays in the Aged Mode, had called for the chorus's first ageuta to be sung in two strains (Table 4). Both of the ageuta discussed previously also contain caesuras—after the *atosue mo* of line 13 and the *inochi nagaraete* of line 42. But these are instrumental breaks, marked by the playing of a characteristic drum pattern, uchikiri, with no grammatical break in the lines before and after. Here we have the reverse: no drum pattern,[42] but a full stop grammatically (*matsu koso medetakarikere* is even stronger than the usual conclusive form because of the emphatic combination of *koso* with the *izenkei* inflection of the adjective).

Thematically, this ageuta contains the strongest expression so far of grateful felicitation for the Emperor's wise and prospering reign. The phrases *eda o narasanu miyo nare ya*, "not a twig is set to rustle in this happy age," and *toki tsu kaze*, "propitious winds," are taken from Chapter 17 of *Lun heng* (Balancing the Discourses) by the Later Han scholar Wang Chong (A.D. 27–90?): "Discussing the auspicious signs of great peace, the Confucians all say, . . . the barrier gates are not closed, no robbers on the roads, the wind rustles not a twig, the rain breaks not a single clod. In five days the wind blows once, in ten days there is a single rainstorm." A line very similar to the first line of this ageuta (*shikai nami shizuka ni shite*) appears in an anthology of medieval songs called *Enkyokushū* (A Collection of Banquet Songs), but both apparently originated in an older work that has not been identified.[43]

This ageuta is relatively simple and straightforward, fittingly so, because it brings to a close the two sections of the development that prepare us for what is to follow: the most complex dan in the play, in both literary and musical terms. The second dan (ha 1) had firmly established the time and place of the play and given the viewer a careful look at the internal world of the shite. The third dan, by contrast, has been completely external and overtly explanatory in approach, thus the frequent appeals to authority in the mondō. The honzetsu of the play has been made explicit with the quotation from and reference to the *Kokinshū* preface, and the various themes of the play, the constancy of the pines, conjugal felicity, the benevolence of the imperial reign, the continuity of tradition in waka poetry, and so on, have all been brought together to lay the groundwork for the narrative heart of the play. Similarly, this dan has been musically faster than the preceding one. Through the gradual, carefully structured, and steady progression from unmetered spoken lines to unmetered song to metered noncongruent song to metered congruent song, the audience's engagement in the play has been heightened (the transition between noncongruent and congruent song as the kakeai ends and the chorus's ageuta begins is particularly stirring), again laying the groundwork for a full appreciation of what is to follow.

In modern performance, the fourth dan begins with a line called the *sasoizerifu*, delivered by the waki:

Sasoizerifu
106 w   Nao nao Takasago no matsu no medetaki iware kuwashiku
        onmonogatarisōrae.

Sasoizerifu
106 w   Tell me yet more of the happy tale of the pine of Takasago.

No line of the sort appears in the 1713 text used for this analysis, but considering its highly formulaic nature and brevity, it may well have been included in early performances, but left out of written texts.

The chorus now enters:

Kuri
107 c   Sore sōmoku kokoro nashi to wa mōsedomo kajitsu no toki o
        tagaezu,
    Yōshun no toku o sonaete nanshi hana hajimete hiraku.

Kuri
107 c   They say that plants and trees have no senses, yet they do not mistake the seasons of flower and fruit;
    Replete with the virtues of the springtime sun, their southern branches first burst into bloom.

In this short shōdan, sung in the musically highly inflected einori style, the language is cast in a highly Sinified mold and includes, in fact, a phrase from a couplet in Chinese by the Heian scholar Sugawara no Fumitoki (899-981):

Who said the colors of spring arrive from the east?
When the dew grows warm, the southern branches first burst into bloom.[44]

The kuri recalls the earlier introduction of the sentient-nonsentient distinction, and here finds a paradox in the fact that the supposedly nonsentient plants do respond to the change of seasons. The shite now delivers the following lines:

Sashi
109 s   Shikaredomo kono matsu wa,
    Sono keshiki tokoshinae ni shite kayō toki o wakazu,
  c   Yotsu no toki itarite mo,

		Issennen no iro yuki no uchi ni fukaku,
		Mata wa shōka no iro tokaeri to mo ieri,
s		Kakaru tayori o matsu ga e no,
115	c	Koto no hagusa mo tsuyu no tama,
		Kokoro o migaku tane to narite,
s		Iki to shi ikeru monogoto ni,
c		Shikishima no kage ni yoru to ka ya.

Sashi

109	s	And yet this pine, for all eternity,
		Stays green. Its needles and flowers make no discrimination of the times,
	c	And even when the seasons pass to winter,
		Its millennial green glows deep in drifts of snow.
		What's more, they say pine blossoms make ten appearances, once every thousand years,
	s	So, awaiting this occasion, the branches of the pine,
115	c	Bear leaves of poetry, shining with dewdrop gems,
		Seeds to polish the mind's sensibility.
	s	Each and every living thing
	c	Draws under the shelter of Shikishima.

The paradox of the kuri is now doubled back on the pine; nonsentient plants and trees sense the change of season to bear flower and fruit, but the pine tree takes no account of the seasons, remaining green all the time. The "seasons" the pine *does* keep come in thousand-year cycles, and its flowers appear for ten of these cycles.[45] While waiting for its flowers, the pine produces poetry; that is, with its constancy, it inspires poets and provides the shelter of poetry for all creatures. (Shikishima, an epithet for Japan here, probably means *Shikishima no michi*, "the way of Shikishima," i.e., the composition of waka poetry.) Images of the pine—its deep green in winter's snow, its needles covered with dewdrops in spring and autumn, the expanse of shade it provides both metaphorically and concretely—dominate the sashi. Into this imagery has been woven further allusion to the *Kokinshū* preface. Lines 115 and 116 allude to the first line of the preface, "Yamatouta wa hito no kokoro o tane to shite, yorozu no koto no ha to zo narerikeru" (The poetry of Japan has its roots in the human heart and flourishes in the countless leaves of words); and line 117 to the third line, "Hana ni naku uguisu, mizu ni sumu kawazu no koe o kikeba, iki to shi ikeru mono, izure ka uta o yomazarikeru" (Hearing the warbler sing among the blossoms and the frog in his fresh waters—is there any living being not given to song?).[46] The transition from the pine's needles to the preface's leaves of poetry is at once made smoother and embellished by a string of engo: *ha*, "leaves" or "pine needles," suggests *kusa* (here, in a compound, pronounced *gusa*), "grass," which leads to *tsuyu*, "dewdrop," and *tane*, "gems," which in turn calls forth *migaku*, "polish." Line 112 quotes part of a Chinese couplet by Minamoto no Shitagō:

AN EPITHET FOR THE PINE TREE

The glory of Duke Eighteen is revealed after the first frost.
Its millennial green glows deep in drifts of snow.[47]

The image evoked, pine green amid the white snow, recalls the imagery of the shite's sashi in the second dan.

Musically, the song is set to noncongruent song. Metrically, however, it shows a tendency to become more regular as it proceeds, and the long lines of the first half gradually give way to more regular 7-5 or 8-5 lines in the second half. This is perhaps because the shōdan itself serves in some sense as a transition to the kuse that follows.

Kuse

119 C	Shikaru ni Chōnō ga kotoba ni mo,
	Ujō hijō no sono koe,
	Mina uta ni moruru koto nashi,
	Sōmoku dosha,
	Fūsei suion made,
	Banbutsu no komoru kokoro ari,
125	Haru no hayashi no,
	Tōfū ni ugoki aki no mushi no,
	Hokuro ni naku mo,
	Mina waka no sugata narazu ya.
	Naka ni mo kono matsu wa,
130	Banboku ni sugurete,
	Shūhakkō no yosōi,
	Senshū no midori o nashite,
	Kokon no iro o mizu,
	Shikō no onshaku ni,
135	Azukaru hodo no ki nari tote,
	Ikoku ni mo honchō ni mo,
	Banmin kore o shōkan su.

[Ageha]

S	Takasago no,
	Onoe no kane mo oto su nari,
140 C	Akatsuki kakete,
	Shimo wa okedomo matsu ga e no,
	Hairo wa onaji fukamidori,
	Tachiyoru kage no asayū ni,
	Kakedomo ochiba no tsukisenu wa,
145	Makoto nari matsu no ha no,
	Chiriusezu shite iro wa nao,
	Masaki no kazura nagaki yo no,
	Tatoe narikeru tokiwagi no,
	Naka ni mo na wa Takasago no,
150	Mat'ndai no tameshi ni mo,
	Aioi no matsu zo medetaki.

Kuse

119 C	Recall, then, the words of Chōnō,
	"Of the many voices of sentient and nonsentient

There is none without its poetry,
In plants and trees, in earth and sand,
Even in wind's voice and water's sounds,
There is that sensibility in which reside all things.
125   A springtime grove
Rustling in the eastern wind, autumn insects
Crying in the northern dew,
Are these not both forms of poetry?"
Among all these, this pine
130   Surpasses other trees,
The decorations of this noble duke
Shine with the green of a thousand autumns
And find no alteration with the passing times.
Of such stature is this tree
135   That the Emperor of Qin gave it peerage,
Abroad then and in our own realm,
Countless peoples proclaim their adoration.
[Ageha]
s   At Takasago
From the peak of Onoe I hear the tolling bell,
140 c   Through the night till dawn;
Even though white frost covers each branch, the needles
Keep their constancy of deepest green.
In morning or at night, although we step into its shade
To rake the fallen needles, there is no end to them.
145   True indeed, the needles of the pine in falling
Never leave the tree completely bare;
Its color still increases, like the trailing laurel vine,
A symbol of our timeless generation.
The most illustrious of evergreens: this pine of Takasago,
150   An example to serve the ages to come,
Happy indeed, the pines that grew up together!

In general kuse are divided into three distinct parts. This one con-
forms to that pattern. The first part begins characteristically with the
connective *shikaru ni*, "so then," and continues through the quotation
about poetic theory, ending with the rhetorical question of line 128. The
second part runs through line 137. The final part begins with two lines
(138-39) termed the *ageha*. This is sung in a higher register by the shite,
and stands apart from the previous parts, which were sung by the chorus
in a lower register. After the shite's ageha, the chorus takes over, return-
ing to a lower register once more to conclude the song.

The musical divisions of a kuse can be accentuated by literary divi-
sions, and Zeami has been careful to do so here. In the first part, he once
again expresses the poetic universalism of the *Kokinshū* preface, drawing
on what purports to be the words of the late-tenth-century poet Fujiwara
no Chōnō.[48] We find two sets of parallel ideas stated in this quotation.
The first is only roughly parallel, the *moruru koto nashi*, "there is none

without," of line 121 corresponding with *komoru kokoro ari*, "there is that sensibility in which reside," of line 124. (This is more obvious in the original, with its sequences of attributive verb, substantive, and sentence final verb/adjective, than it is in the English translation.) The following lines (125-27) are strictly parallel: *haru no hayashi no tōfū ni ugoki*, "A springtime grove rustling in the eastern wind"; *aki no mushi no hokuro ni naku*, "Autumn insects crying in the northern dew." The rhythmic distribution of the syllables of these lines acts something like an enjambment to keep the parallelism from becoming monotonous.

I have chosen to follow the text of the Kanze and Hōshō schools for line 124, which is significantly different from the text used by the other schools (*banbutsu o komoru kokoro ari*, "there is that sensibility that resides in all things") because this is the version that appears in the 1713 text. But a good case can be made for either reading. In any event, the poetic universalism expressed in this passage is a logical development of the ideas of the *Kokinshū* preface; it is a theme that Zeami takes up in other works as well.[49]

Like the transition from kuri to sashi before it, the transition from the first part of the kuse to the second is made by narrowing the focus from nature as a whole to the pine tree in particular. We are treated to two allusions to Chinese sources as Zeami adds to the catalogue of the pine's excellences begun in the preceding sashi. The first of these is made in line 131. My translation for *shūhakkō* is "noble duke," but the literal meaning of the word is Duke Eighteen. This rather odd epithet for the pine is a visual pun: when the Chinese character for pine is divided into its component parts, one gets the characters for "ten," "eight" (therefore eighteen), and "duke," respectively.*

In the second allusion, lines 134-35, Zeami turns to *Shi ji* (Classic of History) to expand on the theme of the pine's nobility: "The First Emperor [of Qin] went to his provinces and districts in the east and in due course climbed Mount Tai. He set up a stone monument there, endowed a shrine, and worshipped. As he was coming down the mountain, a storm suddenly swept over him, so he sought refuge beneath a tree. Consequently he endowed the tree and gave it the rank of Fifth Peer."[50]

There is a clear link between this part of the kuse and the first part. Here Zeami provides a source of authority attesting to the excellence of the pine, just as in the first part he had provided a source of authority

---

* Modern scholars find the locus classicus for this visual pun in the biography of Ding Gu in vol. 3 of *Wu zhi* (Annals of Wu): "At first Gu was secretary. He dreamed he saw a pine tree growing out of his stomach. He said to someone, 'The pine is Duke Eighteen. Does this mean that in 18 years I will be a duke?' Eventually it turned out just as the dream had indicated." (Quoted in Yokomichi and Omote, *Yōkyokushū*, 1: 437 n. 73.)

for his poetic universalism. The last part of the kuse contrasts with what has gone before in its direct appeal to experience.

The shite now sings alone, and at a higher pitch than has been used in the preceding parts.[51] He begins with the word Takasago, which has become an emblem of the entire play by this point, and his lines quote the poem by Masafusa that had earlier been the object of allusive variation. These lines and the choral passage that follows are the high point of the kuse—and also its most dynamic part. Just after the shite delivers his lines, in modern performance, he stands and goes to the front and center of the stage to mime raking up the pine's needles. It is uncertain whether such actions were performed in Zeami's day, but they make a strong impression on stage.

In content, this last part of the kuse is much simpler than the previous two parts, referring once again to the constancy of the pine as a symbol of the continuity of the imperial house. It is important to note that the pine has didactic value: it is "an example to serve the ages to come." Finally, the last line successfully encapsulates the entire experience of the play up to this point in the simple exclamation, *aioi no matsu zo medetaki*, "Happy, indeed, the pines that grew up together!"

The particular care Zeami lavished on this kuse and its compositional mastery are perhaps most apparent in terms of diction. In the first two parts of the shōdan, Zeami uses a highly Sinified vocabulary. This is "stiff language" (*kowaki kotoba*), which he himself had warned against in *Fūshikaden*: "One should choose beautiful poetic phrases, whose meaning is immediately understood. . . . Stiff language usually will not suit the movements." But then he notes that there are exceptions to this rule, indicating that "difficult, unfamiliar words may be used when such language is appropriate to the character being treated."[52] In these parts of the kuse, Zeami treats the conceptual and historical reasons for the choice of the pines as symbols of the great ages of *Man'yōshū* and *Kokinshū*. *Kowaki kotoba* in such a context add a sense of authoritative erudition, so he uses a Sinified phrase such as *banmin kore o shōkan su*, with its aphoristic weight and sonority, instead of, for instance, *tami mina kore o mezuru nari*, which means approximately the same thing and would be metrically acceptable.

From the ageha onward, however, not a single instance of *kowaki kotoba* appears. There is only one Sinified word in the entire third part, *matsudai*, "ages to come," and it is probably there in large part because it allows a pun on *matsu*, "pine." (Noh actors somewhat obscure the pun by pronouncing the word *mat'ndai*, thus my romanization.) Moreover, rhetoric as well as vocabulary is nativized in this final part of the kuse. In contrast to the parallelism and consciously allusive character of the previous parts, purely Japanese rhetorical techniques predominate here. Kake-kotoba abound: *iro wa nao mas(u)/masaki no kazura*, "its color increases/laurel vine"; *na wa taka(ki)/Takasago*, "illustrious/Takasago"; *matsudai/matsu*, "ages to come/pine"; *tameshi ni mo ai/aioi no*, literally "meet with an example," my "example to serve/(pines) that grew up together." An engo appears: *midori* and *tachi*, "green" and "rise"; and the technique of the jo is used: *masaki no kazura nagaki*, "the trailing laurel vine," becomes the "preface" for *yo*, "generation." There are allusions, to be sure—the quote from Masafusa's poem is an allusion of the most exact type, and the *chiriusezu shite*, "never leave the tree completely bare," alludes to the *Kokin-shū* preface yet once more[53]—but unlike the earlier allusions, these are to purely Japanese sources.

The chorus continues:

Rongi

152	C	Ge ni na o etaru matsu ga e no,
		Ge ni na o etaru matsu ga e no,
		Oiki no mukashi arawashite,
155		Sono na o nanoritamae ya,
	S/T	Ima wa nani o ka tsutsumu beki,
		Kore wa Takasago Suminoe no,
		Aioi no matsu no sei,
		Fūfu to genji kitaritari,
160	C	Fushigi ya sate wa nadokoro no,
		Matsu to kidoku o arawashite,
	S/T	Sōmoku kokoro nakeredomo,
	C	Kashikoki yo tote
	S/T	tsuchi mo ki mo,
	C	Waga ōkimi no kuni nareba,
165		Itsu made mo kimi ga yo ni,
		Sumiyoshi ni mazu yukite,
		Are nite machimōsan to,
		Yūnami no migiwa naru,
		Ama no obune ni uchinorite,
170		Oikaze ni makasetsutsu,
		Oki no kata ni idenikeri ya,
		Oki no kata ni idenikeri.

Rongi

152	C	These are justly famous pine boughs.
		These are justly famous pine boughs.
		Reveal your past, as old as these great trees,
155		And let us know your names.
	S/T	What now do we have to keep concealed?
		We are Takasago's, Suminoe's,
		Spirits of the pines that grew up together,
		Come here manifest as man and wife.
160	C	A marvel! The pines of these far-famed sites
		Make known to us a miracle, it seems;

s/t	No mind animates the plants and trees,
c	But in these venerable times,
s/t	simply since they grow within his realm,
c	Even the earth and trees express their hope
165	To live forever under our lord's sway.
	"Now, to Sumiyoshi,
	We will await you there."
	And into a fisher's skiff at the edge
	Of the evening waves they stepped,
170	Commending themselves to the fair wind.
	There! Onto the open sea they disappear,
	Onto the open sea they're gone.

Formally, this shōdan has much in common with the standard ageuta; it is in hiranori sung in the tadautai style. The meter is for the most part regular, and the first and last lines are repeated. The major difference is that most ageuta are sung by one character, or in unison by two or more characters or the chorus, whereas a rongi takes the form of a dialogue, in this case a dialogue between the shite and the tsure on the one hand and the chorus on the other. The chorus, however, never has a personality of its own in noh (as in Greek tragedy), but instead takes the part of the shite or waki or performs a narrative role. Here, it performs all these functions.

Lines 152-61 are clearly a dialogue between the shite/tsure and the waki; the chorus takes the lines that logically belong to the waki. From line 162 on, the division of roles becomes less distinct, and by line 166 the chorus is speaking for the shite and the tsure. Finally, from line 168 on, the chorus becomes narrator to describe the departure of the shite and the tsure from Takasago. (The exclamatory particle of the penultimate line, *ya*, which corresponds to my "There!," may indicate that this is the waki's line.) The point to be made is that the distinction between speakers is blurred here; because of Japanese syntax, this effect is quite natural in the original, and it is a perfect vehicle for the phantasmal nature of the content. The distinctions between characters that were so clear as the shite and the tsure educated the waki (from the third dan through the kuse of this dan) fade away like the shite and the tsure themselves.

The rongi is of a lighter texture than the preceding kuri, sashi, and kuse. There is an allusion, but it is one that is common to many plays and is not obtrusive.[54] There are kakekotoba as well, but they are totally conventional and do not slow the pace of one's understanding.[55] Lines 164-65 have a formulaic air surprisingly reminiscent of the encomia of the Man'yō poet Kakinomoto Hitomaro,[56] and although it is unlikely that Zeami had these in mind, the lexical similarity points to a similarity of function. These lines are shūgen, auspicious words about the power and benevolence of the ruler, and add still more of a sense of propitiousness to the play's theme. The entire song is so relatively simple as to remind us of Zeami's dictum that waki noh should be written in a straightforward manner.

As the chorus finishes singing the rongi, the shite and the tsure leave the stage and the aikyōgen, who took his place on the *hashigakari* (the bridge-like entry to a noh stage) unobtrusively during the chorus's ageuta, is called to the stage proper for the *ai*, a sort of entr'acte. For the text of that piece we must turn to Edo period texts, for though we know from Zeami's holographs that there was some sort of an interlude involving a kyōgen actor in his day, we have no clue to its nature. (I give the translation without the romanization, since only the content, not the actual language used, is relevant here.)

Ai

W	I say, is anybody there?
WT	Yes, here I am.
W	Go get somebody from the area.
WT	Yes, sir. . . . Is there anybody around?
K	Somebody's looking for a resident of the area. I guess I'll go see what he wants. I understand you want to talk to someone. What can I do for you?
WT	There's something my master wants to ask you; come along here.
K	Yes, sir.
WT	I've brought the local resident you called for.
K	Here I am, a man from the vicinity.
W	I am the priest Tomonari from the Aso shrine in the province of Higo in Kyushu. This is the first time I've seen this coast. Tell me what they say around here about the pine of Takasago.
K	This is an unexpected request. Although I do live around here, I'm not very familiar with that sort of thing because it's the concern of more elegant folks than me, but it wouldn't be right to say I don't know anything at all now that you've gone to the trouble of asking for me, so I'll tell you whatever I've heard about it.
W	Yes, please do.
K	Well now, along the coast here the pine most generally referred to as the Takasago pine is this tree right here. That business about the pines having grown up together comes from the preface to *Kokinshū*, where it is recorded, "The pines of Takasago and Suminoe seem just as if they had grown up together." Among all the various trees, the pine, an evergreen, flourishes longest, so the flourishing of the way of poetry is compared to the flourishing needles of the pines of Takasago and Suminoe, as I'm told. Then, there is another version of the story which holds that the gods of this shrine and Sumiyoshi are husband and wife. This being the case, when the goddess of this shrine makes her appearance at Sumiyoshi, she uses this pine for her communication with the god. And again, when the god

of Sumiyoshi appears here, he also uses this pine for his communication with the goddess. From long ago right up to the present day, for ever so long, they've gone back and forth this way, so folks around here have gotten in the habit of calling them the pines that grew up together. Properly speaking, the gods of Sumiyoshi and this shrine are a single deity in two bodies, and their divine powers are alone responsible for the flourishing of the way of poetry as well as the auspicious fulfillment of marriage for a man and his wife, or so I am told. In the language of poetry, I've heard such things as "pebbles grow to maturity to become boulders," and "dust piles up to form mountains," and "though the sand upon the shore be exhausted, the recitation of poetry will never be exhausted," but I really don't know what is meant by the expression "the pines grew up together."

Regarding the auspiciousness of the pines, I'm told that if so much as an inch-long sprig of pine puts forth needles, the tree will be green forever and live to be a thousand or ten thousand years old; there's nothing more auspicious than a pine, and since the gods both planted pines together, the pines are called "the pines that were planted together." I've heard that they will protect this place of ours for five trillion, six hundred and seventy million years.

W   Thank you for your trouble in telling me all this. Before you arrived, an old couple came by, and when I asked them about the Takasago pine, they told me a story just like the one I have now heard from you, and then said they'd be waiting at Sumiyoshi. They boarded a small boat at the water's edge, set out for the open sea— or so it appeared—and vanished.

K   Why, that's astonishing. What you say is miraculous. I suspect that was the god of Sumiyoshi, cleaning up under the pines here with the goddess of Takasago. Since you say they told you they'd be waiting at Sumiyoshi, before they boarded a small boat and set out onto the open sea, I think you ought to make a pilgrimage to Sumiyoshi as fast as you can. I myself have a small boat I made recently, but I haven't taken her out for a maiden voyage yet. Just as I was thinking I must give a ride to some auspicious person, whoever he might be, I meet you, a priest at the great shrine of Aso, and what's more, a man who's conversed with the god of Sumiyoshi. If I were to give a ride to someone as favored of the gods as you are, my boat would reach its destinations successfully for a thousand, or even ten thousand years. Please take a ride in my new boat. I'll man the rudder and accompany you to Sumiyoshi.

W   Well, if that's the case, then I will take your boat to Sumiyoshi.

K   Look! As a mark of the god's great power, a first-class tail wind has started to blow. Hurry into the boat, please.

W   Certainly.[57]

In some plays a break of this sort, which is designed to allow the shite to change his costume, is dispensed with and replaced by an instrumental interlude called a MONOGI, during which the shite changes costume in view of the audience at the rear of the stage. However, in *Takasago*, as in many other plays, an elaborate change of costume is required, so that the aikyōgen's part is essential. In this particular case, though, the aikyōgen does more than merely fill the time. His speech is a commentary on the Takasago pine and includes the identification of the pine itself, a verbal footnote to the *Kokinshū* preface, a short discourse on the things that make the tree an appropriate symbol of constancy, and a brief digression on the conjugal habits of the god of Sumiyoshi and the goddess of Taka- sago. Having been through all this, the aikyōgen admits that he does not really know what it means to say the pines "have grown up together," but then he proceeds to give a possible etymological solution to the problem, explaining that "the pines that grew up together" (*aioi no matsu*) may be nothing more than a mispronunciation of "the pines that were planted together" (*aiue no matsu*). After all this speculation, the aikyōgen seems something of a scholar, providing one of the first commentaries on the play. And this is to say nothing of the touch of individuality that his var- ious interjections and his offer of the boat ride give him.[58]

The second half of the play opens with these lines delivered by the waki and the wakitsure:

Ageuta

173 w/wt	Takasago ya,
	Kono urabune ni ho o agete,
175	Kono urabune ni ho o agete,
	Tsuki morotomo ni ideshio no,
	Nami mo Awaji no shimakage ya,
	Tōku Naruo no oki sugite,
	Haya Suminoe ni tsukinikeri,
180	Haya Suminoe ni tsukinikeri.

Ageuta

173 w/wt	O Takasago!
	Spread the sail above this coastal skiff,
175	Spread the sail above this coastal skiff,
	Out upon the seaward surf, together with the moon,
	Past Awaji Island there reflected in the waves,
	Far out to sea we sail by Naruo,
	Already we arrive at Suminoe,
180	Already we arrive at Suminoe.

This ageuta is, no doubt, the most famous single song in all noh. As noted earlier, it has become standard fare for wedding receptions.[59] In its formal regularity, it resembles the waki's earlier ageuta with the dis- tinction that it has only one part whereas the other had two. It also re- sembles the first ageuta in content: it too is a michiyuki, or travel song. The first words of the song mark the last appearance of the emblem word Takasago; the waki and his retinue are now leaving Takasago be- hind for the shore of Sumiyoshi across the bay. The place names in lines

177 and 178 are kakekotoba hiding *awa*, "bubbles," and *(tōku) naru*, "become (distant)." *Awa* is an engo for *nami*, "waves." *Ideshio*, "the seaward surf," is also a kakekotoba containing an inflection of the verb *izu*, "to go out."

After they have sung this piece, the waki and the wakitsure take their seats. In modern performance the hayashi begins the DEHA, entrance music for the nochijite, who comes to the first pine on the hashigakari to sing the following lines:

Sashi

181 s   Ware mite mo hisashiku narinu Sumiyoshi no,
          Kishi no himematsu ikuyo henuran,
          Mutsumashi to kimi wa shirazu ya mizugaki no,
          Hisashiki yoyo no kamikagura,
185   Yoru no tsuzumi no hyōshi o soroete,
          Suzushimetamae ya miyatsukotachi.

Sashi

181 s   How long I have watched this pine on Sumiyoshi Shore!
          How many generations has it passed here?
          Time enough to make us intimates, my lord. How can you not have
             known?
          Through the ages, here, within these holy bounds, long have they
             danced the dance of gods.
185   Keep a steady beat upon the drums of night tonight,
          Propitiate your master, sacred thralls.

Like the sashi of the second dan, this one quotes waka—in this case, two poems from *Ise monogatari*. The first appears in its entirety in lines 181-82, the second in somewhat modified form in lines 183-84. The original version of the second poem reads:[60]

Mutsumashi to	Through the ages here within these holy bounds,
Kimi wa shiranami	Long have I rejoiced at your reign, my lord,
Mizugaki no	As long, in fact, as white waves have stood upon
Hisashiki yo yori	the seas;
Iwaisometeki	Time enough to make us intimates,
	Or can you not have known?

Zeami has changed the fourth and fifth lines to *hisashiki yoyo no kamikagura* in order to introduce the theme of dance, the major theme of the final dan. *Kagura* is a dance form usually done for the entertainment of the gods, but here the roles are reversed, and the god is dancing in celebration of the Emperor's reign, an understandable transformation, given the generic considerations of waki noh. In modern performance, the shite turns toward the instrumental ensemble as he sings the last part of the sashi, and his words can be taken to refer directly to its members just as if they were the shrine musicians. Mikata Ken assumes that performances of *Takasago* have always had this element, and sees it as a remnant from a time when the division between acting roles and accompanists was not as clear as it is today.[61]

The next shōdan is a jōnoei, a short piece in einori centering on the higher register. It is followed immediately by an *issei.

Jōnoei
187 c   Nishi no umi,
               Aokigahara no namima yori,
     s   Arawareideshi Sumiyoshi no.[62]

*Issei
190   Haru nare ya,
               Nokon no yuki no Asakagata,
     c   Tamamo karu naru kishikage no,
     s   Shōkon ni yotte koshi o sureba,
     c   Sennen no midori te ni miteri,
195 s   Baika o otte kōbe ni saseba,
     c   Jiget'n no yuki koromo ni otsu.

Jōnoei
187 c   Up from the western seas,
               Out of the waves of Laurelfield
     s   The god of Sumiyoshi comes.

*Issei
190   Spring is here.
               A veil of snow remains upon the coast of Asaka Bay
     c   By the seabank where fishers cut jade-like seagrass.
     s   I lean against the pine to rub my hips
     c   And find the green of a thousand years fills my grasp.
195 s   I break a twig of plum to stick into my hair
     c   And find the snow of Midspring falls upon my robes.

The shōdan jōnoei is characteristically used for the recitation of waka in the noh. The waka quoted here is a slight modification of a work by Urabe no Kanenao (late twelfth or early thirteenth century):[63]

Nishi no umi ya	Up from the Western Sea, oh,
Aokigahara no	Out of the tidal paths
Shioji yori	Stretching across Laurelfield
Arawareideshi	The god of Sumiyoshi
Sumiyoshi no kami	Has appeared.

This poem is based on a legend according to which the deity Izanagi gave birth to the god of Sumiyoshi in Awakigahara (or Aokigahara) in Kyushu after his return from the land of Yomi.*

The *issei is slightly irregular melodically;[64] it is also rather irregular metrically, particularly in lines 195-96, where the syllable count is 7-7, 6-

---

* Izanagi and his spouse Izanami were the first two gods to appear from the primordial chaos. When Izanami died and went off to the land of the dead, Yomi, Izanagi followed her longingly. But on discovering the corruption her body had undergone, he fled back to the land of the living, where he gave birth to numerous important deities.

6, probably in preparation for the next item—the dance. It is neverthe-less similar to the earlier issei in that much of its structure relies on par-allelism, though the parallelism is much stricter in this case because it in-volves the verbatim quotation of a Chinese poem by Songyō (Tachibana no Aritsura; late 800's-953?), a priest attached to the Enryakuji:

> I lean against the pine to rub my hips
> And find the green of a thousand years fills my grasp.
> I break a twig of plum to stick into my hair
> And find the snow of Midspring falls upon my robes.*

Alongside this quotation of a distinctly Sinified flavor, Zeami puts three lines displaying more native literary technique. The phrase *nokon no yuki*, "the remaining snow," becomes a jo for Asakagata, "Asaka Bay," by way of the kakekotoba *asa(shi)/Asakagata*, literally, "(the snow) is shallow/Asaka Bay." *Tamamo karu naru*, "(where fishers) gather jade-like seagrass," per-forms a similar function for *kishikage*, "the seabank," although there is no kakekotoba. Instead, the addition of *naru*, implying something like "(fishers) gather . . . , so they say," emphasizes the poetic origins of *ta-mamo karu*, a *makurakotoba* (pillow-word) used as early as *Man'yōshū*.

Still, for all this wordplay, neither of these shōdan is particularly com-plex, probably because the spectators' attention is to be drawn more to the action on stage than the text being sung. This part of the play is pre-sumably the "eye-opening part," or *kaigen*, as Zeami calls it, and in mod-ern performance the shite does indeed perform a number of mimetic and visually effective actions here. These shōdan serve as well to lead into the instrumental dance that is the focal point of the dan. In modern performance this is the KAMIMAI, a fast and vigorous dance during which the taiko (stick drum) joins the ensemble of flute and hand drums. (The taiko is used in *Takasago* only from the DEHA entrance music through the KAMIMAI.) Scholars have yet to determine to what degree the dance of Zeami's day resembles contemporary practice, but it seems quite reasonable to assume that the dance must have been designed to reflect the vigor and felicity of the god of Sumiyoshi.[65]

When the dance is complete, the final shōdan of the play is sung:

Rongi
197 C   Arigata no yōgō ya,
        Arigata no yōgō ya,
        Tsuki Sumiyoshi no kami asobi,

---

* *Wakan rōeishū*, in Kawaguchi and Shida, p. 54. People customarily rubbed their hips on a pine tree on the first day of the rat in the new year to protect themselves from the cold in the coming year. But beyond this surface explanation for the custom, the sexual symbol-ism involved in this movement cannot be ignored, especially since the pine is a Taoist sym-bol for prolonged sexual vigor in old age.

200		Mikage o ogamu aratasa yo,
	s	Ge ni samazama no maibime no,
		Koe o sumu nari Suminoe no,
		Matsukage mo utsuru naru,
		Seigaiha to wa kore yaran,
205	c	Kami to kimi to no michi sugu ni,
		Miyako no haru ni yuku beku wa,
	s	Sore zo Genjōraku no mai,
	c	Sate banzei no
	s	omigoromo,
	c	Sasu kaina ni wa,
210		Akuma o harai,
		Osamuru te ni wa,
		Jufuku o idaki,
		Senshūraku wa tami o nade,
		Manzairaku ni wa inochi o nobu,
215		Aioi no matsukaze,
		Sassat'n no koe zo tanoshimu,
		Sassat'n no koe zo tanoshimu.

Rongi

197	c	O marvelous apparition,
		O marvelous apparition,
		The moon shines clear, the god of Sumiyoshi dances:
200		This vision is a wonder to behold.
	s	The voices of all kinds of dancing maidens
		Ring out clearly over Suminoe's pine,
		Reflected, glittering, on the sea:
		Is this not "Blue Ocean Waves"?
205	c	The paths of prince and god run straight
		And lead to spring in the capital:
	s	This dance must be "Back to the Citadel."
	c	Then dressed in festive robes
	s	that augur ten millennia
	c	He spreads his arms wide,
210		Quelling demons,
		Draws his hands back
		Full of wealth and long life.
		"The Music of a Thousand Autumns" caresses the people,
		"The Music of Ten Thousand Years" extends our lives.
215		The pines that grew together dance to the wind,
		Resounding with the rustling voice of joy,
		Resounding with the rustling voice of joy.

This grand finale brings the play to a close in a sort of Ode to Joy.[66] After three lines (one of which is repeated) expressing the wonderment of those privileged to see the manifestation of the god, the text turns to a description of the scene and the god's dance. The words provide much opportunity for mimetic gesture as a foil to the almost entirely abstract dance that precedes this rongi. The song incorporates the titles of four *bugaku* (court dance music) pieces: "Seigaiha" (Blue Ocean Waves), "Gen-jōraku" (Back to the Capital), "Senshūraku" (The Music of a Thousand Autumns), and "Manzairaku" (The Music of Ten Thousand Years).

The rongi is basically structured into sets of parallel passages. The first set, lines 201-4 and 205-8, is parallel only in the loosest sense; the first member is both longer and more interrogative than the second. Notice, all the same, how each member starts with lines allowing mimetic interpretation by the shite and ends with lines identifying his actions as a bugaku piece: "Is this not 'Blue Ocean Waves?'" and "This dance must be 'Back to the Citadel.'" The second set (lines 209-10 and 211-12) is perfectly parallel, and the syllable counts are identical, 7-7 and 7-7. The third set (lines 213 and 214) is not metrically identical, and although the extra particle *ni* in the second member keeps the lines from being perfectly parallel, they are very nearly so. Furthermore, the correspondence of the bugaku titles in the two lines seems to make up for the slight imbalance caused by the metrical difference and the extra *ni*. The next line (215) sets apart the last two lines of the song from what precedes, and those last two lines form a parallel couplet of the most perfect kind: exact repetition.

As was pointed out earlier, it is standard for the first and last lines of a rongi to be repeated. But Zeami's intent here seems grander than mere conformity to convention. The final two lines of the play are, in fact, the last set of parallel couplets in the sequence described above, and as such, an extension of the sense of the earlier lines in that sequence. Thus, just as the first three sets of parallel passages describe the festive song and dance of the god's apparition, so also do the last lines describe song and dance. This time, the song and dance are the music of the entire natural world. They are therefore more profound and more widely encompassing than the manifestation of a single god, but at the same time, they represent a return to the real world after an excursion into the supernatural.[67] The return puts the waki and all the rest of us back in our own world; now, however, this world of ours is invested with all the magic and wonder of the play, and the theme of poetic universality is given a musical parallel. This is the true meaning of shūgen, and this kind of shūgen can be as meaningful to the modern viewer as it was to Zeami's contemporaries. It accounts for *Takasago*'s popularity in an age when most waki noh are seen as meaningless relics from the feudal past.

Although none of Zeami's other noh in the Aged Mode has matched *Takasago*'s popularity, each in its own way reveals further aspects of his style, expanding the aesthetic territory of the mode without crossing its generic boundaries. Moreover, our understanding of *Takasago* itself is significantly enhanced by considering other plays in the same mode. As mentioned earlier, Zeami picks out five plays in addition to *Takasago* as representative of the mode. Those plays, *Yumi Yawata, Oimatsu, Yōrō, Aridōshi,* and *Tōru,* can be treated in Zeami's terms, first according to thematic material, or shu ("the seed"), then structure, or saku, and finally, rhetorical technique, sho.

Yumi Yawata centers on a warrior's bow wrapped in a brocade bag. The maejite, an old man, appears with the bow at the Iwashimizu Hachiman Shrine in Kyoto and presents it to the waki, a retainer of the Ex-Emperor GoUda (1267-1324, r. 1274-86), to be offered up to His Majesty. As the shite explains: "Among the historical precedents of the land of China, brought to peaceful rule under the Zhou, one finds the precedent of wrapping one's bow and arrows in a bag and shutting away one's lance and shield. Accordingly, I have stuffed this bow into a bag and put my sword away in a box; these very actions are a sign of our lord's age of great peace."[68]

The play is a paean to imperial rule and to the peace that it has brought to the land. As such, it contains many of the traditional commonplaces of tranquility and prosperity, some of which it shares with *Takasago.*[69] The kusemai offers a disconnected recitation of the legendary martial feats of Empress Jingū and the peace they brought to the reign of Emperor Ōjin, as well as a very tenuously related reference to the founding of the Iwashimizu Hachiman Shrine by Emperor Kinmei. The theme of the play is limited to praise for the Emperor's peaceful reign, and it is in this sense "straightforward," but the lack of broader concerns, more subtly articulated, must in part account for the play's failure to arouse much interest in the modern viewer; it is not performed frequently.

Thematically, *Oimatsu* is, of all Zeami's plays, the closest to *Takasago.* As its title suggests, the pine tree is a central theme. But *Oimatsu* places almost equal emphasis on the plum tree. It displays greater thematic consistency and develops more imagistic interest than *Yumi Yawata,* but its theme is not as finely developed as *Takasago*'s, and it lacks that play's breadth of concern. As might be expected, *Oimatsu* also shares a number of auspicious commonplaces with *Takasago,* but it does not extract from them the joy of conjugal fidelity, the conviction that poetry is universal, or the sense that the universe is a sort of celebration, all elements of *Takasago*'s success.

Yōrō, the next play on the *Sandō* list, is based on the legend of a spring of eternal youth in the hinterlands of the province of Mino. The play shows the strongest Confucian coloring of any of Zeami's works: the existence of the spring is itself a mark of cosmic favor for the benevolence of the imperial rule, and it inspires the most upright Confucian behavior. The mood is consistently auspicious, a tone that is capped by the enactment of a miracle at the end of the play: the heavens flash, the gurgle of the spring turns to music, flowers fall from the sky. The chorus, with naïve understatement, announces, "This is not just an ordinary event" (*kore tadagoto to omowarezu*), whereupon the nochijite, the god of spring, appears and does a dance in honor of the Emperor's reign.[70]

Aridōshi is unique among the plays in the Aged Mode, quite different not only in structure and language, as we will see, but also in theme. The shite is a god, an old god, to be sure, but a deity of a different order from the gods in *Takasago*, *Yumi Yawata*, and *Oimatsu*. There is a threatening air about the god in *Aridōshi*, and this lends some sense of conflict to an essentially simple plot. The play opens with the *Kokinshū* compiler Ki no Tsurayuki, the waki, on a journey to Tamazushima. As he is riding along, the sky suddenly goes dark, a thunderstorm overtakes him, and his horse collapses. He is at a complete loss and, poet and litterateur that he is, compares himself to the ill-fated Xiang Yu, alluding to the famous Chinese general's last poem. While Tsurayuki is taken up with his erudite worries, an old man, the shite, approaches, carrying a torch and an umbrella. This exchange between the two of them elucidates Tsurayuki's problem:

Mondō

1	w	Nōnō ano hi no hikari ni tsuite mōsu beki koto no sōrō,
	s	Kono atari ni wa oyado mo nashi ima sukoshi saki e otōri are,
	w	Ima no kurasa ni yuku saki mo miezu,
		Shikamo noritaru koma sae fushite,
5		Zengo o bōjite sōrō nari,
	s	Sate geba wa watari mo nakarikeru ka,
	w	Somo ya geba to wa kokoroezu,
		Koko wa bashō no naki tokoro ka,
	s	Ara motaina no onkoto ya,
10		Kore wa Aridōshi no myōjin tote,
		Monotogame shitamō ongami no,
		Kaku zo to shirite bashō araba,
		Yo mo onninochi wa sōrō beki.[71]

Mondō

1	w	Ahem, you there in the torchlight, I would like to ask you a question.
	s	There's no lodging around here. Be on your way.
	w	It has gotten so dark just now I can't see where I'm going,
		And what's more, even my horse has collapsed.
5		I don't know what I'm going to do.
	s	You mean you failed to dismount to go by here?
	w	What! Well, I didn't know I ought to . . .
		Isn't one allowed to stay mounted here?
	s	Good heavens, no!

10   This is the shrine of the god of Aridōshi, a quick-tempered god,
    And if, knowing this was his shrine,
    You had still dared to stay mounted as you passed
    You certainly would no longer be alive.

Having been informed of his unwitting sacrilege, Tsurayuki begins to be able to make out the silhouette of a shrine in the darkness. The old man asks who he is, and when he finds that the unwitting traveler is the poet Tsurayuki, suggests that a poem may help appease the god. Tsurayuki thinks carefully and composes the following:

Mondō (cont.)
  w Amagumo no tachikasanareru yowa nareba,
    Ari to hoshi to mo omō beki ka wa.[72]
Mondō (cont.)
  w On a night like this, when rain clouds rise in layers all through the
    sky,
    How was I to know if there were stars?

The poem contains a pun: *ari to hoshi*, a grammatical inversion of "there were stars," which sounds like the name of the shrine, Aridōshi. The old man is so delighted with the poem that Tsurayuki goes on to discourse at some length about the history and nature of waka poetry. The old man, in turn, recites a showy prayer and does a short dance. The play ends with general rejoicing as the old man vanishes and Tsurayuki, resuming his journey, rides off into the sunrise.

Aridōshi bears some thematic resemblance to *Takasago* to the extent that both praise the wondrous powers of waka poetry, but this resemblance is generally overshadowed by the play's many eccentricities. It seems in some ways rather unlike Zeami, and in fact in *Sarugaku dangi*, Zōami is reported to have commented on Zeami's performance of it, saying that the first part of the play was done in the style of the old dengaku master Kiami. Zeami himself acknowledges this debt, and this seems to confirm the theory that *Aridōshi* is a reflection of older dramatic forms. (There is something playful about *Aridōshi*, too, and I would venture to say that it is, at least in places, a gentle parody of the conventions of noh. See, in particular, line 2 of the mondō quoted above. The shite's abrupt "There is no lodging around here. Be on your way" is an intriguing manipulation of the very common exchange in which a waki begs lodging of a shite who says he would be glad to oblige, but is embarrassed by his own humble residence and so must refuse.) This thematic irregularity, as much as the structural irregularity in which it is mirrored, distinguishes *Aridōshi* from *Takasago*, *Yumi Yawata*, *Oimatsu*, and *Yōrō*. According to the modern classification, it is not considered a waki noh like most plays in the Aged Mode, but is instead put in the group "miscellaneous plays."

Tōru is not a wàki noh either. Zeami sets it under the rubric yūkyoku ("elegant music") in his *Go on* rather than under shūgen ("congratulatory music"), where most plays in the Aged Mode would be expected to appear.[73] This is eminently reasonable considering the play's theme of elegant nostalgia. The maejite is an old man of the capital, who insists on talking about Shiogama, a famous place far away on the northeastern coast of Honshu. The waki finds the old man a little peculiar, and his questions earn him a detailed account of the Heian-period Epicurus, Minamoto no Tōru.* Tōru had had the gardens at his estate in the capital transformed into a replica of Shiogama through the almost Egyptian labors of a gang of workmen and coolies. Much of the first half of the play is taken up with the old man's reminiscences of his estate. In the last act of the play, the old man reveals himself as the ghost of the great aesthete and illustrious courtier of bygone days. This part of the play bears some resemblance to the auspicious dancing of the end of a more orthodox play in the Aged Mode, but it replaces the exuberance and majesty of a god with the elegance and beauty of the Heian court. In this respect, it resembles the plays in the Woman's Mode.

There is irony in the fact that most of these plays fall under the category of the *Aged* Mode. In none of them except *Oimatsu* is the nochijite actually an old man, or, indeed, an old god. (*Aridōshi* is a one-act play with, therefore, no nochijite.) They are, then, plays in the Aged Mode without aged characters in the last act. This fact has provoked some scholarly debate. Yokomichi Mario has suggested that perhaps the nochijite of *Takasago* and *Yumi Yawata* originally were old gods, but the Kanze school actor and scholar Mikata Ken disagrees, arguing that the final act of these plays can take a (young) male god and should be sung rhythmically and lightly with increasing speed.[74]

The entire controversy does not seem all that important, however, for by the time the nochijite appears in *Yumi Yawata* or *Takasago*, or any of the other plays in the Aged Mode discussed, the play is all but over. The most highly articulated part of each play, in terms of both rhythm and narrative, comes in the first half, and it is the form of the shite during this part of the play that determines the play's classification in Zeami's Three Modes system. This is supported by a quick consideration of the plays Zeami classifies under the Martial Mode. Of the six plays he lists as basic to this class, four (*Michimori*, *Tadanori*, *Yorimasa*, and *Sanemori*) take old men as their maejite; yet none of these plays falls in the Aged Mode. This is because in each case the rhythmic and narrative high points come in the second half.

---

* Minamoto no Tōru (822-95) was the son of Emperor Saga. His estate at Kawara no In was by far the largest private estate of the time, occupying an area of almost 20 acres, some eight times the size of the standard estate allocated to a high-level courtier.

To summarize then, the thematic characteristic that most typifies plays in the Aged Mode is the choice of an old man as the shite for the narrative and musical center of the play. In most cases this results in an emotional tenor of congratulations or auspiciousness (shūgen), and such an emotional tenor usually qualifies the play in question as a waki noh. *Takasago* and *Yumi Yawata* conform most closely to this pattern. *Oimatsu* and *Yōrō* fall in line behind these, and *Tōru* and *Aridōshi* are variations on the theme.

Does the structure of the noh in the Aged Mode reflect these thematic characteristics in some way? This question is of particular concern in this mode because of its ritualistic significance and association with the notion of congratulations and auspiciousness. Form and content can never of course be separated entirely in any work of art, but in these plays formal orthodoxy is inextricably linked to thematic orthodoxy, the necessity that the honzetsu of the play be appropriate and decorous. Such concomitance provides a useful means of contrasting and comparing the plays in the category.

The six basic noh in the Aged Mode can first be compared structurally by a simple charting of the sequences of shōdan in each play. Since Zeami designated *Yumi Yawata* as the most straightforward play in this mode, let us assume for the moment that it is the most orthodox in structure and take it as our model. Table 5 arrays the other five plays from left to right according to the degree to which they depart from the norm.

There is no need to go into tedious detail about each and every difference in the structural organization of those five plays.[75] For our purposes, it suffices to note the order of their divergence from *Yumi Yawata*: *Takasago*, *Oimatsu*, *Yōrō*, *Tōru*, and *Aridōshi* (notice that the last two plays have switched places from the thematic lineup). This exercise is meaningless, however, if *Yumi Yawata* should prove a faulty model. To determine whether the play is indeed structurally orthodox, we must return once more to Zeami's principle of structural organization, jo-ha-kyū. According to that principle, every day's program, every play, every dan within a play, every shōdan within a dan, and even every word delivered on stage is to have its own jo-ha-kyū progression. Structural orthodoxy results from the smooth and regular development of jo-ha-kyū in each dan of a play.

Is this the case with *Yumi Yawata*? Let us once again consider the shōdan sequences in Table 5, this time focusing on that play alone. The last significant shōdan of each dan is either an ageuta or a rongi, shōdan with very similar formal characteristics. Even the aikyōgen interlude conforms in this respect. (The tsukizerifu of the first dan is a highly conventionalized and very brief shōdan of little significance.) But this is only the most obvious continuity among the dan. Dan 1, 2, and 4 each begin with a short song and then proceed to longer shōdan. This may seem a trivial point at first, but the literary function of any given shōdan is greatly influenced by its length, so there is some significance to this pattern. A shidai, or issei, or kuri, is unsuitable for an extended passage of either a lyric or a narrative nature. These songs are instead used for prefatory thematic or contextual statements.*

The shōdan set in the middle of each dan are devoted to the careful verbal development of literary subtleties, whether narrative, lyric, or dramatic. This is especially true of dan 2-4, and it is even true to some extent of the nanori of dan 1. The major exception is dan 5, where aural interest is replaced by visual interest and the dance occupies the central position.

There are still other formal continuities among the dan,[76] but by now it is already apparent that a basic symmetry, created through the principles of jo-ha-kyū, informs the structure of each dan. This is not of course an exact symmetry (perfect symmetry would be perfectly boring, as Leonard Bernstein has admirably demonstrated[77]), but the underlying principle of symmetry is both technically practical and artistically effective.

Each dan, then, is the playing out of the idea of dan, and the dynamic principle behind the idea of dan is a progression through jo-ha-kyū, more or less smooth and regular in accordance with the formal orthodoxy of the play in question. Each dan must of course be constructed with due allowance for its place in the overall structure of the entire play—for example, the first dan, the jo of the whole play, is weighted toward jo and even its central shōdan remains uncomplicated—but at the same time each dan is a cycle that begins anew with each successive dan.

Significant breaks in this formal patterning, especially in waki noh in the Aged Mode, may very likely result from special thematic concerns, and should be examined in such light. The major structural differences in *Oimatsu* provide a good example. Both pine and plum must be treated in its central narrative, so the kuse of the fourth dan is extended to embrace both subjects while other shōdan are either shortened or omitted altogether in what Yokomichi calls a bold design.[78] The fifth dan departs even more substantially from the *Yumi Yawata* model. The central dance

* Thus in *Takasago*, the shidai gives a thematic preface of freshness and felicity to the first dan and indeed to the play as a whole; the issei gives the play a temporal and spatial context; and the kuri specifies the narrative context. All these shōdan serve as the jo of their respective dan, and the same can be said of the sashi of dan 5 (recall how much shorter this sashi is than the sashi of dan 2 and 4, and also what a different literary function it serves).

TABLE 5   *The Shōdan Sequences of Zeami's Six Model Plays in the Aged Mode*

Dan (section)	Yumi Yawata	Takasago	Oimatsu	Yōrō	Tōru	Aridōshi
1 (jo)	SHINNOSHIDAI Shidai Nanori Ageuta Tsukizerifu	SHINNOSHIDAI Shidai Nanori Ageuta (Tsukizerifu)	SHINNOSHIDAI Shidai Nanori Ageuta (Tsukizerifu)	SHINNOSHIDAI Shidai Nanori Ageuta (Tsukizerifu)	NANORIBUE Nanori Sageuta Ageuta Tsukizerifu	SHIDAI Shidai Nanori Ageuta X
2 (ha 1)	SHINNOISSEI Issei Sashi Sageuta Ageuta	SHINNOISSEI Issei Sashi Sageuta Ageuta	SHINNOISSEI Issei Sashi Sageuta Ageuta	SHINNOISSEI Issei Sashi Sageuta Ageuta	ISSEI Issei Sashi Sageuta Ageuta (*Tsukizerifu)	ASHIRAIDASHI Sashi
3 (ha 2)	Mondō Kakeai Ageuta	Mondō Kakeai Ageuta	Mondō Uta	Mondō Kakeai Ageuta	Mondō Ageuta	Mondō Uta
4 (ha 3)	Sasoizerifu Kuri Sashi Kuse Rongi	(Sasoizerifu) Kuri Sashi Kuse Rongi	(Sasoizerifu) Sashi Kuse	(Sasoizerifu) Kuri Sashi Sageuta Ageuta Sageuta Rongi Kakeai Ageuta	(Sasoizerifu) Katari Uta Ageuta Mondō Uta Rongi	Mondō Kakeai Sageuta Ageuta Kuse

				RAIJO		
				Nanori		
				Shaberi		
			SHINNOJONOMAI	SANDANNOMAI		
Aikyōgen	Mondō	Mondō	Mondō	Noriji	Mondō	X
	Katari	Katari	Katari		Katari	
	Ageuta	Ageuta	Ageuta	DEHA	Ageuta	Kakeai
	DEHA	DEHA	DEHA	Sashi	DEHA	Notto
	Sashi	Sashi	Kakeai	Kakeai	Sashi	TACHIMAWARI
		Jōnoei		*Issei		X
	Issei	*Issei	*Issei	Noriji	*Issei	Noriji
	Noriji		Noriji		HAYAMAI	Uta
5 (kyū)	KAMIMAI	KAMIMAI	X	KAMIMAI		
			Noriji	Waka		
	Rongi	Rongi		Wakauke	Rongi	
			Noriji	Noriji		

NOTE: The shōdan in small caps are instrumental pieces, including dances. Parentheses indicate a highly conventional shōdan that was omitted from old texts but was probably included in performances; X indicates an unspecified shōdan; and an asterisk indicates that a shōdan is irregular.

is a SHINNOJONOMAI instead of a KAMIMAI, in keeping with the age of the nochijite (in *Oimatsu* the nochijite and the maejite are both characters in the Aged Mode). Then, instead of a rongi, there are two shōdan in ōnori rhythm separated by two lines in noncongruent rhythm. The noriji at the end of the play, which upsets the symmetry of the fifth dan, is held to be a remnant of the earlier performing art Ennen no furyū, in which the appearance of gods, plant spirits, and demons was accompanied by ōnori rhythm.[79]

The fifth dan of *Yōrō* also ends with a noriji passage reflecting Ennen no furyū influence. Indeed, the influence is perhaps even greater than in *Oimatsu*, because the shōdan immediately preceding the dance in this play is also a noriji. But the most uncharacteristic dan of *Yōrō* is the fourth: the play contains no kuse. One finds instead the sequence sageuta-ageuta-sageuta-rongi. And the dan ends with a kakeai and an ageuta instead of *Yumi Yawata*'s rongi.

The sageuta-ageuta-sageuta-rongi sequence seems, in this case, to reflect some uncertainty. Perhaps Zeami found the tale of the spring alone insufficient for a full noh. At any rate, he uses that sequence, as well as the sashi before it, to augment the original theme with various allusions and references to related legends. The sashi is in large part a quotation from the beginning of Kamo no Chōmei's *Hōjōki* (Record from a Ten-Square-Foot Hut) describing the flow of water. The first sageuta is an exhortation to draw water from the spring. The ageuta jumps to the Seven Sages of the Bamboo Grove and their legendary affection for wine. The second sageuta refers, by way of a Chinese poem,[80] to the elegant diversion of drinking wine from shells floating in an ornamental stream. The rongi then switches to the legend of Peng Zu, a Chinese fairy who gained immortality by drinking the dew off chrysanthemum petals. Finally, at the end of the rongi the original theme returns. In the kakeai the waki expresses his happiness at finding the spring and says he is going to go report to the Emperor. Then comes the miracle mentioned earlier: the heavens rain flowers, there is a flash of light, and so forth. As Yokomichi points out, this shōdan should logically be followed directly by the last dan of the play and the appearance of the god.[81] Instead, the aikyōgen appears. This kink in the progress of the story again reflects structural instability, and the fact that the maejite and nochijite in *Yōrō* are entirely different characters—not merely different manifestations of the same character as in *Oimatsu* and *Yumi Yawata*—suggests that the play was written before Zeami had firmly established the structural principles he sets out in *Sandō*.

Tōru is much like *Yumi Yawata* in its general contours, but differs considerably in the fourth dan. The differences, however, are due not to uncertainty and stylistic instability, as they appear to be in *Yōrō*, but rather to dramatic design. The dan opens with a long narrative shōdan delivered by the shite. His first lines read:*

Katari

1	s	Mukashi Saga no tennō no ontoki,
		Tōru no otodo to mōshishi hito,
		Michinoku no Chika no Shiogama no chōbō o kikoshimeshioyobare,
		Miyako no uchi ni utsushioki,
5		Ano Naniwa no Mitsu no Hama yori mo,
		Higoto ni ushio o kumase,
		Koko nite shio o yakasetsutsu,
		Isshō gyoiu no tayori to shitamō.

Katari

1	s	Long ago, in the reign of Emperor Saga,
		A man called Minister Tōru heard
		Of the famous view of Shiogama in Chika of the Far North.
		He transferred the scene to the capital
5		And from Naniwa's far Coast of Mitsu,
		Each day he had brine drawn,
		And here he had salt water boiled.
		He took lifelong pleasure in the scene.

The shite soon falls into a sad reverie and bitterly contrasts the glories of Tōru's past with the ruins of the garden around him. After the katari, the shite continues his plaint in an uta. The chorus then comes in (continuing the uta and proceeding into an ageuta), voicing the shite's sharply nostalgic longings:

Uta (cont.)

23	c	Urasabishiku mo arehatsuru,
		Ato no yo made mo shiojimite,
25		Oi no nami mo kaeru yaran,
		Ara mukashi koishi ya.

Ageuta

	c	Koishi ya koishi ya to,
		Shitaedomo nagekedomo,
		Kai mo nagisa no urachidori,
30		Ne o nomi naku bakari nari,
		Ne o nomi naku bakari nari.

Uta (cont.)

23	c	All is gone to desolation and stark ruin,
		But I stay soaked with the tides of tears even in these latter days,
25		The waves of age crash down upon me still.
		Oh, how I long for the past.

Ageuta

	c	"How I long, how I long for the past," I sigh,
		But my yearnings and complaints
		Come to no end, and at the water's edge,

---

* Only portions of the dan will be quoted here; a full translation is provided in Appendix B.

30   The plover cries and cries,
          The plover cries and cries.

Now the waki effects a sudden change in mood with a request of the shite:

Mondō
32   w   Ika ni jōdono,
          Miewataru yamayama wa mina meisho nite zo sōrōran onnoshie
               sōrae,

Mondō
32   w   Now then, old sir,
          I suppose all the mountains we see from here are famous places.
          Tell me about them.

There follows a catalogue of the entire panorama of the old capital from east to south to west. The passage is a tour de force, interweaving description, folk etymology, literary lore, and allusion. The shite loses himself in the natural scene for some while, finally returning to self-consciousness only to disappear:

Rongi (cont.)
85   c   Arashi fukeyuku aki no yo no,
          Sora suminoboru tsukikage ni,
     s   Sasu shiodoki mo haya sugite,
     c   Hima mo oshiteru tsuki ni made,
     s   Kyō ni jōjite,
90   c   Mi oba ge ni,
          Wasuretari aki no yo no,
          Nagamonogatari yoshi na ya,
          Mazu iza shio o kuman tote,
          Matsu ya Tago no ura,
95   Azuma karage no shiogoromo,
          Kumeba tsuki o mo,
          Sode ni mochijio no,
          Migiwa ni kaeru nami no yoru no,
          Rōjin to mietsuru ga,
100   Shiokumori ni kakimagirete,
          Ato mo miezu narinikeri,
          Ato mo miezu narinikeri.

Rongi (cont.)
85   c   The gale blows late through the autumn night,
          The sky grows clear, the moon climbs.
     s   Already now the high tide turns.
     c   Although my time is short,
     s   I've been enticed by the shining moon,
90   c   Delighting in the moment's magic,
          I forgot myself this autumn night
          In long tales, to no useful end,
          But now I'll dip salt water, he says,
          And picks up his pail.

95   Hiking up his tide-soaked robe,
    He reaches into the water to catch the moonbeams
    On his sleeve,
    Then standing on the land's edge while the high tide crashes in
     falling waves,
    The old man—or so I thought him—
100   Hides himself away in a cloud of sea mist
    To disappear from sight,
    To disappear from sight.

This dan is remarkable not only because of its highly affecting poetry and carefully calibrated changes in emotional tenor, but also because its form mirrors these qualities with a beautiful precision. First, the theme of nostalgia for Tōru's past glories is articulated in the katari, uta, and ageuta sequence. The mondō, uta, and rongi that follow sing instead of the beauty of the scene from east to south and west of Kyoto. The common thread running through the two sequences is the evanescence of beauty. The glories of Tōru's past are gone, as the katari, uta, and ageuta plainly show. The glories of the early autumn dusk are here now, to savor, but they too are not to last long; thus the emphasis on the advance of time, from dusk to nightfall and from early fall to later in the season, in the mondō and rongi. (This thread is taken up again in the fifth dan, where Tōru's ghost appears again, this time in his former glory, to dance for a fleeting moment beneath the full moon.)

The two subthemes are both significant enough and distinctive enough to merit separate treatment; the fourth dan, therefore, is actually doubled; it contains two subsections, both exhibiting the characteristics of dan symmetry and jo-ha-kyū (see Table 6).

The formal symmetry of the two subsections is evident in the move

TABLE 6 *The Subsections of the Fourth Dan of Tōru*

Category	Shōdan	Subject
Subsection 1		
Jo	Katari, lines 1-8	Tōru's garden at its height
Ha	Katari, lines 9-15	Tōru's garden now
	Katari-uta, lines 16-26	Poem by Tsurayuki and the shite's reaction
Kyū	Ageuta, lines 27-31	The shite's reflection on the situation
Subsection 2		
Jo	Mondō, lines 32-43	Mount Sound-on-Wings
Ha	Mondō-uta-rongi, lines 44-81	Seiganji through Fukakusa
Kyū	Rongi, lines 82-102	Description of the moment and disappearance of the shite

from kotoba (at the beginning of the katari and the mondō) to noncongruent song (later in these shōdan) to congruent song (in the two uta, the ageuta and rongi). This musical structuring is heightened by the fact that the first part of each subsection is delivered in shite and waki solos, whereas the last part is sung in the eight-voice unison of the chorus.

A less precise symmetry can even be discerned in the content of the two subsections. In both, the jo is relatively matter-of-fact and generalized, the ha takes on a more subjective cast in extended descriptive passages, and the kyū directs the audience's attention to the shite (either to his longing or to his movements and disappearance). No longer do we have a "straightforward" structure like that of *Yumi Yawata*, but instead the kind of subtle formal and thematic interaction one expects of the plays in the Woman's and Martial Modes.

As a one-act play, *Aridōshi* is bound to be the most structurally distinct of all the plays. As mentioned earlier, there is more conflict in this play than in most noh, and it has a recognizable plot, unlike *Takasago*, for example. That plot is introduced, developed, and brought to a conclusion through the interaction of the waki with the shite during a single continuous stretch of time. The element of dance in the play is minor, and there is consequently no need for a section like the fifth dan of the other plays. The waki is far more important in *Aridōshi* than in the other plays; he in fact becomes the central character in the fourth dan, with the shite taking on the subordinate role of questioner that the waki plays in *Takasago*, *Yumi Yawata*, and so on. Here it is the shite who asks the waki's identity, and the waki who provides the lyric and narrative interest of the dan, first by composing a waka, then by discoursing on the history and composition of poetry. The kuse is sung mostly by the chorus, as usual, but it is sung from the point of view of the waki, and he sings the lines usually reserved for the shite, the ageha. The fifth dan, however, belongs to the shite. It centers on his delivery of the *notto*, which is followed by his short but flashy dance, the TACHIMAWARI. The difference in balance between waki and shite, though carried to the fullest in the fourth dan, affects the structure of the first two dan as well. For instance, an unspecified shōdan follows the typical shidai-nanori-ageuta sequence of the first dan. This is where the action of the play begins; it grows dark, it rains, Tsurayuki's horse collapses, and Tsurayuki finds himself stranded. No such shōdan exists in the other plays in the Aged Mode, nor could it. Similarly, in contrast to the long, lyrical second dan of the other plays (the dan in which the shite appears and, as it were, sings to himself of his state of mind, the scenery, and so on), *Aridōshi*'s second dan is short and uncomplicated. When the shite appears, it is simply in response to Tsurayuki's transgression. In *Takasago*, by contrast, one feels that the old man and woman come every evening to sweep under the pine; in *Yōrō* the old man and his son seem to go to the spring every day, whether there happens to be an imperial messenger in the area or not. It is precisely the autogenous appearance of the shite in these plays and others in the Aged Mode that permits their second dan to be devoted to a long lyrical expansion of the play between the shite's emotions and his perceptions of the surrounding landscape. This is impossible in *Aridōshi* because any lyrical digression by the shite (other than the few lines with which he begins his sashi) would kill the budding plot of the first dan. Consequently, the second dan consists of nothing more than the shite's entrance music and his sashi.[82]

Takasago, as we saw in Table 5, seems almost structurally identical to *Yumi Yawata*, and certainly far more like that play than the increasingly divergent *Oimatsu*, *Yōrō*, *Tōru*, and *Aridōshi*. Yet Zeami takes care to mention its irregularity, its "fins," as he puts it. What is it about *Takasago* that incites such special mention?

True enough, there is a sashi-jōnoei-*issei sequence leading to the KA-MIMAI in the last dan instead of *Yumi Yawata*'s sashi-issei-noriji sequence.[83] But it is hard to believe that Zeami would find any "fins" in a difference as minor as this. We must therefore take a closer look at the shōdan themselves to see why he might consider the play eccentric. Some of the shōdan do in fact differ considerably from their *Yumi Yawata* counterparts. For instance, all of *Yumi Yawata*'s ageuta are perfectly regular: metrically 5, 7-5, (7-5), . . . 7-5, (7-5). Only half of the ageuta in *Takasago* are. The shite's ageuta in dan 2 parses 4-5, (4-5), 7-5, . . . 7-5, (7-5), and the chorus's ageuta in dan 3 is even more irregular: 5-5, 7-5, . . . 7-5, (7-5). Similarly, the rongi in *Takasago*'s fourth dan contains more metrically irregular lines and more half-lines than *Yumi Yawata*'s. There are irregularities in other shōdan as well.[84]

Even these differences seem minor, but to Zeami's audience, such irregularities were perhaps more obvious.[85] Formal orthodoxy was one of the pleasures to be appreciated when viewing waki noh, and deviations from standard form—at least in the most successful plays—must have been taken as conscious artistic choices for specific aesthetic purposes. If it has become increasingly difficult for modern theater-goers to find much pleasure in waki noh, this must be, in part, because the modern audience is not attuned to structural conventions that were apparent to earlier audiences. We fail to see the trees for the forest, or the fins for the fish, as it were.

In *Sandō*, when Zeami spoke of the final stage in the construction of the play as the "writing" (i.e., sho), he apparently meant the writing of the music as well as the text. The music is, by and large, beyond our purview for reasons stated earlier; we therefore confine our discussion to

Zeami's literary techniques. For these we turn to an examination of the plays themselves. They show an interesting blend of rhetorical devices, combining devices drawn from the classical Japanese and Sino-Japanese traditions, particularly from waka and renga poetry, with a variety of literary innovations not found, at least in precisely the same form, in earlier works.

Three traditional techniques that Zeami uses generously are the kakekotoba, the engo cluster, and the jo (or jokotoba). These often appear in perfectly conventional constructions, such as the wordplay we saw earlier on the term matsu, which can mean both "wait" and "pine tree." They tend to appear most frequently in the metered passages of plays, and although they abound in tadautai songs such as ageuta, the most sophisticated use of them often comes in metered but noncongruent shōdan like the sashi and issei. The maejite's first sashi in *Takasago* is a splendid example, and others are not difficult to find.[86]

Zeami often uses these three techniques to create long passages of psychological description. Such passages might even be called streams of consciousness, because they delineate the internal world of a character through his mental associations in what sometimes seems a highly idiosyncratic and almost random manner. But that term belongs to another sort of criticism and may prove confusing here. Moreover, the literary structure of these passages is often governed by an artful and highly developed set of conventions, so that what seems random at first is not random at all. Certain Japanese scholars, Kōsai Tsutomu most prominently, have identified these passages as "renga-like progressions." I will borrow this term.[87]

One of the best examples of such a passage in all the plays in the Aged Mode is the shite's first sashi in *Takasago*, discussed above. Another fine example is this sashi from *Yōrō*:

Sashi

1	S	Kojin nemuri hayaku samete,
		Yume wa musoji no hana ni sugi,
	S/T	Kokoro wa bōten no tsuki ni usobuki,
		Mi wa bankyō no shimo ni tadayoi,
5		Hakudō no yuki wa tsumoredomo,
		Oi no yashinō takigawa no,
		Mizu ya kokoro o kiyomuran.[88]

Sashi

1	S	An old man wakens early,
		His dreams, in threescore years of flowers, passed.
	S/T	His heart chants to the moon that leaks down through the thatch.
		His body wanders over a frost-laden bridge.
5		The snows of white hair pile deep upon his head,
		But in that spring which gives life to the old,
		His heart is purified.

This is not an easy passage, and does not seem to lead anywhere if read as discursive narrative.[89] It makes more sense as a stream of reflections on old age held together by a series of associations of the type common to renga. Thus, *nemuri*, "sleep," leads to *yume*, "dream"; *hana*, "flower," to *tsuki*, "moon"; *kokoro*, "mind," to *mi*, "body"; *bōten*, "thatched hut," to *bankyō*, "plank bridge"; *shimo*, "frost," to *yuki*, "snow"; and finally, *hakudō*, "white head," to *oi*, "old age." The associations between waking and dreaming, and mind and body, are obvious. Less so, is that between flowers and the moon, but it is pervasive in the tradition. The association of the thatched hut and the plank bridge is made through allusion to a poem by the ninth-century Chinese poet Wen Ting-yun.[90]

The entire song is built up by a renga-like progression and association of images through which the shite can express his emotions. The technique can be used for other types of description as well—for example, in the shite's ageuta in *Oimatsu*, this sort of association and progression is used to compare a natural scene to the way of poetry—but it seems particularly effective for highly lyric passages, and for this reason, it is frequently found in sashi, songs often sung on the shite's entrance to set the emotional tone of a play.[91]

Parallelism is another of the traditional techniques Zeami frequently uses. Indeed, the passage just quoted contains a parallel construction. This probably comes more from the Sino-Japanese tradition than the native, but by Zeami's time it had been thoroughly nativized and could be used with varying degrees of Chineseness. A short song, such as an issei, is easily created entirely of parallel lines.[92] But Zeami sometimes uses the technique for longer passages as well. The end of the second rongi of *Takasago* is a masterly example of this sort of extended parallelism. It is used to less effect in this passage from the fourth dan of *Oimatsu*:

Sashi

1	W	Mazu shadan no tei o ogamitatematsureba,
		Kita ni gagataru seizan nari,
	C	Rogetsu shōhaku no naka ni eiji,
		Minami ni sekisekitaru keimon nari,
5		Shajit' chikukan no moto ni sukeri,
	S	Hidari ni kaen no rintō ari,
	C	Suichō kōkei no yosōi mukashi o wasurezu,
		Migi ni koji no kiuseki ari,
		Shinsho sekibon no hibiki tōru koto nashi.[93]

Sashi

1	W	First, when you lift your eyes unto the holy site,
		On the north, green peaks rise with steep majesty;
	C	The veiled moon casts down its beams among pines and birches.
		On the south, a bramble gate stands with deep tranquility;

5   The setting sun projects its image through to the roots of the
             bamboo grove.
s   To the left, a five-tiered stupa encircled by a halo of flame;
c   The appointments of viridian screen and scarlet chamber forget not
             the past.
           To the right, fallen remnants bequeathed by an ancient temple;
           The reverberations of morning bell and evening chime cease not to
             resound.

The language here is overbearing and at times inappropriate to the object of the description—"the appointments of viridian screen and scarlet chamber" really belong to a lady's bedroom and not to a venerable temple—but the passage is nevertheless a good example of Zeami's parallelism at its most Sinified extreme. This is very difficult language for the ear, *kowaki kotoba*, and may not have been entirely understood even by Zeami's audience,[94] but the weight and formal precision it bears provide an appropriate setting for the discourse on the flying plum and the following pine of the immediately succeeding shōdan, the kuse. In this, the passage resembles the first part of the kuse of *Takasago*, where Zeami uses similar, but not quite so stiff, parallel constructions. As was mentioned earlier, Zeami objects to the overuse of *kowaki kotoba*, so passages like the *Oimatsu* sashi are not too common. But he often combines stiffly Sinified and strictly parallel couplets with more softly Japanese, loosely parallel couplets to form sequences. The best example of this in the Aged Mode is the sequence at the end of *Takasago*.

Another literary device Zeami uses to great advantage and with great variety is allusion (I include direct reference under this rubric). Broadly speaking, he uses three basic types of allusive technique. The first is the simple borrowing of a poetic tag from the tradition for the ornamentation of a passage or for the reinforcement of the general tone of a passage. An example of the former is an allusion to Lao-zi's dictum, "A journey of a thousand leagues begins with the ground you are standing on," in the first sageuta in *Tōru*: *chisato mo onaji hitoashi ni*, "It is all the same for a journey of a thousand leagues, step by step it proceeds." Such allusions are frequently so inconsequential that one wonders whether they were intended at all—and an unintended allusion is not an allusion. On the other hand, sometimes these surface allusions play a part in elevating the tone of a passage or indeed a whole play. Throughout the waki plays in the Aged Mode one finds allusions to Wang Chong's *Lun heng* (this work, *Kokinshū*, and *Wakan rōeishu* are the three most common sources of allusion in this mode). Never are these *Lun heng* allusions actually central to the plays in question, but they enhance the mood of shūgen by evoking that ideal Confucian realm where the passes are all open and where even the weather is good out of gratitude to the sage Emperor.

Similarly, near the beginning of *Aridōshi* Zeami uses this technique not because it is crucial to our understanding of the play, but because it adds to the sense of Tsurayuki's dilemma:

Unspecified shōdan
1   W   Tomoshibi kurō shite wa sukō Gushi ga nanda no ame no,
        Ashi o mo yukazu Sui yukazu,
        Gu ikaga su beki tayori mo nashi,
        Ara shōshi ya zōro.[95]

Unspecified shōdan
1   W   The torchlight wanes and in the many pacing streams of Yu shi's
          raining tears
        No longer can I trudge ahead, no further budges dappled Zhui.
        Yu, I have no notion what to do,
        Oh, what a terrible predicament!

The first line alludes to *Wakan rōeishu* 694: "The torchlight wanes; many streams of Yu shi's tears./The night deepens; on all sides the voices of Chu song." And the second is an allusion to Xiang Yu's song in *Shi ji*: "My strength uprooted hills, yes, my spirit blanketed the generation./Now the times are unpropitious, yes, dappled Zhui won't budge./Dappled Zhui won't budge, no, what am I to do?/Oh Yu, my Yu, what now becomes of you?"[96]

The second kind of allusive technique Zeami uses is to hark back to some important work, by allusion, quotation, or reference, to lend authority to a given pronouncement. The many references to the *Kokinshū* preface in *Takasago* are examples of this practice, as is the reference to Chōnō.[97] This technique is generally used in dialogues like the mondō and kakeai and in extended narrative passages like the kuse, and it is more than mere ornament. The quotations from sutras and other religious texts that one finds so often in noh serve a similar purpose.

Finally, and most important, is Zeami's use of allusion as the centerpiece of a play. As has often been the case in this investigation, the best example is found in *Takasago*. It is the Masafusa poem the shite quotes in his ageha in the kuse (lines 138-40). As the reader will recall, the poem reads as follows: "Takasago no/Onoe no kane mo oto su nari,/Akatsuki kakete,/Shimo wa okedomo"—(At Takasago/From the peak of Onoe I hear the tolling bell,/Through the night till dawn;/Even though white frost [covers each branch]). Aside from the last line, which reads *shimo ya okuran* in the original, this is a direct quotation. But the full quotation, as we have seen, was presaged in the first words of the shite and the tsure on their appearance from behind the entrance curtain. The multiple appearance of an allusion, in varying forms, is a clue that the allusion is very closely related to the play's central theme, and is one of the principal features of Zeami's mature style. In the case of *Takasago*, this poem is actually only one of four waka that are central to the theme of the play.

The others are "Tare o ka mo," "Ware mite mo," and "Mutsumashi to" (lines 23-24, 181-82, and 183-84, respectively). Those poems work together to make Takasago and Sumiyoshi, and their pines, real for the spectator, and along with what I have called the play's emblem word, "Takasago," they unify and direct the lyric energy of the play.

Similar allusive use of waka can be seen in other plays in the Aged Mode. In *Yumi Yawata*, for instance, although the use of the allusion is not so meaningful and well articulated as in *Takasago*, the poem by Urabe no Kanenao that was introduced by the shite in dan 2 reappears at the beginning of the chorus's last continuous passage at the end of the play.

Examples such as these serve to illustrate Zeami's conviction that important poems should be put only in conspicuous places, and then only in the mouth of the main character (but the latter stipulation does not seem to preclude those places where the chorus speaks for the shite). The issei in *Takasago* is of course conspicuous because it is the shite's first song.[98] The ageha, likewise, attracts attention because it is the shite's only solo part in the kuse. In *Yumi Yawata* the poem is given weight initially by its position in the shite's first extended hiranori passage and is later noticed because it stands at the head of the last continuous piece of singing in the play.

The bulk of Zeami's artistic heritage, according to Zeami himself, came from his father Kannami. If this is true, then we should be able to find some similarity between the plays of father and son, especially when comparing plays of the same general category. Unfortunately, there are very few plays that can be definitely attributed to Kannami, and even these are likely to have been revised by Zeami.[99] The only play that may have been written by Kannami, and that also fits into the category of the Aged Mode is *Kinsatsu*.[100]

Kinsatsu takes its name from a golden tablet that falls from the sky during the first act of the play, a miracle on which the rudimentary plot turns. As the story goes, a retainer of Emperor Kammu is commissioned to visit the village of Fushimi, where a shrine is under construction. When he arrives, he finds an old man among the worshippers and questions him. The old man has come to express his thanks for long life and peace and order in the imperial realm. He sings a seemingly unrelated song about "cutting things" and trees (more about this shortly), whereupon a miracle occurs. A golden tablet falls to earth with a divine message inscribed on it. The waki and the shite debate about the meaning of the tablet, and the shite, having won the debate, disappears with the tablet. Just as he leaves, he reveals himself as the god Amatsu Futodama and encourages the waki to have a building added to the shrine to house the golden tablet. The aikyōgen appears and relates what has happened, adding that a decision has been made to do as the god directed. Then the nochijite, Amatsu Futodama undisguised, appears with exhortations to recognize and respect the special relationship between Emperor and god. He explains that he has manifested himself to protect the Emperor and chase away demons. He does a short dance, a MAIBATARAKI, and the play comes to an end with felicitous remarks about the Emperor's reign.

The theme of the play is appropriately auspicious, and one finds the general tone of felicitation and thanksgiving to the sage Emperor that is standard in waki plays. But *Kinsatsu* differs from *Takasago*, *Oimatsu*, *Yōrō*, and *Yumi Yawata* in that the first half of the play centers not around a narrative, but around an event, a "happening." This is not to say, however, that the play is altogether lacking in literary interest. In fact, the following shōdan sequence is quite ingenious, if seemingly unrelated to the "plot":

Ageuta
1   C   Haru wa kazan no ki o kireba,
            Haru wa kazan no ki o kireba,
            Tamoto ni kakaru shirayuki,
            Fukaki ikeda o kiru naru wa,
5   Ransei no tsurubenawa,
            Mata Taisan no yamashita mizu,
            Sono ganseki o kiri ishi,

Rongi
      C   Kuruma o tsukuru shii no ki,
            Kuruma o tsukuru shii no ki,
10 S   Fune o sakusuru yōriu,
      C   Ko no ma ni nasan tsuki no ki,
      S   Sore wa aki tatsu kiri no ki,
      C   Kimi ni yowai o yuzuriha ya,
      S   Chitose no matsu wa kirumaji,
15 C   Na wa haru no ki no eda nagara,
            Hana wa nado sakakiba,
            Kore wa kami no yadoriki,
            Osore ari kirumaji.[101]

Ageuta
1   C   In spring I cut the trees on a flowered hill,
            In spring I cut the trees on a flowered hill,
            And on my sleeve the white snow falls so thick.
            The thick beams of the well frame are cut away by
5   The bucket's frayed rope drawn across the railing,
            And drops of water from Mount Tai
            Make cut stone out of boulders down below.

Rongi
      C   Pasania is the wheelwright's tree.
            Pasania is the wheelwright's tree.

10	s	And willow is for shipwrights.
	c	The moonbark tree shines bright among the woods.
	s	And there's paulownia that rises in the autumn mist.
	c	Here is the tree that grants years to His Majesty,
	s	You mustn't cut the thousand-year-old pine.
15	c	Those over there are spring tree branches, but why don't
		Flowers ever spring from them?
		Sakaki tree—that is the tree the gods live on.
		I'd be too afraid to cut it down.

These two songs have hardly any connection to the central theme of the play (I am not persuaded by Omote's suggestion that they hint at the future construction of the shrine).[102] They are instead to be enjoyed purely for verbal interest and are, in fact, *monozukushi*, "catalogues," that is, lists of things strung together in ingenious ways using puns and other literary and popular conceits. (They are consequently of little interest in translation.)

One looks in vain for a true monozukushi in the six Zeami plays in the Aged Mode we have discussed, but there are passages that in some ways resemble monozukushi. The kuse of *Aridōshi* is suggestive of one in its listing of poetic forms from the Chinese preface to *Kokinshū*. Again, the mondō-uta-rongi sequence of *Tōru* (quoted on pp. 250-51) has something in common with a monozukushi.[103] But in neither of these passages does Zeami indulge in wordplay for its own sake. Instead, he subordinates that technique to thematic consistency. In *Aridōshi* it is perfectly appropriate thematically that the eminent poet Tsurayuki discourse on chōka, tanka, and sedōka, and in *Tōru* it is not only appropriate, but essential that the shite turn away from the phantasm of his nostalgia for Shiogama to the real world before him, the landscape around Kyoto. Indeed, one has only to look at Figure 10, which matches the modern place names to the features Zeami "catalogues" in *Tōru*, to recognize how thoroughly he repressed the tendency toward extraneous wordplay; the landscape he describes is precisely the landscape one sees today to the east, south, and west of the city. Judging from *Kinsatsu*, Kannami did not feel so sharp a need to subordinate verbal play to thematic integration.

Another rhetorical device frequently encountered in *Kinsatsu* but rare in Zeami's plays in the Aged Mode is the makurakotoba. In *Kinsatsu* one finds *aoni yoshi (Nara)*, "(Nara) rich in green earth," and *sabae nasu (arafuru kami)*, "the gods, rambunctious like flies at summer's head," among others. I find no makurakotoba in *Aridōshi*, by contrast, and even in *Takasago*, where I do find one (*tamamo karu*, "cut jade-like seagrass," in the issei of the final dan), it is tied into the rest of the song with *naru*, which alters its function as a makurakotoba to make it a modifier consciously evocative of a poetic style heavily reliant on that device. It turns

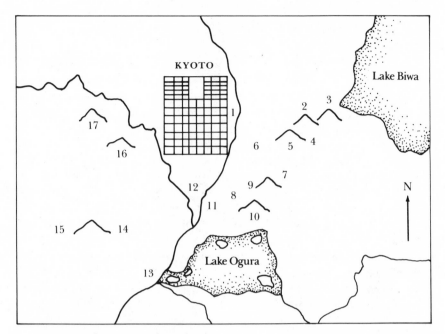

1. Kawara no In
2. Mount Otowa (Sound-on-Wings)
3. Mount Ōsaka (Meeting Pass)
4. Uta no Nakayama (Middlemount of Poetry)
5. Seiganji
6. Imagumano
7. Mount Inari
8. Fuji no Mori (Wisteria Grove)
9. Fukakusa (Deep Grass Mountain)

10. Kowata
11. Fushimi
12. Yodo
13. Toba
14. Ōhara
15. Oshio
16. Matsuno O (Pine's Tail)
17. Arashiyama (Gale Mountain)

Fig. 10   Places mentioned in the fourth dan of the play *Tōru*. The sequence of numbers follows Zeami's description.

out to mean something like, "where, *so they say*, the fishers cut jade-like seagrass" (my emphasis).[104]

If Zeami did not choose to use wordplay as much as his father in these plays, Kannami did not use allusion as much as his son. There are few identifiable allusions in *Kinsatsu*, and certainly none so central to the theme of the play as "Takasago no" is to *Takasago*. One allusion that has been identified is found in the monozukushi quoted above. It comes from Mei Cheng's "Jian Wu Wang Shang Shu" (Admonitions to the King of Wu):[105]

> A trickle from Mount Tai bores through rock,
> A well bucket's frayed rope cuts through a tree trunk.

> Water is not an awl for rock;
> Rope is not a saw for wood;
> Constant application makes them so.

This is certainly the Chinese source of Kannami's *fukaki ikeda o kiru naru wa* (in line 4 of the ageuta' quoted above), but notice how it has been nativized. The line is not, like many of Zeami's allusions, merely a Japanese reading (*kakikudashi*) of the Chinese text, but a complete recasting of the original. It is not difficult to imagine that Kannami never knew the source of his allusion and merely picked it up out of the vernacular. Whether this was in fact the case or not, this example supports the theory that Kannami's learning came through his ears from the language of his contemporaries, and not through his eyes from the manuscripts in a Kyoto aristocrat's library.

From this admittedly very limited comparison it seems that there are more differences than similarities between the Aged Mode styles of father and son. Kannami is interested in play with language and the excitement of a happening enacted onstage, and he is willing to sacrifice structural cohesiveness and thematic integration to these considerations. Zeami is generally true to his creative hierarchy of seed-structure-writing (shu-saku-sho), and strives to create a play in which literary and rhetorical techniques, as well as structural molding, are subordinated to theme and content.

What, then, of plays in the Aged Mode outside the Kanze tradition? For comparative purposes, the most obvious examples in the modern repertory are *Ema* (The Votive Tablet), *Sakahoko* (The Inverted Spear), *Himuro* (The Ice House), *Mekari* (Harvesting Seagrass), and *Chikubushima* (The Isle Where Bamboo Grows). The authorship of these plays is difficult to establish confidently, but they all seem to date in their original form from a period roughly contemporaneous with Zeami.[106] In any case, they can easily be considered a group, for they share several characteristics: all are mugen noh in two acts; in all the maejite is an old man and is accompanied by a tsure; in all a nochitsure appears in the second act to perform his own dance before the nochijite's dance; in all the second act features a long passage in ōnori rhythm during which the nochijite does a highly mimetic dance; and in all except *Ema*, the nochijite dances the quick and rather mimetic HATARAKI or MAIBATARAKI preceded by the nochitsure's TENNYONOMAI, an abbreviated form of the CHŪNOMAI.[107] Zeami's more orthodox plays in the Aged Mode share the first two characteristics, but not the rest.

The appearance of a nochitsure in each of the five plays suggests some connection with the Kamakura and Muromachi performing art Ennen no furyū. So do the long ōnori passages of the second act, where the audience is treated, through the shite's dance, to such spectacles as the creation of the islands of Japan by Izanagi and Izanami (*Sakahoko*), the parting of the seas in a Shinto and syncretic Buddhist miracle (*Mekari*), and Amaterasu's emergence from the cave where she had secluded herself on the High Plain of Heaven (*Ema*). Indeed, much of the pleasure these plays offer resides in the action, the color, and the mime of the second act alone. This, it seems, is the attraction of monomane, that central core of the old Yamato tradition.

The fact that one finds a MAIBATARAKI in most of these works is also instructive. The MAIBATARAKI is a dance of an entirely different character and tradition from the KAMIMAI, SHINNOJONOMAI, and BANSHIKI HAYAMAI of Zeami's plays in the Aged Mode. It is also commonly performed in demon plays,[108] and its use in these plays in the Aged Mode betrays the demonic cast of their shite. This was apparently quite common in early Yamato sarugaku, as Zeami himself acknowledges: "There is something menacing about the role of a god and, depending on the god being portrayed, this role may be cast in the demonic mode."[109]

Zeami is familiar with this kind of god, and implicitly recognizes the demonic play as legitimate waki noh. The shite in *Aridōshi* owes something to this demonic sort of god, and *Yōrō* and *Oimatsu* also show similarities with the plays from outside the Kanze tradition.[110] But for all this, there is something very different about Zeami's plays when they are viewed alongside these works, something that becomes apparent with a return to and reexamination of Zeami's notion and use of the Aged Mode as exemplified in *Takasago*.

What is most notably different about the non-Kanze plays mentioned above is that they have no counterpart to the shite's first sashi in *Takasago*. As the reader will recall, that is the song where we first noticed Zeami setting out to paint a vivid picture of the shite's internal world. The creation of this internal world distinguishes (especially) *Takasago* and *Tōru* from the non-Kanze plays. It is to this end that Zeami uses his renga-like associations, emblem words, and imagistic unity. It is for this purpose that he is so careful to observe the creative hierarchy of shu-saku-sho. It is with this in mind that he subordinates the representational external mimesis of monomane to the more expressive abstract and therefore more emotionally malleable arts of dance and song for the aesthetic ideal of yūgen.

This is not to deny the value of *Sakahoko*, *Chikubushima*, and the other non-Kanze plays,[111] but merely to point out Zeami's tendency to forsake the interest in the supernatural beings on which those plays are based for a more humanistic reality and stronger psychological orientation.

It is in the Woman's and Martial modes that this humanistic reality and psychological profundity come into full flower. After all, the shite of most of the plays in the Aged Mode are still gods in human disguise, not men. Yet we find the first hints of these two qualities in Zeami's development of the Aged Mode; and the lasting appeal of *Takasago* foremost among the plays of that mode is a direct result of those very qualities. The achievement of such humanism and profundity in a public context—a context that has all too often become entirely convention-bound in the Japanese tradition—is a fitting indication of Zeami's genius.

CHAPTER 4

Nyotai:
The Woman's Mode

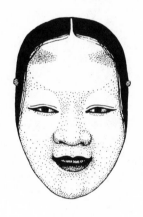

MANY of the truly great plays of the noh theater fall into Zeami's category nyotai, the Woman's Mode. *Matsukaze*, *Izutsu*, and *Teika*—plays about love so persistent that it manipulates even the lovers' ghosts—would certainly be classed under this rubric. But so would *Dōjōji* and *Aoi no Ue*—plays cast instead around the persistent malevolence of hate and jealousy. The most technically revered plays in the repertory, *Higaki*, *Obasute*, and *Sekidera Komachi*, are in the Woman's Mode, as are *Sumidagawa*, *Hyakuman*, and *Hanjo*, plays about disoriented sensibility somewhat inappropriately termed "mad-woman plays." The category claims plays about heavenly maidens and plays about women suffering the worst torments of hell; plays about goddesses and plays about mendicant entertainers; plays about bodhisattvas and plays about seductresses. In fact, there is probably more breadth among the plays of this category, in both theme and treatment, than any other.

In *Sandō* Zeami mentions nine plays as models of the Woman's Mode: *Hakozaki*, *Unoha*, *Mekurauchi*, *Shizuka*, *Matsukaze Murasame*, *Hyakuman*, *Ukifune*, *Higaki no onna*, and *Komachi*.[1] The first two are no longer performed. *Mekurauchi* is lost. *Shizuka* is probably the old play *Yoshino Shizuka*, and *Matsukaze Murasame* is *Matsukaze*. The titles of *Hyakuman* and *Ukifune* have not changed over the centuries, and *Higaki no onna* is now known simply as *Higaki*. *Komachi* is apparently *Sotoba Komachi* (Komachi on the Gravepost).[2] Not all these plays are Zeami's, but the group does illustrate to some extent the breadth of the mode; among them one finds a relatively primitive genzai noh (*Yoshino Shizuka*), one of the greatest mugen noh masterpieces (*Matsukaze*), a mad-woman play (*Hyakuman*), an old-woman play (*Higaki*), and so on. The greater breadth of this category of noh goes hand in hand with a generic fuzziness of a kind not found in Zeami's six exemplary plays in the Aged Mode, all of which are mugen noh.

Writing in *Sandō* on the "shape" of plays in the Woman's Mode, Zeami says:

One must write making allowances for visual display. This is the most basic kind of play, that in which song and dance play a central role. Yet among the plays of this category, one finds displays of the very highest order. For instance, when writing of women of noble rank, such as His Majesty's ladies, and Lady Aoi, Yū-gao, and Ukifune, the writer must remember that the noble bearing of such characters exhibits a grace and elegance quite unequaled among ordinary people. For this reason, the writer must carefully consider the music and appearance appropriate to the characters, and be careful not to fashion them after professional entertainers. A character of such rank should be of the most refined bearing, entrancing, and of the highest level of mysterious beauty; the quality of her voice, her movements, and the very atmosphere of her presence should be unsurpassed. The slightest deficiency will spoil the effect.

In such a character, one finds, as it were, a jewel among jewels. Over and above the sheer visual beauty of such noble persons, one has rare and valuable material here: Lady Aoi bewitched by Rokujō, Yūgao captivated by a malevolent spirit, the possession of Ukifune—in these and like situations there is a seed for the blossoming of sublime mysterious beauty. It is a seed more rare than the one that, as the old poem says, "combines the scent of plum and the blossom of cherry and sets them to bloom on a willow branch." This being the case, one has to admit that a performer who can effectively manage such a style is a complete master of his audience's feelings.

In addition to the above, there are such characters as Shizuka, Giō, and Gijo. Since they are *shirabyōshi* dancers, they should chant a waka, intone an *issei*, and sing in a high register, staying strictly in time. Then, stamping their feet, they should make their exit dancing. It is appropriate for such characters to leave the stage with the feeling of a quiet *kiribyōshi* [ōnori].

Then again, there are characters such as Hyakuman and Yamanba who are fairly easy to create because they can be cast as Kusemai dancers. Of the five *dan* of the play, the *jo* and *kyū* can then be shortened. The *ha* becomes the mainstay and the *kusemai* is put in an eye-catching place. The second half of a double *kuse* is speeded up and concentrated, and the part is written carefully, just like a professional Kusemai. The dancing stops with a *shidai*.

There are also plays in the mad-woman style. Since these are, after all, about people in a state of aesthetic derangement, it is best to take pains with the visual potential and write the music with attention to details appropriate to the movements to be performed. As long as the character is mysteriously beautiful, whatever is done should be interesting. The character's appearance should be beautiful, the melody skillfully inflected, the actor's technical skill pushed to its limit, and the play colorful. Write with these considerations in mind.

The writer who makes distinctions according to the character portrayed—whether she is a paragon of elegance and beauty, a noble lady, a *shirabyōshi* dancer, a *kusemai* dancer, or a mad woman—and furthermore, assigns the appropriate artistic qualities to the role, is a writer who truly understands the way to construct a play.[3]

Several important points are made in this passage. First and foremost, plays in the Woman's Mode are plays "in which song and dance play a central role." Second, three types of women are appropriate for treatment in this mode: the highly refined aristocrat from the imperial court (who shows the greatest dramatic potential when she is possessed); the professional entertainer; and the *monogurui* or *kyōjo*, the woman who, because of some great emotional trauma, is not completely in touch with reality, but is instead highly distracted and susceptible to irrational

Fig. 11   Illustrations for plays in the Woman's Mode from a 1441 manuscript of Zeami's *Nikyoku santai ningyōzu*. "The Woman's Mode. Make [your] sensibility the basis [of your acting] and reject [any show of] strength." *Courtesy of the Noh Theater Research Institute, Hōsei University.*

flights of aesthetic engagement. Third, the visual aspect of performance takes on a significance that was not remarked on earlier, and the writer is advised to keep the visual potential of the character in mind as he writes his play. This third point is related to the fourth and final point: the emphasis on the mysteriously beautiful, yūgen. Yūgen is, as we have seen, one of Zeami's favorite aesthetic terms, and he attaches great importance to its embodiment in the plays of the Woman's Mode. Note that in this case he is concerned primarily with the substance of the plays and does not go into the matter of structure, as he did in his remarks on the Aged Mode, except for a few observations about plays concerning professional entertainers.

Zeami's brief remarks about the Woman's Mode in *Nikyoku santai ningyōzu* further confirm the link between dance and song and this mode, and identify it as the origin of yūgen in a performance. As in the section on the Aged Mode, he illustrates his remarks with two sketches (Fig. 11). The first, a naked (but modest) representation of posture for the Woman's Mode, is accompanied by a brief note: "Make certain that you completely understand how to handle such a role: make your sensibility the basis of your acting and reject any show of strength. The most important thing in dramatic representation is this. You can, in fact, say that this is the basic form of *yūgen*. Whatever you do, do not forget about your posture." The second sketch pictures a character bent gently forward with fan in hand, dancing under a shower of plum blossoms.[4] This sketch too is annotated: "The dance in the Woman's Mode is of particularly elevated style and allows a vision of the sublime form of *yūgen*. The Woman's Mode is supreme among the Two Arts . . . and the Three Modes. Do not forget to make sensibility the basis of your acting and reject strength, and carry this disposition over into your dance and singing; it is the highest manifestation of these in our art. Such elegant style as this allows the fusion of dance and song for a unified apprehension of profound beauty."[5]

The importance of the Woman's Mode as the preeminent mode for the creation of yūgen is obvious here, but again one finds few specifics with which to begin an analysis.[6] It seems best, therefore, merely to select a play in the mode to analyze and refer back to these remarks as they become relevant.

The play *Izutsu* must be a much later work than the plays discussed in the previous chapter. Zeami took great pride in it, but the first we hear of it is in *Sarugaku dangi* (1430).* In any event, his remarks in that work show his confidence in the play: "Aside from the congratulatory plays, *Izutsu* and *Michimori* and the like are straightforward noh. . . . *Izutsu* is of the highest flower."[7]

"The highest flower" is the top level of the aesthetic scale Zeami set forth in *Kyūi*; few modern critics would take issue with this high estimation of the play. The other comment about *Izutsu*, that it is a "straightforward noh," is of more immediate use now. ("Straightforward" is my translation of *sugu naru*. It is the same term Zeami applied to *Yumi Yawata* and probably implies formal orthodoxy here as it did there.[8]) This formal regularity and the play's superb quality are reason enough to choose it as the central work for analysis in this chapter, but there is another reason as well. This is the simple fact that there are not a great many other typical plays in the Woman's Mode that can confidently be attributed to Zeami. Among the other great plays in the mode that come immediately to mind, none really qualifies. *Matsukaze*, it is true, is partially the work of Zeami, but it is also the work of at least two other writers, Kiami and Kannami. *Eguchi* is of disputed authorship, as is *Nonomiya*. *Kakitsubata* and *Yūgao* are traditionally attributed to Zeami, and might very well be his plays, but there is no solid evidence to support his authorship. *Yuya* and even *Hagoromo* are also sometimes said to be Zeami's, but again there is no real evidence to support such a claim, and in fact a good deal of reason to think otherwise. On the other hand, many of the plays in the

* Had it been written by 1423, Zeami almost certainly would have included it in his list of distinguished plays in *Sandō*. He quotes the play in *Go on* (1430), and it is listed among the plays in the undated *Nōhon sanjūgoban mokuroku*.

Woman's Mode that *can* be confidently attributed to Zeami are hardly typical: *Kinuta* is part genzai noh and part mugen noh; in *Higaki* we find a combination of the Woman's Mode and the Aged Mode; in *Taema* the maejite and nochijite are different beings; and *Hanjo* is a mad-woman play.

The modern performance of *Izutsu* begins with a NANORIBUE, the waki's entrance music, after which the waki introduces himself in the following *nanori, sashi,* and *uta*:[9]

Nanori

1	W	Kore wa shokoku ikken no sō nite sōro,
		Ware kono hodo wa Nanto ni mairite sōro,
		Mata kore yori Hatsuse ni mairabaya to zonjisōro,
		Kore naru tera o hito ni tazunete sōraeba,
5		Ariwaradera to ka ya mōshisōrō hodo ni,
		Tachiyori ikken sebaya to omoisōro.

Sashi

		Sate wa kono Ariwaradera wa,
		Inishie Narihira Ki no Aritsune no sokujo,
		Fūfu sumitamaishi Isonokami naru beshi,
10		Kaze fukeba okitsu shiranami Tatsutayama to eijiken mo,
		Kono tokoro nite no koto naru beshi.

Uta

		Mukashigatari no ato toeba,
		Sono Narihira no tomo to seshi,
		Ki no Aritsune no tsune naki yo,
15		Imose o kakete tomurawan,
		Imose o kakete tomurawan.

Nanori

1	W	I am a traveling priest, wandering through the provinces to see what I can see.
		I have made my way to the Southern Capital,
		And from here I intend to go along toward Hatsuse.
		I have made inquiries about this temple,
5		And have been told that it is the Ariwara Temple,
		So I am going to go a little closer and look around.

Sashi

		This Ariwara Temple is in Isonokami,
		The very place where Narihira and the daughter of Aritsune Lived as man and wife.
10		That poem—"The wailing wind, strong enough to raise white waves out upon the sea . . . ,"—
		That must have been composed here.

Uta

		Ki no Aritsune, named "the Constant" in his day, has passed away;
		As have his daughter and his friend, her lover, Narihira.
		But since I've come here where one still hears their tale of long ago,
15		I'll say a prayer for man and wife, to set their souls to rest.
		I'll say a prayer for man and wife, to set their souls to rest.

These three shōdan make up the whole of the first dan. From the very beginning, we find a play quite substantially different from *Takasago*. Instead of the dignified, almost majestic SHINNOSHIDAI, the waki in *Izutsu* makes his entrance to a solo flute playing the highly reflective and enigmatic NANORIBUE. The waki then begins his performance not with song, but with the spoken nanori. He reveals much less about his identity than Tomonari did in *Takasago*, mentioning merely that he is a priest on his way to the Shingon temple Hasedera in Hatsuse (a common site for religious pilgrimages) who has stopped at the Ariwara Temple. In the sashi he recalls a poem associated with the temple, then, reflecting that the subjects of the poem, as well as its author, are long since gone, he decides to pray for them.

Izutsu's first dan, though shorter and generally less obtrusive than *Takasago*'s, is more striking in one particular place. That is in the sashi, where the waki quotes part of the poem he recalls (line 10). The poem is to appear in its entirety later and will be more fully discussed in due course. For now we need only note its appearance here: it is one of the few poems that form the honzetsu of the play, and it forges a close connection between the jo and the ha, where the poems play a central role.

The ha begins with the entrance of a beautiful woman, the shite, to the instrumental piece SHIDAI, which is followed by the tadautai shōdan of the same name:

Shidai

17	S	Akatsuki goto no aka no mizu,
		Akatsuki goto no aka no mizu,
		Tsuki mo kokoro ya sumasuran.

Shidai

17	S	On the water offered here each morning with the dawn,
		On the water offered here each morning with the dawn,
		Clearly shines the moon; so may it clarify my heart.

The shidai is formally regular and presents no musical difficulties.[10] It introduces the important image of the moon's reflection on water; this is a common metaphor for the return of a bodhisattva to the world of unenlightened existence to save sentient creatures.[11] *Akatsuki*, "the moon at dawn," provides a head rhyme with *aka no mizu*, "water for offering." A sashi follows:

Sashi

20	S	Sanaki dani mono no samishiki aki no yo no,
		Hitome mare naru furutera no,
		Niwa no matsukaze fukesugite,
		Tsuki mo katamuku nokiba no kusa,
		Wasurete sugishi inishie o,
25		Shinobugao nite itsu made ka,
		Matsu koto nakute nagaraen,

> Ge ni nanigoto mo omoide no,
> Hito ni wa nokoru yo no naka kana.

Sashi

20 s   The autumn night is lonely as it is, but more so here,
         For no one comes to this old temple garden where the wind blows,
             deepening night.
         In whispers through the pines, the moon inclines to slanting eaves
         Covered with forgetful grass: The now forgotten past
         I once again recall in ferns of recollection;

25   But how long will I live on in ivied remembrance, with nothing to
             await?
         All things lead to memories, and
         Memories alone remain to me
         In this world remaining on though he is gone.

As he did in *Takasago*, Zeami uses this sashi to illuminate the inner world of the shite. It is an interior monologue leading from the immediate scene to the shite's emotions, presenting the first lyrical exposition of her character. Again, renga-like association is used as one of the structuring devices of the text: *tera* (in *furutera*), "temple," leads to both *niwa*, "garden," and *nokiba*, "eaves." (*Aki no*) *yo*, "(the autumn) night," suggests *tsuki*, "moon," as well as *fukesugite*, "deepening." *Fukesugite* sounds very much like *fukisugite*, "blows through," which relates back to *matsukaze*, "the wind in the pines."[12] The pines, of course, are tied to *niwa*, "garden."

The most important set of associations in the song starts with *nokiba*, "eaves," commonly described as covered with moss or vegetation of some sort. Here, *nokiba* sets off the string of engo associated with *kusa*, "grass": *wasure(gusa)*, "forgetful grass," *shinobu(gusa)*, "ferns of recollection," and *itsumade(gusa)*, "ivied,"* all of which provide a pivot whereby the text moves from the external world of the temple garden to the internal world of the shite's emotions, so relentlessly dominated by memories of the far-off past. The topic of remembering and forgetting, introduced by the grasses, leads to the memories (*omoide*) that "remain" (*nokoru*). *Nokoru* harkens back to *matsu*, "await" (as well as "pine") and *nagaraen*, "live on."

The sashi is followed by a sageuta and an ageuta:

Sageuta

29 s   Tada itsu to naku hitosuji ni,
30   Tanomu Hotoke no mite no ito,
         Michibikitamae Nori no koe.

Ageuta

         Mayoi o mo,
         Terasasetamō onchikai,
         Terasasetamō onchikai,

---

* Wasuregusa, not to be confused with wasurenagusa (the forget-me-not), is actually a kind of licorice plant. Shinobugusa is a fern, and itsumadegusa is a variety of ivy.

35   Ge ni mo to miete ariyake no,
     Yukue wa nishi no yama naredo,
     Nagame wa yomo no aki no sora.
     Matsu no koe nomi kikoyuredomo,
     Arashi wa izuku to mo,
40   Sadame naki yo no yumegokoro,
     Nani no oto ni ka sametemashi,
     Nani no oto ni ka sametemashi.

Sageuta
29 s But every moment I must pray
30   That threads from Buddha's hands may guide me
     Out of this delusion. Hear the Dharma's voice!

Ageuta
     Buddha's promise casting light
     Through the night in which we've gone astray,
     Through the night in which we've gone astray,
35   Shines indeed upon the moon it seems.
     It inclines to mountains in the west
     Setting as dawn breaks,
     But my gaze wanders undirected 'round the autumn sky.
     I hear only voices in the pines,
40   Rustled by a wind I cannot find, for I find nothing certain
     In this world. My heart lives a fleeting dream,
     So to what sound shall I one day awake?
     So to what sound shall I one day awake?

With the sageuta, the shite makes a conscious move away from her recollections to a prayer for release from delusion, placing her faith in the Buddha's vow to enlighten all sentient existence. The vow is again symbolized by the moon, here, *ariake no (tsuki)*, "the moon at dawn" (*"ariyake"* on stage). The movement of the moon west provides hope that the shite herself may "go west" (i.e., to the paradise of Amida Buddha). Ironically, however, her concentration on the prayer is destroyed by the very scene she sees as she gazes westward. As her eyes wander across the autumn sky her thoughts return to memories of her long-dead lover. The sights of autumn lead to the sound of the wind; the shite again tries to set her mind on salvation and the sound to which she will one day awaken. This quite regular sageuta-ageuta sequence brings the second dan to a close.

This dan is structured much like *Takasago*'s second dan and serves the same function: the presentation of the shite's inner world and the exposition of the play's theme. In this case the theme is the confusion of a soul caught between a desire for release from the bonds of a past love and an inability to forget that love. Back and forth the text moves, from the wish expressed in the shidai through the tormented memories of the sashi to the prayer and wanderings of the heart and the final question of the sageuta-ageuta sequence.

The third dan opens with the waki posing his first question to the shite in a mondō. The chorus's ageuta follows their exchange:

Mondō

44	w	Ware kono tera ni yasurai kokoro o sumasu orifushi,
		Ito namamekeru nyoshō niwa no itai o musubiage hanamizu to shi,
		Kore naru tsuka ni ekō no keshiki mietamō wa,
		Ika naru hito nite mashimasu zo,
	s	Kore wa kono atari ni sumu mono naru ga,
		Kono tera no hongan Nariwara [sic] no Narihira wa yo ni na o tome-shi hito nari,
50		Sareba sono ato no shirushi mo kore naru tsuka no kage yaran,
		Ware mo kuwashiku wa shirazu sōraedomo,
		Hanamizu o tamuke kayō ni tomuraimōshisōro,
	w	Ge ni ge ni Narihira no onkoto wa yo ni na o tomeshi hito nari sarinagara,
		Ima wa haruka ni tōki yo no,
55		Mukashigatari no ato naru o,
		Shikamo nyoshō no onmi to shite,
		Kayō ni tomuraitamō koto,
		Sono Ariwara no Narihira ni,
		Ikasama yue aru onmi yaran,
60	s	Yue aru mi ka to towasetamō,
		Sono Narihira wa sono toki dani mo,
		Mukashi Otoko to iwareshi mi no,
		Mashite ya ima wa tōki yo ni,
		Yue mo yukari mo aru bekarazu,
65	w	Mottomo ōse wa saru koto naredomo,
		Koko wa mukashi no kiuseki nite,
	s	Nushi koso tōku Narihira no,
	w	Ato wa nokorite sasuga ni imada,
	s	Kikoe wa kuchinu yogatari o,
70	w	Katareba ima mo
	s	Mukashi Otoko no.

Ageuta

	c	Na bakari wa,
		Ariwaradera no ato furite,
		Ariwaradera no ato furite,
		Matsu mo oitaru tsuka no kusa,
75		Kore koso sore yo naki ato no,
		Hitomura susuki no ho ni izuru wa,
		Itsu no nagori naruran.
		Kusa bōbō to shite,
		Tsuyu shinshin to furutsuka no,
80		Makoto naru kana inishie no,
		Ato natsukashiki keshiki kana,
		Ato natsukashiki keshiki kana.

Mondō

44	w	In this temple as I rest and clear my mind,
		A lovely woman appears and, drawing water from the wooden well,
		Readies it for offering with flowers she has brought.

139

Who are you to perform memorials before that mound?

    s   I am simply someone who lives nearby,

But the man for whom this temple is named was Ariwara no Nari-
hira, whose fame lives on in the world.

50   A marker for him stands here in the shadows of this mound, I
think,

And although I know little else about him

I come to offer flowers and to pray for his soul's rest.

    w   Narihira was indeed a man whose fame lives on;

But now his time is long since passed,

55   So why should a fair woman like yourself offer prayers

Before these remnants of a legend

From the far-off past?

You must have some reason, I would guess,

Some connection to this man perhaps?

60 s   You ask if I have some connection to this man?

Why, even then, they used to call him "The Man from Long Ago,"

And he is all the more distant now.

How could I have any connection to him?

65 w   What you say, of course, makes sense,

But this is an ancient site and . . .

    s   Although the man himself is far away,

    w   His traces still remain,

    s   Stories keep his fame untarnished.

70 w   Even now we tell of . . .

    s   "The Man from Long Ago."

Ageuta

    c   His name alone lives on,

Ariwara Temple has now fallen into ruin.

Ariwara Temple has now fallen into ruin.

An ancient pine is rooted in the mound,

75   Grasses spread in wild profusion and

A single stalk of plume grass stands tall,

Blades of memories, what do they recall?

Grasses thick and overgrown,

Dewdrops fallen on the ground;

80   Gazing at this ancient grave I'm filled with

Longing for a love so long passed on.

Longing for a love so long passed on.

    The waki's attention is drawn immediately to the woman making prayer offerings before him.* She is reluctant to admit any reason for her devotions other than Narihira's undying fame, but the waki persists against her hesitancy, and by the end of the mondō, the shite and the waki are exchanging parts of the same line, and sharing the same

---

* In the waki plays in the Aged Mode, by contrast, objects, not the shite, capture the waki's interest: the pine in *Takasago*, the plum and pine in *Oimatsu*, the bow in *Yumi Yawata*. The waki gains information about the shite merely because the shite, as he discusses an object, volunteers that he is its spirit. The obvious observation to be made is that the plays in the Woman's Mode are more humanistic than the waki noh in the Aged Mode.

thoughts. The language of the text has meanwhile changed from metrically irregular prose to 7-5 and 7-7 verse. The characters stop speaking and start singing at line 65. At line 71 the chorus breaks in with its first song, a standard two-part ageuta. This movement from prose to poetry, from spoken lines to noncongruent song to congruent song, was found in the corresponding section of *Takasago* and is used to much the same effect in *Izutsu*. The spectators are caught up in the song, and their involvement in the dramatic action is increased.

The dan introduces and frequently refers to the contrast between Narihira's fame and gravesite, which remain in the world, and the man himself, long dead. The contrast operates primarily through the repeated use of such words as *na*, "name," "fame," and *ato*, "remains," *mukashi*, "long ago," and *tōki*, "far away." Ariwara no Narihira's name itself is put to use in the contrast: in line 72 the *ari* of his surname is understood as "to exist" ("his name exists, but he is long dead"), and in line 67 the *nari* of his given name is combined with *tōku* to give *tōku nari*, "has grown far away."

Imagistically, there is little to mention in the mondō, but the ageuta is built on several important images. Ariwara no Narihira's ruined grave is shown surmounted by an ancient pine, a symbol of longevity stretching, ironically, over the poet's last remains. Below spread dew-drenched grasses and a single stalk of *susuki*, "plume grass" or "pampas grass," a graceful symbol of fragility and evanescence. In modern practice a stalk of grass is tied onto the bamboo framework intended to represent the temple well. There is no proof that this was done in Zeami's day, or even that a bamboo "well" was set on stage, but it is difficult to imagine the play without these simple props.

The dan as a whole is very simple and "straightforward." It has none of the intellectual pretensions and Sinified expressions of *Takasago*'s third dan and very little literary flourish.* It is dominated by the few images of the ageuta. The following dan, however, is more complex, as one might expect, since it is the play's narrative center. It begins with the waki's sasoizerifu, an entirely conventional line asking for more information on Narihira, leading to the chorus's kuri:

Sasoizerifu
83   w   Nao nao Narihira no onkoto onmonogatarisōrae.
Kuri
     c   Mukashi Ariwara no Chiujō,
             Toshi hete koko ni Isonokami,

---

  * There are a few kakekotoba; the ones that work on Narihira's name mentioned above, as well as *oitaru*, which can mean both "grow old" and "grow" (as a plant), in line 74; *susuki no ho/ho ni izuru*, "a stalk of plume grass"/"recall" or "reveal," in line 76; and *tsuyu furu/furutsuka*, "the dew falls"/"ancient grave," in line 79.

Furinishi sato mo hana no haru,
Tsuki no aki tote sumitamaishi ni.

Sasoizerifu

83   w   Tell me more of Narihira.

Kuri

c   Long ago, Lieutenant Narihira
Spent many years in this old village, Isonokami,
Watching the flowered spring
And the autumn of clear moonlight.

The kuri identifies the hero of the narrative, Narihira, and provides a spatial setting. Part of an old poem is written into lines 85-86,[13] but this seems to be little more than a superficial embellishment of the text. The flowers of spring and the autumn moon are mentioned as evidence of Narihira's sensibility. A sashi follows:

Sashi

88   s   Sono koro wa Ki no Aritsune ga musume to chigiri,
Imose no kokoro asakarazarishi ni,

90   c   Mata Kawachi no kuni Takayasu no sato ni,
Shiru hito arite futamichi ni,
Shinobite kayoitamaishi ni,

s   Kaze fukeba okitsu shiranami Tatsutayama,

c   Yowa ni ya kimi ga hitori yukuran to,

95   Obotsukanami no yoru no michi,
Yukue o omō kokoro togete,
Yoso no chigiri wa karegare nari,

s   Ge ni nasake shiru utakata no,

c   Aware o nobeshi mo kotowari nari.[14]

Sashi

88   s   In those days he made a lover's pledge with Aritsune's daughter,
And although no shallow love was theirs,

90   c   Still he kept a mistress in Kawachi, in Takayasu village,
And splitting his attentions,
Followed a furtive path to love.

s   "The wailing wind, strong enough to raise white waves out upon the sea

c   Blows down now from Tatsuta. Will you cross the mountains all alone in dark of night?"

95   While waves of restive apprehension broke upon her mind, she sang this poem,
And he for his part recognized her fears
And let his other romance wither in estrangement.

s   So with good reason had she made her feelings known in poetry,

c   Which plumbs the depths of love in words as fragile as the ocean foam.

In lines 93-94 we find a full quotation of the poem that the waki referred to in dan 1, followed by a partial explanation of the circumstances under which it was composed. The poem is one of three from Episode 23 of *Ise monogatari* that provide the honzetsu for *Izutsu*, and it is to appear again in the rongi and the aikyōgen's katari. After the poem is quoted, the rhetorical texture of the song becomes slightly denser, and engo and kakekotoba appear. *Obotsukanami*, "apprehension," harkens back, through its final syllables, to *nami*, "waves," in the poem. This in turn calls up *yoru*, "(waves) break (upon the shore)," which is homophonous with *yoru*, "night," and also refers back to *yowa*, "dark of night." The final two lines contain the phrase *utakata no aware*, which has the double meaning, *uta no aware*, "feelings (made known) in poetry," and *utakata no awa*, "bubbles of foam."

The kuse follows in the standard three parts:

Kuse
100 C   Mukashi kono kuni ni,
            Sumu hito no arikeru ga,
            Yado o narabete kado no mae,
            Izutsu ni yorite unaiko no,
            Tomodachi kataraite,
105   Tagai ni kage o mizukagami,
            Omote o narabe sode o kake.
            Kokoro no mizu mo sokoi naku,
            Utsuru tsukihi mo kasanarite,
            Otonashiku hajigawashiku,
110   Tagai ni ima wa narinikeri,
            Sono nochi kano mame otoko,
            Kotoba no tsuyu no tamazusa no,
            Kokoro no hana mo iro soite.

[Ageha]
s   Tsutsu izutsu,
115   Izutsu ni kakeshi maro ga take,
C   Oinikerashi na,
            Imo mizaru ma ni to,
            Yomite okurikeru hodo ni,
            Sono toki onna mo kurabe koshi,
120   Furiwakegami mo kata suginu,
            Kimi narazu shite,
            Tare ka agu beki to,
            Tagai ni yomishi yue nare ya,
            Tsutsu izutsu no onna to mo,
125   Kikoeshi wa Aritsune ga,
            Musume no furuki na naru beshi.

Kuse
100 C   Long, long ago,
            Here before their houses,
            Two young children used to play,
            Leaning on the well curb,
            Telling stories, looking far below,
105   There to see their faces mirrored, shining in the well.
            They were the best of friends.

		Their hearts to one another were translucent pools,
		Bright with sun by day, and moon by night;
		But days and nights turned months to years,
110		And years brought shyness. Guilelessly enamored now,
		The boy composed a poem.
		He strung his words like beads of dew,
		Love's flowers blushed throughout his heart:

[*Ageha*]

	s	"Well curb, on the well curb,
115		On the well curb once we marked our height,
	c	But I've grown taller since I saw you last,
		Well past those marks we left
		Upon the well."
		And to his poem she answered,
120		"Side by side we stood
		Comparing our locks then,
		But now my hair hangs far below my shoulders.
		If not for you, for whom shall I tie it up one day?"
		Because of these poems they made for each other
125		Aritsune's daughter came to be called
		The woman by the well curb.

The kuse opens onto two children playing in the yard before their houses. The focus of the narrative starts on the well where the children used to look down at their mirrored faces. (There is a kakekotoba in line 105: *kage o mi/mizukagami*, "look to . . . reflection"/"mirror of water.") The depth of the water in the well becomes a metaphor for the depth of their affection in the second part of the kuse (lines 107-13), and the text narrates how the children grew up and learned to be bashful. The concluding lines introduce a poem. These lines (112-13) provide an excellent example of a text generated by word associations. Most important, perhaps, is *kotoba/kokoro*, "words"/"heart," standard vocabulary from poetic criticism dating back to *Kokinshū*. Embedded in *kotoba* is *ha*, "leaves," which connects to *tsuyu no tama*, "beads of dew"; *ha* also associates with *hana*, "flower," and *iro*, "color." The syntax of the sentence is itself a sequence of word-beads strung together by the particle *no* and the kakekotoba *kotoba/ha no tsuyu/tsuyu no tama /tamazusa*, "(leaves) of words"/"dew on leaves"/"drops of dew"/"love letter." The rhetorical heightening of these lines prepares the way for the shite's ageha (lines 114-15) to begin the final part of the kuse.

The third part of the kuse contains two more poems from Episode 23 of *Ise monogatari* (in lines 114-17 and 119-22). The shite delivers the first half of one of these in her ageha. This poem is of particular significance: it gives the play its name and reappears several more times in important places (again in the kuse at line 124; at the end of the rongi, in line 140; in the aikyōgen's interlude; in the sashi of the fifth dan, in line 154; and at the head of the noriji that concludes the play, in line 169). It is comparable in this respect to "Takasago ya" and "Takasago no" in *Takasago*, but is, if anything, more striking because the internal rhyme of its first eight syllables creates an unmistakable word music.

This dan, then, completes the exposition of the honzetsu. Before proceeding further, let us look at the *Ise* tale itself:

Long ago, the children of certain people with affairs in the provinces used to come out to play around the well, but when they got older, both of them, a young man and a young woman, grew bashful. Even so, the young man intended to make the young woman his wife, and the young woman, for her part, was filled with thoughts of the young man; although her father would introduce her to other suitors, she would have nothing to do with them. Eventually, a poem came from the young man next door:

Tsutsu izutsu	Well curb, on the well curb,
Izutsu ni kakeshi	On the well curb once
Maro ga take	We marked our height,
Oinikerashi na	But I've grown taller since I saw you last,
Imo mizaru ma ni[15]	Well past those marks we left upon the well.

The young woman responded,

Kurabe koshi	Side by side we stood,
Furiwakegami mo	Comparing our locks then,
Kata suginu	But now my hair hangs far below my shoulders.
Kimi narazu shite	If not for you, for whom
Tare ka agu beki	Shall I tie it up one day?

And at long last, the two became man and wife, just as they had wished.

As the years went by, the woman's father died. As long as the man spent all his time with the woman, he had little chance to satisfy his ambitions, so he sought out someone he could visit in Takayasu village in the province of Kawachi.

His wife showed no signs of discontent, though, and let him go on his way, and he began therefore to suspect she was so compliant because she had taken a lover herself. One day he pretended to go off to Kawachi, but actually hid behind bushes in the garden. His wife made herself up quite beautifully and, with a sigh, recited a poem:

Kaze fukeba	The wailing wind,
Okitsu shiranami	Strong enough to raise white waves
Tatsutayama	Out upon the sea
Yowa ni ya kimi ga	Blows down now from Tatsuta. Will you cross
Hitori yukuran to	The mountains all alone in dark of night?

When the man heard this, his love for his wife was rekindled, and he did not go to Kawachi anymore.[16]

The most important poems in the play come directly from this passage, but Zeami has rearranged the narrative order. He introduces the second part of the story first, and treats it in his sashi. Only then does he turn back to the first part of the tale, filling it out with far more detail than the original contained. Notice, in particular, his reference to the surface of the water in the well; it is a mirror capturing the experience of the two playmates as well as the passing days and months and years (in the reflections of the sun and moon).

The dan is brought to a close with a rongi:

Rongi

127	C	Ge ni ya furinishi monogatari,
		Kikeba tae naru arisama no,
		Ayashi ya nanoriowashimase,
130	S	Makoto wa ware wa koigoromo,
		Ki no Aritsune ga musume to mo,
		Isa shiranami no Tatsutayama,
		Yowa ni magirete kitaritari,
	C	Fushigi ya sate wa Tatsutayama,
135		Iro ni zo izuru momijiba no,
	S	Ki no Aritsune ga musume to mo,
	C	Mata wa Izutsu no onna to mo,
	S	Hazukashinagara ware nari to,
	C	Iu ya shimenawa no nagaki yo o,
140		Chigirishi toshi wa tsutsu izutsu,
		Izutsu no kage ni kakurekeri,
		Izutsu no kage ni kakurekeri.

Rongi

127	C	This is a tale of long ago, a tale that holds great charm,
		But listening to it fills me with suspicion.
		Tell me who you are.
130	S	Actually I wander here in robes of love,
		Am I Aritsune's daughter?
		Who might know? From Tatsuta of the white waves,
		Through the dark night, all alone I've come.
	C	A strange reply: Aritsune's daughter comes blushing with love's revelation,
135		Crimson as the leaves of Tatsuta.
	S	Ashamed though I am to admit it,
	C	I'm also called the woman by the well curb,
	S	Bound in ropes of love, like the twisted braids at a sacred shrine.
	C	Long are the years uncoiled since then when
140		At nineteen I first pledged love with him, she said,
		And vanished in the shadows of the well curb.
		And vanished in the shadows of the well curb.

The waki finally coaxes the shite's identity out of her, but it comes only gradually and through a series of wordplays. First she hints that she may be Ki no Aritsune's daughter, leading into Ki, the proper name, through the word *kiru*, "wear," which is introduced by *koigoromo*, "robes of love." But no sooner does she hint at being Aritsune's daughter than she obscures her identity again with another wordplay, *isa shira(zu)/shiranami no*, "Hmm, (I) really do not know"/"white waves." This leads to a variation on lines from the poem "kaze fukeba" quoted earlier: *shiranami Tatsutaya-*

ma yowa ni, "from Tatsuta of the white waves through the dark night." Tatsutayama is famous for red maples and suggests *momijiba,* "maple leaves," to the waki. In lines delivered for him by the chorus, he mentions them, but the attributive phrase he attaches, *iro ni zo izuru,* literally "coming out in color," suggests not only the redness of the leaves, but also the love of the woman and Narihira; this, because *iro,* "color," implies sexual love. *Momijiba* suggests *ki,* "tree," as well as the surname Ki to the shite, and she finally admits unequivocally that she is the daughter of Ki no Aritsune. She further identifies herself as *Izutsu no onna,* "the woman by the well curb."

The chorus responds with yet another wordplay: *iu ya/iu ya shimenawa,* "(as soon as) she says"/"Oh, weave the rope." The latter interpretation of this phrase serves as a jo to *nagaki,* "long," which modifies the vows of love the shite made with Narihira. Still another play on words occurs in *tsutsu* (line 140), or more accurately, *tsuzu,* an archaic word actually meaning "ten," but frequently misunderstood to mean "nineteen" in medieval Japan. (The shite made her vow of love when she was nineteen.)[17] This meaning is naturally doubled with *tsutsu izutsu* of the play's central poem, which fits into this specific context to mean "well curb" in "she vanished in the shadows of the well curb." The rongi is artfully constructed, but at the same time easier to follow, and less evocative and serious, than the preceding kuse. There is something almost playful about it, and it serves to bring a quick and adept closing to the fourth dan.

An aikyōgen interlude follows. Lacking any notion of what this may have consisted of in Zeami's day, we must settle for the translation of a modern version:

Ai

K   I before you am a man of Ichinomoto. I often go up to Ariwara Temple with certain things to pray for, and on this very day I'm headed there. Hmm. There's a priest over there I've never seen here before. Where might you be going, reverend sir? I see you're resting here now.

W   I am a wandering priest. Do you live nearby?

K   Yes, sir.

W   Good. Come a little closer. I've got something to ask you.

K   Yes, sir. Now what exactly did you have on your mind?

W   This question may surprise you, but could you tell me something about Narihira and Ki no Aritsune's daughter? You must know something about them.

K   I never expected you to ask anything like that. Well, actually, even though I live near here, I don't really know much about them, but I can't very well refuse your request, so I'll tell you what I've heard.

W   Very well.

K   Well now, they say that Narihira was the youngest child of Prince Abo. He lived nearby when he was just a little boy, and he used to play with Ki no Aritsune's daughter here, looking down at the re-

An actor of the Konparu school as the nochijite in *Izutsu*. The mask is of the type known as *koomote*, and the shite wears a light, gold-embroidered dancing robe (*chōken*). The hat is called an *uikanmuri*, and the feathery attachments to it that shade the sides of the mask are termed *oikake*. *Photograph by Masuda Shozoh, courtesy of the Noh Research Archives of Musashino Women's College.*

flections on the surface of the water in the well. As they grew up, though, they both became very bashful and they didn't see each other for a long while. Then Narihira sent her a poem:

> Well curb, on the well curb,
> On the well curb once we marked our height,
> But I've grown taller since I saw you last,
> Well past those marks
> We left upon the well.

She replied with another poem:

> Side by side we stood
> Comparing our locks then, but now
> My hair hangs far below my shoulders.
> If not for you, for whom
> Shall I tie it up one day?

They were married before long and were very much in love. But at that time, Narihira had a mistress in Takayasu he would visit now and again. His wife had no desire to appear jealous, so she always saw him off cheerfully when he was going to Takayasu. Narihira found this very suspicious. He thought she might have taken a lover. Once he pretended to go off to Takayasu, but merely hid himself behind the plume grass near the well to see what would happen. His wife dressed more beautifully than ever, burned incense, and arranged a bouquet of flowers, then went out on the veranda. Gazing far off toward Takayasu, she recited this poem:

> The wailing wind,
> Strong enough to raise white waves out upon the sea,
> Blows down now
> From Tatsuta. Will you cross the mountains
> All alone in dark of night?

Then she went back inside looking ever so dejected. Narihira saw this and realized how faithful she was, so he stopped going to Takayasu. After both Narihira and his lady were dead, a temple was built here, named after them. That's about all I know, but why do you ask?

w   I appreciate your story. I don't have any particular reason to ask except that a woman appeared here a while ago. She took water from the well for some flowers she had, lit incense, and made an offering to that mound. And when I asked her what she was doing, she told me the very story you just related. But she spoke as if she were talking to herself. Then I lost sight of her behind the well.

k   She must be the ghost of Aritsune's daughter. Why don't you stay awhile and pray for her?

w   That is what I thought I'd do. I'll recite a sutra for her.

k   Let me know if you need anything.

w   Thank you.

k   Don't mention it.[18]

The aikyōgen interlude ends with the waki's song of waiting written as a formally regular ageuta:

Ageuta
143 W　　Fukeyuku ya,
　　　　　Ariwaradera no yoru no tsuki,
145　　　Ariwaradera no yoru no tsuki,
　　　　　Mukashi o kaesu koromode ni,
　　　　　Yume machisoete karimakura,
　　　　　Koke no mushiro ni fushinikeri,
　　　　　Koke no mushiro ni fushinikeri.

Ageuta
143 W　　Far into the night
　　　　　Over Ariwara Temple still the bright moon shines.
145　　　Over Ariwara Temple still the bright moon shines.
　　　　　Inside out I turn my robe to call the past to mind,
　　　　　And wait for dreams. I sleep
　　　　　On a traveler's bed, on a mat of sedge rolled out upon the moss.
　　　　　On a traveler's bed, on a mat of sedge rolled out upon the moss.

The song contains a kakekotoba in line 146: *mukashi o kaesu* means "turn the past (into the present)" and *kaesu koromo* means "a robe turned inside out." The latter expression refers to turning a robe inside out as one goes to sleep in order to dream of one's lover.

　　Like the corresponding ageuta in *Tōru*, this song explicitly sets the rest of the play in the context of a dream. In *Izutsu* the dream begins with the shite's entrance to the instrumental ISSEI, followed by a sashi:

Sashi
150 S　　Ada nari to na ni koso tatere sakurabana,
　　　　　Toshi ni mare naru hito mo machikeri,
　　　　　Kayō ni yomishi mo ware nareba,
　　　　　Hito matsu onna to mo iwareshi nari,
　　　　　Ware tsutsu izutsu no mukashi yori,
155　　　Mayumi tsukiyumi toshi o hete,
　　　　　Ima wa naki yo ni Narihira no,
　　　　　Katami no nōshi mi ni furete.

Sashi
150 S　　"Cherry blossoms have a name for faithlessness, they scatter
　　　　　　　fruitlessly,
　　　　　Yet they have waited, as have I, for one who comes so rarely
　　　　　　　through the year."
　　　　　It was I who wrote this poem,
　　　　　So they call me the woman who awaits her lover;
　　　　　Many years have come and gone since I was nineteen,
155　　　Many times the bowed moon has grown full,
　　　　　And Narihira died so long ago.
　　　　　Now I wear this robe he wore, something left me, his remembrance.

The first two lines quote a poem from Episode 17 of *Ise monogatari*, which calls up by association allusions to other poems in the same work: to one in Episode 23, through the now highly resonant *tsutsu izutsu* (line 154), and to one in Episode 24, which is quoted in part in line 155.[19] The sashi is the nochijite's self-introduction, and the mention of yet another of her nicknames, *hito matsu onna,* "the woman who waits for her lover," completes the catalogue of names begun in the rongi (lines 136-37). Narihira, though dead, comes onto the scene through the clothes he has left his lover, and she begins to turn into him, as the next lines of the play reveal:

Issei

158	s	Hazukashi ya,
		Mukashi otoko ni utsurimai,
	c	Yuki o megurasu hana no sode.

Issei

158	s	Embarrassed though I am,
		I am transformed into the man from long ago, in dance,
	c	And wave my flowered sleeves through swirling snow. . . .

Utsurimai in line 159 is a dance done in imitation of someone else, but here *utsuri* must also be taken with *mukashi otoko ni* (*utsuri*) to mean "I am transformed into the man from long ago" (i.e. Narihira).

In closing on the image of sleeves raised in dance, the song leads directly to the shite's dance, in modern performance a quiet, elegant JONO-MAI. This is followed by a *waka* shōdan, whose dominant image—the shining moon—calls to mind Narihira's most famous poem. The shite then goes on to quote part of that poem in lines 166-67.[20]

Waka

161	s	Koko ni kite,
		Mukashi zo kaesu Ariwara no,
	c	Terai ni sumeru,
		Tsuki zo sayakeki,
165		Tsuki zo sayakeki.

Unidentified shōdan

	s	Tsuki ya aranu
		Haru ya mukashi to nagameshi mo,
		Itsu no koro zo ya.

Waka

161	s	Coming here
		Recalls the past to me.
	c	In the well near Ariwara Temple,
		Shines the dazzling moon.
165		Shines the dazzling moon.

Unidentified shōdan

	s	When was it Narihira said,
		"That is not the moon,
		Nor is this the spring of years gone by . . ."?

The shite's short shōdan, though it has no name, serves an important transitional role between the preceding *waka* shōdan and the noriji that is to follow. Furthermore, it continues the string of poems from *Ise mono-*

gatari, which have become so dominant in this dan. "Tsuki ya aranu" is particularly effective here because of a reversal effected by Zeami. In the original context, Narihira delivers the poem recalling a lost love. Here, however, the shite sings the poem recalling Narihira. The irony is readily apparent, but over and above the ironic contrast spreads the common experience of love. The moon, which is so central to the original poem, is no less important to the play, and its reappearance here is yet one more in a chain of references that began, as the reader will recall, in the maejite's first song.

The next shōdan is the all-important noriji mentioned earlier:

Noriji

169	s	Tsutsu izutsu,
	c	Tsutsu izutsu,
		Izutsu ni kakeshi,
	s	Maro ga take,
	c	Oinikerashi na,
	s	Oinikeru zo ya,
175	c	Sanagara mimieshi,
		Mukashi otoko no,
		Kamuri nōshi wa,
		Onna to mo miezu,
		Otoko narikeri,
180		Narihira no omokage.

Noriji

169	s	"Well curb,
	c	On the well curb,
		On the well curb
	s	Once we marked our height.
	c	But I've grown taller since I saw you last . . ."
	s	I've grown old, so many years have passed,
175	c	My reflection in his clothes,
		Looks like the "Man from Long Ago."
		Courtier's hat and palace robes
		Make me look no longer like myself,
		No longer woman, now I am a man,
180		Narihira's image.

The song begins evocatively with the echoing and re-echoing of the phrase *tsutsu izutsu.* This leads to the quotation of three-quarters of the play's central poem, but the words *oinikerashi na* call up *oinikeru zo ya* here instead of the original *imo mizaru ma ni.* This is possible, in part, because *oinikerashi,* "I've grown up," and *oinikeru,* "I've grown old," are homonyms, but there is more here than a simple play on words. Both words describe the passing of time, but whereas the former indicated a fulfillment of the temporal conditions necessary for love, the latter marks the end of the physical capacity for that (sexual) love. The similarity of sound and immediate juxtaposition here underscore the ironic discrep-

ancy between states of life. The image of Narihira that the shite sees in-
carnate in herself is obviously a phantasm, but she has been so caught up
in love that she is exquisitely deranged and achieves a complete unity
with Narihira in the world of phantasms, thereby conquering time and
space, if only for an instant of ecstatic perception. As the last lines of the
noriji are sung, she gazes down into the well on stage to see herself as her
lover. This is the climax of the drama, a moment of silence where time
and space are transcended for the character and, in great performances,
for the audience as well.[21] The play then closes with an uta:

Uta
181   s   Mireba natsukashi ya,
     c   Ware nagara natsukashi ya,
           Bōfu hakurei no sugata wa,
           Shibomeru hana no
185   Iro nōte nioi,
           Nokorite Ariwara no,
           Tera no kane mo honobono to,
           Akureba furutera no,
           Matsukaze ya bashōba no,
190   Yume mo yaburete samenikeri,
           Yume wa yabure akenikeri.

Uta
181   s   Reflected there, his image reawakens all my love,
     c   I see myself, his image reawakens all my love,
           The spirit dressed in robes her lover wore
           Fades from sight, the wilted flower's color gone,
185   Its fragrance lingers on.
           The temple bell tolls,
           Night fades with the dawn,
           The morning wind plays around rustling pines,
           Here before the ancient cloister, ripped like plantain leaves,
190   My dreams are torn away, I wake,
           My dreams are torn away, dawn breaks.

Line 181 is a spontaneous exclamation, but with line 182 the shite re-
turns to self-consciousness. Then the waki's dream, which has made up
this part of the play, begins to evaporate. The shite's spirit fades like a
wilting flower. Here again the text is structured more by association than
discursive narrative: *shibomeru*, "wilt," "fade," is associated with both *su-
gata*, "shape," and *hana*, "flower." *Hana* suggests *iro*, "color," and *nioi*, "fra-
grance."[22] *Nokorite ari*, "linger on," leads to *Ariwara no tera*, "the Ariwara
temple." *Tera* calls up *kane*, "bell," which leads to *honobono*. This word is
not conventionally familiar as onomatopoeia for the tolling of bells, but
it may represent this sound here. It also modifies *akureba*, "(dawn)
breaks," in which context it suggests dawn breaking gradually and qui-
etly. *Furutera*, "the old temple," is linked to *matsu*, "pines," and *bashōba*,
"plantain leaves"; and, finally, the plantain leaves, so easily ripped by the

wind, become symbols for the dreams (*yume*) ripped away by dawn. The play's final word, *akenikeri*, "dawn breaks," harkens back to *akureba*, "when dawn breaks," in line 188.

Izutsu is a play of far less breadth than *Takasago*. In place of that play's themes of poetic universality, conjugal felicity, imperial benevolence, and so on, *Izutsu* has only the tension between love and time. What the play lacks in breadth, however, it more than makes up for in depth. No single step in Zeami's process of composition, neither seed (shu), nor structure (saku), nor writing (sho) can solely be credited with his success here. The depth he achieves comes from the complete integration of the three stages of creation. How has this been accomplished?

For the source material (or honzetsu), as we already know, Zeami selected several poems from *Ise monogatari*. "Tsutsu izutsu" is the most important, but "Kaze fukeba" and "Kurabe koshi" both hold prominent positions in the play; and at the beginning of the fifth dan, still more waka from *Ise* appear to enrich the play's thematic texture.

The use of waka in the noh theater did not originate with Zeami. Kannami frequently quoted famous old poems (as in, for example, *Yoshino Shizuka*, just after the JONOMAI), and waka or parts of waka can be found in such old noh as *Ukifune*, *Aoi no Ue*, and *Unrin'in* (the original version). Even among the earliest extant records of sarugaku performances, one finds mention of plays that must have included waka. Notes on a performance of 1349, for example, speak of one piece in which "Norikiyo [the poet Saigyō] chants ten poems at the palace of Emperor Toba," and of another in which "Murasaki Shikibu visits the ailing Izumi Shikibu."[23] The first is specifically said to contain waka, and the second could hardly have been performed without some poetry, given the identity of its two main characters.

But Zeami uses waka in an altogether original way. Here in *Izutsu* we find that each time a waka appears and reappears it is in a different temporal context. The waki's partial quotation of "Kaze fukeba" in his sashi identifies that poem with the play's setting. The poem reappears in the sashi of the fourth dan, quoted in full, and now it juxtaposes the context in which it was composed (Narihira's nighttime departure and his lover's worries about his safety) against the waki's encounter with the shite. "Tsutsu izutsu" first appears in the kuse (lines 114-17) with "Kurabe koshi" (119-22) to bring alive the moment when the two childhood friends, Narihira and the daughter of Ki no Aritsune, became lovers.[24] When "Tsutsu izutsu" reappears just a few lines later, that moment is set against the longer expanse of time during which Aritsune's daughter came to be known as "the woman by the well curb." In the rongi, part of "Kaze fukeba" is quoted again, but now it is the ghost of Aritsune's daughter who has come "through the dark night, all alone," to meet the waki. At the end of the rongi, "Tsutsu izutsu" appears once more. This time, however, the line from the poem describes the disappearance of the shite near the same well curb where she and her lover made their pledge so long ago.

The aikyōgen's narrative sets all three poems into the quasi-historical context of legend, providing the only objective perspective on the poems. The beginning of the last dan then layers "Tsutsu izutsu" in with (at least) three other poems from *Ise monogatari*. First, in line 150, "Ada nari to" is quoted. The shite claims this as her own poem (although it is attributed to an unknown lady in *Ise monogatari*), thereby introducing another incident in the lives of Narihira and Aritsune's daughter. This poem must also be understood in the immediate context of the nochi-jite's appearance in the waki's dream. One of the most dominant characteristics of the shite in this play—and one direct link with the conventional view of love in the Japanese aristocratic tradition—is that she is always waiting; this is made explicit here.

The span of time from that moment at the well curb until the dramatic present of the waki's dream is then delineated in lines 154-55, where the shite sings *tsutsu izutsu no mukashi yori . . . toshi o hete ima . . .*, "Many years have come and gone . . . since I was nineteen and now . . ." Again this is accomplished with poems: "Tsutsu izutsu" and "[Azusa yumi]/mayumi tsukiyumi." Finally, after the JONOMAI, the shite recalls Narihira's poem "Tsuki ya aranu," and as she wonders when Narihira composed it, she is thrown into an elegant state of derangement in which she becomes Narihira and escapes for a moment from the bounds of time and space. This passage is—of course—introduced by "Tsutsu izutsu."

Throughout the play, then, one experience, one time, is set against another through the use and reuse of waka. A diagram of the various appearances and reappearances of waka as they relate to the time line from Aritsune's daughter's lifetime through the play's dramatic present may serve most efficiently to summarize all this layering (Fig. 12). By this technique, Zeami creates a new context for each occurrence of these poems, and the ambiguity resulting from the new context allows a new interpretation of each poem. The new interpretation, however, does not invalidate an earlier one, so the waka become more and more evocative as the play progresses and the honzetsu expands beyond the naïve poetic encounter of *Ise monogatari* to encompass a broad range of experiences of love. This technique is akin to, if not identical with, the allusive variation we encountered in *Takasago*.

As Figure 12 shows, the waka in *Izutsu* tie together the various poetic occasions in the lives of Narihira and Aritsune's daughter with the realization of the daughter's ghost in the waki's dream. I should more cor-

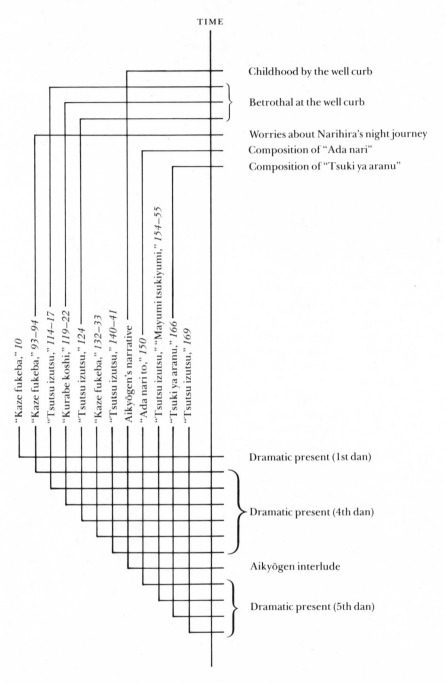

TIME

Childhood by the well curb

Betrothal at the well curb

Worries about Narihira's night journey
Composition of "Ada nari"
Composition of "Tsuki ya aranu"

"Kaze fukeba," 10
"Kaze fukeba," 93–94
"Tsutsu izutsu," 114–17
"Kurabe koshi," 119–22
"Tsutsu izutsu," 124
"Kaze fukeba," 132–33
"Tsutsu izutsu," 140–41
Aikyōgen's narrative
"Ada nari to," 150
"Tsutsu izutsu," "Mayumi tsukiyumi," 154–55
"Tsuki ya aranu," 166
"Tsutsu izutsu," 169

Dramatic present (1st dan)

Dramatic present (4th dan)

Aikyōgen interlude

Dramatic present (5th dan)

Fig. 12   The layering of time through the use of waka in the play *Izutsu*. The italic line numbers are keyed to the text analysis.

rectly say, "part way through the waki's dream," for waka do not by themselves bring about the shite's ultimate identification with her long-dead lover. That comes not with words alone, but with action on stage. The chorus sings, "No longer woman, now I am man, Narihira's image," and as the shite brushes aside the plume grass at the well curb and gazes down to the water below, she comes to realize that identification. Her actions here recreate the experience of her youth with the boy Narihira *before* either had enough self-consciousness to compose any poems. The nochijite's gaze down into the well here recalls the experience of the children as they "lean[ed] on the well curb, telling stories, looking far below, there to see their faces mirrored, shining in the well" (lines 103-5).

An entirely literary approach to *Izutsu* would miss this, the climax of the play, and although I have frequently cautioned against the facile assumption that modern performance practice accurately reflects practice in Zeami's day, there seems to be sufficient justification to assume that this much of the performance of *Izutsu* has remained constant since the fifteenth century. I say this recalling Zeami's instructions on plays in the Woman's Mode.*

As far as structure is concerned, *Izutsu* follows much the same format as *Takasago*. The most important differences, as Table 7 shows, come in the fifth dan, with its waka, unspecified shōdan, and noriji between the dance and the final shōdan in tadautai style.[25] In *Takasago* the dance is followed immediately by the tadautai shōdan.

The reader will recall that in the third chapter I noted that ōnori rhythm was originally used for the appearance of furyū characters, that is, nonhuman characters; and that this introduced a contradiction, for in *Takasago*, although the shite is a god, a nonhuman character, no ōnori is used. Now, in *Izutsu*, where the shite *is* human, or more accurately, the ghost of a human, the contradiction is compounded, for ōnori does appear. What is it about *Izutsu* that justifies the use of this rather particular rhythm? Is there some connection to furyū? These questions must be held in abeyance until more of Zeami's plays in the Woman's Mode have been discussed; I bring them up here only because the noriji in *Izutsu*'s final dan is one major structural difference between this play and *Takasago*.

There is, however, another structural irregularity in the play that does not appear in the shōdan sequence—the narrative inversion in the fourth dan. A normal narrative sequence would proceed just as the ai-

---

* "One must make allowances for visual display," he declares in *Sandō* (p. 137). Later on, speaking specifically of plays about people in a state of emotional derangement (*kuruimono*), he says, "It is best to take pains with the visual potential and write the music with attention to details appropriate to the movements to be performed" (*ibid.* p. 138). *Izutsu* is not a *kuruimono*, but there is sufficient reason to consider it within the context of such plays. I will return to this issue later.

TABLE 7   *The Shōdan Sequences of Izutsu and Takasago*

Dan (section)	*Izutsu*	*Takasago*
1 (jo)	NANORIBUE	SHINNOSHIDAI
		Shidai
	Nanori	Nanori
	Sashi	
	Uta	Ageuta
		(Tsukizerifu)
2 (ha 1)	SHIDAI	SHINNOISSEI
	Shidai	Issei
	Sashi	Sashi
	Sageuta	Sageuta
	Ageuta	Ageuta
3 (ha 2)	Mondō	Mondō
		Kakeai
	Ageuta	Ageuta
4 (ha 3)	Sasoizerifu	(Sasoizerifu)
	Kuri	Kuri
	Sashi	Sashi
	Kuse	Kuse
	Rongi	Rongi
aikyōgen	Mondō	Mondō
	Katari	Katari
	Ageuta	Ageuta
5 (kyū)	ISSEI	DEHA
	Sashi	Sashi
		Jōnoei
	Issei	*Issei
	JONOMAI	KAMIMAI
	Waka (shōdan)	
	X	
	Noriji	
	Uta	Rongi

NOTE: The shōdan in small caps are instrumental pieces, including dances. Parentheses indicate a highly conventional shōdan that was omitted from old texts but was probably included in performances; X indicates an unspecified shōdan; and an asterisk indicates that a shōdan is irregular.

kyōgen's narrative does, from the shite's childhood, to the betrothal poems, to the incident in which Aritsune's daughter composed "Kaze fukeba." But Zeami chooses to put the "Kaze fukeba" incident ahead of the earlier events. This inversion is not particularly striking when one reads or sees the play, but Zeami seems to have made it consciously. It illustrates very well a remark of his from *Sarugaku dangi*:

As one is writing, there is a tendency to become caught up in trying to produce a beautiful text, and, as a consequence, to write over-long lines. One must rid oneself of this tendency in writing. The "Song of Susanoo" is well written. It says, "In the age of the gods, he appeared as the brother of the goddess Amaterasu; in the age of men, Prince Yamato Takeru chastised the barbarians," and then, although one would have expected the story about the Eastern Regions, that story is omitted; at the end of the *kusemai*, the story of the Palace of Eight Swords and so on appears; thus the narrative is inverted, and the most promising material is written into the *kuse*. If this were written straight through from beginning to end, it would be too long and ineffective.[26]

The "Song of Susanoo" is lost, so it is difficult to determine how effective the particular inversions Zeami refers to may have been there. But his comments are still relevant to our analysis because they show a clear and conscious selection of materials from the honzetsu for a specific narrative focus. In putting the "Kaze fukeba" episode out of chronological order, Zeami makes the most temporally remote incidents of the honzetsu the centerpiece of the play's narrative, sharpening the focus on the span of time from those incidents to the play's dramatic present.

Is it paradoxical that such care and attention are given to the choice and placement of narrative materials while, in the wording of many individual passages, the narrative element is subordinated to nondiscursive associations? Renga-like associations, as we have seen, occupy much of the *Izutsu* text. The shite's first sashi—as in *Takasago*—provides an excellent example; or again, the last shōdan of the play, the uta. The mechanics of these individual passages were discussed earlier, but consider now the similarity between these associations on their small scale and the layering of poems and parts of poems on a larger scale throughout the play. In both instances, the literary effect of the text is created by juxtaposition, not by discursive exposition. As a consequence, the viewer (reader) apprehends the play by leaping from image to idea to emotion, and so on, rather than by following the logic of a particular story line. Perhaps this is what has prompted the frequent comparison of noh with dream and film. Is this not, in fact, the very reason why a more chronological unfolding of the honzetsu is avoided?

This brings us to the last of Zeami's three stages—the act of writing the play itself. *Izutsu* has none of the highly Sinified vocabulary of *Takasago*; it would of course be inappropriate to use such *kowaki kotoba* in a play as delicate as this. Parallelism, too, is much less apparent in the text, though some examples can be found (including the strictest type of parallelism possible, exact repetition).[27] In lines 112-13, for instance, one finds *kotoba no tsuyu*, "dew of words," parallelled by *kokoro no hana*, "flowers of heart"; here the rhetorical correspondence underscores the conventional association of *kotoba* with *kokoro* and *tsuyu* with *hana*.

A more interesting use of loosely parallel lines is to be found at the beginning of the final uta (lines 181-82). *Mireba natsukashi ya* is roughly parallel to *ware nagara natsukashi ya*. The repetition of *natsukashi ya* (which I have very loosely translated as "his image reawakens all my love") after dependent clauses (one temporal, one concessive) suggests a similarity of meaning more substantial than sound alone, and indeed the same longing is intended both times. There is, however, an ironic tension between these lines, because in line 181 the shite is still caught up in the deranged notion that she is Narihira, whereas in the next line she has returned to self-consciousness, and her moment's precious union with her dead lover is over.

Zeami must have been interested in this existential dilemma: the conflict between consciousness of self and total engagement in experience. He uses the same literary technique in other plays for the same effect. Take, for example, this passage from *Tōru* (lines 26-29, quoted in Chapter Three): *Ara mukashi koishi ya. Koishi koishi ya to, Shitaedomo nagekedomo, kai mo na(gisa)* (Oh, how I long for the past. "How I long, how I long for the past," I sigh, but my yearnings and complaints come to no end). Here the shite is not longing for a lover, but for a time in his own past. The dynamics of the passage are, nevertheless, identical. The shite's total absorption in his emotions calls forth the exclamation *ara mukashi koishi ya*, but immediately he becomes self-conscious (he even quotes himself) and admits that his longings cannot return to him what he has lost. The simple parallelism in the repetition of the words *koishi ya* ironically highlights the contrast between mental states, between complete absorption in emotion and self-awareness.[28]

Zeami finds a honzetsu for *Izutsu* in the poetry of early classical Japan, but poetry is not the only source for his plays. Among the noh in the Woman's Mode, there are works based on myths from Japan's early "histories" (i.e., *Kojiki, Nihongi,* and so on), on episodes from prose fiction, and on popular legends and anecdotes associated with famous places. And on occasion one finds a play without any particular previous source, an entirely original play.

Unoha is an early work that draws on a story in *Kojiki*; and *Tōboku* (which is likely one of Zeami's works but cannot be categorically ascribed to him) finds its honzetsu in the poetic associations of a once-famous place.* Another, far greater play, *Taema,* also centers on a famous place, but in this case Zeami concentrates on a legend associated with the place instead of the diffuse and rather inchoate associations used in *Tōboku*. *Taema* is most likely a work of Zeami's last years,[29] and he shows himself at his masterly best in his manipulation of its source materials.

---

* The place is Tōboku no In, a temple that had been the residence of Michinaga's daughter Shōshi, consort of Emperor Ichijō. The only mention of *Tōboku* in Zeami's writings is found in *Nōhon sanjūgoban mokuroku*.

The honzetsu of *Taema* is the story of the miraculous creation of the Taema mandala, a tapestry illustrating the Buddhist cosmos. Zeami's immediate source is unknown, but a version in *Genkō shakusho* (Commentaries of the Genkō Era), one of several works he may have used, tells the following tale:

The deeply religious daughter of one Fujiwara no Yokohagi had long refused to marry. In 763 she vowed she would not leave the grounds of the Zenrin (or Taema) Temple in Yamato until she had seen Amida Buddha in his true form. Several days after she made this vow, a beautiful nun of noble bearing appeared at the temple promising to show her Lord Amida if she would gather a hundred stalks of lotus. Yokohagi's daughter had the lotus stalks sent from the palace and gave them to the nun. She split them into threads and dyed them in five colors. Several days later another beautiful nun arrived and took the dyed thread off to a corner of the temple hall. She began weaving at dusk, and before daybreak the next morning, she had woven a 15-foot-wide tapestry depicting the majestic sights of Amida's Pure Land. The nuns handed the tapestry over to Yokohagi's daughter, and the second nun mysteriously disappeared. The first nun composed a hymn, made obeisance to the tapestry, and said, "According to the teachings of Kāśyapa, there is a karmic reason for the appearance of things related to Buddhism. I have come here out of admiration for your worthy endeavors and now that I have arrived, there will be no suffering for a long while." Yokohagi's daughter asked who the nun was, and she replied, "Who else could I be! I am Dharma Master of the West and the other woman was the great lord Kannon." With that she disappeared to the west, and Yokohagi's daughter spent the remaining years of life with greater devotion than ever before.[30]

At the opening of the play *Taema*, the waki, a priest of one of the devotional sects, stops at the Zenrin Temple on his way to Mikumano. While resting there, he notices two women, the shite and the tsure, coming into the temple gardens. As he listens, they exchange lines from the sutras in the hope of attaining buddhahood:

Sashi

1	S	Ichinen Midabus' sokumet'n muryōzai to mo tokaretari,
	T	Hachiman shoshōgyō kai ze Amida to mo arige ni sōro,
	S	Shaka wa yari,
	T	Mida wa michibiku hitosuji ni,
5	S/T	Kokoro yurusu na Namu Amidabu to.

Issei

	S	Tonōreba,
		Hotoke mo ware mo nakarikeri,
	T	Namu Amidabu no,

		Koe bakari
	s	suzushiki,
10		Michi wa
	s/t	tanomoshi ya.[31]

Sashi

1	s	A single call on Buddha's name erases countless sins, they say.
	t	Eighty thousand tomes of sacred writ are all contained within the name of Amida.
	s	Shakyamuni points the way,
	t	And Amida leads souls to Paradise upon a single thread,
5	s/t	Pray intently, do not slacken in your heart.

Issei

	s	For when you call upon the name of Amida,
		There is no buddha as there is no self,
	t	Just the sound of
		"Turn your heart to Amida." With this
	s	we set our hopes
10		Upon the freshening way
	s/t	to Paradise.

The waki asks the women about the temple, and they tell him about a particularly lovely cherry tree in its precincts. He then asks about the Taema mandala, whereupon they relate the story of Chūjōhime, the daughter of Yokohagi, who vowed she would not leave her grass hut until she had seen the living Buddha. One evening, as she pursued her solitary devotions in the light of the full moon, an old nun suddenly appeared:

Kuse (cont.)

1	c	Kore wa ika naru hito naran to,
		Tazunesasetamaishi ni,
		Rōni kotaete notamawaku,
		Tare to wa nado ya oroka nari,
5		Yobeba koso kitaritare to,
		Ōserarekeru hodo ni,
		Chūjōhime wa akiretsutsu.

[Ageha]

	s	Ware wa tare o ka yobu kodori,
	c	Tasuki mo shiranu yamanaka ni,
10		Koe tatsuru koto tote wa,
		Namu Amidabu no tonae narade,
		Mata taji mo naki mono o to,
		Kotaesasetamaishi ni,
		Sore koso waga na nare koe o,
15		Shirube ni kitareri to,
		Notamaeba himegimi mo sate wa,
		Kono gan jōju shite,
		Shōshin no Mida nyorai,
		Ge ni raikō no jiset'n yo to,
20		Kanrui kimo ni meijitsutsu,

Kirae no onsode mo,
Shioru bakari ni mietamō.

Kuse (cont.)

1   C   When she asked
          Who this person might be,
          The old nun replied,
          "Why do you ask? . . . Such foolishness!
5   I only came because you called my name."
          And when she said this,
          Chūjōhime was struck with amazement.

[*Ageha*]

     S   "Whose name did I call! Hardly a bird
     C   Cries in this mountain wilderness;
10   And if I made any sound at all,
          I sang, 'Turn your heart to Amida'
          And not another thing."
          When she had so replied, the nun said,
          "There you have it, that is my name,
15   And hearing it, I came."
          At last the princess realized
          Her wish was granted.
          The living Buddha Amida
          Had come for her.
20   Grateful tears were etched into her memory.
          Her brilliantly dyed sleeves
          Were fully drenched.

The waki remarks what a wonderful story he has heard, and the shite
and tsure inform him that it is the anniversary of Chūjōhime's assumption
into Amida's paradise. They tell him that they are none other than
the mysterious women from the story; and then, in a scene reminiscent
of the miracle in *Yōrō*, the chorus announces, "Hikari sashite / Hana furi
ikyō kunji, / Ongaku no koe su nari" (A flash of light / Flowers rain from
above, incense fills the air, / Somewhere sound the voices of music), and
the two women mount a purple cloud and disappear.

This marks the end of the fourth dan. The aikyōgen then appears to
retell the story, this time including the episode about the weaving of the
tapestry. In the second half of the play Chūjōhime herself appears as the
bodhisattva of song and dance. She explains her transformation, reads
from a sutra, and then, handing it to the waki, begins her dance, a HAYA-
MAI.[32] As she finishes dawn breaks, and the waki awakens from his
dream.

One striking difference between this play and *Izutsu* or *Takasago* is the
change in the shite's identity from the first to the second act. In both *Ta-
kasago* and *Izutsu*, and in fact in most of Zeami's mugen noh, the shite's
identity remains constant throughout the play, although his form often
changes. Here, however, the maejite is the old nun, and the nochijite is
Chūjōhime as the bodhisattva of song and dance. This change is a direct

reflection of the play's honzetsu carried to its logical end. In the original story it is, of course, Chūjōhime herself who encounters the two mysterious women. That encounter leads to her own salvation and metamorphosis into a bodhisattva. In the play the waki takes the place of Chūjōhime as host to the mysterious visitors; they deliver the Buddhist message to him. The truth of this message is then demonstrated by the appearance of Chūjōhime herself, and the waki becomes her follower on the path to Amida's paradise. With this manipulation of the honzetsu, the form of the drama is made to imitate its content. The waki can be seen to represent any being who has taken the first step toward the Dharma, and the play can be taken as an illustration of the process of salvation. This is made explicit in the maejite's issei quoted above: "There is no Buddha as there is no self." This comes to mean: "There is no distinction between the Buddha and the self, and all creatures are destined for enlightenment."

Such an interpretation of *Taema* makes one wonder whether it may not in fact be Zeami's personal testament to his faith. It seems to have been written very late in his life, and in addition to the ingenuity with which it illustrates the process of salvation in devotional Buddhism, the play contains an interesting clue about Zeami's personal investment in the work. The tsure's first line, "Eighty thousand tomes of sacred writ are all contained within the name of Amida," comes from an unidentified source, probably a sutra.[33] As an expression of the standard belief that chanting the name of Amida is sufficient for salvation, it might be passed over were it not for the fact that Zeami has signed his own name to the play with this quotation: "hachiman shoshōgyō kai ze Amida to." With his careful attention to sound in language, Zeami cannot have missed this repetition of his own name.* Then, too, the omission of any mention of the tapestry itself in the narrative of the play proper (as distinct from the aikyōgen's narrative) suggests that Zeami's concern was salvation as opposed to the material appurtenances of religion.

There are other examples of Zeami's skillful manipulation of a honzetsu as the seed of a play. *Higaki*, to name one example, uses a poem as honzetsu to great effect. Among the plays for which the honzetsu seems to be entirely Zeami's own creation, *Kinuta* is the most outstanding example. It is, moreover, a play that would be well worth an exhaustive study in its own right.

In turning from Zeami's use of source materials in the plays in the Woman's Mode to the question of structure, we are faced with a prob-

* Zeami's full name was Zeamida (or Zeamidabutsu). Although the character *ze* in the quotation ("this," which can also be read *kore*) is different from the character customarily used in Zeami's name, one does on occasion see his name written with it. As we will see later, this is not the only instance of wordplay on personal names in Zeami's noh.

lem. Zeami has very little to say on the subject in *Sandō*. In these circumstances the best standard to use in a structural analysis of these plays must remain the most structurally orthodox of the plays in the Aged Mode, *Yumi Yawata*. In Table 8, therefore, I have arranged five model plays of the Woman's Mode by the degree to which they depart from that standard.

It takes no more than a glance at the table to see that there is considerable variation among these plays. None of them follows the *Yumi Yawata* pattern exactly, but *Izutsu, Unoha,* and *Taema* are closer to it than *Hanjo* and *Higaki* in taking the basic five-dan structure.[34] In the case of *Izutsu*, the most notable departure is in the first dan, which proceeds from the waki's entrance music directly to a nanori, then to a sashi—there is no equivalent sashi in *Yumi Yawata*—and finally to an uta.[35] The sashi adds an element of song not present in *Yumi Yawata*, giving *Izutsu* a more lyrical opening than that play and at the same time creating a more direct link between this section—the jo—and the ha.

Both *Izutsu* and *Unoha* are much like *Yumi Yawata* in their second dan, but *Taema* is very different structurally with its two extra shōdan. The sashi and issei just after the shite's entrance compose a semi-discrete unit preceding the shidai-sashi-sageuta-ageuta sequence of the rest of the dan. The general function of the second dan, as we have seen, is to introduce the shite's physical environment and emotional world. This function is performed satisfactorily by the last four shōdan in *Taema*. Why, then, has Zeami added the other two?

The answer, I think, is that the sashi and issei serve to thicken the religious atmosphere enveloping the play. Roughly half of the lines of these two shōdan are written in the distinctive sort of Sino-Japanese found in Buddhist scriptures. This language is not easy to understand aurally. It must have been much like the Latin of the old Catholic liturgy, which imparted a musical sanctity quite apart from the discursive meaning its words contained yet concealed. These words are *kowaki kotoba*, stiff, difficult language, something Zeami warned against in *Fūshikaden*, but their effect here has an almost instrumental quality, providing background music for the temple setting. When native Japanese does surface in these two shōdan, its meaning is all the more transparent and important. Take, for example, the issei's line *hotoke mo ware mo nakarikeri*, "There is no Buddha as there is no self." This condenses the spiritual thrust of the play into five words, and it is the key to what is to occur. These two shōdan, then, provide a general texture for the shite's entrance and an overall statement of the play's theme before the specifics of the shite's identity and personality are introduced.

After this irregularity *Taema* proceeds through its third and fourth dan following more or less the same path as *Izutsu* and *Yumi Yawata*. But *Unoha*, which has been perfectly regular throughout its first two dan,

TABLE 8   *The Shōdan Sequences of Zeami's Five Model Plays in the Woman's Mode*

Dan (section)	Yumi Yawata	Izutsu	Unoha	Taema	Higaki	Hanjo
1 (jo)	SHINNOSHIDAI Shidai Nanori Ageuta Tsukizerifu	NANORIBUE Nanori Sashi Uta	SHIDAI Shidai Nanori Ageuta	SHIDAI Shidai Nanori Ageuta Tsukizerifu	NANORIBUE *Nanori	Nanori Mondō Kudoki Sageuta Ageuta ASHIRAINAKAIRI SHIDAI Shidai Nanori Ageuta Mondō Tsukizerifu
2 (ha)	SHINNOISSEI Issei Sashi Sageuta Ageuta	SHIDAI Shidai Sashi Sageuta Ageuta	ISSEI Issei Sashi Sageuta Ageuta	ISSEI Sashi Issei Shidai Sashi Sageuta Ageuta	NARAINOSHIDAI Shidai Sashi Sageuta Ageuta	ISSEI *Sashi KAKERI Issei Sashi Sageuta Ageuta
3 (ha 2)	Mondō Kakeai Ageuta	Mondō Ageuta	Mondō Katari Kakeai Ageuta	Mondō Kakeai Ageuta		Mondō Uta
4 (ha 3)	Sasoizerifu Kuri Sashi	Sasoizerifu Kuri Sashi	*Kuse Rongi Mondō	Sasoizerifu Kuri Sashi		Kuri Sashi

4 (ha 3) (cont.)	Kuse / Rongi	Kuse / Rongi	Kakeai / Uta	Kuse / Rongi	Kuse
Aikyōgen	Mondō / Katari	Mondō / Katari	?	Mondō / Katari	Mondō / Katari / X
	Ageuta	Ageuta	Ageuta	Ageuta	Ageuta
5 (kyū)	DEHA / Sashi / Issei / Noriji / KAMIMAI / Rongi	ISSEI / Sashi / Issei / JONOMAI / Waka / X / Noriji / Uta	DEHA / Sashi / Issei / Noriji / CHŪNOMAI / Noriji / HANOMAI / Rongi (?)	DEHA / Sashi / Issei / X / Noriji / X / Noriji / HAYAMAI / Uta	NARAINOISSEI / X / *Sashi / *Kuri / Uta / Kakeai / Shidai / Kuri / Sashi / Kuse / Susoguse / Ei / *Waka / JONOMAI[a] / Waka / Noriji / Uta / Mondō / Uta / Rongi

NOTE: The shōdan in small caps are instrumental pieces, including dances. Parentheses indicate a highly conventional shōdan that was omitted from old texts but was probably included in performances; X indicates an unspecified shōdan; and an asterisk indicates that a shōdan is irregular. The dan or sectional divisions in the table stub do not hold for *Higaki* and *Hanjo*, for reasons discussed in the text.

[a] Or CHŪNOMAI.

now differs in the third and fourth. In this play the main narrative takes place in the third dan, rather than in the kuri-sashi-kuse sequence of the fourth dan familiar from the plays referred to so far. This narrative takes the form of a katari, a spoken shōdan, and the immediate effect is to make the third dan undramatic, in the sense that the information imparted does not come gradually through a series of questions and answers, but is delivered all at once in a direct narrative. Because of this shift, the fourth dan must provide some other kind of interest. It does that in its rongi:

Rongi

1	C	Haya iugure no aki no sora,
		Nami mo chiru nari shiratsuyu no,
		Tama o tsuranete fuku to ka ya,
	s/T	Noki no ame,
5		Furuki koto no ha torisoete,
		Tamuke zo makoto matori sumu,
		Unade no mori no ochiba o,
		Hiroiage iza ya fukō yo,
	C	Hirō shiohi no tamatama mo,
10		Ori o etari to iugure no,
	s/T	Tsuki sude ni ideshio no,
		Kage nagara fukō yo,
	C	Kage mo shigeki no yaezakaki,
		Hairo o soete fuku hodo ni,
15	s/T	Kasanaru noki no shinobugusa,
		Wasuretari fukisashite,
		Sukoshi wa nokose,
	C	Na o kiku mo,
		Fukiawasezu no,
20		Kami no ogariya,
		Fukinokose fukinokose,
		Shikamo tsuki no yosugara,
		Kage morotomo ni ware mo ite,
		Moru kage wa Amaterasu,
25		Kamiyo no aki no tsuki o,
		Iza ya nagameakasan.[36]

Rongi

1	C	Already dusk settles over the autumn sky,
		Over there the waves fall, tossing white gems of water high into the air,
		A foamy thatch of sea spray, as it were.
	s/T	It rains upon the eaves,
5		And I add age-old leaves of words,
		To make my offering true like the true eagles of
		Unade Forest where I pick up fallen leaves.
		Come now, let's thatch the hut!
	C	The time is right to pick up jewels
10		Upon the beach at low tide, so they say,
	s/T	So as the evening moon comes out, then,
		In the light that shines upon the ebbing surf, let's thatch the hut.

> c The moonlight scatters everywhere, lush like *sakaki* leaves,
>   And as we add bright-hued feathers to the thatch
> 15 s/t Of layered eaves where forgetful grasses grow—
>   Oh, I had forgotten—as you thatch,
>   Leave part uncovered,
> c For by his name we know him as
>   The God of
> 20 The Half-Thatched Hut.
>   Leave part uncovered, part uncovered,
>   That way the moon can shine in all night long.
>   And I too can bask in its reflection.
>   Oh, let's gaze upon
> 25 The moonbeams leaking through the half-thatched roof,
>   The autumn moonbeams lighting up the sky.

In the rongi of the fourth dan of *Izutsu, Takasago, Yumi Yawata, Taema,* and so on, the shite reveal their identities and leave the stage. *Unoha's* rongi serves an entirely different purpose. It is a song constructed so as to include the word *fuku,* "to thatch," in as many contexts as possible. This is not unrelated to the legend from *Kojiki,* the play's honzetsu; a half-thatched hut figures prominently there. Here, however, narrative content takes second place to verbal ingenuity. One finds repeated use of engo (e.g., *shigeki,* "lush," *yaezakaki,* "eight-fold *sakaki* tree," and *kasanaru,* "layered"), makura kotoba (e.g., *matori sumu,* "true eagles live," for *Unade no mori,* "the Unade Forest"), kakekotoba (e.g., *etari to iu/yūgure,* "the time is right, they say"/"evening"), and other native rhetorical devices. The song is closest in function to the monozukushi, "catalogues of things," in the rongi of *Kinsatsu,* providing an opportunity for ingenious wordplay only tangentially related to the story line. Since it does not serve the usual purposes of the rongi, namely, to identify the shite and allow her to disappear, those purposes must be served by other shōdan: the mondō, kakeai, and uta that follow the rongi.

The final dan of *Unoha* is formally very similar to that of *Yumi Yawata,* the only differences being the extra dance, the short HANOMAI, added after the CHŪNOMAI, and the bridge between the two dances, a noriji.[37] This difference does not alter the fundamental nature of the dan; it still begins with entrance music, proceeds through songs of varying rhythmic and melodic character to its high point in dance, and ends with a tadautai shōdan.

The fifth dan of *Taema,* by contrast, departs rather severely from the model in its series of unspecified shōdan and noriji. The most surprising thing is to find the play ending not with a tadautai song such as an ageuta or a rongi, but with a noriji. This perhaps relates to the nature of the nochijite. As I mentioned earlier, ōnori rhythm was originally used in the depiction of nonhuman beings from another dimension of existence, furyū characters. Since Chūjōhime has at this point become a bodhisatt-va, which is to say, a nonhuman being, ōnori fits with her dramatic character. But if this is true, we come back face to face with the problem of the noriji shōdan in *Izutsu*: a song form that evolved specifically for the depiction of nonhuman characters is used at the dramatic climax of a play about a character who is struggling with the all-too-human emotions of love and yearning for someone long dead.

A strikingly similar use of noriji can be found in the play *Matsukaze*. Again, the shite is obsessed with the memory of someone long dead; and just as in *Izutsu*, she dances in her dead lover's clothes. She then recites a poem he originally composed and falls into a state of derangement. In *Izutsu* this derangement results in the shite's mistaking herself for her lover when she gazes down into the well. In *Matsukaze* the shite mistakes a pine tree for her lover and tries to embrace it.

The single-most-important similarity here is the temporary derangement of the two shite, and this is the key to understanding why a noriji can be used for the expression of human emotions. In the noh theater the derangement caused by the loss of a lover or a child often seems to release the mind of the bereaved from logical constraints and set it loose to what we would call free association. This kind of mind wandering was considered interesting, and a fit object of aesthetic appreciation, perhaps because of its similarity to the association of ideas and words in comic linked verse.[38] Zeami himself, in fact, identifies the role of the *monogurui*, or deranged person, as the "kind of performance with the most potential for arousing interest."[39]

Derangement, then, makes for interest, removing human characters (or their ghosts) from the dimension of normal human existence so that they can be considered furyū; their derangement, therefore, can be cast in ōnori rhythm without seriously violating its traditional conventions. This reasoning may seem a bit too facile without practical examples, but consider it in the light of the following passage from the mad-woman play *Hanjo*. Again we find a noriji following a dance (a JONOMAI or CHŪ-NOMAI) and the recitation of part of a poem—a Chinese poem by Bo Ju-i (Po Chü-i) this time instead of a waka:

*Waka

1	c	E ni kakeru

JONOMAI

Waka (cont.)

	s	Tsuki o kakushite futokoro ni,
		Mochitaru ōgi.

Noriji

	c	Toru sode mo miegasane,
5	s	Sono iroginu no,
	c	Tsuma no kanekoto,
	s	Kanarazu to iugure no,
		Tsukihi mo kasanari,

	c	Akikaze wa fukedomo,
10	s	Ōgi no ha no soyo to no,
		Tayori mo kikade,
	c	Shika no ne mushi no ne mo,
		Karegare no chigiri,
		Ara yoshi na ya.[40]

Waka

| 1 | c | The moon is gone. |

JONOMAI

Waka (cont.)

| | s | I hide it here with my painted fan |
| | | Next to my breast. |

Noriji

	c	The sleeve that holds it is threefold,
	s	And like the hem on that bright silk sleeve,
	c	My lover made me a pretty promise.
	s	He said he would come back for me
		But the days and months pass by
	c	And now the winds of autumn blow.
10	s	I hear hardly the rustle of reeds,
		Much less any word from him.
	c	The cries of stags and the cries of insects
		Weaken like the bonds that held us.
		Oh, what a senseless pity!

This shite is hardly as deranged as her counterparts in *Izutsu* and *Matsukaze*. Her sad longing has not so much distorted her senses as sharpened them—an ironic fact considering that *Hanjo* is a full-fledged mad-woman play. Nevertheless, there is more than mere archness in her comment that she hides the moon; her perceptions are not normal, but heightened by emotional distraction, and to some degree at least this gives her an element of furyū. One finds similar use of noriji in *Kinuta* and *Sekidera Komachi*, two plays that can reasonably be attributed to Zeami.[41]

Hanjo and *Higaki* are balanced differently from the plays discussed so far. The major narrative in both comes only after the shite has made a first appearance and then left the stage to appear again later. The shite's first appearance, then, merely serves to set the scene, and the important kuri-sashi-kuse sequence we observed before the aikyōgen interlude of the more orthodox *Izutsu*, *Takasago*, and *Yumi Yawata* comes almost immediately before the dance in these two plays. Indeed, in both *Hanjo* and *Higaki* the major portion of the ha as well as the kyū comes only after the shite has reappeared, having once left the stage.* This is easy to see in Table 9, which compares the functions of the shōdan in the latter half of *Higaki* with the shōdan of dan 2-5 of *Yumi Yawata*. The overall sequence

---

* *Hanjo*, in fact, contains something like dan 1 of a more orthodox play after the shite's reappearance, as we shall shortly see.

TABLE 9 *The Shōdan Sequences of Yumi Yawata and Higaki Compared by Function*

Yumi Yawata (Dan 2-5)	Higaki (latter half)	Function
Dan 2		
SHINNOISSEI	NARAINOISSEI	Shite's entrance
Issei	X	
Sashi	*Sashi	Lyric monologue
Sageuta	*Kuri	
Ageuta	Uta	
Dan 3		
Mondō		
Kakeai	Kakeai	Interaction between waki and shite
Ageuta	Shidai	
Dan 4		
Sasoizerifu		
Kuri	Kuri	
Sashi	Sashi	Narrative sequence
Kuse	Kuse	
Rongi	Susoguse	
Aikyōgen part		
Dan 5		
DEHA		Nochijite's entrance
Sashi		
Issei	Ei	Introduction to dance
Noriji		
KAMIMAI	JONOMAI	Dance
	Waka	
	X	Closing
Rongi	Uta	

NOTE: The shōdan in small caps are instrumental pieces, including dances. X indicates an unspecified shōdan, and an asterisk indicates that a shōdan is irregular.

of dramatic events, the dramatic contours of the two plays, are in the end very similar despite various minor differences.

Hanjo at first seems to differ quite strikingly from the *Yumi Yawata* pattern. This is in large part because it is a genzai play. Its first six shōdan, for one thing, have no counterpart in any of the plays we have studied so far. They are designed merely to set the play in context. Similarly, the last three shōdan allow for the reconciliation of the shite and her long-lost lover, and have no counterpart in the mugen plays studied so far. An important similarity between *Hanjo* and those plays, however, can be discerned in the other shōdan. Beginning with the shidai, the play falls into basically the same five-dan structure we have become familiar with. From that piece through the tsukizerifu, we find a rough equivalent of the first dan of a more standard play. The ISSEI, *sashi, and KAKERI sequence of the next dan is somewhat unusual, but the issei-sashi-sageuta-ageuta sequence that follows is structurally identical with the second dan of *Yumi Yawata*, and *Unoha*, and very similar to the same dan of *Izutsu*. More important, it fulfills the same function of psychological description as the second dan of a more formally orthodox play. And thereafter the play's shōdan sequences, with only some minor differences, follow the standard pattern. In sum, what we find in *Hanjo* is basically a formally regular play with the addition of a kind of prelude and coda.[42] As in *Higaki*, the main narrative comes in the second half. This feature is common in plays in the Martial Mode and will be covered in some detail in the next chapter.

Zeami uses many of the same rhetorical techniques in the plays in the Woman's Mode as he uses in the plays in the Aged Mode. Renga-like association, for example, is employed to great advantage in the plays under study. We saw several examples in the analysis of *Izutsu*. Another vivid example is to be found in the first half of the kuse of *Higaki*:

Kuse

1	C	Tsurube no kakenawa,
		Kurikaeshi uki inishie mo,
		Kōka no haru no ashita,
		Kōyō no aki no yūgure mo,
5		Ichijit'n no yume to haya narinu,
		Kōgan no yosōi,
		Bujo no homare no ito semete,
		Sa mo utsukushiki kōgan no,
		Hisui no kazura hana shiroi,
10		Katsura no mayu mo shimo furite,
		Mizu ni utsuru omokage,
		Rōsui kage shizunde,
		Midori ni mieshi kurokami wa,
		Dosui no mokuzu chiri akuta,
15		Kawarikeru,
		Mi no arisama zo kanashiki. . . .[43]

Kuse

1	C	The rope on the well bucket winds round and round
		Like the time wound painfully out since yesteryear.
		Spring mornings with their scarlet blossoms,
		Autumn dusks with scarlet leaves,
5		They've all become the dreams of a single night.
		The scarlet cheeks made up so fair
		Were a dancer's pride, so enchanting,
		Yes, those scarlet cheeks;
		But my once opalescent hair has lost the bloom of youth
10		And frost has fallen on my eyebrows, once as delicate as the crescent moon.

173

My reflection on the water sinks away,
Foundered in the frail decrepitude of age,
My tresses, once blue-black, hang
Dull and drab like litter drowned in mud.
15 This being of mine,
So changed, so pitiful. . . .

Associations such as *haru no ashita*, "spring mornings," and *aki no yūgure*, "autumn dusks," made with opposites arranged in parallel couplets, or *hisui no kazura*, "opalescent hair," and *katsura no mayu*, "eyebrows delicate as the crescent moon," made with homonyms, are clever and effective, but not particularly remarkable given the similar associations seen earlier. In lines 3-8 at the beginning of the passage, however, the progression *kōka*, "scarlet blossoms," *kōyō*, "scarlet leaves," *kōgan*, "scarlet cheeks," *kōgan*, "scarlet cheeks" (again), is a short catalogue of red things reminiscent of the monozukushi of early noh. It appears, however, not merely for its verbal interest (like many of the catalogues in early noh), but also for its thematic value. The rich sensuousness of these bright-red images, combined with the opalescence and blue-black sheen of hair in the middle of the passage, provides a wonderfully effective contrast with the colorlessness of the last lines. This technique is not qualitatively different from the renga-like associations pointed to earlier, but is more striking because the associations are not made through convention-blessed word categories from the elite poetic tradition, but are made through associations found in the popular catalogue form. Moreover, the associations contribute to the whole in a way most of the catalogues in pre-Zeami noh do not.

The shite's first ageuta in *Taema* provides yet another example of mastery of rhetorical technique fully integrated into thematic content:

Ageuta (cont.)
1　S　Tamatama kono shō ni ukamazu wa,
　　　Mata itsu no yo o matsu no to no,
　　　Akureba idete kururu made,
　　　Nori no niwa ni majiru nari,
5　　　Minori no niwa ni majiru nari.

Ageuta (cont.)
1　C　Had my soul not floated up by karma's chance to this, my present
　　　　incarnation,
　　　Then in what world would I find the pine-branch door
　　　I pass through to the dawning day
　　　To stay until night falls in the garden of the Law?
5　　　To stay until night falls in the garden of the Good Law?

Here Zeami ties four lines together through the use of three kakekotoba and two renga-like associations. The kakekotoba are *itsu no yo/yo o matsu*, "in what world"/"wait through the night"; *yo o matsu/matsu no to*, "wait through the night/pine-branch door"; and *yo o . . . akureba/to no akureba*, "wait (until dawn)"/"open the door." The renga-like associations are *akureba*, "dawn breaks," with *kururu*, "night falls," and *matsu no to*, "pine-branch door," with *niwa*, "garden." The result is a passage that at one and the same time creates a picture of the shite coming out of a hut into the garden to spend the day and makes a statement about the fortunate soul whose incarnation as a human provides a chance for enlightenment.

Countless other examples of Zeami's rhetorical mastery are to be found in the plays in the Woman's Mode, but an enumeration of them will not change the results of this investigation. It is time, then, to turn away from Zeami's plays in this mode to take a brief look at those written by other playwrights. We begin, as before, with Zeami's father. In this case we have more room for comparison than we had in examining the plays in the Aged Mode, since Kannami is known to have had a hand in the creation of such masterpieces of the genre as *Matsukaze*, *Eguchi*, and *Motomezuka*. The problem now is not a lack of material for comparison, but the fact that all of Kannami's works passed through Zeami's hands, and he apparently felt no compunction at all about revising them for his own ends in any given performance. Thus, it is certain that he composed at least part of *Matsukaze*. *Eguchi* too, although it was once considered Kannami's play by even the most rigorous scholars, has been reexamined within the past few years, with the result that much of it is now thought to be Zeami's work.[44] The attribution of *Motomezuka* to Kannami has also been challenged, but it still remains the best play for examination at this point in our investigation.[45]

The honzetsu of the play is the story of the Maid of Unai, known to the modern reader from *Man'yōshū* and *Yamato monogatari*.[46] It relates how a young woman of marriageable age has two suitors and cannot choose between them. In their competition for her hand, the suitors agree to shoot at the same target, a mandarin duck in a nearby river, to determine which will win the maiden. But as it happens, both archers hit the bird simultaneously. In her distress at still being unable to choose, the maiden drowns herself. She is buried on the banks of the river, after which, according to the version of the story used in the play, the two suitors come to blows at the foot of her tomb and kill each other.[47]

This story is told by the shite in the first half of the play, providing its narrative center. The shite then disappears, the aikyōgen comes on stage for an interlude, and once again the shite appears, this time in her true form. She is now the spirit of the Maid of Unai suffering the torments of hell for having caused the death of her two lovers and the mandarin duck. This is a familiar structure for a noh play, but we have left something out of our discussion up to this point. Just after the shite makes her first appearance on stage, she and the tsure who accompanies her sing a long series of lyrics about picking spring shoots on the fields of Ikuta. The name Ikuta means "Living Field," and seems bitterly ironic given the plot, but the rest of the passage seems unrelated to the play as a whole and creates a disturbing disunity. Kannami, it seems, chose to include a song of purely verbal interest in the play; consequently, the first part does not quite seem to belong with the rest. The structure and shō-dan sequence reflect this. After a standard first, second, and third dan,[48] one finds a sageuta and a rongi. The rongi is a *wakanazukushi*, or "catalogue of young shoots." This is reminiscent of the rongi of *Unoha* and the first part of the kuse of *Higaki*, both of which are catalogue songs of a sort, but in the Zeami plays, the catalogues are integrated satisfactorily with the honzetsu. This is not the case with *Motomezuka*.[49]

In terms of structure, the second half of *Motomezuka* deviates from the standard pattern in many ways. Most important, it lacks an instrumental dance altogether. There is, to be sure, a good deal of dancing, but it is all accompanied by vocal as well as instrumental music, and is highly mimetic. The act is a vivid depiction of the sufferings of the Maid of Unai in hell; this part of the play is extremely moving and brilliantly constructed, but it is unlike the last half of any Zeami play in the Woman's Mode,[50] and seems to have contributed more to the development of the Martial Mode than the Woman's Mode.

Motomezuka seems to lack thematic unity when seen in the light of Zeami's most successful plays in the Woman's Mode. This is indeed the case with many of Kannami's plays when we look for artistic integration in them. Any number of carefully constructed poetic passages can be found, but they often seem to have been inserted into a particular play for their cleverness, not because they are thematically appropriate. This seems a defect in the literary quality of some of his works, but we should not forget that much of Kannami's success as an actor came as the result of his great versatility, and what we see as a lack of integration may have been the perfect vehicle for his variety-show mentality. On the other hand, probably all the plays attributed to Kannami have been through numerous revisions and dismemberments. Perhaps a unity once present is now lost. Whatever the case, there are many questions about Kannami's influence on his son that must await further research. Among the more intriguing is what part Kannami played in the development of mugen noh. The authorship of *Eguchi* is open to question, and *Matsukaze* owes its present structure to Zeami, so if it were not for *Motomezuka* (and *Kayoi Komachi*) there would be very little reason to doubt that the mugen noh was entirely Zeami's invention.[51]

What influence Kannami had on Zeami's rhetoric is difficult to say. The rongi from *Unoha* and the first part of the kuse in *Higaki* are cer-

tainly developments from the catalogue song, and as has been demon-
strated, Kannami was very adept at such songs. What about the lyric pas-
sages with their streams of association that figure so importantly in
Zeami's plays? It is tempting to assume that they were born of contact
with renga through Yoshimoto and his literary acquaintances. On occa-
sion, however, one finds passages in Kannami's plays that show the same
use of association to move the text in combination with a high degree of
lyricism. A good example is the sashi from *Matsukaze*, a passage Zeami
unequivocally attributes to his father, which occupies the same structural
position in that play as "Sanaki dani" and "Tare o ka mo" do in *Izutsu* and
Takasago.[52]

If the distinction between father and son is not always easy to see in
the case of Kannami and Zeami, it is clear enough in the case of Zeami
and *his* son, Motomasa. There are no mugen plays confidently attribut-
able to Motomasa, and even if one takes monogurui, so-called mad-
woman plays, into consideration, only one play appears relevant to this
discussion: *Sumidagawa*. And even then one finds little ground for com-
parison; *Sumidagawa* contains no kuri-sashi-kuse, no instrumental dance
at the end of the play, and in fact very little dance at all. The climax
comes not through highly charged lyric apprehension on the part of the
shite, but through a tragic, or perhaps I should say pathetic, encounter
between a mother and the insubstantial, unreachable ghost of her child.*

Zeami had the highest regard for Motomasa's potential as an actor,
and presumably as a writer as well. Nevertheless, the father's artistic in-
fluence is much more easily seen in the son-in-law, Konparu Zenchiku,
than in the son, Motomasa—assuming, that is, that our examples are in-
deed Zenchiku's. For once again we have to rely on slim evidence in at-
tributing the plays to be examined—*Bashō*, *Teika*, *Yōkihi*, and *Tamaka-
zura*—to Zenchiku.[53] (For convenience, let us accept him as the author
without qualification.)

The subjects Zenchiku selected for these four plays could have been
treated in a great many ways, but he chose to depict them in a mono-
chromatic, sad and pessimistic manner that seems to owe more to the

* An anecdote in *Sarugaku dangi* about this play perhaps best illustrates the aesthetic
difference between father and son. Motomasa designed the play with the intention of hav-
ing a child actor actually appear on stage as the dead child's ghost. Zeami allowed that such
an appearance might succeed, and that one would not know for certain until it had been
tried. But he thought the noh would be more interesting without any representation of the
ghost at all. He preferred, in other words, to have the audience's attention focused exclu-
sively on the deranged shite chasing after a dead child who remained invisible to the other
characters and the audience. This would make the play more like *Izutsu* and *Matsukaze*. To-
day, the play is almost always done as Motomasa wished and sometimes it is extremely mov-
ing. More often, however, the child actor's presence calls forth a kind of banal sentimental-
ity totally inappropriate to the play ("Oh, look, that's Rokurō *sensei*'s little boy. Isn't he
darling! And what a good little trouper to put up with that costume for so long!").

aesthetic of Yoshimasa's age than to the earlier Muromachi period. *Teika* explores the tormented souls of Princess Shokushi and Fujiwara no Teika, considered lovers according to popular tradition. *Bashō* centers on the fragility of the plantain, or bashō plant. *Tamakazura* treats in a vague, unsatisfying way the character of the same name from *Genji monogatari*. *Yōkihi*, which takes the ghost of the Chinese siren Yang Gui-fei as its heroine, is the best case in point. With such a subject, the play could have been almost gaudily sensuous and colorful, but Zenchiku had other ideas, and even though he sets the play in the Taoist paradise of the Isles of Peng-lai, the shite hardly appears as a carefree immortal. She is instead inseparably attached to her unreachable love and obsessed with the law that all who meet must part. The narrative center of the play deals with decay, not the delights of paradise, and in the final scene the shite does not disappear into the air, but collapses in a distraction of longing on her jeweled dais in paradise.

Zeami too deals with the themes of longing and sadness, but it is difficult to imagine him trying to treat these emotions from the viewpoint of a character who dwells in the Isles of the Blessed. This fact points to a frequently mentioned characteristic of Zenchiku's, his inability or lack of desire to clearly delineate the honzetsu of his plays. As Yokomichi puts it: "Works connected with Zenchiku do not have a clear theme running through them as Zeami's plays do. He characteristically depicts things as if seen through a veil."[54]

Even Zenchiku's best play, *Teika*—and it is a very great play indeed—exhibits this characteristic; yet somehow in this case, it seems not to detract from the play but to add to it. The play begins at dusk in the chilling drizzle of early winter. The waki, a priest come to the capital, finds himself at the Shigure (i.e., "chilling drizzle") Pavilion built by the famous poet Teika. The shite appears and tells the priest about the pavilion, then asks him to come with her to a nearby gravesite. Once there, the priest finds the gravestone so choked by vines that he cannot see who is buried there. After informing him that it is the grave of Princess Shokushi, the shite relates the story of Shokushi's love affair with Teika, emphasizing the pain and shame it caused. She also tells him how Teika's undying attachment to Shokushi turned into a creeping vine after her death and coiled around her tombstone. Then the shite admits that she is the ghost of Princess Shokushi and disappears. In the second half of the play, the ghost of the princess returns in response to the prayers of the waki. There is an exchange about the universality of salvation and, in anticipation of that salvation, the princess tries to recreate in dance some of the beauty she had in life. Her beauty cannot be recreated, and ultimately she can only turn back to her grave, which stands, as before, strangled with vines.

Structurally, *Teika* follows the general five-dan pattern of the typical Zeami play. There are important variations, however. The second dan, for instance, instead of providing a lyric monologue like that in *Izutsu* or *Takasago*, begins with a mondō between the waki and the shite concerning the Shigure Pavilion. This mondō leads to the chorus's first ageuta, with the same sort of carefully proportioned movement one often finds in Zeami's third dan. But since the play's honzetsu, the love affair between Teika and Shokushi, has not yet been mentioned, the entry of the chorus cannot prepare the audience for the narrative center of the play (the kuri-sashi-kuse sequence), as it would in a Zeami play, but must serve as a bridge to the introduction of the honzetsu. Thus, following the chorus's ageuta we find another mondō, and there, after two exchanges with the waki, the shite begins to tell the story of Teika and Princess Shokushi. This then leads to the kuri-sashi-kuse sequence, where the narrative is completed. Finally, in the rongi, just as in a typical Zeami play, the shite identifies herself and disappears.

There are several differences in the last dan of the play, too. Most striking is the ending. The play's last shōdan is a noriji. (*Bashō* and *Yōkihi* also end with a noriji; *Tamakazura* ends with a chūnoriji.) We have already seen that Zeami uses the noriji for the appearance of nonhuman furyū characters or characters in the grip of some sort of aesthetic derangement or illusion. In *Teika*, on the other hand, the noriji appears when the shite *fails* to create the illusion she intends:

Noriji

1	s	Omona no mai no,
		Arisama ya na,
	c	Omona ya omohayu no,
		Arisama ya na,
5	s	Moto yori kono mi wa,
	c	Tsuki no kaobase mo,
	s	Kumorigachi ni,
	c	Katsura no mayuzumi mo,
	s	Ochibururu namida no,
10	c	Tsuyu to kiete mo,
		Tsutana ya tsuta no ha no,
		Kazuragi no kamisugata,
		Hazukashi ya yoshi na ya,
		Yoru no chigiri no,
15		Yume no uchi ni to,
		Aritsuru tokoro ni,
		Kaeru wa kuzu no ha no,
		Moto no gotoku,
		Haimatowaruru ya,
20		Teika kazura,
		Haimatowaruru ya,
		Teika kazura no,

Hakanaku mo,
Katachi wa uzumorete,

25   Usenikeri.[55]

Noriji

1 s   A shameful sight,
        My dancing figure,

    c   So shameful that
        I cannot hold my head upright.

5 s   This body before you

    c   Once had a face that shone like the moon,

    s   But now the moon is clouded,

    c   My crescent eyebrows sparse,

    s   Matted with tears.

10 c   Even though my life is gone, like morning dew by midday,
        I come here, bound in clinging vines, a wretched sight,
        The image of the ugly god of Kazuragi.
        So shameful and so useless!
        The night's pledge between us

15   Is accomplished only in dreams,
        So now I go back where I was,
        There among the leafy creepers,
        Just as before
        Strangled

20   By the Teika vines,
        Strangled by
        The Teika vines
        Grow round the gravestone while this insubstantial
        Ghostly figure's buried there below

25   And disappears.

In the Zeami plays we have looked at, the music changes from ōnori rhythm to tadautai rhythm (in an uta or rongi) as the shite's perceptions return to normal, but in *Teika*, the shite fails to create the illusion she wants, and the play ends with ōnori rhythm, which serves to intensify the inescapable suffering of her reality. The great actor Kanze Hisao held that the use of ōnori to end a play is characteristic of Zenchiku and contended that this was consistent with his ideas about the cyclical nature of noh.[56] I am not qualified to speak to this point, but I do think there is an obvious difference in the use of this particular shōdan in the works of Zeami and Zenchiku studied here. This observation requires us to consider a play that I have been at pains to avoid mentioning so far, *Nonomiya*.

The shōdan sequence of *Nonomiya* is identical to that of *Izutsu* until the last dan. Some scholars, looking at the similarity, argue that the work must be Zeami's; others point to the disparity as evidence that it is not.[57] There is something to be said for both sides of the argument, but it becomes obvious in studying the two sides that the shōdan lineup alone cannot resolve this controversy. One telling feature of the play, however, is that the fifth dan ends with a noriji. In purely structural terms, this makes *Nonomiya* much more like *Teika*, *Bashō*, and *Yōkihi* than *Izutsu*, *Higaki*, *Matsukaze*, and *Unoha*.

The last few words of *Nonomiya* also seem to place it among Zenchiku's works. *Izutsu*, *Higaki*, *Matsukaze*, *Unoha*, and *Taema* all end with either the dissolving of the dream of the final dan or a request for prayer; the last lines of these plays all impart a sense of release. But *Teika*, *Bashō*, and *Yōkihi* all close in concentration on a specific image: *Teika* on the gravestone wrapped in creeping vines, *Bashō* on the ripped leaves of the bashō plant, and *Yōkihi* on the pathetic figure of Yang Gui-fei's ghost prostrate and weeping on her jeweled dais. Although in modern performance the final line of *Nonomiya* varies (the Kanze and Hōshō texts have *kataku no kado*, "the gate of the burning house"; the Kongo text has *kataku no kado o*, "[out of] the gate of the burning house"; and the Kita and Konparu texts have only *kataku*, "the burning house"[58]), these differences seem minor. In all versions the focus at the end is, as in Zenchiku's plays, on a single image. This feature suggests that Zeami did not write *Nonomiya*. At the same time, the structure of the play clearly places it in what Konishi Jin'ichi calls "the Zeami group." If it was not written by Zenchiku, then it might well be the work of one of Zeami's sons, maybe Motoyoshi.[59]

Zenchiku was a highly literate man who counted among his acquaintances such cultured men as the scholar Ichijō Kanera, the last great classical waka poet Shōtetsu, and the ordination priest of Tōdaiji Temple, Shingyoku.[60] He had more than a passing familiarity with Zen, Neo-Confucianism, and the other intellectual currents of his day, and this is reflected in his treatises, which are held by many to be more philosophically comprehensive and consistent than Zeami's. Like Zeami, Zenchiku was familiar with renga and participated in renga gatherings himself. For this reason one might expect to find a frequent use of renga-like association in his plays, and indeed that technique is apparent in the passage from *Teika* quoted above. There is, nevertheless, a more explanatory, less evocative character to his writing than to Zeami's. By way of illustration, recall the lyrical monologue in the second dan of *Izutsu*, with its string of associations, and contrast this with the replacement in the second dan of *Teika*—a prosaic question-and-answer session about the Shigure Pavilion.

In Zenchiku's plays, one finds, if anything, more use of waka than in Zeami's. There are quotations of or allusions to at least eight waka in the kuri-sashi-kuse sequence alone in *Teika*.[61] Sometimes, in fact, it seems that Zenchiku is trying to substitute quantity for quality, and we find nothing like Zeami's repeated use of a few highly resonant poems, with the rich accumulation of meaning that is so affecting in *Izutsu*.[62] Zenchiku's breadth of knowledge seems to have gotten in the way here. This is even more apparent when he is bent on demonstrating his knowledge of Chinese literature. As Yokomichi notes, the play *Bashō* suffers because of ill-considered and unexplained allusions to *Lie zi* and to a certain story about Wang Wei painting a bashō plant in the snow.[63]

Another prominent feature of Zenchiku's style is a predilection for head rhymes and other word music such as assonance and alliteration. These are found in the works of other writers as well, but not with the frequency of, for example, the noriji from *Teika*. There he writes *omona/ omona/omohayu* and *tsutana ya/tsuta no*. In the kuse of the same play I find *adashi/ada naru*, as well as *otome/todome*, and *kokoro zo/morotomo*.

Of all the noh playwrights, Zenchiku is probably the closest to Zeami stylistically, yet he seems to have preferred darker, gloomier subject matter and to have paid less attention to the creative hierarchy of shu, saku, and sho than his father-in-law. The first characteristic places Zenchiku in the mainstream of the monochromatic artistic world of Higashiyama aesthetics, the world of Sōgi and Sesshū. The second seems to have weighed his plays down; they labor under heavily allusive texts that impede the development of the drama and stagnate in over-long, difficult, and ornamented passages.

The major playwrights of the next generations, Nobumitsu, Nagatoshi, Zenpō, and even the earlier (?) Miyamasu, do not seem to have written plays with anything like the aesthetic focus of Zeami's and Zenchiku's noh. Their works are usually plot-centered, and frequently the shite is either some sort of demon or a living warrior out to avenge the death of a relative. Since they seem to have found the Woman's Mode uncongenial, they are best discussed in connection with the last of Zeami's Three Modes, the Martial Mode, the subject of the next chapter.

CHAPTER 5

Guntai:
The Martial Mode

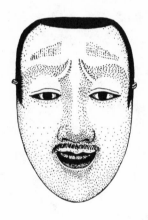

THERE ARE sixteen noh plays in the Martial Mode in the current repertory, all classified as "second-category plays" (*nibanmemono*) or *shura* noh, warrior plays. Zeami states unequivocally that he wrote five of these: *Atsumori*, *Kiyotsune*, *Sanemori*, *Tadanori*, and *Yorimasa*.[1] He also mentions a play called *Yoshitsune*, known today as *Yashima*; it too is likely to be his composition. Of the remaining ten plays, six were traditionally attributed to him: *Ebira* (The Quiver), *Kanehira*, *Tamura*, *Tomoakira*, *Tomonaga*, and *Tsunemasa*. *Michimori*, Zeami says, was written by one Seiami (or Iami) and revised by Zeami. The remaining three plays, *Ikarikazuki* (Shouldering an Anchor), *Ikuta Atsumori* (Atsumori at Ikuta), and *Shunzei Tadanori* (Shunzei and Tadanori), appear to be the work of later playwrights.

There is such consistency and continuity in the classification of these plays throughout the five-and-one-half centuries since Zeami's death, that Zeami's classification "Martial Mode" can be translated into today's "shura noh" without misrepresenting or distorting either term. This fact reveals a sort of generic stability not present in the plays in the other two modes, and suggests an interesting hypothesis about the plays in the Martial Mode: they were created and perfected by Zeami, and his successors had either too little success or too little interest in them to develop the genre further. The accuracy of this thesis will be tested after an examination of several of these plays.

Zeami has this to say about the "shura" role in *Fūshikaden*:

This too is one of the objects of dramatic imitation. Even though you perform the role well, there is little of interest in it. It should not be performed often. However, if you take a famous character from the Genji or the Heike and bring out the connection between him and poetry and music, then—so long as the play itself is well written—it will be more interesting than anything else. It should contain some particularly colorful places.

Among the energetic movements of the *shura* of this genre, there are some that verge on demonic animation and there are others that are close to dance. If the piece reflects the style of the Kusemai, then dancelike movements are appropriate. The character should carry a sword and wear a quiver, and these weapons should lend the role dignity. You should inquire into the way to hold them and use them so that you can manipulate them correctly. Be very careful to distinguish which places are appropriate for demonic movement and which for dancelike movement.[2]

The famous characters from the Genji and the Heike to which Zeami refers are warriors who made their names in the twelfth-century battles between those two clans. Zeami saw great dramatic potential in such characters when they were treated in a poetic and musical manner. Why, then, does he begin the article with the puzzling statement that the role of shura offers little of interest even when performed well?

The word shura is a shortened Sino-Japanese transliteration for the Sanskrit *asura*, a term designating spirits mad with jealous rage and doomed to constant battle. Among the warriors consigned to this existence are those titans who assault the heavenly kingdoms of Brahmadeva and Śakra-devānām Indra, two guardians of the Buddhist universe.[3] In Zeami's view, these shura are demon-hearted demons who are terrifying rather than interesting when accurately portrayed.* Consequently, he discourages his heirs from portraying them, promoting instead human-hearted shura, that is, the heroes of the Genpei wars, further softening and civilizing them with the graces of poetry and music. Already, then, in *Fūshikaden*, Zeami sees "the warrior" as a master of the arts as well as war.

In his article on the Martial Mode in *Sandō*, Zeami seems to assume this basis for characterization, although he does not say so outright, concentrating instead on technical matters in the construction of the plays:

The configuration of a play in the Martial Mode. If, for example, the play is to be created around a famous general of the Genji or the Heike, you should take special care to write the story just as it appears in *Heike monogatari*.

You should also plan the musical proportions and arrangement of the five *dan*. Moreover, if the *shite* is to leave the stage part way through the play to reappear later in a different guise, then the *kusemai* and so on should be set in the latter half of the play. In this way, the *ha* runs over into the *kyū*. Such a noh may also be written in six *dan*, or again, if the *shite* does not leave the stage, it may be written in four *dan*. It depends on the particular play. The first half of the play should be abbreviated and written to be as short as possible.

The characteristics of a play in the Martial Mode vary considerably according to the *honzetsu*, and there is no single specific way to write it. Musical passages should be brief, and in the *kyū*, the *shite* should make his exit in *chūnori* of the

---

* Zeami does not seem to have had much regard for the entertainment potential of terror. Although he was still speaking in positive terms of the portrayal of demons as late as 1428 (in *Shūgyoku tokka*), what he had reference to was not true demon-hearted demons, but demons with the hearts of men. Zeami came increasingly to exclude true demons and titanic shura from the subject matter he considered proper to noh. There are, nonetheless, several plays that very successfully treat the great battles of these cosmic shura, including *Shari*, *Daie*, and *Dairokuten*.

shura style. In certain cases, it is appropriate to portray a character with de-monic fury. The melody should be heroic and complex. When he appears dressed as a warrior, the *shite* should definitely make a self-introduction. Take care in writing it.[4]

This article falls somewhere between the one on the Aged Mode and the one on the Woman's Mode in its degree of specificity. Although not as detailed as the article on the Aged Mode, with its exact measurements for dan and prescriptions for the sequence of shōdan, neither is it as ab-stract as the article on the Woman's Mode, which says almost nothing about structure. A play in the Martial Mode is more directly reliant on its original source than plays in the other two modes. This is partly because the plays in the Martial Mode are typically more narrative in nature than those plays; that characteristic will become apparent later. Even at this point, however, the close connection between the mode and its source is obvious, witness Zeami's caution to take "special care to write the story just as it appears in *Heike monogatari*."

The comment about calculating the arrangement of the dan and measuring the length of the music does not seem any more significant than Zeami's other frequent reminders to be aware of the structure and

Fig. 13   Illustration for plays in the Martial Mode from a 1441 manuscript of Zeami's *Nikyoku santai ningyōzu*. "The Martial Mode. Make strength the basis [of your acting] and infuse your movements with subtlety." *Courtesy of the Noh Theater Research Institute, Hosei University.*

length of a play, but the recommendation that the kusemai come in the second act of the play is important. This obviously changes the narrative balance of the play, and is the reason why such plays as *Tadanori*, *Yorimasa*, *Yashima*, and *Sanemori* are put in the Martial Mode category instead of the Aged Mode; for even though the maejite in each case is an old man, not a warrior, the shite is a warrior in the play's narrative center. The placement of the kusemai in the second half often changes the number of dan in the play and has a direct effect on the type and length of any dance it may have. Usually, the only instrumental dances in plays in this mode are the short KAKERI or TACHIMAWARI, though long instrumental dances are not ruled out altogether; in both *Atsumori* and *Ikuta Atsumori* the shite dances a CHŪNOMAI or OTOKOMAI.[5]

The lack of a major dance in these plays is reflected in the *Nikyoku santai ningyōzu* article on the Martial Mode, as well. Unlike the previously mentioned articles in that brief work, the article on the Martial Mode is accompanied by just one sketch—an endearingly clumsy picture of a man with froglike legs wearing only a loincloth and a hat and carrying a sword and a fan (Fig. 13). Brief notes beneath the sketch state: "This is the Martial Mode, but since a concern for elegant sensibility persists, it ought to retain the last blossoms of the child's training in the Two Arts. Be certain that you completely understand how to handle the mode: make strength the basis of your acting and infuse your movements with subtlety. Get a firm grasp on the physical and mental disposition of the character from the sketch."[6]

It would be difficult to choose a single play to analyze from among Zeami's many fine noh in the Martial Mode, but fortunately he does the job for us, commenting in *Sarugaku dangi*: "The three plays *Michimori*, *Tadanori*, and *Yoshitsune* [i.e. *Yashima*] are good plays in the *shura* style. Among these, *Tadanori* is probably of the highest flower."[7] (Still, much as Zeami esteems *Tadanori* among the plays in the Martial Mode, he does not single it out as the most "straightforward" of those plays, a distinction that he awards to *Michimori*.[8])

Tadanori opens with a five-shōdan sequence, beginning with a shidai by the waki and the wakitsure:

Shidai
1   w/wt   Hana o mo ushi to sutsuru mi no,
              Hana o mo ushi to sutsuru mi no,
              Tsuki ni mo kumo wa itowaji.

Nanori
     w   Kore wa Shunzei no miuchi ni arishi mono nite sōrō,
5   Sate mo Toshinari nakunarasetamaite nochi,
           Kayō no sugata to narite sōrō,

Mata Saikoku o mizu sōrō hodo ni,
Saikoku angya to kokorozashite sōrō.

Sashi

Seinan no rikiu ni omomuki miyako o hedatsuru Yamazaki ya,
10   w/wт   Sekido no shuku wa na nomi shite,
Tomari mo hatenu tabi no narai,
Uki mi wa itsu mo majiwari no,
Chiri no ukiyo no Akutagawa,
Ina no ozasa o wakesugite.

Sageuta
15   Tsuki mo yado karu Koya no ike,
Minasoko kiyoku suminashite.

Ageuta

Ashi no hawake no kaze no oto,
Ashi no hawake no kaze no oto,
Kikaji to suru ni uki koto no,
20   Sutsuru mi made mo Arimayama,
Kakurekanetaru yo no naka no.
Uki ni kokoro wa adayume no,
Samuru makura ni kane tōki,
Naniwa wa ato ni Naruogata,
25   Okinami tōki obune kana,
Okinami tōki obune kana.[9]

Shidai
1   w/wт   One weary of the flowers casts it all away,
One weary of the flowers casts it all away,
He doesn't care if clouds eclipse the moon.

Nanori
      w   I am a man who was in the service of Lord Shunzei,
5   But now that he has passed away,
I have come to this.
I have never seen the west country,
So now I set out on a westward pilgrimage.

Sashi

We make our way toward the southern palace, past Yamazaki,
     parted from the capital by hills.
10   w/wт   The lodging house at Sekido remains in name alone,
We pass it without resting; our traveling by its nature never ends.
This weary world of dust pervades our wearied being,
And we cross the littered river Akuta,
To file through bamboo grass at Ina,

Sageuta
15   There, in Koya pond, the moon itself finds humble lodgings,
Radiating clarity throughout the water's depths.

Ageuta

The rustling breeze blows over leaves of reeds,
The rustling breeze blows over leaves of reeds—
A sound I had resolved I would not hear, yet this troubled murmur
20   Makes itself heard even here; and though I leave the world behind,
I cannot hide away. It's always there, even in the hills of Arima.

My heart aggrieved by insubstantial dreams
I wake; a bell tolls far away.
Leaving Naniwa I come to Naruo Bay.
25   A fisher's skiff floats far out on the open sea,
A fisher's skiff floats far out on the open sea.

This shōdan sequence is not fundamentally different from the sequences in the first dan of *Takasago* and *Izutsu*, though it is longer and more gradually modulated.[10] But Zeami pays much more attention to the waki in this passage than he accords to the waki in those two plays, and this is a feature that carries over to other plays in the mode as well. Where the waki in *Izutsu* is nameless and unobtrusive, and the waki in *Takasago*, although he is given an identity, is emotionally opaque (a fittingly "straightforward" expression of uncomplicated auspiciousness), the waki here is not only given an identity, as one of Shunzei's retainers, but also portrayed in some depth. As a retainer of the great twelfth-century poet, the waki is himself connected to poetry.[11] He is now masterless, however, because Shunzei is dead. He has taken the tonsure and, as he says, left the world behind. This should imply a total commitment to the way of Buddha. Indeed, in the shidai, the waki forswears artistic ambition by denying attachment to the two natural phenomena most dear to the heart of the classical Japanese poet, the moon and flowers (specifically, cherry blossoms). A few lines later, however, he readily admits that the "weary world of dust pervades [his] wearied being," and when he comes to Koya pond, he cannot help noticing the moon's reflection on the face of the water. His resolution not to hear the wind rustling sadly across the leaves (at Naniwa?[12]) is a concession to his abiding poetic sensibility. As he says, he cannot escape, and the bell tolling (with the Buddhist message) is far away indeed. In fact, as soon as he arrives at Suma, the setting for the play, he goes off to see a flowering cherry.

The introduction of the play's theme—the conflict between poetic sensibility and the desire for Buddhist release—at this early stage works to make the first dan much more dynamic emotionally than the first dan of either *Takasago* or *Izutsu*. A lyrically charged context for the play is created even before the shite appears. Perhaps this accounts for the length of the dan and the inclusion of a sashi-sageuta-ageuta sequence, so frequently found in other lyric contexts in Zeami's plays.

The shite, an old woodcutter, makes his entrance in the next dan, coming on stage to the ISSEI to deliver the following monologue:

Sashi
27   S   Ge ni yo o wataru narai tote,
Kaku uki waza ni mo korizu ma no,
Kumanu toki dani shioki o hakobeba,
30   Hosedomo hima wa naregoromo no,
Urayama kakete Suma no umi.

Issei

Ama no yobikoe hima naki ni,
Shiba naku chidori ne zo tōki.

*Sashi

Somosomo kono Suma no ura to mōsu wa,

35 Sabishiki yue ni sono na o uru,
Wakurawa ni tō hito araba Suma no ura ni,
Moshio taretsutsu wabu to kotae yo,
Ge ni ya isari no ama obune,
Moshio no kemuri matsu no kaze,

40 Izure ka sabishikarazu to iu koto naki.
Mata kono Suma no yamakage ni hitoki no sakura no sōro,
Kore wa aru hito no naki ato no shirushi no ki nari,
Kotosara toki shi mo haru no hana,
Tamuke no tame ni gyakuen nagara.

Sageuta

45 Ashibiki no,
Yama yori kaeru origoto ni,
Takigi ni hana o orisoete,
Tamuke o nashite kaeran,
Tamuke o nashite kaeran.

Sashi

27 s Making my way in this hard world
Leaves me not a moment's rest from wearying toil,
And when I am not dipping brine, I carry logs to burn.

30 Though I spread out my sea-soaked rags, there is no time for them
to dry.
I spend my days between the mountains and the sea at Suma shore.

Issei

The fishers' shouts are ceaseless;
The plovers' cries sound far away.

*Sashi

Ah yes, this Suma coast

35 Has gained its name from desolation:
"If, by chance, someone should ask for me,
Tell them that I live in lonely poverty on Suma coast, soaked
through with the brine."
How true! The little fishing boats,
The smoke of brine-soaked seagrass, wind rustling in the pines,

40 Which of these is anything but sad?
And in the shadows of the coastal hills there is a single cherry tree,
A tree standing in memory to someone.
Since this is the blossoming of spring
I will go make some offering there although it is but chance that
brings me.

Sageuta

45 Whenever I come back here
Footsore from the mountain path,
I always bring a branch of blossoms with my bundle of wood
To leave in offering before I go,
To leave in offering before I go.

Many of the features of this, the entire second dan of *Tadanori*, will be familiar to the reader already from the analyses of *Takasago* and *Izutsu*. The passage is a lyric monologue in which the shite gives voice to impressions of the external world and feelings about his inner world. The text is built by renga-like association as well as discursive logic. For example in lines 30-31, the kakekotoba *hima wa na(shi)/naregoromo*, "there is no time / sea-soaked rags," leads to *ura*, "lining." This is a homonym for *ura*, "coast," which in turn suggests *yama*, "mountain," and Suma, the place name. Suma is associated with *sumu*, "to live," by sound.

Much attention is devoted to the description of Suma, the setting for the play. Fishing boats are shown bobbing on the water, fishers' calls to one another stand out over the more distant plaintive cries of the plover; both of these punctuate the ceaseless soughing of the wind through coastal pines. Trails of smoke rise along the coast from fires kindled by the poor folk who eke out their existence in the arduous extraction of salt from sea water. These coastal peasants are among the few types of commoners whom Zeami permits to appear in noh. Their activities have a certain pastoral poetic value because they are associated with an aesthetically positive kind of loneliness, *sabi*.[13] Indeed the whole scene is so perfect an example of loneliness that the shite credits that loneliness with the very naming of the place, quoting a famous waka by Ariwara no Yukihira (818-93) as evidence.[14]

One new feature is the shite's complaint about the hard work he is required to do. Although the shite and the tsure in *Takasago* and the shite in *Izutsu* were both engaged in a sort of work—cleaning up around the base of a pine in the one case and carrying water for a religious offering in the other—they seemed to accept these tasks as a matter of course. But here the shite is left "not a moment's rest from wearying toil." This awareness of physical suffering in everyday activities is a common feature of noh in the Martial Mode. In the sageuta we see what transforms this suffering into beauty: a provocative contrast emerges between the shite who sweetens his labors with poetry and flowers, and the waki who professes to be trying to escape the snares of poetry for pure religious devotion.[15]

Formally, the second dan of *Tadanori* is regular in its gradual move from instrumental music (the ISSEI) through noncongruent song (the two sashi and the issei) to congruent song (the sageuta). The actual shōdan sequence, however, is somewhat idiosyncratic: one would have expected the issei to follow directly on the ISSEI; the second *sashi is musically a bit irregular (it mixes tsuyogin and yowagin, for one thing); and instead of the longer, more formally distinct ageuta typical of the end of these sections, one finds a short sageuta. None of these irregularities is really jarring. On the contrary, as Yokomichi so aptly puts it: "This play follows the established pattern of *mugen* noh for the most part, but attention to its specific parts reveals unique inventions in practically all the *dan*. This is an artfully constructed play."[16]

The third dan is unusually long. It opens with a mondō and an ageuta:

Mondō

50	w	Ika ni kore naru rōjin okoto wa kono yamagat'n nite mashimasu ka,
	s	Sanzōrō kono ura no ama nite sōro,
	w	Ama naraba ura ni koso sumu beki ni,
		Yama aru kata ni kayowan no ba,
		Yamabito to koso iu bekere,
55	s	Somo amabito no kumu shio oba yakade sono mama okisōrō beki ka,
	w	Ge ni ge ni kore wa kotowari nari,
		Moshio taku naru iukemuri,
	s	Taema o ososhi to shioki toru,
	w	Michi koso kaware satobanare no,
60	s	Hito oto mare ni Suma no ura,
	w	Chikaki ushiro no yamazato ni,

Ageuta

	s	Shiba to iu mono no sōraeba,
	c	Shiba to iu mono no sōraeba,
		Shioki no tame ni kayoi kuru,
65	s	Amari ni oroka naru,
		Osō no gojō kana ya na.
	c	Ge ni ya Suma no ura,
		Yo no tokoro ni ya kawaruran,
		Sore hana ni tsuraki wa
70		Mine no arashi ya yamaoroshi no,
		Oto o koso itoishi ni,
		Suma no wakaki no sakura wa,
		Umi sukoshi dani mo hedateneba,
		Kayō urakaze ni,
75		Yama no sakura mo chiru mono o.

Mondō

50	w	You there, old man, are you one of the mountain people from around here?
	s	Yes, I am one of the sea folk who live on this coast.
	w	One of the sea folk ought indeed to live on the coast,
		But someone who goes back and forth into the mountains
		Should be called one of the mountain people.
55	s	So then, do you think the sea folk should draw brine and simply leave it sitting!
	w	I see, I see. You have a point there.
		The trails of evening smoke that rise from fires kindled in the seaweed
	s	Must not be allowed to cease, so we hurry after firewood,
	w	Although the path leads far away from the sea.

60   s   There, too, the sounds of human voices are too few,
     w   In a village in the mountains just behind the Suma coast,
Ageuta
     s   They have something they call "brushwood."
     c   They have something they call "brushwood."
         And I go off there to bring it back to burn.
65   s   This priest's fine distinctions
         Make no sense in these surroundings,
     c   For the coast of Suma
         Is not like most places: As anybody knows,
         The bane of cherry blossoms is the gale off mountain peaks,
70   Or the gusts that race down mountainsides;
         Their very sound is hateful.
         But the young cherry on the coast of Suma
         Stands here just at seaside,
         And even in the coastal breeze
75   This mountain cherry scatters all its blossoms.

Shunzei's retainer seems to have some sort of difficulty communicating with the shite here, much as the priests did with the shite in *Takasago* and *Izutsu*. In the one case Tomonari could not, at first, grasp why pines in places as far from each other as Sumiyoshi and Takasago could be called *aioi no matsu*. In the other the priest had trouble understanding the shite's reasons for praying before Narihira's grave. What puzzles this priest is how to classify the old man he has happened upon. To his question, "Are you one of the mountain people?," the shite answers, "Yes, I am one of the sea folk."

The ageuta reintroduces Suma, which is characterized as a place unlike most others, tying this dan to the previous one, where Suma was pointed out as a particularly lonely place. But the focus is now narrowed to the young cherry tree on the coast. Unlike the cherry trees in poetic lore, which are blown bare by *mine no arashi*, "the gale off mountain peaks,"[17] or *yamaoroshi*, "the gusts that race down mountain sides," this cherry sheds its blossoms in the soft coastal breeze. The situation is unusual, or at least Zeami wants to make it seem unusual. The cherry is a bit out of place; it is a *yama no sakura*, "a mountain cherry," but it blooms on the seacoast. Already there is a hint that the shite himself is out of place, like the cherry tree. His answer to the waki's question was one indication of this, and his line *shiba to iu mono no sōraeba*, "They have something they call 'brushwood,'" is another. That line is an undistinguished one, but Zeami's audience would have recognized it as an allusion to the "Suma" chapter of *Genji monogatari*.[18] *Suma no wakaki no sakura*, "the young cherry on the coast of Suma" (line 72), is also apparently an allusion to that chapter.[19]

So far, there is nothing particularly unusual about the structure of this dan except that the last line of the ageuta is not repeated; the mondō-ageuta shōdan sequence is perfectly regular. But now Zeami inserts another mondō and a rongi, extending the exchange between the waki and the shite.

Mondō

76	w	Ika ni jōdono haya hi no kurete sōraeba,
		Ichiya no yado o onkashisōrae,
	s	Utate ya na kono hana no kage hodo no oyado no sōrō beki ka,
	w	Ge ni ge ni kore wa hana no yado naredomo,
80		Sarinagara tare o aruji to sadamu beki,
	s	Yukikurete ko no shita kage o yado to seba,
		Hana ya koyoi no aruji naramashi to,
		Nagameshi hito wa kono koke no shita itawashi ya,
		Warera ga yō naru ama dani mo,
85		Tsune wa tachiyori tomuraimōsu ni,
		Osōtachi wa nado gyakuen nagara tomuraitamawanu,
		Oroka ni mashimasu hitobito kana,
	w	Yukikurete ko no shita kage o yado to seba,
		Hana ya koyoi no aruji naramashi to,
90		Nagameshi hito wa Satsuma no kami,
	s	Tadanori to mōshishi hito wa kono Ichi no Tani no kasen ni utarenu,
		Yukari no hito no ueokitaru shirushi no ki nite sōrō nari,
	w	Ko wa somo fushigi no chigu no en,
		Sashi mo sa bakari Toshinari no,
95	s	Waka no tomo tote asakaranu,
	w	Yado wa koyoi no,
	s	Aruji no hito.

Rongi

	c	Na mo tada nori no koe kikite,
		Hana no utena ni zashitamae,
100	s	Arigata ya ima yori wa,
		Kaku tomurai no koe kikite,
		Bukka o en zo ureshiki,
	c	Fushigi ya ima no rōjin no,
		Tamuke no koe o mi ni ukete,
105		Yorokobu keshiki ni mietaru wa,
		Nani no yue nite aru yaran,
	s	Osō ni towaremōsan tote,
		Kore made kitareri to,
	c	Iube no hana no kage ni nete,
110		Yume no tsuge o mo machitamae,
		Miyako e kotozute mōsan tote,
		Hana no kage ni yadoriki no,
		Yuku kata shirazu narinikeri,
		Yuku kata shirazu narinikeri.

Mondō

76	w	Now then, old sir, already dusk begins to fall,
		So would you lend me a night's lodging?

	s	Such foolishness! Where would you find a place to sleep as fine as the foot of this tree?
	w	Ah yes, these are flowery lodgings,
80		But who would be my host then?
	s	"If I travel till dusk falls, and lodge beneath the cherry boughs,
		The blossoms might play host to me tonight."
		The one who first recited this poem lies beneath the moss here; how sad!
		And even seaside peasants like myself
85		Come all the time to pray for him.
		I know you priests just come by chance, but why don't you pray for him!—
		How negligent these people are! . . .
	w	That poem you mentioned, "If I travel till dusk falls, and lodge beneath the cherry boughs,
		The blossoms might play host to me tonight,"
90		That was composed by the lord of Satsuma.
	s	Tadanori was his name, he died here in the battle of Ichi no Tani.
		This tree was planted to mark the spot by some relation of his.
	w	What a strange coincidence! a karmic link,
		A man so close to my lord Toshinari,
95	s	A friendship made through poetry, no shallow bond,
	w	These lodgings tonight,
	s	This host,

Rongi

	c	His name is Tadanori: just listen to the Dharma's voice,
		And seat yourself upon a pedestal of flowers.
100	s	This is a marvel, from now on
		To hear the comforting voice of prayers,
		To reap the fruit of Buddhahood delights me.
	c	This is strange, this old man
		Takes the prayers I say to be for his sake,
105		And he seems to be rejoicing.
		What, I wonder, is the cause of this?
	s	From the first, I came here
		Just to have you pray for me.
	c	Lie down beneath these blossoms
110		And wait to see what dreams will bring.
		I will bear a message to the capital, he said,
		Then without a trace, into the blossoms, hiding,
		Like the bark-bound roots of mistletoe, he disappeared.
		Like the bark-bound roots of mistletoe, he disappeared.

It is quite common for the waki to ask for lodgings sometime during his exchange with the shite. It happens in *Matsukaze, Yashima, Kantan, Adachigahara, Nue, Funabashi,* and many other plays, far too numerous to mention. There is nothing surprising, then, about the waki's request at the beginning of the mondō. What is unusual is the shite's response: "Such foolishness! Where would you find a place to sleep as fine as the foot of this tree?" The shite often refuses the waki lodging, claiming that his own hut is far too humble or offering some similar excuse. But in this case the waki's request draws an almost sarcastic retort. It reveals the same attitude as lines 55 and 65-66 in the first part of the dan. There, the shite complained of the waki's lack of understanding of the circumstances of a seaside peasant's life. Here, he marvels at the waki's lack of sensibility, for since the time of *Kokinshū*, at least, anyone with the slightest poetic sensibility has known that there is no finer place to spend the spring night than at the foot of a blossoming cherry.[20]

The waki's reply to this retort ("But who would be my host then?") reveals either a hopelessly obtuse literal-mindedness or a belated awakening of poetic wit.[21] In any event, it leads to the shite's recitation of Tadanori's poem "Yukikurete." This poem is at the center of the play's honzetsu, as will become apparent later. (It comes from Book Nine of *Heike monogatari*, in the episode "Tadanori no saigo," "Tadanori's death.") Here it serves to introduce the play's central figure, Tadanori, leading to a rather petulant request for prayers (lines 86-87), a brief identification of Tadanori as both warrior and poet (lines 91, 95), and a hint that the old man himself has something to gain from any prayers said for Tadanori (lines 100-106).

The dan closes with the conventional request that the priest go to sleep and wait for dreams, and the disappearance of the maejite. Line 111, "I will bear a message to the capital, he said," is puzzling at this point, but will make sense later.

Structurally, this part of the third dan is almost as regular as the first part. It leads from the spoken word to noncongruent song to congruent song in a perfectly standard manner, including even the metrical and musical tapering at the end of the mondō that was noticed in the analyses of *Takasago* and *Izutsu*. The rongi rather than the expected ageuta seems appropriate, for these two shōdan are very similar formally, and the dan would have otherwise had two ageuta. As mentioned above, the third dan is unusual because Zeami has extended it by repeating the usual sequence of shōdan. It is comparable in this respect to the fourth dan of *Tōru*, which was discussed in Chapter Three. In that play the shōdan sequence consisted of a katari, an uta, and an ageuta followed by a mondō, an uta, and a rongi. Although this is a longer sequence than the mondō-ageuta-mondō-rongi sequence of *Tadanori*—indeed, it should be, since it is the narrative center of *Tōru*—they are similar because both match two consecutive passages of different but not unrelated content with two structurally parallel shōdan sequences leading from speech to noncongruent song to congruent song. In *Tadanori* the third dan is unified by a common thread: the superiority of the shite's understanding to the waki's. In the mondō-ageuta sequence the waki's narrow view of who is a mountain dweller and who is a seacoast dweller is superseded by the shite's practical understanding of the life of a peasant on the coast; in the mondō-rongi sequence the waki's obtuseness is corrected by the shite's poetic sensibility. These two articulations of a common idea are allotted separate shōdan sequences, as were the two subthemes in the passage from *Tōru*.*

One more feature of this dan should be noted before we move on. That is the wordplay in line 98. Tadanori, the name of the play's central character, is hidden in *tada nori*, "just . . . the Dharma." There is nothing particularly profound in this, but it is a technique we have seen before in *Taema*, and Zeami also uses it in two other plays in the Martial Mode, *Yashima* and *Kiyotsune*.† Perhaps this signaling of the shite's identity was intended to foreshadow the more complete self-introduction that Zeami prescribes for the second half of his plays in the Martial Mode.

The maejite leaves the stage at the end of the rongi, and the aikyōgen comes forth for the following dialogue with the waki:

K   I before you am a resident of the coast of Suma. Today I am intend-
     ing to go off to see the young cherry tree. Well now, there's a priest I
     have never seen here before. Where have you come from, Your
     Reverence?
W   I am a priest from the capital. Do you live around here?
K   Yes, I do.
W   Well then, come over here a minute. I have something to ask you.
K   Certainly. Now what was it you wanted to ask me?
W   This may take you by surprise, but I'd like you to tell me about this
     young cherry tree and the fate of Tadanori, if you know anything
     about them.
K   I didn't expect you to ask me anything like that. I do live around
     here, but I don't really know very much about these matters. Never-
     theless, it wouldn't be proper to say I don't know anything at all
     about what you've asked—especially since this is the first time I've
     met you—so I'll tell you what I've been told.
W   Very well.
K   There was, at one time, a Heike courtier named Tadanori, the lord
     of Satsuma. He was a man outstanding even among the Heike for
     his martial prowess and his cultured refinement, and he was a good
     general, so they say. Now, when Tadanori was about to leave the

---

* Interestingly, in both *Tōru* and *Tadanori* the dividing line between the two subthemes is marked by the same phrase—*ika ni jōdono*, "Now then, old sir."

† In *Yashima* (YK, 2: 270) the shite is hesitantly identified as Minamoto no Yoshitsune just before he leaves the stage for the aikyōgen interlude: "Tatoi nanorazu to mo nanoru to mo *yoshi tsune* no uki yo no yume ba shi samashitamō na yo" (What difference does it make whether I make my name known to you or not? Don't waken from the dream of this vain world [but pray for me]). In the final lines of *Kiyotsune* (YK, 1: 256), the chorus sings, "Ge ni mo kokoro wa Kiyotsune ga, bukka o eshi koso arigatakere" (How marvelous that Kiyotsune, in his purity of heart, should gain the fruit of Buddhahood), punning *kokoro wa kiyo[shi]* ("the heart is pure") on Kiyotsune's name.

capital, he went to Lord Shunzei and told him he had made waka poetry his chief interest and would like to be recognized as a poet. Shunzei replied that that would be impossible, since he was under imperial proscription.

Tadanori, however, repeated his request with great conviction, and returning all the way from Yamazaki, he went to Shunzei's residence. He provided him with examples of his poetry and requested that his poems be included in the imperial anthology if they were worthy. After this, they say, he went off to the country to join his clan. Later, during the reign of the Retired Emperor GoShirakawa, when Shunzei was compiling the *Anthology of a Thousand Ages*, he did include one of Tadanori's poems, but he listed it as an anonymous composition.

Now, regarding Tadanori's fate. A great many of the Heike had taken refuge here; the Genji in their efforts to destroy the Heike had divided their forces of 60,000 men into two wings, and Yoshitsune and Noriyori drove these wings against the Heike from both sides and defeated them handily. Many courtiers were killed; the rest fled in great confusion. Tadanori was a general of the western ranks, and when these were defeated—even before the main ranks—he began to make his escape among the foot soldiers. Okabe no Rokuyata Tadazumi, however, picked him out as a worthy opponent and chased after him with seven or eight horsemen. Tadanori finally had to fight with Rokuyata, and being as strong as he was, he about had Rokuyata down when one of Rokuyata's retainers killed him. Everyone thought this a terrible pity and wept, so I'm told. As for this cherry tree, some say Tadanori had it planted, and others say Hikaru Genji did. That's what I've been told. I wonder, though, why you ask all this.

w   You've been very kind to tell me this. The reason I've asked is none other than that I am a retainer of Lord Shunzei, and now that he has passed away, I have taken the tonsure, as you see. Before you appeared, an old man came by here and when I spoke to him, he told me about the old cherry tree just as you have now. He spoke of Tadanori as if he were speaking of himself, and then, saying he was off to bear a message to the capital, he disappeared.

K   This is peculiar. I think Tadanori's ghost must have come to talk with you. Do please stay awhile and say some prayers for him.

w   I will stay awhile and recite the miraculous sutras and pray for him as you request.

K   If you should need anything, don't hesitate to ask.

w   Thank you.

K   You're most welcome.[22]

As usual, the aikyōgen part cannot be considered a part of the original text. There are, in fact, certain details in it that seem slightly inconsistent with the rest of the play, but they need not detain us here. The transition between this interlude and the last half of the play takes the form of an unspecified shōdan and the typical ageuta sung by the waki and his companion. These can be considered part of the original text, and are quoted and translated below:

Unidentified shōdan
115 W   Mazu mazu miyako ni kaeritsutsu,
           Teika ni kono koto mōsan to.

Ageuta
    w/wt Iuzuki hayaku kagerō no,
           Iuzuki hayaku kagerō no,
           Ono ga tomo yobu murachidori no,
120   Ato mienu isoyama no,
           Yoru no hana ni tabine shite,
           Urakaze made mo kokoro shite,
           Haru ni kikebaya oto sugoki,
125   Suma no sekiya no tabine kana,
           Suma no sekiya no tabine kana.

Unidentified shōdan
115 W   I must rush back to the capital
           To report this to Teika, but even as I say so,

Ageuta
    w/wt The evening moon already hides in darkness,
           The evening moon already hides in darkness,
           The plovers in their flocks cry back and forth to one another,
120   Now unseen below the coastal range.
           I sleep beneath the night-clad blossoms,
           Troubled that the faint sea breeze might scatter them away.
           Is it spring that makes that rustling sound so ominous?
           Ah, so this is "a traveler's sleep at the Barrier House of Suma."
125   Ah, so this is "a traveler's sleep at the Barrier House of Suma."

The waki's resolution to return to the capital to convey the news of his experience to Teika, Shunzei's son, is broken by encroaching darkness, and he lies down for an unsettling night beneath the cherry tree.

This ageuta is less directly related to the content of the play than its counterparts in *Takasago* and *Izutsu*, and it is perhaps for this reason that the Konparu, Kongō, and Kita schools have replaced it with an almost completely different song.[23] It is, nevertheless, a highly evocative passage effectively capturing the traditional association of Suma with sadness and loneliness,[24] and is thus well suited to this position in the play.

The nochijite makes his entrance at the beginning of the next dan, coming on stage to the instrumental ISSEI to sing the following lines:

Sashi
126 S   Hazukashi ya naki ato ni,
           Sugata o kaesu yume no uchi,
           Samuru kokoro wa inishie ni,
           Mayō amayo no monogatari,
130   Mōsan tame ni konpaku ni,
           Utsurikawarite kitaritari.

*Kudoki
           Sanaki dani mōshiu ōki shaba naru ni,
           Nani nakanaka no *Senzaishiu* no,

135

140

Uta no shina ni wa iritaredomo,
Chokkan no mi no kanashisa wa,
Yomibito shirazu to kakareshi koto,
Mōshiu no naka no daiichi nari,
Saredomo sore o senjitamaishi,
Toshinari sae munashiku naritamaeba,
Onmi wa miuchi ni arishi hito nareba,
Ima no Teika kimi ni mōshi,
Shikaru beku wa sakusha o tsukete tabitamae to,
Yume monogatari mōsu ni Suma no,
Urakaze mo kokoro seyo.

Sashi
126 s

130

How it shames me
To return to this, my former figure,
Now within a dream,
My mind awakened wanders lost in the past.
I appear to tell a rainy night's tale,
Taking on this ghostly form I come.

*Kudoki

135

140

As it is, delusion fills the world,
Yet, to be but half recognized; my poem included
In the ranks of the *Anthology of a Thousand Ages,*
But by that poem to read this note: poet unknown.
This is the misery of imperial proscription.
And this is the foremost of the delusions tormenting me.
But now even Toshinari, who chose the poems for that anthology,
Has passed on to empty death,
But you, who once served in that house,
You must speak to Teika, the lord there now,
And have the author's name set down beside his poem, as it should
  be.
I relate these things in a tale told through a dream,
So you, too, take heed, coastal breeze of Suma.

Buddhist doctrine holds that existence is suffering, and that suffering is caused by delusive attachment (*mōshū*; in noh, *mōshiu*) to impermanent things. Buddhism as it is used in the noh theater further postulates that strong attachments binding an individual at death will impede the progress of his soul to a subsequent stage of existence (or extinction). Thus, the nochijite in *Tadanori* comes on stage singing lines about the foremost of the delusions tormenting him. There is nothing strange about this until one realizes that the foremost cause of delusive attachment for Tadanori's spirit is not a warrior's furious desire for vengeance, but a dissatisfaction with a politically influenced editorial decision to omit his name from a famous poetic anthology.

The story behind the decision is this. In the second month of 1183, the Retired Emperor GoShirakawa (1127-92) ordered the poet Fujiwara Shunzei (or Toshinari) to compile the seventh imperial anthology of Japanese poetry. In the seventh month of the same year, the Taira, or Heike, clan was forced to abandon the capital, and its members came under imperial proscription. Thus, when Taira no Tadanori risked his life to bring a collection of poems to Shunzei for consideration, the compiler was faced with a dilemma: how could the poems of a man under imperial proscription be included in an imperially sponsored anthology? Shunzei eventually chose to use one of Tadanori's poems,[25] but decided it should be included anonymously.

To make this a matter of anguish for Tadanori may seem rather strained to the modern reader, but having one's poetry selected for an imperial anthology was a great honor, and Tadanori was not the only poet to go to great lengths to have a work included.[26] In Zeami's day the audience would have readily accepted such a situation. What is important to note, in any event, is that in choosing this as the foremost of Tadanori's delusive attachments, Zeami has shown no interest in developing his protagonist as a demonic shura figure, but has concentrated instead on "establishing the connection between [Tadanori] and poetry," thus following his own advice in *Fūshikaden*. There is some connection to the warring spirits of the older shura role, however, in the fierce pride that animates Tadanori, even though that pride is directed toward poetic rather than martial accomplishments.[27]

The play now turns to narratives about Tadanori, in the form of a kuri-sashi-sageuta-ageuta sequence:

Kuri

145 C   Ge ni ya waka no ie ni 'mmare,
Sono michi o tashinami,
Shikishima no kage ni yosshi koto,
Jinrin ni oite moppara nari.

Sashi

w   Naka ni mo kono Tadanori wa bumpu nidō o uketamaite sejō ni manako takashi,

150 C   Somosomo GoShirakawa no In no gyō ni *Senzaishiu* o erawaru,
Gojō no sammi Shunzei no kyō,
Uketamawatte kore o senzu.

Sageuta

Toshi wa Juei no aki no koro,
Miyako o ideshi toki nareba.

Ageuta

155   Sa mo isogawashikarishi mi no,
Sa mo isogawashikarishi mi no,
Kokoro no hana ka rangiku no,
Kitsunegawa yori hikikaeshi,
Toshinari no ie ni yuki,

160   Uta no nozomi o nagekishi ni.
Nozomi tarinureba,
Mata kiusen ni tazusawarite,
Saikai no nami no ue,

		Shibashi to tanomu Suma no ura,
165		Genji no sumidokoro,
		Heike no tame wa yoshi nashi to,
		Shirazarikeru zo hakanaki.

Kuri

145	C	Indeed, to be born into a poetic house,
		And practice that vocation,
		Finding one's place in the shade of Shikishima,
		This is the greatest good among men.

Sashi

	w	And among such men, Tadanori succeeded to a heritage of both martial valor and cultured refinement, achieving great repute.
150	C	Now, in the reign of Retired Emperor GoShirakawa,
		When Lord Shunzei was called upon to compile the *Anthology of a Thousand Ages*,
		He accepted the commission and began to choose worthy poems.

Sageuta

		It was autumn in the era of Juei,
		When the Heike had already fled the capital.

Ageuta

155		Even in the flurry of his pressing obligations,
		Even in the flurry of his pressing obligations,
		—The blossoms of his sensibility must have required it—
		He turned back from the orchids and chrysanthemums of Fox River,
		And went to Shunzei's home
160		To ask that his own poems be considered for the collection.
		Then, with assurances that his request would be honored,
		He once again took up his bow and quiver,
		And set out on the waves of the Western Sea.
		His clan sought temporary shelter on the coast of Suma,
165		But this was the home of Genji,
		Not a place well suited to the Heike clan.
		Their blindness to this brought their doom.

The kuri states a general proposition about poetry. The content is clearly articulated, if rather surprising in itself. The only difficulty is the mention of *Shikishima no kage*, "the shade of Shikishima," but the reader will recall from the discussion of the second sashi in *Takasago* that Shikishima is an epithet for Japan. *Shikishima no kage* is a metaphor for Japanese poetry. Next, in the sashi we learn that Tadanori is a paragon of the virtues of martial valor and artistic refinement, and that Shunzei is the compiler of *Senzaishū*.

The sageuta gives the specific temporal context for the short narrative that follows. (The era of Juei is the period from 1182 to 1185. The Heike fled the capital in the seventh month, early autumn, of 1183.) The ageuta then proceeds to tell the story of Tadanori's daring return to the capital to submit his poems to Shunzei. The song paraphrases very briefly the events related in "Tadanori's Flight from the Capital," in Book Seven of *Heike monogatari*. Zeami's version of the story does not differ from that account, but neither does it owe its phrasing directly to the earlier work. The Genji named in the last lines of the ageuta is Hikaru Genji, whose exile on the coast of Suma is familiar from *Genji monogatari*. Hikaru Genji shares his surname with the Genji clan, Tadanori's enemies, so his residence on the coast is taken to be an ill omen for Heike fortunes there. This is the second allusion to *Genji monogatari* in the play (the third, counting the aikyōgen's interlude), but these do little more than make the traditional association between Genji and Suma.

As has often been seen before, narrative sequences in noh usually take the form of kuri-sashi-kuse, so it is surprising to find the kuse here replaced by a sageuta and ageuta. Perhaps Zeami's suggestion in *Sandō* that the music of a play in the Martial Mode be kept brief is apposite here. A kuse has certain formal requirements that, when properly met, result in considerable length. Since a longer narrative is to follow in the next dan, this one is better kept short.

Lines 156-58 provide an example of a text generated by renga-like associations. *Kokoro*, "sensibility," is an engo of *mi*, literally "body," and is frequently attached to *hana*, "flower," in the noh (see, for example, line 113 of *Izutsu*). *Hana* calls forth *rangiku*, "orchids and chrysanthemums," and this in turn links to *Kitsunegawa*, "Fox River," by way of an allusion to a couplet by the famous Tang poet Bo Ju-i (Po Chü-i):

> The owl hoots in the branches of pine and cassia,
> The fox hides in clumps of orchids and chrysanthemums.[28]

(One scholar, noting that the Kitsunegawa is a tributary of the Yodo River, seems to find the reference puzzling, since the river is not mentioned in the extant texts of *Heike monogatari*.[29] We might conjecture, however, that Zeami simply chose the name to fit into a chain of associations and not for any specific geographical purpose.)

To sum up, the structure of the fourth dan proceeds through the following shōdan sequence: ISSEI-sashi-*kudoki-kuri-sashi-sageuta-ageuta. The dan serves the double function of bringing the nochijite on stage and presenting a short narrative. The sashi accomplishes the first task, as sashi often do (see *Takasago*, *Yōrō*, *Izutsu*, and *Tōru*, to mention but a few examples). The *kudoki provides a transition from the entrance to the narrative proper, and at the same time relates back to the first half of the play. The kuri-sashi-sageuta-ageuta sequence is used for the narrative, which moves characteristically from the general to the specific. There are irregularities in this dan. In addition to the irregular kuri-sashi-sageuta-ageuta sequence, the *kudoki is irregular both because of its placement and because of its content, according to Yokomichi.[30]

Nevertheless, on the whole, the dan follows the standard pattern in moving from noncongruent song to tadautai. It provides another example of artful variation within the standard parameters of a mugen noh.

A long narrative, a short dance, and two tadautai shōdan bring the play to a close:[31]

*Kuri
168 c   Saru hodo ni Ichi no Tani no kassen,
          Ima wa kō yo to mieshi hodo ni,
170   Mina mina fune ni torinotte kaijō ni ukamu.
*Katari
   s   Ware mo fune ni noran tote,
          Migiwa no kata ni uchiideshi ni,
          Ushiro o mireba,
          Musashi no kuni no jūnin ni,
175   Okabe no Rokuyata Tadazumi to nanotte,
          Roku shichiki nite okkaketari,
          Kore koso nozomu tokoro yo to omoi
          Koma no tazuna o hikkaeseba,
          Rokuyata yagate muzu to kumi,
180   Ryōba ga ai ni dōdo ochi,
          Kano Rokuyata o totte osae,
          Sude ni katana ni te o kakeshi ni.

Uta
   c   Rokuyata ga rōdō,
          Onnushiro yori tachimawari,
185   Ue ni mashimasu Tadanori no,
          Migi no kaina o uchiotoseba,
          Hidari no onte nite,
          Rokuyata o totte nagenoke,
          Ima wa kanawaji to oboshimeshite,
190   Soko nokitamae hitobito yo,
          Nishi ogaman to notamaite,
          Kōmyō henjō,
          Jippō sekai nenbusshujō,
          Sesshu fusha to notamaishi,
195   Onkoe no shita yori mo,
          Itawashi ya aenaku mo,
          Rokuyata tachi o nukimochi,
          Tsui ni onkubi o uchiotosu.
   s   Rokuyata kokoro ni omō yō,
200 c   Itawashi ya kano hito no,
          Onshigai o mitatematsureba,
          Sono toshi mo madashiki,
          Nagazuki goro no usugumori,
          Furimi furazumi sadame naki,
205   Shigure zo kayō muramomiji no,
          Nishiki no hitatare wa,
          Tada yo no tsune ni yo mo araji,
          Ikasama kore wa kindachi no,

Onnaka ni koso arurame to,
210 Onna yukashiki tokoro ni,
Ebira o mireba fushigi ya na,
Tanjaku o tsukeraretari,
Mireba ryoshuku no dai o sue.

Jōnoei

Yukikurete,
215 Ko no shita kage o yado to seba.

TACHIMAWARI

Jōnoei (cont.)
    s   Hana ya koyoi no,
         Aruji naramashi.

Uta
    s   Tadanori to kakaretari,
    c   Sate wa utagai arashi no oto ni,
220 Kikoeshi wa Satsuma no,
         Kami nite masu zo itawashiki.

Uta

Onmi kono hana no,
Kage ni tachiyoritamaishi o,
Kaku monogatari mōsan tote,
225 Hi o kurashi todomeshi nari,
Ima wa utagai yo mo araji,
Hana wa ne ni kaeru nari,
Waga ato toite tabitamae,
Kokage o tabi no yado to seba,
230 Hana koso aruji narikere.

Kuri
168 c   Now, the Battle of Ichi no Tani
         Appeared to have been lost,
170 So everyone was hurrying into boats to set off on the sea.

Katari
    s   And I rode out upon the beach
         So I too might climb onto a boat,
         But when I looked behind me
         A man from the province of Musashi,
175 Announcing himself as Okabe no Rokuyata Tadazumi,
Rode up with six or seven horsemen, chasing after me.
Thinking this was just what I had hoped for,
I reined my horse in and
Rokuyata came to grips with me instantly.
180 We fell with a thud between our horses.
I took that Rokuyata and held him down.
Already I had my hand upon my sword, but

Uta
    c   One of Rokuyata's men
         Came around behind him
185 And cut off Tadanori's right arm
         Even as he stood ready, over Rokuyata.
         With his left hand

Tadanori threw Rokuyata off to the side,
And realizing this would be his end,
190   He ordered everyone out of his way
So that he might face west to pray:
"The holy light shines everywhere,
Throughout the ten directions, all beings who have faith in Amida
Will find salvation, not abandonment."
195   But as he spoke these words—
What a wretched shame!—
Rokuyata drew his long sword
And struck his head off then and there.
s   Now Rokuyata thought to himself
200 c   "What a great pity!"
And gazed down at the corpse:
The fallen warrior's span of years was not yet long
But he would never see the faintly clouded autumn of his life,
When fall showers come and go
205   Unceasingly to dye the leaves into a
Crimson brocade war-robe.
This was no common warrior.
He must have been a courtier,
The son of some great lord.
210   As Rokuyata wondered who the man might be,
He caught sight of his quiver, and to his surprise,
He found a slip of paper with a poem.
The title read "A Traveler's Lodgings."

Jōnoei

"If I travel till dusk falls,
215   And lodge beneath the cherry boughs,

TACHIMAWARI

Jōnoei (cont.)
s   The blossoms might
Play host to me tonight."

Uta
s   The poem was signed "Tadanori."
c   So, there is no doubt,
220   The sound I heard beyond the shrieking wind
Was the lord of Satsuma, how painfully sad.

Uta

Now, as for you,
You stopped beneath this cherry tree
Because I brought nightfall to keep you here
225   To listen to my tale.
Now let there be no doubt that
Flowers fall back to their roots
And as I fall back into darkness, pray for me.
For if you find your travel's lodging underneath a cherry tree,
230   The blossoms might indeed play host that night.

Zeami devotes the major portion of this final dan to the long narra-
tive of Tadanori's death. In *Sandō* he had stressed the importance of writ-

An actor of the Kita school as the nochijite in *Tadanori*. The mask is of the type *chūjō*, and the hat (a *nashiuchi eboshi*) would have been worn under a samurai helmet in medieval Japan. The large right sleeve of the shite's hunting robe has been secured behind him for the battle narrated in the fifth dan. Here we see him reading the poem attached to Tadanori's quiver (lines 214-17). Behind the shite to the left is the *kotsuzumi* player, to the right the *ōtsuzumi* player. *Photograph by Masuda Shozoh, courtesy of the Noh Research Archives of Musashino Women's College.*

ing the story "just as it appears in *Heike monogatari*." But it is clear, on reading the play, that Zeami does not mean by this that the writer should quote the tale directly. Except for a few details to be mentioned below, Zeami's rendition is perfectly faithful to the account of Tadanori's death in Book Seven of *Heike monogatari*. But he not only casts the events of that story into his own language; he takes into consideration the visual implications of his phrasing and carefully manipulates the narrative voice. Thus, where the *Heike* account is entirely in the third person, Zeami has the shite, as Tadanori, speak for himself in the *katari.

Person and number are far less distinct in Japanese than in English, of course, and one might well read the text as a straightforward third-person narrative were it not for the honorifics that begin to appear in reference to Tadanori after the *katari. This change in the level of speech signals a change in narrative voice. Thus, whereas in the *katari itself, Tadanori's actions are described with neutral forms, such as *uchi-ideshi*, "(I) rode out," and *mireba*, "when (I) looked," in the following uta, honorific and therefore third-person forms appear: *onnushiro*, "behind (him)," *ue ni mashimasu*, "(he) stood ready," *oboshimeshite*, "(he) realized," and so on. This change in narrative voice comes just as the tide is turning in Tadanori's battle with Rokuyata, so that when Tadanori is winning, he speaks in the first person. As soon as Rokuyata's man comes along to rescue his master, the narrative voice changes. When Tadanori is beheaded, the narrative voice changes once more. Now, in a characteristically lyrical passage, Zeami presents Rokuyata's interior monologue about the (yet unidentified) warrior he has slain. This point of view is used until the last shōdan when, to great effect, Zeami switches back to Tadanori's own consciousness, again unmistakably in the first person. This final uta also contains direct address in the second person to the waki, something completely new in this position, as far as the plays in this study are concerned.

These changes in point of view juxtapose different visions of Tadanori: Tadanori the proud warrior in the context of *Heike monogatari*; Tadanori the fallen warrior; Tadanori the cultured poet; and finally, Tadanori the ghost seeking salvation. This layering of one aspect of the hero onto another is not unlike the layering of different times in the life of the heroine of *Izutsu*. The means are somewhat different, but the overall effect of heightened lyricism is identical. Just as Zeami uses the poems of Episode 23 of *Ise monogatari* to create a much more profound understanding of the psychology of the woman in *Izutsu*, so he manipulates the viewpoint of the *Heike monogatari* narrative to create a much more psychologically rounded picture of Tadanori than the rather flat narrative style of *Heike monogatari* can provide.

The change in narrative voice may have been necessary to fulfill the visual potential of this dan. That is, the battle scene provides a rich source for monomane, dramatic imitation, but if Zeami had used the first person here, the acting out of the narrative would naturally be limited, lasting only as long as Tadanori was a living, moving warrior. To be sure, Zeami might have written a long, exciting narrative in which Tadanori stayed alive and moving on stage until the end of the play, but he chose instead to disengage the narrative from Tadanori's consciousness even before his death to give full play to the visual mimetic potential of the battle with Rokuyata. This potential is exploited to the fullest in the modern *kata* or actions accompanying the piece. In the Kanze school, for example, from line 197 on ("Rokuyata drew his long sword"), the shite begins to imitate Rokuyata's actions, drawing out a sword (actually he uses a fan), looking down at the severed head, looking back at the body, and so on. Then, at line 222 ("Now as for you, you stopped beneath this cherry tree"), the shite begins to imitate Tadanori's actions. Again, it would be a mistake to suppose that the scene is played now as it was in Zeami's day, but at the same time, it is very difficult to imagine that the shite did not in some way mimetically represent the text being sung, even in the fifteenth century.

The steady discursive narrative that characterizes much of this dan is interrupted by an associative sequence at lines 202-6. *Sono toshi mo mada-shiki naga(karanu)*, "(his) span of years was not yet long," associates with *nagazuki*, "the long month" (i.e., the ninth month, the last month of autumn), which calls up *usugumori*, "faint clouds." This leads to *furimi furazumi sadame naki shigure*, "the fall showers that come and go."[32] These showers were thought (at least in a poetic sense) to turn the trees' leaves red, thus they are linked with *muramomiji*, "mottled crimson leaves." The mention of color in turn leads back to Tadanori, who is pictured in a crimson *hitatare*, or war-robe. This is one of the details that varies from the *Heike monogatari* version of the story.

With the end of the *katari-uta sequence, the narrative that has dominated the dan gives way to the more lyrical text of Tadanori's poem. The last three shōdan retain a strongly lyric character to complete the piece. There is a possible allusion in line 227 to a waka by the Retired Emperor Sutoku:[33]

Hana wa ne ni	Flowers fall back
Tori wa furusu ni	To their roots, and birds return
Kaeru nari	To former nests.
Haru no tomari o	But no one knows
Shiru hito zo naki	Where spring comes to rest.

This can quite reasonably be taken as a metaphorical reference to Tadanori himself. He falls like the blossoms back to the roots of the cherry, and indeed his remains are buried under the young cherry on the coast of Suma, or so one is told in the first half of the play.

The final two lines of the play are a variation on Tadanori's poem, and they suggest the same metaphor: "the blossoms" are Tadanori, and they are also the waki's host. Tadanori's ghost has in fact been a host to the waki, entertaining him through the night in his dreams. The word *hana*, "blossoms," in the last line echoes the *hana* of the first line, further testimony to Zeami's artful construction of the play.

Tadanori is a fine example of a noh based on "a famous character from the Genji or the Heike" in which care has been taken to "bring out the connection between [the character] and poetry and music." Only Yorimasa, the shite in the play of the same name, can rival Tadanori as a warrior-poet, but no single poem in *Yorimasa* holds the significance of "Yukikurete," in *Tadanori*, and Zeami pays far less attention to Yorimasa's poetic achievements than to Tadanori's. The other plays in the mode also contain quotations from famous waka, but in none of them does poetry occupy the central role it does in *Tadanori*.

Zeami's *Atsumori*, however, is to music (and dance) what *Tadanori* is to poetry. Much of the last half of the play is devoted to a description of Atsumori's flute playing on the night before his death.[34] This is then followed by a long instrumental dance. Both the description and the dance attest to the connection between the shite and music in the play, but even in the first half of the play this connection is made obvious. Thus, the mondō-rongi sequence in the first half of *Tadanori* (where "Yukikurete" first appears) finds its counterpart in *Atsumori* in a mondō-kakeai-ageuta sequence. The waki, a priest named Renshō who took the tonsure after having killed the boy Atsumori on the beach at Ichinotani, returns to that place to find a group of reapers. He hears one of them playing a flute with unexpected elegance, and is taught the lesson that artistic sensibility is not dependent on social class.

Mondō

1	w	Ika ni kusakaritachi ni tazunemōsu beki koto no sōro,
	s	Konata no koto nite sōrō ka nanigoto nite sōrō zo,
	w	Tadaima no fue wa katagata no naka ni fukitamaisōrō ka,
	s	Sanzōro warera ga naka ni fukite sōro,
5	w	Ara yasashi ya sono mi ni mo ōzenu waza,
		Kaesugaesu mo yasashiu koso sōrae,
	s	Sono mi ni mo ōzenu waza to uketamawaredomo,
		Sore masaru o mo urayamazare,
		Otoru o mo iyashimu na to koso miete sōrae,
10		Sono ue shōka bokuteki tote,
	s/T	Kusakari no fue kikori no uta wa,

Kajin no ei ni mo tsumoriokarete,
Yo ni kikoetaru fuetake no,
Fushin na nasasetamaiso to yo.[35]

Mondō

1   w   Excuse me, I have something to ask you reapers.

     s   Are you addressing us? What is it you would like to ask?

     w   Was one of you playing the flute I just heard?

     s   Yes, one of us was playing.

5   w   It was so elegant, I would not have expected it of someone of your class.

        It was so very elegant.

     s   You say you would not have expected it of someone of our class, but
It is written, "Neither envy your superiors,
Nor hold inferiors in contempt."

10   Or better yet, woodsmen's songs and pastoral pipes,

     s/T   This is to say, the flutes of reapers and the songs of woodcutters,
Have found a place in poetry.
They are known throughout the world,
So do not be suspicious finding them here.

Despite the shite's protestations about the existence of art among the masses—this is something we will come back to in the concluding chapter—the flute-playing reaper is something of an anomaly; in this he is similar to the shite of *Tadanori*, who sweetens his arduous woodcutting and salt-making with poetry and cherry blossoms. In fact, the shite of many plays in the Martial Mode turn out to be souls of great sensitivity and refinement who are trapped in toilsome and wearying incarnations as peasants. In *Yorimasa* the maejite is by his own admission an *iyashiki Uji no satobito*, "a vulgar inhabitant of Uji village." He is, all the same, capable of considerable verbal wit. Similarly, the maejite in *Yashima* is a busy fisherman, but not so busy that he cannot take time to recite Chinese poetry with his companion, the tsure, as he fishes:

Sashi

1   s   Omoshiro ya tsuki kaijō ni ukande wa,
Hatō yaka ni nitari,

     T   Gyoō yoru seigan ni sōte shukusu,

     s   Akatsuki shōsui o kunde sochiku o taku mo,

5   s/T   Ima ni shirarete ashibi no kage,
Hono miesomuru monosugosa yo.[36]

Sashi

1   s   What a charming scene: With the moon afloat on the ocean's surface,
The breakers look like brushfires.

     T   "An old fisherman takes shelter for the night by the western bank,

     s   At dawn he gathers water from the Xiang River and lights a fire of Chu bamboo."

5   s/T   Now at last I can picture that scene, as I begin to catch sight
Of the reed fires burning in the desolation here.

212

Such complaints, with the unexpected refinement they reveal, are important keys to the character of the shite in these plays, serving much the same function as the shite's first sashi in *Takasago*.[37] These passages intensify the lyrical nature of plays like *Tadanori* and *Atsumori*. Certain other plays in the mode, though by no means lacking in lyricism, subordinate it to narrative interest.

Yashima is one outstanding example of such a play. In its fourth dan we find an exciting battle narrative in the form of a katari-kakeai-uta sequence; then, in the fifth, the shite and the chorus tell the story of Yoshitsune's loss and retrieval of his bow in a sashi-kakeai-sashi-kuse sequence. Both of these narratives owe much to *Heike monogatari*. So does most of the last dan of *Yorimasa*. The shite, Minamoto no Yorimasa, has conspired to depose the Heike, and they have discovered the plot. In a long narrative sequence he first recounts how he escaped from the capital with a co-conspirator, Prince Takakura, and how, when their party reached the Uji bridge, they were forced to take a stand. Then, with help from the chorus, he goes on to tell of the ensuing battle:

Kuse (cont.)

1	C	Ujihashi no naka no ma hikihanashi,
		Shita wa kawanami ue ni tatsu mo,
		Tomo ni shirahata o nabikasete,
		Yosuru kataki o machiitari.

Katari

5	S	Kakute Ujigawa no nanboku no kishi ni uchinozomi,
		Toki no koe yasakebi no oto,
		Nami ni taguete obitatashi,
		Hashi mo yukigeta o hedatete tatakō,
		Mikata ni wa Tsutsui no Jōmyō,
10		Ichirai Hosshi,
		Kataki mikata ni me o odorokasu,
		Kakute Heike no ōzei,
		Hashi wa hiitari mizu wa takashi,
		Sasuga nanjo no daiga nareba,
15		Sō nō watasu beki yō mo nakarishi tokoro ni,
		Tōra no Matatarō Tadatsuna to nanotte,
		Ujigawa no senjin ware nari to,
		Nanori mo aezu sambyaku yo ki,

Chūnoriji

	C	Kutsubami o soroe kawamizu ni,
20		Sukoshi mo tamerawazu,
		Mureiru muratori no tsubasa o naraburu,
		Haoto mo kaku ya to shiranami ni,
		Zazzatto uchiirete,
		Ukinu shizuminu watashikeri,
25	S	Tadatsuna tsuwamono o geji shite iwaku,
	C	Mizu no sakamaku tokoro o ba,
		Iwa ari to shiru beshi,

Yowaki 'mma oba shitade ni tatete,
Tsuyoki ni mizu fusegaseyo,
30   Nagaren musha ni wa yuhazu o torasete,
Tagai ni chikara o awasu beshi to,
Tada ichinin no geji ni yotte,
Sabakari no taiga naredomo,
Ikki mo nagarezu konata no kishi ni,
35   Omeite agareba mikata no sei wa,
Ware nagara fumi mo tamezu,
Hanchō bakari oboezu shisatte,
Kissaki o soroete,
Ima o saigo to tatakōtari.[38]

Kuse (cont.)

1   C   [We] pulled up the planks from Uji bridge.
Below, the river's white waves rushed,
Above, we set white Genji banners streaming in the wind
And waited for the enemy to come.

Katari

5   S   Thus, the armies lined up on the north and south banks of the Uji River,
War cries and the hiss of arrows
Fused with the rush of the waves in one great roar.
We did battle with just the bridge girders between us,
And among our allies Tsutsui no Jōmyō
10   And the warrior-monk Ichirai
Startled both enemy and friend with their bravery.
The bridge was stripped, the waves were high,
It was a treacherous place on the great river,
And it looked as if the Heike forces
15   Would not be able to cross.
But then one of their party raised a shout,
"I, Tōra no Tadatsuna, will be the first on the other side!"
And even as he spoke three hundred horsemen

Chūnoriji

   C   Arrayed their mounts in order, and
20   Lunged into the river waters, without the slightest hesitation.
The splash rose like a flapping flock of birds
As it takes to the air. The horsemen plunged
Into the white waves rank by rank,
Bobbing up and down as they struggled across.
25   S   Tadatsuna directed the troops saying,
   C   "Watch out for the whirlpools,
There are boulders underneath in those spots.
Head the weaker horses downstream,
Break the force of the current upstream with the stronger ones.
30   If anybody falls in, stretch your bow out to him to grab hold of.
We have to keep our efforts unified."
And on the instructions of this single man
The entire force crossed through the great river
To our side without losing a single horseman.
35   When they came up screaming on the bank,

We retreated fifty yards,
Almost without knowing it,
Then we held fast, swords drawn.
Knowing this would be the end, we fought.

This passage is based on two episodes in Book Four of *Heike monogatari*: "The Battle of the Bridge" and "The Prince's Death." Aesthetically, it aims at the same sort of narrative interest as the tale itself.

The play in the Martial Mode, thus, can have either a lyric or a narrative emphasis. None relies exclusively on the one or the other, however, so even a predominantly narrative play like *Yorimasa* ends with a waka, and even *Tadanori*, for all its lyricism, contains long, purely narrative passages.

As we saw, in the first dan of *Tadanori*, Zeami pays more than usual attention to the waki. He is identified as one of Shunzei's retainers, and his avowal to abandon poetry (in the shidai), his shallow understanding of the life of a seaside peasant (in the first mondō), and his lack of sensibility (in the second mondō) give him a personality of sorts. This emphasis is underscored by the direct address to him at the end of the play. Other plays in the Martial Mode also devote more attention to the waki than was remarked in the standard plays of the Aged and Woman's Modes: in *Atsumori*, the most striking example, the waki is the very warrior who killed Atsumori; in *Tsunemasa* the waki is the priest Gyōkai, Tsunemasa's childhood teacher; and in *Kiyotsune* the waki is Kiyotsune's retainer Awazu no Samurō.[39]

The close link between the waki and the shite in so many of these plays, as Kami Hiroshi suggests, may have grown out of popular tales about specific people who took it upon themselves to pray for famous warriors.[40] Not only can one well imagine that such tales might lie behind the creation of these noh, but there is in fact convincing documentary evidence that this was the case in at least one play. That play is *Sanemori*. It is first mentioned in *Sandō* and must consequently have been written before 1423. The waki is an actual historical figure, the Reverend Father Tawami (1375-1437), a disciple of the founder of Ji sect Buddhism, Ippen. In the play he is visited by the ghost of the warrior Sanemori.

Now it so happens that the Shingon priest Mansai recorded the "appearance" of Sanemori's ghost in his diary. In the fifth month of 1414, he wrote: "The ghost of Saitō Bettō Sanemori appeared in Shimowara in the province of Kaga. He met with the Reverend Father Yūgyō and had ten recitations of the holy name said. This happened, they say, on the eleventh of the third month. . . . If it is true it is the occurrence of a remarkable age."[41] "The Reverend Father Yūgyō" usually refers to Ippen himself, but in this case it means his thirteenth successor, the fourteenth Yūgyō, Tawami.[42]

It seems quite clear that Zeami took advantage of the currency of this rumor to write *Sanemori*. There is no evidence that he did the same for the other plays in the mode, but perhaps this gave him inspiration for their composition. At any rate, the convention of having the waki related to the shite and specifically named in the plays of this mode is well established, the only exceptions among plays confidently attributable to Zeami being *Yorimasa* and *Yashima*.

Turning now to the structure of the plays in the Martial Mode, we begin, as usual, by looking at their shōdan sequences. A single glance at Table 10 confirms Zeami's statement that "the characteristics of a play in the Martial Mode vary considerably according to the *honzetsu*, and there is no single specific way to write it." There is far more structural variation among these plays than among those of the Woman's Mode (despite the striking variations of some of the mad-woman plays). For one thing, they have as few as four dan and as many as six. But beyond this, the breaks between dan are often indistinct. By necessity, then, we will look at only the structural variations that seem particularly noteworthy.

In the instructions quoted above, Zeami said: "If the *shite* is to leave the stage part way through the play to reappear later in a different guise, then the *kusemai* and so on should be set in the latter half of the play." Probably no other statement, by Zeami or anyone else, had more to do with the emergence of a distinct Martial Mode in the noh theater, for in it Zeami sets forth a rule that separates these plays from the rest. All the plays in the Martial Mode are heavily weighted toward the last half (or, in the case of the one-act play *Kiyotsune*, toward the last part of the play). Thus, in *Tadanori* both narrative sequences are delivered by the nochijite. As a result, the climax of these plays tends to come not in a lyrical passage, as it usually does in the plays of the Aged and Woman's Mode, but in narrative form. It is quite true that lyric shōdan follow such narrative sequences (e.g., the jōnoei and two uta after the *kuri-*katari-uta sequence of *Tadanori*), but most of the nochijite's time is spent in the description of events rather than emotions, and his dance accompanies that account (and usually mimetically presents those events). Less time is available for abstract movement like the JONOMAI of *Izutsu* or the KAMI-MAI of *Takasago*. Indeed, among the major plays in the Martial Mode, only *Atsumori* has an important instrumental dance. The others either do not have a dance at all or have only a brief one like *Tadanori*'s TACHIMAWARI.[43]

Since the nochijite (supposedly the spirit in his true form) rather than the maejite (the spirit in some sort of disguise) is responsible for the narrative in these plays, we might expect to find less narrative distance in these passages than in plays such as *Izutsu* and *Takasago* where the maejite delivers the narrative. But this is not always the case. We have already seen how narrative distance is purposely manipulated in the second half of *Tadanori*. This is true in *Sanemori* as well. There, three narratives are delivered. The first is the katari of the final dan. The shite, Sanemori, relates that the battle is over, and Tezuka no Tarō Mitsumori has come before his general, Kiso no Yoshinaka. The shite then speaks from the point of view of Tezuka, reporting how he killed a strange warrior whom he cannot identify: "I [Tezuka] thought he might be a great general, but he had no retainers to accompany him, so I wondered if he was a mere soldier. But he was wearing a brocade warrior's robe. I shouted at him to announce himself, but he would not. He spoke with an Eastern accent." The shite goes on to tell the story of the examination and washing of the warrior's head, which eventually reveals that the mysterious warrior is Sanemori. He was not recognized at first because he had dyed his white hair black. This first narrative provides a distant view of Sanemori, switching, as it does, from the third-person point of view to the direct quotation of Tezuka.

The second narrative is cast into a kuse. It is again written in the third person, this time in a discursive style complete with quotations of proverbs and old poems (for explanatory rather than lyrical purposes) and references to Chinese history. It gives Sanemori's reasons for wearing a red brocade robe, and because of its content, gives a rather closer picture of the man than the katari did.

The third narrative gives a far more intimate picture than the second, however. It mixes first and third person, moving directly into Sanemori's mind. Zeami even goes so far as to mimic his Eastern dialect and mild vulgarity.* The passage reads:

Rongi

1	C	Ge ni ya sange no monogatari,
		Kokoro no mizu no soko kiyoku,
		Nigori o nokoshitamō na yo,
	S	Sono mōshiu no shura no michi,
5		Megurimegurite mata koko ni,
		Kiso to kuman to takumishi o,
		Tezuka me ni hedaterareshi,
		Munen na ima ni ari,
	C	Tsuzuku tsuwamono taretare to,
10		Nanoru naka ni mo mazu susumu,
	S	Tezuka no Tarō Mitsumori,
	C	Rōdō wa shiu o utaseji to,
	S	Kakihedatarite Sanemori to,
	C	Oshinarabete kumu tokoro o,
15	S	Appare onore wa Nippon ichi no,
		Kō no mono to kunjōzu yo tote,

---

* Not the blasphemous, sexual, or scatological vulgarity one might find in contemporary English, but a Japanese form of cursing: using intimate or humble forms of second-person pronouns in direct address to strangers.

TABLE 10 *The Shōdan Sequences of Five Zeami Plays in the Martial Mode*

Dan[a] (section)	*Yumi Yawata*	*Tadanori*	*Atsumori*	*Yorimasa*	*Sanemori*	*Kiyotsune*
1 (jo)	SHINNOSHIDAI Shidai Nanori Ageuta Tsukizerifu	SHIDAI Shidai Nanori Sashi Sageuta Ageuta (Tsukizerifu)	SHIDAI Shidai Nanori Ageuta (Tsukizerifu)	NANORIBUE Nanori Ageuta (Tsukizerifu) X	 Nanori Fure Sashi Ageuta	SHIDAI Shidai Nanori Ageuta (Tsukizerifu)
2 (ha 1)	SHINNOISSEI Issei Sashi Sageuta Ageuta	ISSEI Sashi Issei *Sashi Sageuta	SHIDAI Shidai Sashi Sageuta Ageuta	 Mondō Ageuta	 *Sashi	 Mondō Kudoki Sageuta Ageuta
3 (ha 2)	Mondō Kakeai	Mondō Ageuta Mondō	Mondō Kakeai Ageuta Kakeai	Mondō	Mondō	Mondō Kudoki
4 (ha 3)	Ageuta Sasoizerifu Kuri Sashi Kuse Rongi	Rongi	Uta	Ageuta	Ageuta	Uta

Aikyōgen Mondō Katari Ageuta	Mondō Katari X Ageuta	Mondō Katari Ageuta	Mondō Katari X Ageuta	Mondō Katari Fure X Ageuta	Mondō Katari Fure X Ageuta
5 (kyū) DEHA Sashi Issei Noriji KAMIMAI Rongi	ISSEI Sashi *Kudoki Kuri Sashi Sageuta Ageuta *Kuri *Katari Uta Jōnoei TACHIMAWARI Jōnoei Uta Uta	ISSEI Genoei Kakeai Uta Kuri Sashi Kuse Kakeai *Issei CHŪNOMAI X Noriji X Chūnoriji	ISSEI Sashi Genoei Issei Kakeai Ageuta Nanoriguri Sashi Kuse Katari Chūnoriji *Rongi Jōnoei Uta	DEHA X *Issei Noriji Kakeai Ageuta Kuri Sashi Katari Ageuta Kuse Rongi Chūnoriji	KOINONETORI Sashi Genoei Kakeai Ageuta Mondō Sashi Kakeai Sashi Jōnoei Ei Uta Kuse Kudokiguri Genoei Chūnoriji

NOTE: The shōdan in small caps are instrumental pieces, including dances. Parentheses indicate a highly conventional shōdan that was omitted from old texts but was probably included in performances; X indicates an unspecified shōdan; and an asterisk indicates that a shōdan is irregular.

ᵃThe dan numbers for the Martial Mode plays are not necessarily accurate. Because of the irregularity in the number and sequence of the shōdan, they cannot be aligned here as in the analogous tables for the plays in the other modes.

> Kura no maewa ni oshitsukete,
> Kubi kakikitte sutetengeri.[44]

Rongi

1   c   Continue with your tale of penitence
            Leave no trace of muddiness in the depths
            Of the pristine waters of your heart.

       s   The *shura* road leads round and round
5   Through the torments of clinging delusion,
            And I come here to grapple yet again with Kiso Yoshinaka,
            But, held off by that bastard Tezuka,
            Even now I feel resentful rage.

       c   Among the advancing ranks of warriors,
10   Calling out their names, there, he comes forth first,

       s   Tezuka no Tarō Mitsumori.

       c   One of Tezuka's retainers, in defense of his lord,

       s   Drove his own mount between us two,

       c   And thought to match himself against Sanemori.

15   s   "So, y'all mean to set yourself 'gainst
            Me, the strongest warrior 'n all Japan," I said,
            And jammed him down at his saddle
            Took his head off, and dropped his damned carcass.

Zeami never speaks of narrative distance, or anything of the sort, in his comments on creating new plays, and it is impossible to tell whether he was conscious of such a thing or not. He does, however, comment on his positioning of the *Sanemori* narratives. In *Sarugaku dangi*, he says: "If one were to write in usual order, the battle scene should come directly after the head-washing scene, but I inserted the passage beginning *mata Sanemori* [the kuse] instead and put the battle scene at the end of the play."[45] By inserting that passage—the narrative about Sanemori's reasons for wearing a red warrior's robe—he provided an additional perspective on Sanemori for the viewer to use in interpreting the play, thereby creating a depth of characterization and layering of experiences as he had done to such great effect in *Izutsu* and *Tadanori*.

Another interesting variation on the standard narrative is found in *Kiyotsune*. As a one-act play, it is unique among the major plays of the mode on that count alone, but it also has a particularly striking structure of great dramatic power.[46] The play opens with the waki, one of Kiyotsune's retainers, telling the warrior's wife, the tsure, of her husband's suicide. The wife becomes distraught, and when Kiyotsune's ghost, the shite, appears,* she reproaches him for having killed himself. He sets out to explain his actions in a narrative beginning with a sashi:

---

* Table 10 shows a KOINONETORI here. Standard modern performances do not call for an instrumental piece for the shite's entrance. In the variant performance *koi no netori*, however, the shite enters to this unique instrumental piece. Although that variant is rarely seen today, it was originally the more common and standard way of performing the play. (See the record notes by Konparu Sōemon and Masuda Shōzō to *Nōgaku hayashi taikei*, Japan Victor SJL 64-69, p. 74.)

Sashi

1   S   Sate mo Kiushiu Yamaga no gō e mo,
         Kataki yosekuru to kikishi hodo ni,
         Toru mono mo toriaezu yo mo sugara,
         Takasebune ni torinotte Bungo no kuni Yanagi to iu tokoro ni tsuku,

5   C   Ge ni ya tokoro no na o etaru,
         Ura wa namiki no yanagi kage,
         Ito karisome no kōkyo o sadamu,
     S   Sore yori Usa Hachiman ni gosankei aru beshi tote,
     C   Jinme shichihiki sono hoka kongon shuju no sasagemono,
10   Sunawachi hōhei no tame naru beshi.[47]

Sashi

1   S   So then, when we heard that the enemy had come
         As far as the area of Yamaga in Kyushu,
         We took to any available boats immediately, and all night long
         Rode in shallow skiffs until we came to a place called Willow in the province of Bungo.
5   C   The place was well named;
         All along the coast were rows of willows,
         Beneath their threadlike branches we set up a temporary residence for the Emperor.
     S   From there it was decided to make a pilgrimage to the Hachiman shrine of Usa,
     C   And we prepared horses and gold and all sorts of precious offerings
10   To give to the god of the shrine.

When the shite has gotten this far, the tsure suddenly interrupts:

Kakeai

11   T   Kayō ni mōseba nao mo mi no,
         Urami ni nitaru koto naredomo,
         Sasuga ni imada kimi mashimasu,
         Miyo no sakai ya ichimon no,
15   Hate o mo mizu shite itazura ni,
         Onmi hitori o suteshi koto wa,
         Makoto ni yoshi naki koto narazu ya,
     S   Ge ni ge ni kore mo onkotowari sarinagara,
         Tanomi naki yo no shirushi no tsuge,
20   Katari mōsu kikitamae.

Kakeai

11   T   It will sound like my resentment speaking
         When I tell you this, but
         You see there, His Majesty was still alive.
         And you didn't even wait to see the end
15   Of his sacred reign, or the final outcome for our clan,
         But vainly threw your life away.
         Wasn't that completely senseless?
     S   Yes, yes, it seems that way, but all the same
         Listen and I will tell you of
20   The signs I had that all hope in this world was lost.

Only now does the shite complete his narrative (in the highly idiosyncratic sequence sashi-jōnoei-ei-uta-kuse). The audience's expectations have been challenged, and the subsequent narrative is all the more effective for that.

Zeami follows his own suggestion that the shite should make his exit in chūnori of the shura style in *Atsumori, Sanemori, Kiyotsune,* and *Yashima.* And *Yorimasa* at least has a chūnori near the end of the play. *Tadanori* is the exception here, probably because it is the furthest removed from the traditional shura role depicting the sufferings of the warring spirit in hell. In fact, only *Kiyotsune* among Zeami's plays in the Martial Mode is explicit in depicting such sufferings:

Chūnoriji

1	S	Sate wa shuradō ni ochikochi no,
	C	Sate wa shuradō ni ochikochi no,
		Tatsuki wa kataki ame wa yasaki,
		Tsuchi wa seiken yama wa tet'njō,
5		Kumo no hatate o tsuite,
		Kyōman no tsurugi o soroe,
		Jaken no manako no hikari,
		Ai yoku tono i chi tsūgen dōjō,
		Mumyō no hosshō mo midaruru kataki,
10		Utsu wa nami hiku wa ushio. . . .

Chūnoriji

1	S	Then I fell to the hell of warring spirits.
	C	Then I fell to the hell of warring spirits.
		There, the very trees are enemies; it rains arrows.
		The ground reveals sharp swords, the mountains iron citadels.
		Clouds turn to streaming banners, or again, to shields pierced through,
		Arrogance aligns in rows of sabres,
		The light in the eyes of wickedness
		Shines with obsession, greed, covetousness, rage, and stupidity.
		The enmity of benighted delusion pollutes the Buddha nature.
10		Waves crash, the tide rushes out. . . .

This passage can be profitably compared with the end of the now defunct piece *Kasa Sotoba* or *Motomezuka*.[48]

Because discursive narrative figures so large in the plays of the Martial Mode, they tend to have fewer purely lyrical passages than the plays in the other two modes, especially those in the Woman's Mode. But they are not so few as to be considered rare or even infrequent. We encountered several in *Tadanori*. In fact, the dramatic success of these plays owes much to the careful combination of lyrical and narrative shōdan. Consequently, one finds the standard lyric "tools," such as renga-like association and progression, allusive variation, simple allusion, and parallelism, throughout the plays in the Martial Mode.

In his *Sandō* article on plays of this mode, Zeami says, "The melody should be heroic and complex." Despite the danger of assuming that the modern music of noh accurately reflects the music of Zeami's day, one cannot help noticing that many of the plays in the Martial Mode are sung with long passages of neither tsuyogin nor yowagin, but a difficult and subtly articulated mixture of the two called *kongin*. The *sashi in the second dan of *Tadanori* is one such passage. Both sashi in the fourth dan are other examples. In addition, there is a good deal of switching from yowagin to tsuyogin and vice versa in all the major plays. Can this be a remnant of Zeami's "heroic and complex" melody?

The variety and originality of Zeami's noh in the Martial Mode arouse curiosity about the plays of other noh dramatists. Unfortunately, such curiosity finds little reward. Among the sixteen plays in the Martial Mode in the modern repertory, only three can be confidently attributed to writers other than Zeami: *Michimori* was written (at least originally) by Seiami, *Shunzei Tadanori* by Naitō Fujizaemon, and *Ikuta Atsumori* by Konparu Zenpō (1454-1532).[49] (No one has ventured to guess who wrote the infrequently performed *Ikarikazuki*.)

Michimori seems to have preceded Zeami's other plays in the Martial Mode, but what it was like in its original form we do not know because, as Zeami admits, he "cut out the parts that were too long and turned it into a good play."[50] It is based on the story of two lovers, Taira no Michimori and Kozaishō no Tsubone, both of whom die as a result of the Genpei wars, she by her own hand, and he in battle. In the first half of the play, the tsure, the ghost of Kozaishō no Tsubone, relates how she jumped into the sea to drown herself off the coast of Naruto. In the second half the shite, the ghost of Michimori, tells of his own death in battle. The nochijite's narrative seems unduly short; possibly Zeami cut it too much in his eagerness to improve the play.[51] As noted earlier, Zeami calls *Michimori* a straightforward noh, but the play's structure does not seem particularly orthodox, and it has been suggested that what he means is that it is completely faithful to its source in *Heike monogatari*.[52] Unfortunately, *Michimori* offers few clues about the origin of the Martial Mode as a genre, and it was apparently so extensively revised by Zeami that it provides little contrast with the plays he wrote himself.

Shunzei Tadanori is a one-act play that begins when Rokuyata, the waki, takes a poem card he has found on Tadanori's body to Shunzei, the tsure. Once he has given the poem card to Shunzei, he leaves the stage. Then Tadanori's ghost, the shite, appears. He delivers a kuse about the origins of waka poetry, dances a KAKERI, and then exits with a description of the suffering of warring spirits. Sanari Kentarō believes that the insertion of the story about the beginnings of waka in the kuse instead of something more directly related to the shite's own life is an original and dramatically effective way of using the shōdan.[53] I cannot agree. I find the play fragmented and tedious. Neither is it instructive as a counter-example to Zeami's own plays.

Ikuta Atsumori takes as its subject a meeting between Atsumori's orphaned son and the ghost of Atsumori. It is, in other words, a combination of a play in the Martial Mode and a reunion play (a relatively common type of genzai noh). This idea is more interesting in conception than in execution, however, and *Ikuta Atsumori* is not a distinguished work. Again, it offers little instructive contrast with Zeami's plays in the Martial Mode.

This exhausts our list of plays by known authors, leaving one puzzle: why did other playwrights fail to write mugen noh in the Martial Mode? There are numerous plays about living warriors—*Funa Benkei* (Benkei on the Boat), *Ataka*, *Shōzon*, and the Soga plays are but a few examples—but they do not fall into the Martial Mode as Zeami conceived it. Did Zeami's plays somehow fail to please, or was it rather that they were too good to be successfully imitated? Either alternative might have kept other playwrights from trying their own hands at the genre. It is hard to imagine that such works as *Tadanori*, *Atsumori*, *Kiyotsune*, *Yashima*, *Yorimasa*, and *Sanemori* found no admirers,[54] and indeed Omote Akira and Konishi Jin'ichi seem to concur that no one else wrote noh in the Martial Mode like Zeami's because his were impossible to improve on.[55] This may be, but then why did Zenchiku and other authors bother to write plays in the Woman's Mode? It seems unlikely that anyone could improve on *Izutsu* or *Kinuta* either. Whatever the case, Zeami appears to be almost entirely responsible for the development and perfection of plays in the Martial Mode.

Conclusion

Tradition weighs heavily on the arts in Japan, so heavily in fact that many of them have died as arts per se, and they remain, like pressed flowers, brittle and pale reminders of a once brilliant vitality. The art of reciting medieval war narratives, *heikyoku*, is a clear case in point. From its inception in the thirteenth century, heikyoku remained an enormously popular and accessible performing art for some six hundred years. Even the tiniest communities would be visited by itinerant bards, and the tales of martial valor related by such musicians provoked an enthusiastic response in a highly diverse audience. Heikyoku survives to this day, but now it is one of the least accessible of Japan's traditional arts. No one really enjoys it anymore—at least no one without a brilliant imagination and an archaeologist's lust for the gone and all-but-forgotten. The one or two heikyoku singers alive today are very old men. Only scholars know their names.

The case of the noh theater is much more complicated. One can see professional performances of noh almost every night of the week in Tokyo, and there are thousands—no, probably tens of thousands—of practicing amateurs who pour millions (billions?) of yen into recital fees, lessons, costume rental, and so on. The noh is very much alive . . . in a way.

Yet the untimely death of the exciting contemporary noh master, Kanze Hisao, in 1978 left many patrons and aficionados of noh in despair. "There will never be another actor like him now," some said. Or: "The noh has had it. All we have left now is the nepotistic economic superstructure of noh. There's no art left in it. Just money." Or yet again: "The noh now is like penny candy in a priceless lacquer box. Sure, the costumes and masks are wonderful, but these people's performances are atrocious."

The situation cannot be quite as bad as these complaints would have us believe. All the same, the economic prosperity that some schools of noh enjoy has not unleashed a surge of artistic genius. Brilliant performances are rare, exciting ones uncommon. The majority can at best be characterized as competent, and there are many that hardly deserve even that modest nod of approval.

There is little room for anything new in the noh today. Every step, every gesture, is prescribed by the long and long-venerated tradition. There is little new blood in the professional ranks. Father succeeds grandfather, son succeeds father. Admittedly, the noh would hardly have survived into the Tokugawa period, much less into the present, without this strictly exclusive hereditary professionalism and the companion system of patronage by practicing amateurs. But the great irony is that these systems have all too often worked at cross-purposes to the artistic integrity of noh. Many of those professionals were—and are— engaged in noh, not for its artistic potential, but merely because their fathers were. Amateurs, no matter how talented, must overcome formidable obstacles to gain access to the professional stage. The pressures of modern society have exacerbated the problem. A strict concentration on professional training and performance will not pay the bills, but a very comfortable living can be had by the actor who sacrifices most of his time to amateur students, typically wealthy, middle-aged women. The hereditary heads of schools dominate noh economically and artistically whether they are themselves blessed with talent or not; meanwhile, the audience, though wealthy and generous, grows more elderly and elitist.

It seems too early to tell whether noh will survive as a museum piece or whether it will find enough talented and devoted students to stay alive as an art. But the question is more than merely incidental to this study, for the weight of tradition is not a new problem to noh. It is a problem that has persisted since the fifteenth century when noh became noh, and it is in fact so central to the existence of noh that a general understanding of Zeami's style can best be grasped from an examination of his relation to the tradition, or traditions, of noh.

Zeami was a master of several different traditions. His birthright was the art of Yamato sarugaku, but that alone seems to have been of limited appeal to his wealthiest and most powerful patrons, so he made liberal use of the traditions of other successful performers, most conspicuously, Inuō Dōami of Ōmi sarugaku and the dengaku actor Zōami. And then, of course, there is the elite literary tradition of Japan, the waka and renga he learned in the capital from the old aristocrat Nijō Yoshimoto, among others. These traditions were not always harmonious, yet their synthesis in Zeami's plays is such that it is often difficult to discern the original strains of influence.

The most complete documentation of his work with these many "traditions" is to be found in his treatises, but they provide little explicit information by which to gauge the evolution of his literary and musical style. Indeed, as we have seen, the first six decades of his life are almost a complete blank in this regard, so that we are left to guess at the dates of many of his plays.

Yet if, in our search for clues about Zeami's evolution as a playwright, we have no alternative but to turn back to the treatises, this inconvenience may in fact allow us an unexpectedly salutary change of perspective on his work. It has been all too easy for modern scholars, especially in the West, to see Zeami as a literary man, but he was not, at least not primarily. He was always more concerned with performance than with writing, and his Yamato "tradition" and most immediate artistic heritage was popular, nonliterate and nonintellectual, a practical tradition completely dependent on the favor of the masses, untouched by abstract concerns and far removed from the elite culture of the capital. If the Ōmi tradition that he found so useful was somewhat less dependent on the masses, it was, all the same, not a literary tradition, but a performing tradition of visual elegance and beauty. The elite literary tradition, however masterly his use of it, was always a practical tool to him, never an end in itself.

As a member of the Yūzaki troupe, then as its head, and even much later, as a retired but interested adviser, Zeami consistently gave precedence to performance, not to writing; indeed, we can most clearly see the course of his life and the gradual changes in his literary style through three performance-related and extra-literary concerns: dramatic training, patronage, and virtuosity. In a sense, these are merely different aspects of a single inclination of professional intent. Ideally, the one supports the other, giving birth to the third, but it is natural that one concern color a certain span of life most intensely, only to give way, in its turn, to others; so Zeami's attention seems to flow between training and patronage in his youth and middle age to virtuosity in his last decades.

Some conjecture was made about Zeami's training in Chapter One, based on his comments about training the young actor. A constantly recurring theme is the nurture of an actor's ambition and technical skill to sustain him in competition with other troupes. The other troupes of Yamato sarugaku were his most immediate rivals, and the field of battle was monomane, dramatic imitation. "The Yamato style," he maintains, "takes dramatic imitation and discursive interest as fundamental, and the public recognizes our proficiency in the portrayal of roles of impressive appearance or violent action. Such, indeed, has been our traditional aim."[1] In this tradition diversity, the portrayal of as many character-types as possible, was a great virtue. "The basic idea in portraying . . . characters [was] to imitate exactly, without leaving anything out," and although one had to "discriminate what degree of imitation [was] appropriate, depending on the object imitated,"[2] the actor's job was, plain and simply, to present a character mimetically on stage.

Had the Yūzaki troupe confined its performances to the Yamato area, this imitation of demons and other violent characters would probably have remained Zeami's central aesthetic goal, and we would know almost nothing about him. Fortunately for us, when Zeami was hardly ten years old, perhaps even earlier, Kannami's ambitions led his troupe outside of the Nara basin, and its successes in the capital faced him and his son with a great dilemma and a crucial professional stimulus.

Novelty and a certain rustic vigor were probably the greatest virtues of their early performances in Kyoto, but certain adjustments in Yamato style assured continued success in competition against other troupes, particularly against the Ōmi troupe of Inuō Dōami, whose aesthetic aims were well attuned to the aristocratic taste. Kannami's adaptations of other performing arts, such as Kusemai and dengaku, to his own troupe's purposes are indicative of these efforts, and throughout the treatises one finds Zeami picking and choosing from among the most successful approaches to acting he encountered to adapt them for his own noh. He discovered yūgen, or elegant and graceful beauty, probably in the late-fourteenth-century performances of the Ōmi troupes; first, rather disingenuously, he claimed it as a complementary virtue to mono-mane in the Yamato style: "In Ōmi they set *yūgen* as their standard, and dramatic imitation is of secondary importance. Their performances are based on elegance, but in Yamato, dramatic imitation is the first priority; we exhaust every possible type of role and, moreover, we aim for an effect of *yūgen*."[3]

As a young performer restricted to the Yamato tradition, Zeami would have had little to offer on stage. The best Yamato roles, those of "impressive appearance or violent action" (i.e., the demon, the demon-like god, and the *monogurui*, or so-called mad role), were ill-suited to a child. At the same time, the practicalities of life required that the troupe take advantage of whatever assets the boy actor had. His physical beauty was a valuable professional asset—so basic to his early success that in later years he spoke of the child's beauty (in song and dance) as a paradigm for *hana*, "the flower" (i.e., dramatic interest).[4] It may well be that Zeami's first interest in yūgen was a direct result of his own professional capacities as a boy actor. His task was to bring his beauty into play for professional advantage on stage, and so, a search for his "style" in these first years as an actor (and perhaps playwright) is to be found at the nexus between his natural physical advantage, the tools available to him from his Yamato heritage, and anything else he could bring to the stage.

Consider the following characters: Kagetsu, Jinen Koji, Tōgan Koji, Seigan Koji. They are apprentice priests, all proficient in a variety of arts, all attractive boys. Each has lent his name to a noh play, and at least three of these plays date from sometime before 1423.[5] Now, consider what we know of the relationship between Zeami and Yoshimitsu, together with a group of plays encouraging the display of boyish beauty and subtle adolescent homoeroticism. If Zeami did not write these plays,[6] he certainly used them as a drawing card, and they reflect a dramatic milieu with which he was completely familiar as a boy and young man. Furthermore, they provide valuable evidence of a successful dramatic style, and a part of Zeami's heritage, whatever his eventual disposition of it.

Plays like these may have been successful in the capital because they combined monomane, in the imitation of an apprentice priest, with yūgen, in the singing and dancing that he performed. *Kagetsu*, for instance, opens with the self-introduction of an older priest who has taken the tonsure because he has lost track of his son. By the end of the play, the father comes to discover that his son is none other than the boy Kagetsu; their eventual reunion provides a sort of plot. It is, however, the thinnest of excuses for a plot, and audience interest centers rather on verbal ingenuity and a succession of singing and dance performances (a *geizukushi*) that follow one after the other throughout the play. *Jinen Koji* contains a similar succession of songs and dances and a rather more developed melodramatic plot. *Tōgan Koji* uses dances and precocious erudition to similar, if not as successful, effect, and *Seigan Koji* follows its pattern.

Since there is no evidence to prove Zeami's authorship of any of these plays, to take them as representative of his early literary style is pure speculation. But they can confidently be considered representative of his early performance style—a fascinating compromise between monomane and pure dance and song, evidence of the already mixed nature of his heritage and early repertory. Perhaps they account in some measure for the appeal of the Yūzaki troupe in the capital, where the traditional staples of demons and the like may not have been terribly effective.

Zeami may eventually have rejected plays with the loose variety-show format of *Kagetsu*—there is nothing among his later works to suggest a continued commitment to such plays—but the training of a young actor in song and dance and the exploitation of the child's natural beauty played a continuing, in fact an increasing, role in his mature style in both performance and writing. This may be a tacit admission that he was dissatisfied with the Yamato tradition, specifically with the lopsidedness of its "dramatic imitation."

It is clear that new traditions became important to the young Zeami in the capital. His encounters with renga and waka were mentioned in Chapter One, and his familiarity with the elite literary tradition, particularly with *Kokinshū* and *Ise monogatari*, is everywhere apparent in his plays. And Ōmi sarugaku, as embodied in the art of Inuō Dōami, exerted an increasingly strong attraction on him, to the point where, by the 1420's, yūgen had replaced monomane as the primary goal of a performance, a change that was to have far-reaching effects in his subsequent work of both a theoretical and a practical nature.

Whatever the purely aesthetic virtues of Ōmi sarugaku may have been, it held one supreme attraction for Zeami: it was successful with important people. We saw in Chapter One that Dōami stood higher in Yoshimitsu's estimation than Zeami, and the inescapable conclusion must have been that the techniques of Ōmi sarugaku had to be adopted into the Yūzaki troupe. A gradual shift was made, therefore, away from monomane to yūgen. When it was begun is hard to say. Kannami himself, in his practicality and catholicity of taste, probably took notice of the advantages of Ōmi sarugaku during the 1360's or 1370's. In Zeami's mature style, however, the shift is complete, and yūgen has emerged as the central aesthetic goal of performance; its embodiment has become the central object of the actor's training.

The mature style takes documentary shape in the treatises of the early 1420's with *Shikadō* (1420), *Nikyoku santai ningyōzu* (1421), and *Sandō* (1423). I have quoted extensively from the last of these in previous chapters, discussing as well some of the illustrations in *Nikyoku santai ningyōzu*. The first illustration in that work seems to reflect Zeami's early experience in noh. It is not difficult to see Kagetsu in the simple sketch of a boy actor, but the caption accompanying it goes somewhat deeper than the naïve precocity of that play:

In *Shikadō* it says, "The first graceful beauty of the child remains in the Three Modes and the various applications of the Three Modes concretely manifest the myriad pieces." The figure of the child embodies *yūgen*. His arts are dance and song. Once you have mastered these two arts they merge into each other, and you become an accomplished actor of life-long promise and lofty performance. Thereafter, if you transpose the figure of the child into the Three Modes to dance and sing, *yūgen* will be manifest in the Three Modes. Not performing the Three Modes as a child while preserving the overall attractiveness of a child throughout the Three Modes is a profound strategy. Once you have mastered those two first arts of the child, you safely attain an enduring and lofty individual style, which thereafter remains in your applications of the Three Modes to take concrete form in the myriad pieces.[7]

The child's role is now seen as the beginning of a systematic strategy for training and the embodiment of dramatic ideals. Training begins in childhood and the foundation laid by a child's training in singing and dance becomes the kernel of the mature actor's successes.

The nearly sixty-year-old actor has a sizable investment in the past, in his training as a child, but the strains of naturalistic representationalism that colored his earlier work have for the most part given way to a kind of idealism, clearly exemplified in the Three Modes themselves. Zeami's reduction of the many roles mentioned in *Fūshikaden* to the Three Modes discussed in the previous chapters is indicative of an attempt to find stable and reliable artistic values. This had been of some concern to him earlier; in *Fūshikaden* he had frequently warned the young actor to cultivate a "true flower" that would not die as the physical charm of youth faded. His emphasis there was placed on constant training and the refinement of the actor's art.

By the 1420's, however, his attention is directed more toward formulating the ideals of performance, and central to those ideals is a nondiscursive, abstract beauty, verging on the supernatural or sublime, beyond the natural circumstances of physical reality. Recall, for example, his discussion of yūgen in selecting the ideal character for plays in the Woman's Mode: "In such [an ideal] character, one finds, as it were, a jewel among jewels. . . . There is a seed for the blossoming of sublime mysterious beauty. It is a seed more rare than the one that, as the old poem says, 'combines the scent of plum and the blossom of cherry and sets them to bloom on a willow branch.'"[8] The seasonal boundaries of the natural world are transgressed to bring to the stage an ideal synthesis of various types of beauty. An actor who can embody this sort of abstract beauty has nothing to fear from age and diminishing physical capacity. His attainments reach beyond the physical. This goes hand in hand with a new hierarchy of performance styles. On the bottom is the performance to be seen; above it, the performance to be heard; and above all, the performance beyond the senses.[9]

For the playwright this lofty aesthetic ideal is achieved through an increased formalism—through the creation of an abstract beauty apprehended and appreciated much as one appreciates the formal beauty of, say, a well-written classical sonata. This is the primary sense in which Zeami's style can be called "classical." Beauty comes from the balance and grace of the form itself, rather than from the imitation of external reality; thus, the extensive and influential role of the formal orthodoxy of waki noh on the basic configuration of all Zeami's plays.

Consider, in this regard, the technical specificity of the *Sandō* discussions of dramatic structure. Zeami pays meticulous attention to the measured development of a performance through the gradual unfolding of jo-ha-kyū and the principle of dan symmetry because he understands the relation between form and affect much more clearly than his predecessors. From the list of plays in *Sandō*, it is plain that the Aged Mode and the Martial Mode have attained their classic configuration by this point; the most famous plays centering on those modes have been written.

Moreover, as form takes precedence over mimetic diversity and the dramatic process is refined, Zeami finds certain types of performance unacceptable. The Three Modes have become the models to which all other dramatic representations are referred, and as a result, one of the most important roles of the Yamato tradition is unceremoniously rejected: "The demon of violent movement [*rikidōfū no oni*] is demonic in his actions, his appearance, and his mind. It is a heterodox role of naked rage. This style is not acknowledged by our tradition. It is, however, used for superficial effect in the role of the demon of subtle movement [*saidōfū no oni*]."[10]

There is undoubtedly a measure of elitism in this. The demons of which he speaks were popular with the mass audience, and in appealing to the lowest common denominator, took no account of the aesthetic advances that had won noh aristocratic recognition—unlike his father, Zeami unambiguously prefers aristocratic patronage to mass appeal. At the same time, we continue to see his concern with training; he repudiates the demon of violent movement in part because young actors who indulge themselves in such raw and energetic performances can win a temporary success that is detrimental to their long-term artistic development.[11]

In this light, one can reasonably argue that Zeami turned his back on a major part of the Yamato tradition; he unblushingly appropriated the virtues of Ōmi sarugaku to his own use, and narrowed the representational scope of noh in deference to the old court elite. The picture is perhaps unflattering. It is also incomplete. Plays of such quality as *Atsumori*, *Kiyotsune*, *Sanemori*, *Takasago*, and *Tadanori* cannot be explained away as a simple matter of bowing to influence. There is something altogether new here, something bordering on the revolutionary. We catch our first glimpses of it in the treatises, in Zeami's expanding notions of a new level of artistic power and accomplishment through which the actor can rise above his own limitations. Perhaps the most obvious example is the notion of *riken no ken*, "a view removed from [one's own] view," which, in the most practical terms, enables the performer to gain an objective perspective on his performance.[12] One can also point to Zeami's discussion of artistic ranking, the upper ranges of which allow increasingly individualistic and at the same time transcendent performances. Indeed, he contends that the actor may become the very vessel of the universe:

In the *Analects* it is written, "Zi Gong inquired of the Master saying, 'What am I?' The master replied, 'Thou art a vessel.' . . . 'What manner of vessel?' 'A chalice for ancestral offerings.'" . . .

Now then, in terms of our art, this vessel is actually the master who has attained to the myriad pieces from the Two Arts and the Three Modes, that is to say, a vessel of diverse accomplishment. It consists in the artistic power whereby one contains within one's being the full diversity of styles and techniques. When the visual and aural attainments from the Two Arts and the Three Modes are made manifest, extending throughout one's acting for inexhaustible artistic effect, this is the vessel of diverse accomplishment.

If you understand this in terms of Substance and Nothingness, Substance is the visible phenomenon, Nothingness is the vessel. That which manifests Substance is Nothingness. For example, crystal is itself colorless and patternless, but from it come fire and water. How is it that things of such diametrically opposed natures as fire and water can both be born of colorless emptiness?

There is a poem that reads:

Sakuragi wa	Take a cherry tree,
Kudakite mireba	Break it apart and you will find
Hana mo nashi	No blossoms.
Hana koso haru no	Blossoms come to bloom
Sora ni sakikere	Out of the empty springtime sky.

The seeds and flowers of the myriad pieces in the performing arts are born of the mind pervading the performer's artistic powers. Just as crystal gives birth to fire and water out of the air, and a cherry tree bears blossoms and fruit out of its colorlessness, so also does the accomplished master create the phenomenal manifestations of his art out of the intentional content of his mind, and as such, he is indeed a vessel.

Many are the graces of nature that embellish this auspicious and life-stretching art. The universe is the vessel that gives birth to all things, from the seasonal changes of flower and leaf, the snow and moon, mountains and seas, plants and trees, the sentient and nonsentient. In taking these many things as the affective materials of our art, our aim is to make the mind a vessel of the universe, establish that vessel of mind securely in the vast and formless emptiness, and attain the miraculous flower of attainment in the art.[13]

This theoretical inclination finds a practical manifestation in the thematic treatment of identity, most characteristic perhaps of the Martial Mode, but apparent as well in, for instance, the first sashi of *Takasago*. One also sees here that Zeami has in large degree turned away from training and patronage toward the pervasive interest in virtuosity expressed in his late treatises. For example, in *Kyūi* (written by 1428), *Kyakuraika* (1433), and to a lesser extent, *Go on* (probably before 1432), he proposes that the consummate master can go beyond the highest levels of artistic attainment and descend to completely individual and at the same time sublime performances of roles that would normally be unsuitable and uninteresting.

Commentators have frequently and plausibly demonstrated the presence of an element of Zen in these ideas, but there are other elements from the intellectual traditions of East Asia that may have an equally important share in such thought. In the passage above, for instance, we found Zeami quoting Confucius. He borrows from Confucius elsewhere as well, and quotes the *Classic of Poetry* alongside the *Heart Sutra* (which is not in any case exclusively a Zen text). In fact, Zeami's formulation of nine stages of artistic development, positing a complete liberation of individual capabilities through the gradual cultivation of one's talents, seems to point to the first article of the *Analects*: "The Master said, At fifteen I set my heart upon learning. At thirty, I had planted my feet firm upon the ground. At forty, I no longer suffered from perplexities. At fifty, I knew what were the biddings of Heaven. At sixty, I heard them with a docile ear. At seventy, I could follow the dictates of my own heart; for what I desired no longer overstepped the boundaries of right."[14]

The true virtuoso can follow the dictates of his own heart in performance and not overstep the bounds of taste. Such liberation is the natural result of life-long training on the part of the talented actor, and in theory, it provides him with complete security across a full range of dramatic expression without leaving the ethical stability of shūgen: "The straightforward style is *shūgen*. Using it as the base, proceed to the style of *yūgen, aishō, mujōon*, and so on, mastering each in its own way, and as you exhaust the mental devices of the patterned and patternless, you can attain even to the rank of virtuosic transcendence [*taketaru kurai* or *ran'i*]."[15]

Zeami looks back to his father as the exemplary actor of "virtuosic transcendence," and claims for him an artistry that allows access not only to the highest levels of dramatic expression, but also beyond them and back down to the most artless, even crude, levels of inartistic movement, which, from the pinnacle of his virtuosity, he succeeds in investing with sublimity.

The music of virtuosic transcendence [*rangyoku*] is of the highest level. Once you have exhausted your training in the myriad pieces and attained complete proficiency, you mix the positive and negative in the same sound and sing with a voice like, yet unlike, all others. In poetic theory, among the ten styles, in speaking of the strong rank, they mention "the demon-quelling style"; it must be of the same sort of level. This is the transcendent return and is the musical level of singing with complete fruition.[16]

Such attainment is exclusively the province of the solo actor because it is an utterly and uniquely individualistic form of expression; the troupe as a whole is incapable of performing on the level of virtuosic transcendence: "It cannot successfully be sung by a group even though all the members are accomplished in their own right."[17] As the completely individual expression of the master who has perfected his training, it cannot be learned or objectively assimilated by anyone else, just as it is impossible for anyone to appropriate another's shadow.[18]

Although some of the philosophical antecedents of these ideas have been ferreted out of Zen texts by modern scholars, Zeami's treatment of them seems to have the vitality of practical experience behind it, and the circumstances of his life seem to add palpable substance to what might otherwise be rather dry idealism. Behind his aesthetic and ethical philosophizing stands the same successful synthesis of diverse traditions that animates his plays. Zeami's struggle with the issue of virtuosity finally enables him to come full circle and integrate previously rejected elements of his Yamato tradition back into the repertory of his noh. He says, himself, that this is a return: "The demon of violent movement is not to be considered part of our tradition, but Kannami did it on occasion and having learned it, I myself did it only after taking the tonsure. One returns to this role in old age after one's training is complete."[19]

Among the plays listed for the first time in his late treatises, and in the presumably quite late *Nōhon sanjūgoban mokuroku*, we find certain unorthodox plays, and works that fall outside the pale of what he had earlier claimed as the correct domain of his style. These are the exclusive province of the transcendent virtuoso and have been termed *hifū*, the anti-style; the most striking examples are *Nomori*, a play about a demon of violent movement, and *Tokusa*, a monogurui play centering on an old man. The demon of violent movement had been rejected by Zeami in *Nikyoku santai ningyōzu*, and the performance of an old man's monogurui, though not explicitly rejected, is highly unusual; there is no comparable play in the entire repertory.[20] One is left to guess that, in the ruminations of his advanced age, Zeami found it possible to accommodate, through a kind of aesthetic dialectic, what had earlier seemed irreconcilable aesthetic contradictions.

The tragic personal events of his last years seem almost to have broken Zeami; *Museki isshi* and the opening of *Kyakuraika* show him perilously close to complete despair and seem to mock the completeness of his artistic life, but then again, in the "rank of virtuosic transcendence" and the "anti-style," he attains independence from patronage and exhausts the process of training, so perhaps the last words we have from him, those surprisingly cheerful and contented songs of *Kintōsho*, should not be so surprising after all.

Most of the thirty-odd plays ascribed to Zeami seem to bear a distinctive aesthetic imprint that differentiates them from other plays in the modern repertory and gives reasonable validity to the notion that there is an intellectual and artistic personality behind them. One of the most obvious characteristics of that imprint is his concern for form or structure. Although Zeami's creative hierarchy specifies a prior concern for the choice of subject (shu or honzetsu), his comments on structure (saku) and formal organization (using the principles of jo-ha-kyū) are far more detailed and precise. This careful attention to the configuration of the play through time is in fact indispensable to the thematic and imagistic unity that is the hallmark of his style,[21] and it is clearly one of the most important of the characteristics that distinguish his work from that of his predecessors, even his father.

We have seen repeated examples of the disunity of dramatic intent in early sarugaku plays. Some of them use a simple plot merely as a framing device for a sequence of artistic performances that have no other connection. *Kagetsu* is such a play, and whether it was actually written by Zeami or merely used to good advantage by him, it provides a suitable barometer by which to gauge the change he accomplished in developing his mature style. As delightful as the play can be, it is a sort of sarugaku vaudeville act decidedly unlike the more sophisticated plays for which Zeami is known.

Zeami's concern for form and structure had thematic consequences of great importance; it could hardly be otherwise since form and content are ultimately inseparable. We shall discuss that relationship presently, but before we do, let us consider one other aspect of Zeami's formalism. A kind of pleasure comes from the apprehension of form, a pleasure probably most immediately apparent in music and architecture, and indeed the musical side of noh drama had enormous influence on the development of Zeami's style. We have referred repeatedly to the conflict between monomane and yūgen in his theory, and have seen how yūgen emerged as a sine qua non in his mature style through his insistence on singing and dance. His constant awareness of form, however, has an even more important role in the creation of abstract beauty. The gradual progress of a play through jo, ha, and kyū orchestrates a coherent and affectively efficient aesthetic response; dan symmetry provides balance, a sense of repetition with variation, and an internal resonance or self-referentiality that encourages a well-proportioned and graded increase in audience involvement. As each dan plays out its theme, the audience perceives a kind of formal integrity and stability and nonlinear wholeness.

The thematic consequences of such formal concerns were enormous, particularly for the mugen noh.[22] In this type of play Zeami found an extraordinarily malleable and responsive form; a full four-fifths of the plays attributable to him are mugen noh, and many of the rest at least follow the same basic formal configuration. Why?

It is largely a matter of perspective. The appearance of a spirit in a dream or vision is obviously not a direct reflection of everyday reality. It is a privileged experience with broad metaphysical, aesthetic, and emotional potential. The waki noh are quite explicitly extensions of the divine into the world of men, whether straightforward miracles (the appearance of a golden tablet, the manifestation of a god, etc.) or carefully articulated presentations of the divine rationale for order of various sorts in the phenomenal world (marital felicity, imperial benevolence, poetic universality). When the ontological level changes from the divine to the human, as in the plays of the Woman's and Martial Modes, the axis of metaphysical revelation turns instead to lyricism or lyrically charged narrative to present the most profound qualities of an individual human existence from perspectives outside of the individual's life. I say "qualities" because Zeami is consistently more interested in the essential emotions and sensibilities of his characters than in the narrative chronology of their lives. Repeated allusion to a poem, the repetition of a single narrative from different points of view, or, on a smaller scale, the nondiscursive chains of associated thoughts, images, and words within a shōdan, all contribute to filling out the internal world of a character while focusing on a single emotional quality or group of related qualities. And this is accomplished with extraordinary efficiency, usually within a scope of but two hundred verses or so.

In filling out the internal world of a given character from several perspectives, Zeami makes the character of the shite his primary concern; interaction with other characters through a plot is minimized, and dramatic conflict is customarily restricted to the early stages of a play (usually the third dan), where it prompts the shite to reveal certain aspects of his internal world. The play is squarely centered on the shite, and the waki becomes a privileged bystander and sometime interrogator as the shite unfolds his life and relives his obsessions through to an epiphanic climax. The dominant influence of Zeami's style on noh is apparent when one realizes that these very characteristics are often thought to define not only the plays of Zeami, but noh theater in general.[23]

Such a lyric orientation accounts for Zeami's apparent lack of interest in genzai noh. He wrote relatively few genzai plays and even those tend to be monogurui plays structured along the lines of mugen noh, climaxing in the heightened lyricism of emotionally disoriented sensibilities. *Hanjo* and *Hanagatami* are outstanding examples.

There are, to be sure, elements of dramatic conflict and extensive narratives in Zeami's plays. But they are structurally subordinated to the exposition of the shite's emotions, that is, to a lyric exposition. This becomes apparent when one examines the way in which Zeami uses a few key types of shōdan.

The one shōdan form that, in many ways, most typifies Zeami's style comes near the beginning of the typical play, shortly after the shite's entrance. This is, of course, the sashi. Musically unobtrusive, it is delivered with little melodic variation, and the instrumental accompaniment one hears with some sashi bears only the vaguest rhythmic relation to the text. Its importance to Zeami is obvious, however, from the attention he pays it in *Go on*. Sixty-nine different plays or dramatic pieces are mentioned in the treatise, and alongside each title is a passage of text from five or six words to over thirty lines. The quotations are exemplary songs from the plays listed, and some 75 percent of the songs are sashi or sequences that include sashi.

In the oldest extant plays the sashi seems to have served as part of the shite's self-introduction. One of the finest examples is found in the old Konparu play *Ama*:

```
1    s    Kore wa Sanshiu Shido no ura,
          Tera chikakeredomo kokoro naki,
          Amano no sato no kaijin nite sōro.
          Ge ni ya na ni ō Iseo no ama wa iunami no,
5         Uchito no yama no tsuki o machi,
          Hamaogi no kaze ni aki o shiru,
          Mata Suma no amabito wa,
          Shioki ni mo wakaki no sakura o orimochite,
          Haru o wasurenu tayori mo aru ni,
10        Kono ura nite wa nagusami mo,
          Na nomi Amano no hara ni shite,
          Hana no saku kusa mo nashi,
          Nani o mirume karō yo.
```

```
1    s    I am one of the seafolk of the village of Amano
          On the Shido Coast in Sanuki,
          And though a temple stands nearby, I have no mind for religious
              devotion.
          The fisherfolk of famous Iseo await the moonrise
5         Over mountains cradling holy shrines;
          They sense autumn's advent in the winds
          That cross the seaside reeds.
          And fisherfolk at Suma, to remember spring,
          Bring cherry blossoms with the brine-soaked logs they bear.
10        But we at Amano find no poetic consolations,
          No flowers in the grasses.
          What should we gaze on
          As we go off to gather seaweed?[24]
```

Here the shite imparts certain specific items of information to the audience: she is careful to identify herself as a poor resident of the Shido Coast in Sanuki, and she distinguishes herself from the more poetic seafolk of Suma and Ise. Then, following a brief complaint about the barrenness of the area, she announces that she is about to begin her work, cutting seaweed.

In another old play of the Konparu tradition, *Shōkun*, the first sashi is cast, rather superficially, in the form of a dialogue.[25] Its function, however, is almost identical to that of *Ama*; in five short lines, we learn the identities of the speakers and their social class. Then, the circumstances in which the play takes place are explained in some detail. This is the pattern one encounters again and again with the earliest plays in the repertory, nor is it entirely abandoned later. We begin to see certain innovations, however, in some of Kannami's plays. The original version of *Jinen*

Koji, as we know it from *Go on*, casts the shite's first sashi in the form of a sermon:

| 1 | s | Sore ichidai no kyōbō wa,
Goji hakkyō o tsukuri,
Kyōnai kyōge o wakataretari . . . |

| 1 | s | Verily, the Dharma teachings of the first generation
Specified five ages and eight doctrines,
Dividing scriptures from apocrypha.[26] |

No longer do we find an explicit self-introduction. The new approach, however, seems more effective dramatically: the shite is a young priest, and having him deliver a sermon in his first appearance on stage is far more natural than the explicit introductions of *Ama* and *Shōkun*. The audience is directly confronted with the dramatic situation instead of an explanation of that situation.

In the plays of Zeami, we do not find the sashi used to confront the audience with drama, but rather to explore the internal world of the shite. This has been thoroughly discussed in connection with the first sashi of *Takasago*, *Izutsu*, and *Tadanori*, so let us here consider another example, this time from the play *Nue*:

| 1 | s | Kanashiki kana ya mi wa rōchō,
Kokoro o shireba mōki no fuboku,
Tada anjiu ni 'nmoregi no,
Saraba 'nmore mo hatezu shite,
Bōshin nani ni nokoruran.[27] |

| 1 | s | Such aimless misery, my body a caged bird,
My mind a blinded tortoise clinging to a floating log;
Bogwood buried in the sightless black
And yet not fully buried,
Why should my spirit linger on? |

This piece is shorter than some of Zeami's other sashi, but it shows the same exploration of an internal world through traditional rhetorical association. *Mi*, "body," leads to *kokoro*, "mind"; *mōki*, "a blinded tortoise," suggests *anjiu* (*anchū* in modern Japanese), "sightless black"; there is a kakekotoba in *anjiu ni 'nmore*/'*nmoregi*, "buried (in sightless black)" / "bogwood"; and so on. This is a fine and very typical sashi for Zeami. What is unusual is the fact that it is put in the mouth of a demon, the *nue* monster that gives the play its name. The lyric sensibility that so typifies Zeami's style in other plays has even penetrated into the world of the demonic to create this memorable character and make this particular demon an appropriate vehicle for Zeami's noh.

Sashi such as these give the audience greater insight into the psychological state of a character than do the self-introductions of the old plays.

They do not present us with a potentially dramatic situation from contemporary life, as did the sashi from *Jinen Koji*, but aim instead at a lyric experience, providing lyric portraits achieved as the consequence of associations made in the shite's mind on the basis of poetic convention, both elite and popular.

The sashi seems to have reached its maturity with the plays of Zeami. It is frequently employed by later playwrights in a manner that readily attests to Zeami's influence. *Nonomiya*, *Bashō*, and *Ugetsu* contain fine examples.[28] These plays were probably written by Zenchiku or someone else closely associated with Zeami, so there is no surprise in finding Zeami's influence in them. But we might expect less similarity from other later playwrights. Zeami's grand-nephew Nobumitsu, for instance, seems to have had aesthetic aims worlds apart from Zeami's. Nonetheless, in one of his more famous plays, *Momijigari* (Gathering Maple Leaves), we find a sashi cast into a lyric portrait.[29]

Zeami thus radically transformed the sashi, making it into a vehicle for lyric expression far more sophisticated than the simple song of introduction it was in earlier noh. Moreover, his recasting of the form was to extend an influence even into the plays of stylistically much different playwrights. His innovation in the case of another song form, the kusemai, was less a matter of transformation as such than the carefully considered integration of the form into the overall structure of a play.

The introduction of the kusemai into noh was one of Kannami's major contributions, as has been pointed out previously. One finds several examples of well-developed narratives among the kuse of Kannami's plays. *Jinen Koji* and *Eguchi* contain notable examples. Other playwrights as well seem to have had enough success with the form that their efforts either survived independently or were used in later plays. Zeami himself, for instance, borrowed one of his father's kusemai and used it, apparently verbatim, in his play *Hanagatami*.[30] But Zeami takes care to fit the song to the subject matter of the play, contributing to its overall effect, something that Kannami and his contemporaries were little concerned to do. The kusemai in *Jinen Koji*, for example, is merely another of the miscellaneous entertainments the shite offers in that "vaudeville-style" noh play. So is the kusemai in Kannami's version of the famous play *Hyakuman*.[31] The piece is a description of hell (in Japanese it is called *jigoku no kusemai*) with only the most tenuous thematic relation to the play.[32] In revising *Hyakuman*, Zeami wrote a more appropriate kusemai and transferred the *jigoku no kusemai* to a more fitting place in *Utaura*, one of his son Motomasa's works.

Zeami's use of the kusemai not only shows his skill in adapting shōdan forms that had already attained an internal coherence and integrity into the grander structure of the entire play, but also reveals his aesthetic priorities, in that this predominantly narrative shōdan is integrated into the structural framework to further the predominantly lyric ends of the play as a whole. His use of another pair of shōdan, the mondō and kakeai, shows this process of integration yet more clearly.

The mondō and kakeai of the third dan represent in some sense the most strictly dramatic part of a Zeami play. It is usually the only place where the shite and the waki interact line by line, and it sometimes contains an element of mild dramatic conflict. Here too, though, the drama of the shōdan is subordinated to the overall, ultimately lyrical structure. The exchanges of question and answer with which the sequence begins are gradually blended into an alternating recitation of the successive phrases of a single sentence. Two, often opposing, viewpoints are thus blended into a single harmonious assertion; the strains of dramatic conflict are braided together into a single strand of thought; and this is then handed over to the full chorus, to be instilled with the power of a full complement of eight voices and instrumental accompaniment in congruent song. The process has been illustrated in our discussions of *Takasago*, *Izutsu*, and *Tadanori*. One can find analogous examples in a great many other plays. But not a single one of these plays can be confidently said to predate Zeami.[33]

In earlier chapters more was said about Zeami's use of certain specific shōdan and the techniques that distinguished him from his predecessors and successors. Far more could yet be said, but there would probably be little alteration in the general conclusion to be made from what we have already seen. It is already clear that Zeami's first interest was in the emotional world of the shite; the strongly lyrical orientation of his plays is a natural consequence of this interest, and it seems unnecessary to review his use of other shōdan merely to emphasize the point. The lyric thrust of his work, however, is evident even in shōdan for which there is no written text. In contrast with his Yamato predecessors, who used the *hataraki* and similar mimetic dances to strengthen the monomane of their plays, Zeami chose instead the more abstract and expressionistic mai dances.

Yet Zeami was an adapter as well as an innovator. Indeed, this was part of his genius. The predominantly lyrical character of his works owed much to the elite literary tradition, which was overwhelmingly lyrical. It was heavily indebted as well to the strongly lyrical performance styles of Ōmi sarugaku and Zōami's dengaku. And in the end we must not forget that for all the changes Zeami made in sarugaku, he effected them on a popular art.

From a modern perspective, it is obvious that by the fifteenth century the elite tradition of waka was moribund. Only a strong infusion of popular vitality could resurrect it. Zeami's noh and the renga of Shinkei and Sōgi eventually made the elite tradition their own and extended its life by centuries. In the process, the tradition was inexorably and radically transformed; Zeami left it much different than he found it. This brings us to our final consideration of him, to reflections on the intellectual and ethical entity that invests the theory with coherence and creates an identifiable style in the plays.

Lyricism implies a human voice, so it is no surprise that in Zeami's noh, humanistic concerns come to dominate. His plays become explorations of the inner world of human beings. There were, of course, plays that centered on certain states of the human mind, obsession, longing, rage, and the like, before Zeami, but in his plays, the human psyche comes to dominate the thematic range of noh, eventually to the exclusion of the supernatural. This is ironic when one realizes that most of Zeami's plays deal with human experience from the perspective of death—the majority of his shite are ghosts, supernatural characters. But this otherworldly perspective is not adopted to illuminate the other world. It is a means of enriching and deepening our understanding of life and its significance. We see, therefore, a decrease in plays about miraculous occurrences, and when gods and demons appear in Zeami's plays, they are depicted with distinctly human features. The denigration of the role of the demon-hearted demon is merely the other side of the coin.[34]

Zeami's plays are, moreover, ruminations on the problem of identity. He betrays his fascination with this problem by plumbing the depths of the individual psyche through repeated allusions to a poem, the repetition of a single narrative from different points of view, and nondiscursive chains of associated thoughts. The characters he creates have little faith in the efficacy of human action. A tortured but inescapable absorption in the self, an inability to escape the ties of a past life, love, hate, longing, and pride—these characteristics persecute Zeami's shite. Yet they are the very characteristics that can give birth to a great performance and provide an opportunity for the uninhibited individual expression of an actor's attainment.

Zeami balances deftly between the vanity of subjective expression and the power of artistic transcendence. His art is a dialectic process, the synthesis of lyric sensibility and virtuosic mastery to the end that, in his own words, technique serves as the seed for the flower of the mind (*hana wa kokoro, tane wa waza nari*).[35] The attainment of Zeami's master actor embraces human experience not only thematically, then, in plays exploring the human psyche, but also technically, so that what is presented on stage is the actor's sensibility made available to the audience through the attainments of his training. Zeami's plays concentrate attention on the essential nature of an individual's experience; the goal of their aesthetic is the lyric exfoliation of identity. The corollary to this in his treatises focuses on the creation of a professional identity of virtuosic attainment. The expression of a character's fundamental essence thus parallels the virtuoso's expression of individual accomplishment. This is the nexus between the aesthetics of the "flower" and the ethics of the Way. This is where we find Zeami's style.

Reference Matter

Zeami's Technical Terminology

Technical terminology can be a frustrating obstacle to analysis and understanding of the structural components of the noh theater. The reasons for this are varied. Noh grew up in a milieu in which secret traditions were highly respected. Zeami himself says, "Secrecy itself provides the flower" (FSKD, p. 61), meaning that an air of secrecy surrounding performance techniques adds a kind of aesthetic mystique with considerable practical advantage. Some of the obscurity of noh terminology must, indeed, be part of the actor's secret bag of tricks. Other factors have also played a role, however. Simple linguistic change over the course of six hundred years, the need for a professional jargon (whether secret or not), the enormous gap between medieval aesthetics and our contemporary mentality, all these things have played a part in making the technical language of noh difficult to understand. Be that as it may, it is nonetheless important to gain some familiarity with *sashi, tsuyogin, yūgen*, and the like in order to study noh. It is hoped that the Glossary, pp. 291-300, and the explanations in the Introduction will help the reader to do so. Here, I append a translation of one of Zeami's most technical passages from *Sandō* (pp. 136-37), along with a note explaining the relationship between his terminology and the technical language used in noh today. I hope that these will further help clear up the muddy waters of noh jargon for interested readers.

The Aged Mode. This is generally cast in the form of the *waki* noh. First, in the congratulatory style, a play takes the following configuration: The *waki* appears and delivers the first section from the *shidai* through the *hitoutai* singing in a meter of 5-7-5/7-5/7-5, etc., for a total of seven to eight verses [*ku*]. One verse consists of a seven-syllable line and a five-syllable line, but a standard *tanka* (5-7-5/7-7) counts as two verses.

    Then the *shite* appears. (From here on comes the first section of the *ha*.) As in the instance of the old couple [in *Takasago?*], after an *issei* of 5-7-5/7-5 and a *ninoku* of 7-5/7-5, the *sashigoe* proceeds for about ten verses of 7-5/7-5. There are about ten verses to the *hitoutai* from the part in a lower register [*sagete*] through the part in a higher register [*kōnomono*]. (Next comes the second section of the *ha*.) Now there is a *mondō* between the *waki* and the *shite*, which should not exceed four or five exchanges between the two. (In this *mondō*, the old couple are asked about the area and they make their explanations. This should not exceed two or three exchanges apiece.) Then, in the *kōnomono*, from the point where the chorus joins in (this might be an ear-opening point), through to where they stop, there should be about ten verses sung in two strains. (From here on comes the third section of the *ha*.) Thereafter, if there is a *kusemai*, there should be about five verses of *agurukoe*, five of *sashigoe*, then, in the lower register [*sagete*] about five to six verses to the cadence. The *kusemai* should probably consist of twelve to thirteen verses and the *kōnomono* perhaps twelve to thirteen. Then there should be two to three exchanges in the *utairongi*, which should close briskly and lightly. (Now comes the *kyū*.) Here the *shite*, whether heavenly maiden or male god, sings a *kōnomono* or *sashigoe* flowingly from the *hashigakari* and delivers the *issei*, the last verse of which is accompanied by the chorus and sung mellifluously and fully and brought down to cadence. The two or three exchanges in *semerongi* are sung rhythmically and lightly with increasing speed. In some cases, depending on the sort of dance the *shite* does in character, the play should close with a *kiribyōshi* section. In any case, it should not be too long. One should plan the length by the number of musical verses.

This is the general outline of a noh of the first category. Since it is most appropriate for an old man to appear in the *waki* noh, this category is classified as the Aged Mode. In addition to this, the Aged Mode can be used in other ways, depending upon the material.

Plays of a congratulatory nature in the Women's Mode also take the same five-*dan* configuration.

Much of this passage can be put into modern terms:

1. *Kōnomono* means something sung in a high register (see Kōsai, *Nōyō*, 303; and zz, p. 136). Zeami uses it to mean two different things. In dan 1 and 3 it refers to what is now called an ageuta, a song sung in tadautai style in a high register. In dan 4 it refers to the last third of the kuse from the point where the shite sings a line (or two lines), again in high register, called the ageha, "the start of the high part."

2. *Ninoku* refers to the two 7-5 verses that follow an issei in standard waki noh. The first of these is delivered by the tsure and the second by the shite and the tsure together. The term is still used today and is paired with issei. For simplicity's sake, I have followed Yokomichi's lead, using issei to indicate both the issei proper and the ninoku. (see YK, 1: 16).

3. *Kusemai* is used by Zeami in two ways. In the broader sense he refers not only to the single shōdan kuse, but to the long sequence of songs of which the original Kusemai is composed. The most important of these are the kuri, the sashi, and the kuse. In the narrower sense he means the first half of the modern kuse, i.e., the part in a lower register from the point where the rhythm changes to congruent rhythm up to the point where the shite sings the ageha.

4. *Agurukoe* ("high-pitched song") corresponds to the modern kuri, a shōdan in einori sung in a high register with several rises to the pitch level called kuri pitch. See also kuse and kusemai in the Glossary.

5. *Sashigoe* refers to the modern sashi.

6. *Sagete* further specifies that part of the sashi or other shōdan that falls to a lower register. Zeami distinguishes several types of rongi (see Omote's excellent note, zz, p. 464). *Utai rongi* corresponds to a standard modern rongi. *Semerongi* seems to indicate a rongi sung at a fast pace, used characteristically at the end of a play.

7. The hashigakari is the bridge to the stage over which the actors make their entrance. On modern stages this bridge enters from the back left corner of the stage (from the viewer's perspective). On mid-Muromachi stages the hashigakari apparently attached to the middle of the back edge of the stage.

The Fourth Dan of 'Tōru'

The text for this passage comes from YK, 1: 295-302. It is based on a text copied by Shimomura Nagamasa in 1609. I have also compared this text with that portion of the dan quoted in Zeami's *Ongyoku kuden*, zz, pp. 79-80. For a discussion of the play and of this dan in particular, see pp. 112-16, above.

Katari

1   S   Mukashi Saga no tennō no ontoki,
        Tōru no otodo to mōshishi hito,
        Michinoku no Chika no Shiogama no chōbō o kikoshimeshioyobare,
        Miyako no uchi ni utsushioki,
5   Ano Naniwa no Mitsu no Hama yori mo,
        Higoto ni ushio o kumase,
        Koko nite shio o yakasetsutsu,
        Isshō gyoiu no tayori to shitamō,
        Shikaredomo sono nochi wa sōzoku shite moteasobu hito mo
            nakereba,
10   Ura wa sono mama hishio to natte,
        Chihen ni yodomu tamarimizu wa,
        Ame no nokori no furuki e ni,
        Ochiba chiriuku matsukage no,
        Tsuki dani sumade akikaze no,
15   Oto nomi nokoru bakari nari,
        Sareba uta ni mo,
        Kimi masade,
        Kemuri taenishi Shiogama no,
        Urasabishiku mo miewataru kana to,
20   Tsurayuki mo yomete sōro.

Uta

    C   Ge ni ya nagamureba,
        Tsuki nomi miteru Shiogama no,
        Urasabishiku mo arehatsuru,
        Ato no yo made mo shiojimite,
25   Oi no nami mo kaeru yaran,
        Ara mukashi koishi ya.

Ageuta

        Koishi ya koishi ya to,
        Shitaedomo nagekedomo,
        Kai mo nagisa no urachidori,

249

30   Ne o nomi naku bakari nari,
Ne o nomi naku bakari nari.

Mondō

w   Ika ni jōdono,
Miewataru yamayama wa mina meisho nite zo sōrōran onnoshie
    sōrae,

s   Ontazune sōrae oshiemōshisōrōran,

35 w   Mazu are ni mietaru wa Otowayama zōrō ka,

s   Sanzōrō are koso Otowayama zōrō yo,

w   Otowayama oto ni kikitsutsu Ōsaka no,
Seki no konata ni to yomitareba,
Ōsakayama no hodo chikō sōrōran,

40 s   Oše no gotoku seki no konata ni to wa yomitaredomo,
Anata ni atereba Ōsaka no,
Yama wa Otowa no mine ni kakurete,
Kono hen nyori wa mienu nari,

w   Sate sate Otowa no mine tsuzuki,

45   Shidai shidai no yamanami no,
Meisho meisho o kataritamae,

s   Katari mo tsukusaji koto no ha no,
Uta no Nakayama Seiganji,
Imagumano to wa are zo ka shi.

50 w   Sate sate sue ni tsuzuketaru,
Sato hitomura no mori no kodachi,

s   Sore o shirube ni goranzeyo,
Madaki shigure no aki nareba,
Momiji mo aoki Inariyama,

55 w   Kaze mo kureyuku kumo no ha no,
Kozue ni shiruki aki no iro,

s   Ima koso aki yo na ni shi ō,
Haru wa hana mishi Fuji no mori,

w   Midori no sora mo kage aoki,

60   Noyama ni tsuzuku sato wa ika ni,

s   Are koso iu sare wa,
Nobe no akikaze,
Mi ni shimite,
Uzura naku naru

65   Fukakusayama yo.

Uta

c   Kowatayama Fushimi no Takeda,
Yodo Toba mo mietari ya.

Rongi

       Nagameyaru,
Sonata no sora wa shirakumo no,

70   Sonata no sora wa shirakumo no,
Haya kuresamuru tōyama no,
Mine mo kobukaku mietaru wa,
Ika naru tokoro naruran,

s   Are koso Ōhara ya,

75   Oshio no yama no kyō koso wa,

Goranjisometsurame,
Nao nao towasetamae ya,
c Kiku ni tsukete mo aki no kaze,
Fuku kata nare ya mine tsuzuki,
80 Nishi ni miyuru wa izuku zo,
s Aki mo haya,
Aki mo haya,
Nakaba fukeyuku Matsu no o no,
Arashiyama mo mietari,
85 c Arashi fukeyuku aki no yo no,
Sora suminoboru tsukikage ni,
s Sasu shiodoki mo haya sugite,
c Hima mo oshiteru tsuki ni made,
s Kyō ni jōjite,
90 c Mi oba ge ni,
Wasuretari aki no yo no,
Nagamonogatari yoshi na ya,
Mazu iza shio o kuman tote,
Matsu ya Tago no ura,
95 Azuma karage no shiogoromo,
Kumeba tsuki o mo,
Sode ni mochijio no,
Migiwa ni kaeru nami no yoru no,
Rōjin to mietsuru ga,
100 Shiokumori ni kakimagirete,
Ato mo miezu narinikeri,
Ato mo miezu narinikeri.

Katari

1 s Long ago, in the reign of Emperor Saga,
A man called Minister Tōru heard
Of the famous view of Shiogama in Chika of the Far North.
He transferred the scene to the capital
5 And from Naniwa's distant Mitsu Coast,
Each day he had brine drawn,
And here he had salt water boiled.
He took lifelong pleasure in the scene.
But afterwards there was no one to carry on with this diversion
10 And the banks were barren at ebb tide.
Where the lake had been, what water remained
Was only what was left by passing rain, fallen in the ancient cove.
Dead leaves scattered down, to float across the pine's reflection,
Where even the moon no longer shines, and only
15 The rush of the autumn wind remains.
It was just as in the poem
That Tsurayuki himself composed:
"With you no longer here,
The trails of smoke at Shiogama fade.
20 I gaze across the lonely banks and sigh."

Uta

c And when I gaze out there, it's true,
Shiogama's kettles are filled with nothing but the moonlight,

251

All is gone to desolation and stark ruin,
But I stay soaked with the tides of tears even in these latter days,
25   The waves of age crash down upon me still.
Oh, how I long for the past.

Ageuta

"How I long, how I long for the past," I sigh,
But my yearnings and complaints
Come to no end, and at the water's edge,
30   The plover cries and cries,
The plover cries and cries.

Mondō

w   Now then, old sir,
I suppose all the mountains we see from here are famous places.
    Tell me about them.
s   Ask what you like and I'll tell you what I can.
35 w First, is that one over there Mount Sound-on-Wings?
s   That is correct. That is indeed Mount Sound-on-Wings.
w   A poet once said, "Mount Sound-on-Wings I have heard of on the
    wings of rumor,
But I have stayed on this side of Meeting Pass,"
So Mount Meeting Pass must also be nearby.
40 s Just as you say, a poet once so sang, but
Mount Meeting Pass is over the range,
Now hidden by the peak of Sound-on-Wings,
And it cannot be seen from here.
w   Well then, following across from the peak of Sound-on-Wings
45   Mountain after mountain stands in line.
Tell me all about the famous places there.
s   Not all the leaves of speech could tell it all,
But there is Middlemount of Poetry and Seigan Temple,
And Imagumano is that spot over there.
50 w As you follow from the mountain's edge, then, there,
That stand of trees beside the village, . . .
s   Set your gaze right there,
For autumn's come, but the rains that dye the leaves are yet to fall;
And that is Mount Inari, still green with autumn leaves.
55 w The wind blows off toward dusk near those clouds,
Autumn colors glow distinctly in the treetops . . .
s   Yes, it's autumn now, but spring bears fame to
Those flower-laden bowers, that's Wisteria Grove.
w   Under the indigo sky the light shines blue,
60   Across the fields and hills to a village there,
s   That's where "night's fall
Hastens autumn's wind across the moors
To permeate my soul:
Deep-grass Mountain,
65   Where, they say, the quails cry."

Uta

c   Mount Kowata, Takeda in Fushimi,
Yodo, Toba, all there to be seen.

Rongi

<table>
<tr><td></td><td></td><td>I spread my gaze</td></tr>
<tr><td></td><td></td><td>Across the sky to white clouds.</td></tr>
<tr><td>70</td><td></td><td>Across the sky to white clouds.</td></tr>
<tr><td></td><td></td><td>What are those far-off hills,</td></tr>
<tr><td></td><td></td><td>Darkening already,</td></tr>
<tr><td></td><td></td><td>With their tree-covered peaks?</td></tr>
<tr><td></td><td>s</td><td>That is Ōhara</td></tr>
<tr><td>75</td><td></td><td>And Mount Oshio, this must be</td></tr>
<tr><td></td><td></td><td>The first time you have seen them.</td></tr>
<tr><td></td><td></td><td>Ask me more.</td></tr>
<tr><td></td><td>c</td><td>As I ask, the autumn wind blows</td></tr>
<tr><td></td><td></td><td>That way, again to a row of peaks.</td></tr>
<tr><td>80</td><td></td><td>What place is that to the west?</td></tr>
<tr><td></td><td>s</td><td>Already autumn is half gone by:</td></tr>
<tr><td></td><td></td><td>Already autumn is half gone by:</td></tr>
<tr><td></td><td></td><td>The wind blows off</td></tr>
<tr><td></td><td></td><td>To Pine's Tail, and Gale Mountain, you see there,</td></tr>
<tr><td>85</td><td>c</td><td>The gale blows late through the autumn night,</td></tr>
<tr><td></td><td></td><td>The sky grows clear, the moon climbs.</td></tr>
<tr><td></td><td>s</td><td>Already the high tide turns.</td></tr>
<tr><td></td><td>c</td><td>Although my time is short,</td></tr>
<tr><td></td><td>s</td><td>I've been enticed by the shining moon,</td></tr>
<tr><td>90</td><td>c</td><td>Delighting in the moment's magic,</td></tr>
<tr><td></td><td></td><td>I forgot myself this autumn night</td></tr>
<tr><td></td><td></td><td>In long tales, to no useful end,</td></tr>
<tr><td></td><td></td><td>But now I'll dip salt water, he says,</td></tr>
<tr><td></td><td></td><td>And picks up his pail.</td></tr>
<tr><td>95</td><td></td><td>Hiking up his tide-soaked robe,</td></tr>
<tr><td></td><td></td><td>He reaches into the water to catch the moonbeams</td></tr>
<tr><td></td><td></td><td>On his sleeve,</td></tr>
<tr><td></td><td></td><td>Then standing on the land's edge while the high tide crashes in fall-
ing waves,</td></tr>
<tr><td></td><td></td><td>The old man—or so I thought him—</td></tr>
<tr><td>100</td><td></td><td>Hides himself away in a cloud of sea mist</td></tr>
<tr><td></td><td></td><td>To disappear from sight,</td></tr>
<tr><td></td><td></td><td>To disappear from sight.</td></tr>
</table>

Notes

Complete authors' names, titles, and publication data for the works cited in short form are given in the Bibliography, pp. 301-8. Unless otherwise noted, all citations of Zeami's works are drawn from Omote and Kato, *Zeami, Zenchiku*, abbreviated as zz. Other abbreviations used in the Notes are:

Dangi	Zeami, *Sarugaku dangi*, in zz
FSKD	Zeami, *Fūshikaden*, in zz
GSIS	*Goshūishū*
KKS	*Kokinshū*
MYS	*Man'yōshū*
NKBT	*Nihon koten bungaku taikei*
SKKS	*Shinkokinshū*
YK	Yokomichi and Omote, *Yōkyokushū*

INTRODUCTION

1. See Yokomichi in Kōsai, *Nōyō*, p. 289.

2. I have chosen *Hagoromo* for this and later examples because it is a very well-known play and because the greater part of it is widely available in the West on phonograph recordings: *Japanese Noh Music*, by the Kyoto Nohgaku Kai (Lyrichord LLST 7137); and the Unesco Collection, *A Musical Anthology of the Orient: Japan II*, Barenreiter Musicaphon (BM 30 L 2013). The text of the play can be found in YK, 2: 326-29. For a detailed study, see Yasuda, "Structure."

3. I borrow the terms from Flindt and Hoff, pp. 38ff.

4. YK, 2: 328. The notation I use is only approximate. Pitch notation for noh is difficult because there is no absolute pitch, and considerable variation occurs according to the particular piece being performed and the performer himself. Even within a single piece, the same jō pitch, for example, can vary depending on a number of factors. The problem is further complicated by the fact that modern-day pitch is not necessarily the same as the pitch used at any particular point in the history of noh. This problem will be dealt with below. What I am concerned with here are the contours of the phrases in question; these remain unchanged regardless of the method of notation or the historical changes the music has undergone. My notation follows the Kanze school's rendering.

5. The text of the passage shown in Fig. 3 can be found in YK, 2: 77. See also Yokomichi's discussion of the passage on p. 5 of the same volume. Here I have written the text out according to the modern count. In Zeami's day there would have been differences, as will be discussed in Chap. 2.

6. See YK, 2: 8, for the metric pattern of ōnori and chūnori.

7. The half-beats are left "open" in the sense that they can either be used for an extension of the previous syllable in the text or be left without any vocalization (but with perhaps a beat on one of the drums or some other musical sound). Virtuoso performers sometimes purposely obscure the relationship between the 12 syllables of the text and the 8 beats of the measure to avoid a sing-song monotony, just as good readers of English poetry will not overemphasize the iambic pentameter when reading, for instance, a Shakespearean sonnet. A useful discussion of this technique and the general musical structure of noh itself can be found in Bethe and Brazell.

8. There are, of course, certain irregularities in the setting of syllable to beat. Sometimes such irregularities are nothing more than a slight stretching of the rules to allow for metrical irregularities such as *jiamari* (hypercatalexis) in waka. Sometimes they are intentional moldings of the text for an artistic purpose similar to syncopation in Western music. On occasion, 8-beat measures are truncated to 4 beats (this is called a *tori*) or, more rarely, 6 beats (*kataji*).

9. Zeami himself says as much in *Dangi*, p. 276.

10. Examples from *Hagoromo* will make my explanation clearer. First, note the syllabic structure of this piece, the chorus's first ageuta, in standard tadautai style (syllable count is given to the left):

7-5	Karyōbinga no/narenareshi
7-5	Karyōbinga no/narenareshi
7-5	Koe imasara ni/wazuka naru
5-5	Karigane no/kaeriyuku
7-5	Amaji o kikeba/natsukashiya
7-5	Chidori kamome no/oki tsu nami
7-5	Yuku ka kaeru ka/harukaze no
7-5	Sora ni fuku made/natsukashiya
7-5	Sora ni fuku made/natsukashiya

There is only one metric irregularity in the entire song, and that is minor. But now consider the last part of the kuse from the same play:

0-5	Kimi ga yo wa
7-5	Ama no hagoromo/mare ni kite
7-5	Nazu to mo tsukinu/iwao zo to
7-5	Kiku mo tae nari/Azumauta
5-5	Koe soete/kazukazu no
4-5	Shōchiku/kinkugo
7-5	Koun no hoka ni/michimichite
5-5	Rakujitsu no/kurenai wa
8-4	Someiro no yama o/utsushite
7-5	Midori wa nami ni/ukishima ga
7-5	Harō arashi ni/hana furite
5-4	Ge ni yuki o/megurasu
8-4	Hakuun no sode zo/tae naru

At first glance, this passage too seems to have a preponderance of regular lines, but in fact lines 9 and 13 are irregular, even though they have 12 syllables, as is clear when they are written out in 8-beat measures:

8	1	2	3	4	5	6	7	8
so me –	i	ro no ya	ma –	o –	u	tsu shi –	te	•
ha ku –	u	n no –	so	de zo –	ta	e na –	ru	•

(In both cases the line starts on the 8th beat of the preceding measure, the first 8 syllables come before beat 5, and the last 4 syllables fill out the last 4 beats because of a hold on the penultimate syllable. Thus, less than half the lines in this piece are regular, and yet it is still set to hiranori. The result is rhythmically interesting.

CHAPTER ONE

1. *Dangi*, p. 301.

2. Little is known of Naami. Zeami calls him a "skillful composer," offering as evidence a brief anecdote. It seems that Naami set certain lyrics of an exiled renga poet, Tamarin, to music. He had Zeami sing them, and they so impressed the shogun that Tamarin was granted a pardon (*Dangi*, p. 277). Naami seems to have been a careful observer of the noh. It was, for instance, through him and the well-known general Sasaki Dōyo (1306-73) that Zeami learned about the style of the earlier master Itchū (*ibid.*, p. 261). Zeami's references to Naami show great respect: he always refers to him as Naamidabutsu, using the most polite and honorific form of the *-ami* name (see Kōsai, *Zeami*, p. 50). Some have called Naami one of Yoshimitsu's *dōbōshū*, or custodians of taste, but the role of dōbōshū in the early Muromachi period has been called into question by Kōsai (*Zeami*, pp. 69-96), and it seems unlikely that Naami can confidently be identified as such. Earlier scholars called Kannami and Zeami dōbōshū as well, but Kōsai (*ibid.*, pp. 283-87) demonstrates that there is no evidence to support this.

3. *Dangi*, p. 293. The Imagumano shrine is located in southeast Kyoto in Higashiyama-ku.

4. The Okina referred to above is one of the three central roles in *Shikisanban* (The Three Rites), a ceremonial play dating back to the late Heian period. Because the play was performed at the beginning of formal programs of noh and had a strong ritualistic significance, the role of Okina was traditionally given to the oldest member of the troupe. In replacing the oldest member of the troupe with the most skillful performer, the central purpose of the play is itself altered.

5. My discussion of the origins of sarugaku is of necessity limited to Zeami's immediate forebears. For a much fuller account in English, see O'Neill, *Early Nō*.

6. From the "Kanze Kojirō Nobumitsu gazō no meimon" quoted in Kobayashi, *Yōkyoku*, pp. 2-3. This inscription provides the basic information for later accounts of the early history of the Kanze troupe. The portrait and the inscription were both completed before Nobumitsu's death.

7. See, for example, "Jō Yūzakigoza no koto," in *Dangi*, p. 308.

8. *Dangi*, p. 302.

9. Hattori could be a place name, but it is more likely that it is a family name because of the previously mentioned account and because there was, indeed, a Hattori clan in Iga that claimed descent from the Heike.

10. The genealogy belongs to a certain Kamijima family, originally of Iga. It is a copy made in the early 19th century from an original now lost. As such, it lacks a degree of credibility, but nonetheless raises some rather startling possibilities that, on further reflection, fit extremely well with certain other facts about Kannami and Zeami. In the reproduction of the genealogy in the Kubo article on which Fig. 4 is based, Iemitsu and his three sons, including Kannami, are lined up as if they were all brothers. This is clearly a misprint, as the notes under Kannami's name show. See also Kubo, "Kannami," p. 24, which quotes a similar, if less-detailed document from the same source, reprinted with Iemitsu as Kannami's father.

11. FSKD, p. 19. JŌRAKUKI, a death register of notables for the period 1295-1467, puts the exact date at the 19th of the 5th month (cited in Kobayashi, *Zeami*, p. 23).

12. Zeami writes of himself as 70 years old in 1432 (*Museki isshi*, p. 242). By Japanese reckoning, this places his birth in 1363. Such a date is supported by a note in an unnamed diary, which tentatively suggests that Zeami was 16 in 1378 (see Ijichi). On the other hand, Zeami says that at age 12, he attended a special noh performance in Nara (*Dangi*, p. 261), and this performance could only have taken place in 1375. For this reason, Omote once set forth the theory that Zeami was actually born in 1364. He has since changed his mind (see his notes in ZZ, p. 498), and now ascribes Zeami's statement to a faulty memory. (See also Matsuda, pp. 23-31.)

13. Kubo, "Kanze-Fukuda keizu." Motokiyo, as noted earlier, was one of the many names Zeami was known by in his lifetime. This text presents some problems. Obata is in Iga and was perhaps the place where Kannami first established his saragaku troupe. If so, Zeami might well have been born there. Recently, however, this view has been challenged by Kōsai (*Zoku Zeami*, pp. 64-69). His argument hinges on the interpretation of the following sentence from *Dangi*, p. 301: "Iga Obata nite za o tatesomerareshi toki Iga nite tazuneidashitatemasshi men nari." Kōsai maintains that the previous interpretation—"It is a mask acquired in Iga when Kannami first established his sarugaku troupe in Obata in Iga"—is wrong. He argues that the sentence should be read, "It is a mask acquired in Obata, in Iga, around the time when Kannami first established his sarugaku troupe," and asserts that the troupe was founded in Yamato even though the mask was acquired in Iga.

14. FSKD, p. 15. Zeami refers to age seven, which would be younger by Western reckoning.

15. *Ryūgen Sōjō nikki*, the diary of the Shingon bishop Ryūgen, mentions the performance. The diary entry was not made until 1424, but refers to a performance during the administration of the bishop Kōsai (Kitagawa, *Zeami*, pp. 26-27). Kōsai served as abbot of Daigoji for three separate terms: 1357-60, 1363-74, and 1375-79. Kitagawa does not specify which of these terms is referred to, but the middle seems the most logical.

16. *Gogumaiki*, quoted in Kobayashi, *Yōkyoku*, p. 101.

17. Imaizumi, pp. 55, 65 n. 9.

18. The letter is quoted with arguments for its authenticity in Fukuda. It is addressed to a *sonshōin*, the title of a high officer in one of the esoteric sects at either Enryakuji, Tōdaiji, or Ninnaji. A certain Kyōben, the sonshōin at Tōdaiji, seems the most likely candidate, since Yoshimoto's second cousin was his superior there and the style of the letter indicates that it was sent to an inferior (see Nishi, "Nō," p. 107). Yoshimoto's vocabulary is of interest. He refers to Zeami as *hokehoke to shite*, *hokete*, and *hokeyaka* (my "charming," "entrancing," and "captivates," respectively). All three words come from a word originally meaning "unclear" or "vague." One meaning became "to have one's heart/mind stolen away and to be lost in a trance." Yoshimoto uses hokehoke in his treatises on renga. For instance, in his *Jūmon saihishō* (in Imoto and Kidō, p. 115) he says, "Now probably the best of all is to achieve a quality of *hokehoke* and permeation." He considers this ability to entrance an important quality in poetry. Here he has transferred it out of the rather abstract critical category to describe Zeami's appearance. Furthermore, the word *hana*, "flower," appears twice in the letter (my "blossoming of his ap-

pearance" and "the flower of the heart"). This word became one of the most important terms in Zeami's early noh theory, and its appearance here cannot but make one speculate about Yoshimoto's influence on Zeami. Similarly, one should note the use of the word yūgen, which may mean something like "mystery and depth" here. This is another of Zeami's favorite aesthetic terms. Yoshimoto's reference to *Genji* comes from the chapter entitled "Wakamurasaki" (NKBT, 14: 185).

19. Toita, "Uguisu," discusses the possibility that Kannami's fourth prohibition for the Yūzaki troupe, that against raising bush warblers, was actually a discreet way of prohibiting homosexual relationships between troupe members. He links this to the encouragement of such relationships between them and wealthy and powerful men in the hope of gaining their patronage of the troupe. The article is in large part conjecture, but thoughtfully written and well argued.

20. Omote, "Yoshimoto." In this article Omote admits that he once doubted the letter's authenticity because it was too long and flowery, too full of praise, and so on, and though he has come to agree with Fukuda that Yoshimoto is probably the author, he now questions Yoshimoto's motives.

21. *Dangi*, p. 264.

22. FSKD, pp. 15-16. The translation for yūgen here is intended to convey the meaning of that word in Zeami's earliest theory, and is quite different from the translation I choose for his later uses of the term.

23. Entry for 25 iv Eiwa 4 (1378) from an unidentified manuscript in *Sukōin Jōkō gyoki* (the diary of the Retired Emperor Sukō; r. 348-51), quoted in Ijichi, p. 5.

24. Ijichi, p. 6.

25. *Dangi*, pp. 261-62.

26. There was no costume-donation performance at the Hōon'in in 1374, but there were two in 1375 (ZZ, p. 499).

27. FSKD, pp. 16-17. "Using your voice in a manner appropriate to the time of day" refers to Zeami's belief that one must hold back a bit in the morning and sing with full power only later in the day. See his *Ongyoku kuden*, p. 76.

28. FSKD, p. 19.   29. FSKD, p. 17.

30. FSKD, pp. 17-18.   31. FSKD, p. 18.

32. The 1394 performance is recorded in *Kasuga gokeiki* and *Kanenori Kyō ki* (the diary of Lord Kanenori; 1366-1429) and the 1399 performances in *Geiyōki* (the diary of Higashibōnojō Hidenaga), quoted in Kobayashi, *Zeami*, pp. 25-26.

33. Entry for 14 iii Ōei 1 (1394) in *Kasuga gokeiki*, quoted in *ibid.*, p. 26.

34. Takegahana is now known as Takigahana and is located in northwest Kyoto near Kitano shrine.

35. *Kadensho*, the title Yoshida Tōgo gave the work when he first made it available to the general public in 1908, is easily confused with the homophonous word meaning merely any treatise handed down within a family. It is also easily confused with a homograph meaning "a treatise on flowers."

36. Secs. 1-3 are dated 13 iv Ōei 7 (1400). Sec. 4 is not dated, and sec. 5 bears the date 2 iii Ōei 9 (1402), but there is some question whether this date is authentic. Omote thinks the postscript to sec. 5 may be a later addition by someone other than Zeami, and speculates that the section itself may not have taken its present form until after the death of Yoshimitsu in 1408 (ZZ, pp. 435-36). The postscript to secs. 6 and 7 relates that they were transmitted to an otherwise unidentified man named Mototsugu in 1418. (This may have been an earlier name

for Zeami's son Motomasa or the name of one of his other sons; see Kubo, "Kanze-Fukuda keizu," pp. 58, 62-63.) The same postscript also notes that this was the second transmission; these two books were probably written earlier. The first transmission was apparently to Zeami's younger brother Shirō, but no date is given for the event.

37. Indeed, it was in large part due to a musical—specifically rhythmical—innovation, the introduction of the *kusemai*, that Kannami achieved his great success.

38. Quoted in Kobayashi, *Zeami*, pp. 34-35. One phrase is ambiguous, and the text may read "the actors of this vocation" instead of "Dō[ami]'s actors." The Japanese text reads *Dō[ami] no monodomo* or *michi no monodomo*, depending on one's interpretation. Dōami was another name for the Ōmi sarugaku actor Inuō.

39. *Dangi*, p. 300.   40. zz, p. 500.
41. *Dangi*, pp. 306-7.   42. *Dangi*, p. 303.

43. See Omote's note, zz, pp. 500-501, as well as his article "Zeami no shōgai," especially pp. 20-23.

44. Nonomura, "Zeami."

45. Quoted in Narushima Yoshinori, *Nochikagami*, as cited in Kobayashi, *Zeami*, p. 187.

46. *Mansai jugō nikki*, quoted in Kitagawa, *Zeami*, pp. 38-39. Kanze Shirō has not been positively identified. Kitagawa assumes he is a member of Zeami's own troupe. He may, however, be Zeami's younger brother, also known as Motonaka, to whom the final book of *Fūshikaden* was originally transmitted. If so, there is no guarantee that Zeami was involved in this performance; Shirō may have had his own troupe. The quotes for the next two performances are from the same source.

47. *Kōfukuji nikki*, quoted in *ibid.*, p. 39.

48. *Mansai jugō nikki*, quoted in Kobayashi, *Zeami*, p. 44; also in Kitagawa, *Zeami*, p. 39. The identity of Kanze Saburō is not certain, but Kobayashi argues (not entirely convincingly) that he is Zeami. Kanze Gorō has not been identified.

49. These performances have been mentioned in the course of the discussion. They total five in all: 1372(?), Kannami and Zeami at Daigoji; 1374, Imagumano performance; 1394, Kōfukuji, Ichijōin performance; 1399, Daigoji Sanbōin performance; 1399, Ichijō Takegahana performance. If Zeami performed during the Emperor's visit to Kitayama in 1408, another item can be added to this list, but, as mentioned earlier, his participation is problematical.

50. *Mansai jugō nikki*, entry for 17 iv Ōei 31 (1424), quoted in Kobayashi, *Zeami*, p. 46.

51. This is the majority opinion, that of Kobayashi (*Yōkyoku*, pp. 113-14; *Zeami*, pp. 45-48), Nishi (*Zeami*, p. 233), and Omote (zz, p. 545). Kitagawa dissents (*Zeami*, pp. 43-45).

52. Kitagawa, *Zeami*, pp. 38-39.

53. *Kashū* is also known as *Kashū no uchi nukigaki*. It should not be confused with sec. 6 of *Fūshikaden*, which is known as "Kashu" (with a short "u"—On Preparing for the Flower). *Ongyoku kuden* is also known as *Ongyoku kowadashi kuden*. *Sandō*, a work on the composition of noh plays to be discussed in more detail later, is also known as *Nōsakusho*. Three other undatable treatises also appeared in the early to mid-1420's. They are *Fushizuke shidai* (On Composing Music), a technical and poorly understood work; *Fūgyoku shū* (The Collection on Fine Music), another difficult musical treatise; and *Goi* (The Five Ranks), a predecessor of *Kyūi* (discussed later).

54. *Nikyoku santai ningyōzu*, pp. 124-28.

55. Motoyoshi's note is written at the end of a collection of auspicious songs, *Shiki shūgen,* the only copy of which is now in the possession of the head of the Kanze school (see zz, pp. 467-68 n. 81, 555-56).

56. Konishi, *Zeamishū*, p. 14.

57. *Ibid.,* pp. 14-17.

58. *Dangi*, p. 263.

59. zz, p. 350. The poem is kks 56.

60. Shinkei, *Hitorigoto,* in Hayashiya, p. 474; *Dangi,* p. 262, where Zeami mentions a noh play now lost in which Zōami played the shakuhachi.

61. See *Nō kyōgen men,* pp. 46, 75-76, for photographs and notes on the mask.

62. *Dangi*, p. 262.

63. Kōsai, *Zeami,* p. 23.

64. Among others one finds *mui no kurai,* "the rankless rank," *mumon no mon,* "the patternless pattern," and *mukyoku no kyoku,* "the melody without melody" (*ibid.,* pp. 23-39).

65. The temple register will be discussed later. There is also mention of the priest at this temple in a letter from Zeami to Zenchiku, dated the 14th day of the first month of an unspecified year after 1428 (see zz, p. 316; and Kōsai, *Zeami,* pp. 3ff).

66. Earlier scholars (Kanai Kiyomitsu, in particular) have tried to link Zeami to the Ji sect of Pure Land Buddhism, purely because the suffix -*ami* was frequently taken by Ji believers. Kōsai and Omote have shown quite clearly, though, that there is no convincing evidence of the suffix's having been taken *exclusively* by Ji believers. Their care in refuting the Ji sect connection, however, has deserted them when discussing Zeami's supposed Zen ties, and Kōsai, in particular, seems bent on establishing Zeami as a Zen worthy (Kōsai, *Zeami,* pp. 40-68).

67. fskd, p. 19.

68. *Kakyō,* pp. 108-9; Konishi, *Zeamishū,* p. 192.

69. Yoshimochi was the fourth Ashikaga shogun. He put his son Yoshikazu in the position for a time as the fifth. The son died shortly afterwards, so Yoshinori became the sixth shogun even though his rule followed directly on that of the fourth.

70. *Mansai jugō nikki,* entry for 13 v Eikyō 1 (1429), quoted in Kobayashi, *Yōkyoku,* p. 116. The previous day's entry says that a sarugaku performance might be held there any time. Kobayashi speculates that the Cloistered Emperor Gokomatsu had asked Yoshinori for permission to see Kanze sarugaku, and that the entry for the 12th granted permission for a performance by one of the Kanze clan whom Yoshinori understood to be Zeami's nephew Onnami. Gokomatsu, however, wanted to see Kanze Motomasa and Zeami. When Yoshinori found this out, he rescinded his permission, sending the order mentioned in the entry for the 13th. Later, Onnami did appear at the Sentō Palace, but this must have been only because of Yoshinori's order, for the diary succinctly records the event as follows (10 i Eikyō 2 [1430]): "This is not the sort of performance His Majesty enjoys." (See Kobayashi, *Yōkyoku,* p. 116; and Kobayashi, *Zeami,* pp. 54-55.)

71. *Mansai jugō nikki,* entry for 17 iv Eikyō 2 (1430), quoted in Kobayashi, *Yōkyoku,* p. 117.

72. *Dangi,* p. 310. Motoyoshi memorialized his move into the religious life with three waka.

73. *Museki isshi,* p. 242. According to Kubo, "Kanze-Fukuda keizu," p. 58, Motomasa was murdered by an Ashikaga retainer, Shiba Hyōe Saburō.

74. *Kintōsho,* p. 250.

75. His descendants lived on in Ochi after his death until the end of Muromachi, when their line died out and a successor was brought in from the Kyoto branch of the Kanze clan. Some of Zeami's treatises passed through these Ochi Kanze. (See zz, p. 549.) Furthermore, Motoyoshi is thought to have returned to secular life on the death of his brother to join the family in Ochi (*Nō* [1978], p. 68).

76. A color photograph can be found in *Nō* (1978), p. 38.

77. Enami was Motomasa's predecessor at the Kiyotaki shrine, "the former director who committed an offense."

78. Nishi, *Zeami,* pp. 55-61. The plays mentioned include *Koi no omoni* (The Heavy Burden of Love), *Kurama tengu* (The Goblin from Kurama), *Taisan Pukun* (Archdemon Taisan), and *Ukai* (The Cormorant Fisher). Onnami also seems to have played the shite role in *Hōkazō* (The Dancing Priest), a vendetta play, several times.

79. Nishi (*Zeami,* pp. 75-81) suggests that similar circumstances lay behind Yoshinori's selection of Asukai Masayo (1390-1452) as compiler of *Shinzokukokinshū* over Reizei Tameyuki (1393?-1439). But Nishi's argument is not terribly convincing. He quotes no poems to support his assertion that Yoshinori rejected Kyōgoku-Reizei style for Nijō style, and he fails to mention the strong possibility that in this selection Yoshinori was merely following a pattern set generations earlier.

80. Nishi, *Zeami,* pp. 55-61. The plays are *Matsukaze* (Wind in the Pines), *Kakitsubata* (Iris Blossoms), *Yūgao* (Evening Faces), and *Nonomiya* (The Shrine in the Fields). This *Nonomiya,* however, may not be the play known by that name today.

81. *Mansai jugō nikki,* entry for 18 iv Ōei 22 (1415), cited in Kobayashi, *Zeami,* p. 48.

82. Entry for 13 v Eikyō 1 (1429), quoted in *ibid.,* p. 53.

83. zz, p. 318. By the middle of his career, Zeami had already begun to distinguish between the demon-hearted demon, which he thought inappropriate to the stage, and the human-hearted demon (see his *Nikyoku santai ningyōzu,* pp. 128-29).

84. Onnami is first recorded as head of the Kanze troupe in *Mansai jugō nikki,* entry for 17 iv Eikyō (1433). (See Kobayashi, *Yōkyoku,* p. 124 n. 17.) Onnami is officially considered the third head of the Kanze line. Motomasa is ignored.

85. *Museki isshi,* pp. 242-43. P. G. O'Neill translates and discusses the work, which he calls "A Page on the Ruin of a Dream," in his article "The Year of Zeami's Birth."

86. *Kyakuraika,* p. 246; my emphasis. See Nearman's translation of this work for an interesting commentary that draws on his own experience as an actor.

87. Imaizumi, in his discussion of the issue of the editorship of *Shinzokukokinshū* (see especially pp. 59-60), comes to more satisfying conclusions than Nishi (see n. 79, above). He points out that when Reizei Tameyuki refused to hand over certain family materials to Asukai Masayo to use in compiling the collection, Yoshinori confiscated some of his estates. If such a refusal resulted in these consequences for a court aristocrat like Tameyuki, it is not difficult to imagine that a similar refusal could have resulted in the exile of someone of much lower social position like Zeami.

88. See Nearman, "Zeami's *Kyūi,*" for a translation. There is some doubt about the authenticity of *Rikugi.* It is the most colorless of the treatises mentioned and seems to have been produced at the request of Konparu Zenchiku, and not because Zeami himself wanted to write it (zz, p. 564). Various *"rikugi"* exist in the

history of Japanese literary criticism, the earliest being that found in the prefaces to *Kokinshū*, a confusing attempt to impose Chinese genre theory on the native tradition. The existence of a rikugi for noh may have added to its prestige because of the tie to the *Kokinshū* rikugi, and this may be one reason the treatise was written.

89. O'Neill, "Letters," translates these two letters, as well as the one from Jūni Gonnokami to Zeami mentioned earlier.

90. For a translation and a study of the work, see Matisoff, "*Kintōsho*," and Matisoff, "Images of Exile."

91. Konishi, *Zeamishū*, pp. 10, 13-14, argues that to understand Zeami's later thought one must study Zenchiku's treatises, where Zeami's influence is very strong. This, however, is beyond the compass of my study.

92. According to the tale, the plays were *Teika, Miidera, Yuya, Tōboku* (The Northeastern Hall), *Higaki* (The Cypress Fence), *Miwa*, and *Izutsu* (The Well Curb). The other versions add *Bashō* (The Plantain), *Matsukaze*, and *Yamanba* (The Mountain Hag). Several of these plays were probably not written by Zeami, and even those that are definitely his were undoubtedly written before his exile.

93. Kobayashi, *Yōkyoku*, pp. 132-34.

94. The register from Fuganji is not itself contemporaneous with Zeami, but dates from 1572. Kōsai, *Zeami*, pp. 56-68, argues persuasively for its authenticity, however.

CHAPTER TWO

1. Shinkei, *Hitorigoto*, in Hayashiya, p. 474.

2. The work, *Hachijōbon kadensho*, can be found in Hayashiya, pp. 511-665.

3. Nose, p. 1321.

4. The works are, according to Yoshida's titles, *Kadensho, Kadensho besshi kuden, Kakushū no jōjō, Kyūi shidai, Yūgaku shūdō kenpūsho, Shikadōsho, Nikyoku santai ezu, Nōsakusho, Fushizuke sho, Fūkyokushū, Shūdōsho, Zeshi rokujū igo sarugaku dangi, Museki isshi, Zeshi shichijū igo kuden*, and *Kintōsho*. The first two items are actually both part of *Fūshikaden*, and *Kakushū no jōjō* is a fragment of *Kakyō*.

5. Kawase, *Tōchū Zeami*. Kawase's additions are *Nō jo ha kyū no koto, Go on, Rikugi, Yūzaki geifū goi, Shūgyoku tokka, Ongyoku goi*, and *Ongyoku no uchi muttsu no daiji*. The last two are spurious, and Kawase's *Shūgyoku tokka* text has been superseded by a more accurate version discovered in 1956. The *Go on* in this work is not complete; the full version was not made available to the public until 1963.

6. There are a total of 255 plays (excluding new noh such as Yokomichi's *Takahime*) performed in the five schools of noh today, slightly fewer than the number performed when Yoshida triggered new scholarly interest in Zeami.

7. The most important of these lists are *Nōhon sakusha chūmon, Jika denshō, Nihyakujūban utai mokuroku, Kayō sakushakō*, and *Ihon ōkyoku sakusha*. All of the following material on these works is drawn from Kobayashi, *Yōkyoku*, pp. 254-94.

Nōhon sakusha chūmon was compiled by Yoshida Kurōdo Kanemasa in 1524 on the basis of conversations with Kanze Yajirō Nagatoshi (1488-1541). Kobayashi argues that it is probably accurate—except for a few detectable errors in copying—insofar as it deals with the plays of Nagatoshi himself, his father, Nobumitsu, and a contemporary of Nagatoshi's, Konparu Zenpō. The list contains no attributions to Kannami or Motomasa; their plays are believed to be subsumed under Zeami's name. It attributes 154 plays to Zeami. Of these, 40 are mentioned in Zeami's treatises as either composed or revised by him, and 15 are mentioned as the works of other writers.

Jika denshō is part of a three-part text known as *Kaze no kuchi* that was handed down in the Konparu school. It ends with the signature, "A day of the twelfth month of 1442, Zeami wrote this." This signature cannot possibly be authentic for a number of reasons, not the least of which is that some of the plays listed were written long after Zeami was dead. Kobayashi, after discussing the many—mostly false—signatures in the work, concludes that it was written around 1516. He gives it some credence merely because it is old, but one cannot help doubting the reliability of a document shown to contain counterfeit signatures.

Nihyakujūban utai mokuroku was compiled to accompany the Meiwa (1764-72) revisions of noh texts carried out by the fifteenth Kanze tayū, Motoakira (1722-74). Given Motoakira's position, he should have had access to any of Zeami's texts in the possession of the Kanze line, in particular, *Sarugaku dangi* and *Go on*. Unfortunately, the list of attributions he prepared proves that even if he did have access to those texts, he did not read them carefully. It seems he relied on *Jika denshō* and *Nōhon sakusha chūmon*, among other lists of attributions, and consequently his work is of no additional help in the search for documentary evidence relating to Zeami. *Kayō sakushakō* and *Ihon ōkyoku sakusha* belong to the same tradition as *Nōhon sakusha chūmon*.

8. This is the authoritative opinion of Omote (*Nōgakushi*, pp. 483-504).

9. *Sandō*, p. 142.

10. The practice of writing music for someone else's text appears to have been irregular; it seems likely in such circumstances that Zeami would have made a note to this effect, as he does in *Go on* for "Kaidō kudari" and "Saikoku kudari" (pp. 226, 228).

11. Omote, *Nōgakushi*, p. 485.

12. The most interesting case in point is *Eguchi*, which has long been thought to be the work of Kannami because of an attribution to him in *Go on* (p. 210). The quotation with the attribution is from the kuri, which would have been the first part of a full kusemai, and it is possible that Kannami wrote only this kusemai and Zeami composed the rest of the play. This is supported by the fact that the autograph text of *Eguchi*, although it contains the most detailed musical notation of all the handwritten texts, has no notation for the kusemai.

13. The section is undated, and several theories have been advanced to explain how it relates to the other sections (see Nishi, *Zeami*, pp. 89-100).

14. FSKD, pp. 47-49.

15. Kōsai, *Zeshi*, p. 328, asserts that honzetsu can mean "reliable information, a reliable opinion, or a reliable hypothesis."

16. Consider, for example, the following passage in FSKD, p. 20: "The main point behind dramatic imitation [monomane] is to present a comprehensive likeness of the object portrayed. However, . . . the actor must take into consideration the degree to which such a likeness is fitting. . . . Dramatic imitations of His Imperial Majesty and his courtiers, as well as the shogun and the military aristocrats, are very difficult because these persons are not available for actors of our class [to observe]. Nevertheless, we must make every effort to inquire into and research the language and manner of such persons and seek their criticisms after they have seen our performances. In addition, we may imitate very precisely the higher courtiers and their accomplishment in poetry and music, but it will not do to imitate too accurately the vulgar habits of farmers and the like. The poetic as-

pects of the lives of woodcutters, reapers, and charcoalmakers are appropriate for imitation, but the actor must not imitate every last detail of such commoners' manners; this would not be proper to present before the eyes of higher-class spectators. . . . It would be too vulgar and would contain nothing to draw their interest. . . . According to the social quality of the object portrayed, one must adjust the degree of faithfulness of imitation."

17. The success of noh at this time was very much dependent on a star performer. This was the point of Naami's suggestions about the *Okina* performance at Imagumano shrine. See Omote's helpful note 6 in zz, pp. 429-30.

18. *Sandō*, p. 144. The Ōei era dates from 1394 to 1428, so Zeami was still in the midst of the era as he wrote these words.

19. *Sandō*, p. 134.

20. *Ibid.*

21. Giō, Gijo, and Shizuka are *shirabyōshi* dancers; Hyakuman is a Kusemai dancer; Jinen Koji, Seigan Koji, Tōgan Koji, and Kagetsu are priest-entertainers; and the heavenly maidens, goddesses, and priestesses, mentioned last, are appropriate as a general class because they dance kagura, Shinto ritual dance (*ibid.*).

22. *Ibid.*, p. 135.

23. When jo-ha-kyū first appears in *Fūshikaden*, Zeami already sees it as a universal process: "In all things there is *jo-ha-kyū*, and *sarugaku* is no exception" (FSKD, p. 29). But in *Kakyō* he takes up jo-ho-kyū as it relates to an entire day's performance (pp. 90-91): "The *jo*, since it is the beginning, provides the basic configuration. . . . It should consist of the correct rendering of a straightforward and auspicious but not terribly detailed theme. . . . [The *ha*] directs the straightforward correctness of the *jo* toward fine nuance. . . . What I mean by the *kyū* is the end. It is the parting for the day and as such it has an air of, finality. . . . The *kyū* is the last stage and completely exhausts the *ha*." The ideas set forth here are obviously developed out of those in "Kashu." But the separation of jo, ha, and kyū into five dan does not occur until *Nikyoku santai ningyōzu*, where dances are discussed in these terms; and their separation into the five parts of a play does not appear until *Sandō*.

24. Yokomichi uses this term of his own devising (see Kōsai, *Nōyō*, p. 289) throughout his introduction to the two volumes of noh he co-edited with Omote. Excerpts from that introduction are translated in Flindt and Hoff.

25. As the table shows, Zeami's sashigoe corresponds with what is now known as the nanori. One might expect sashigoe to be equivalent to the modern sashi instead of to the nanori, now a spoken passage. It was the practice in Muromachi times, however, to begin the nanori in sashinori, so there is no great difficulty here. Zeami's mai is a dance of a rather elegant, abstract sort, as compared with the more vigorous and mimetic hataraki. The degree to which specific examples of the modern mai and hataraki resemble the dances to which Zeami refers is a question to be dealt with later, but the general distinction between the two genres seems to have continued unchanged from his day to the present. Incidentally, both dances are accompanied by instrumental, not vocal, music.

26. As *Dangi*, p. 289, says, "Kiribyōshi [i.e., *ōnori*] is for the purpose of showing off the dance."

27. *Sandō*, pp. 135-36.

28. *Bōoku* is written in kana in all texts but one (both ばうをく and ぼうをく appear); in the variant text it appears as 亡臆, "a devastated heart." Scholars have read 望憶, "longing thoughts," and 亡憶, "devastated thoughts," as well, and some versions of the original text write 茅屋 alongside the original kana. This means a

sedge-thatched hut and is to be taken as a metaphor for the life of lonely poverty that gives birth to the emotion in question. None of these characters really makes very good sense, and it has been suggested that Zeami actually meant *bōkoku no on* 亡國之音, "the music of a land about to fall," but did not say what he meant because the phrase was bad luck. *Bōkoku no on* is a likely candidate, because it is one of the kinds of music mentioned in the Mao preface to *Shi Jing* (Classic of Poetry), which is quoted at some length in Zeami's *Go ongyoku no jōjō* (p. 202): "The music of a land about to fall is mournful and thought-provoking. Its people are suffering."

29. Especially in *Go ongyoku no jōjō* and *Go on*. The five types of music he lists in these works are *shūgen* ("congratulations"), *yūkyoku* ("elegant music"), *renbo* ("romantic longing"), *aishō* ("mourning"), and *rangyoku* ("consummate music"). *Bōoku* in a broad sense is mentioned as the complement to *shūgen*. Shūgen remains constant, yūgen becomes yūkyoku, koi becomes renbo, and shukkai and bōoku (in the narrow sense) both become aishō. Rangyoku refers not to any particular emotional state as expressed in music, but to the music of an accomplished master that embraces and transcends all the other types.

30. The holograph texts are dated as follows:

a, Naniwa, -vii Ōei 20 (1413)	*g, Matsura,* x Ōei 34
b, Morihisa, 20 viii Ōei 30 (1423)	*h, Akoya . . . ,* xi Ōei 34
c, Tatatsu, 18 i Ōei 31 (1424)	*i, Furu,* ii Ōei 35 (1428)
d, Eguchi, 20 ix Ōei 31	*j, Kashiwazaki,* n.d.
e, Unrin'in, 7 xi Ōei 33 (1426)	*k, Yoroboshi,* Shōchō 2 (1429),
f, Tomoakira, 25 ii Ōei 34 (1427)	copied 22 xi Shōtoku 1 (1711)

The minus sign on the month vii for text *a* indicates an intercalary month, but 1413 did not have an intercalary month. Perhaps Zeami meant Ōei 21, which did. The *Yoroboshi* text, which was copied by Takeda Gonnohyōe Hirosada, has a note to the effect that he copied it directly from a holograph in his possession and had given the copy to Konparu Yazaemon in return for having been allowed to copy two Zeami holograph noh texts that Yazaemon possessed. Texts *a, g, h,* and *i* are in the possession of Kanze Motomasa, the present head of the Kanze school; the rest belong to Hōzanji Temple in Ikoma (west of Nara). At least *d, f,* and *j* are addressed to Konparu Tayū (i.e. Zenchiku). The texts are all written almost entirely in katakana. Some have brief stage directions and notes on costuming and also, interestingly enough, parts for the *okashi* (i.e. kyōgen actor). Texts *b, d,* and *e* contain relatively detailed musical directions, but the rest make very few references to music. Some of the texts (especially *b*) contain numerous revisions. Texts *b–f, j–k* are printed in Kawase, *Zeami jihitsu*, pp. 150-265, but texts *b, d, e,* and *j* are more readily available in Gotō et al., pp. 102-35. YK, vol. 1, has texts for *b, d, e, h,* and *k* based on the holographs, along with helpful notes identifying modern departures from the originals. The entire text of *d* and excerpts of the others are reproduced in *Nō* (1978), pp. 110-14.

31. *Morihisa* and *Yoroboshi* are the work of Motomasa (*Go on*, pp. 214-15), though Zeami is identified as the composer of the kusemai in the latter. Kannami is listed as composer of the kuri of *Eguchi* (probably standing for the entire kusemai) and as author of the chorus's first ageuta in *Furu* (*Go on*, pp. 209-10). And Zeami himself admits to revising *Kashiwazaki* from an original by Enami no Saemon Gorō (*Dangi*, p. 291). *Akoya no matsu* and *Unrin'in* were also probably revised, not written, by Zeami.

32. There have recently been experimental "revivals" of *Furu* and *Matsura*, but these plays cannot yet be considered part of the repertory.

33. Zeami's original version is reprinted in YK, 1: 50, 459. The modern Kanze text is found in *Kanzeryū* 1, p. 529.

34. The *Genna uzukibon* text, an early Edo text, is identical with the modern Kanze (also Hōshō) version here.

35. See the list of differences in YK, 1: 459.

36. YK, 1: 51.

37. ZZ, pp. 462-63 n. 69.

38. But the original has been standardized and weakened somewhat. For example, the nanori, as in *Eguchi*, has been changed:

ZEAMI TEXT (YK, 1: 148)

Kore wa Tsu no kuni Ashiya no sato ni Kinmitsu to mōsu mono nari. Ware jakunen no inishie yori *Ise monogatari* o sōden shi akekure moteasobisōro. Aru yo no yume ni toaru hana no moto ni sokutai tamaeru otoko kurenai no hakama mesaretaru nyoshō kano *Ise monogatari* no sōshi o goranjite kokage ni tachitamō o atari ni arishi okina ni toeba sore koso *Ise monogatari* no konpon zaichūjō Narihira nyoshō wa Nijō no kisaki tokoro wa Miyako Murasakino no Kumo no Hayashi to kataru to omoite yume samenu. Amari ni arata naritsuru yume nareba isogi Miyako ni nobori kano tokoro o mo tazunebaya to omoitsutsu. (I am Kinmitsu from the village of Ashiya in the province of Tsu. Long ago when I was young, I was initiated into the secret traditions of *Ise monogatari*, and I have taken constant pleasure in the work ever since. One night I dreamed that a man in formal court attire and a woman wearing scarlet trousers [*hakama*] were standing beneath a flowering cherry somewhere, reading a scroll of that work. When I asked an old man nearby about them, he told me that the man was the hero of the tales, Lieutenant Narihira, the woman Empress Nijō, and the place the Grove of Clouds in Murasaki Plain in the capital. And then I awoke. The dream was so startling that I am going to go up to the capital and search out the place.)

MODERN KANZE TEXT
(Taiseiban; *Kanzeryū* 1, p. 711)

Kore wa Tsu no kuni Ashiya no sato ni Kinmitsu to mōsu mono nite sōro. Ware itokenakarishi koro yori mo *Ise monogatari* o tenaresōrō tokoro ni aru yo fushigi no reimu o kōmurite sōrō hodo ni tadaima Miyako ni noborabaya to zonjisōro. (I am Kinmitsu from the village of Ashiya in the province of Tsu. Ever since I was young I have read *Ise monogatari*. One night I had a marvelous dream, and I am off to the capital now.)

One is immediately struck by how disjointed the modern version is. It is impossible to tell what connection the dream may have to Kinmitsu's trip to the capital, and the beautiful scene from the dream in the original has been lost. The language has even been standardized into the medieval formal language, *sōrōbun*, whereas the original mixed the older *nari* language with sōrōbun. The original version seems to prefigure the events of the play that follows.

39. *Ise monogatari*, episode 11.

40. The original play shows several archaic characteristics. The shite and tsure of the dream sequence might be considered two shite. (A similar argument can be made for *Kayoi Komachi* by Kannami.) There is a strong element of monomane and not any mai at all. The argument with poetic allusions is reminiscent of other old plays, such as *Sotoba Komachi* and Zeami's admittedly old-fashioned *Aridōshi* and *Saigyōzakura*. The modern reworking follows the five-dan standard form

more closely, but has been clumsily revised. Probably one of the major reasons it survives is that it is one of the two plays—the other is *Oshio*—in which a young man dances the elegant JONOMAI. It is unfortunate that the original has not been revived in more than a merely experimental way.

41. The oldest printed noh text with vocal notation is the so-called *Kurumaya-bon* of 1600. It includes a version of *Unrin'in* almost identical to the modern version. (See Nishi, *Zeami*, pp. 101-17.)

42. Further information on modern performance practice (in Japanese) can be found in the three books by Miyake Kōichi listed in the Bibliography. Information in English is available in Bethe and Brazell and in Flindt and Hoff. Tamba Akira's study in French has recently been translated as *The Musical Structure of Nō* (Tokyo, 1983) by Patricia Matore.

43. Lecture, Tōkyō Geijutsu Daigaku, Nov. 16, 1978.

44. Thus the hiranori passage in Fig. 3 would have been sung somewhat differently, as indicated below (the modern version is written in lower-case letters and the reconstructed original in capitals):

1	2	3	4	5	6	7	8
cho — o ryo o		— ku	tsu o	— sa	sa ge	tsu tsu	•
CHO O — RYO O KU		— TSU	O SA	— SA	GE TSU	TSU	•
n — ma no u		— e	na ru	— se	ki ko	o ni	•
N MA — NO U E		— NA	RU SE	— KI	KO O	NI	•
ha — ka se ke		— ru	ni zo	— ko	ko ro	to ke	te
HA KA — SE KE RU		— NI	ZO KO	— KO	RO TO	KE	TE

(See YK, 2: 5.) Yokomichi also identifies a new pattern that has begun to appear in the Kita school:

1	2	3	4	5	6	7	8
cho o	ryo —	o ku	tsu —	o sa	sa —	ge tsu	tsu

All this shifting of the beat has come about as a result of the rhythmic tension between the 12-syllable line and the 8-beat measure. Those half-beats marked with dashes between, for instance, MA and NO in line 2, would not be left blank by a skilled actor. Using an advanced technique known as "hiding the holds" (*mochi o kakusu*), he would sing the syllable before the dash slightly later than beat 1 and fill in the hold left at beat $1\frac{1}{2}$. As this process continues, the syllable is sung later and later until it eventually falls between the beat where it originally fell and the following beat. All the syllables originally on beats 1, 3, and 5 are thereby moved to beats $1\frac{1}{2}$, $3\frac{1}{2}$, and $5\frac{1}{2}$, and the original structure is transformed into the modern structure. It is important to notice that the syllables falling on even beats do not, and cannot, shift. They provide stable points that keep one line from intruding on the next, a stability that, fortunately, allows the reconstruction of the original rhythmic structure. (Lecture by Yokomichi, Tōkyō Geijutsu Daigaku, Nov. 6, 1978.)

45. Yokomichi, notes to the record set *Nō* (Japan Victor SJ 3005 and SJ 3006), p. 12. Zeami does, however, distinguish between *ō no koe*, "the horizontal voice," and *shu no koe*, "the vertical voice," and some think these are the prototypes of

tsuyogin and yowagin. Yokomichi traces the modern distinction between tsu-yogin and yowagin back to the Genroku period (1688-1704).

46. For example, in the modern (Taiseban) text of the Kanze school, "kuru" always indicates a rise to kuri pitch, but in the handwritten texts, the word often seems to indicate merely a rise from one pitch to another.

47. My transcription of the two texts. The modern original is in *Kanzeryū* 1, p. 536. There are mistakes in the printed version of the holograph text in Gotō et al., p. 107, but a photograph of the manuscript appears in *Nō* (1978), p. 112.

48. As have the structures of *Morihisa*, *Tomoakira*, *Yoroboshi*, *Naniwa*, and *Kashiwazaki*. *Unrin'in*, as we have seen, has changed radically.

49. The oldest extant instrumental notation is to be found in *Kō Masayoshi densho*, which dates from the early 17th century. Kō Masayoshi lived from 1547 to 1626.

50. Hagiwara (part 2, p. 30), who discusses the origins of the drums used in noh, notes that Zeami simply refers to *tsuzumi* (in *Shūdōsho*, pp. 236-37) without any distinction in terms, but argues that both the kotsuzumi and the ōtsuzumi might have been used by the time Kannami adopted Kusemai into noh. It is uncertain whether the flute used in Zeami's day had undergone the unusual modifications in the bore that give the modern *nōkan* its characteristic sound, or whether a flute more like the gagaku transverse flute (the *ryūteki*) was in use.

51. Lecture by Yokomichi, Tōkyō Geijutsu Daigaku, Dec. 12, 1978.

52. The oldest comprehensive *katatsuke* (compilations of notes on staging noh) are to be found in *Sōsetsu shimaizuke*, written by the eighth Kanze school head (including Motomasa) and dating from the first half of the 16th century.

53. Takemoto suggests that the JONOMAI performed in the modern *Eguchi* (and indeed all of the mai in modern noh) can be traced to a specific dance of Ōmi sarugaku, the *Tennyonomai*, or "Angel's Dance." He thinks Zeami was here, as in other cases, influenced by Inuō Dōami of Ōmi sarugaku. (The *Tennyonomai* mentioned here is to be distinguished from the modern TENNYONOMAI, which is simply a variant of the CHŪNOMAI.)

54. *Dangi*, pp. 301-2.

55. Aside from the Three Modes, the most important of these was the *go on* (Five Sounds), discussed in n. 29, above. The *go on* system is not well understood by modern scholars, however.

56. zz, pp. 88, 112-19, 122-32, 136-39.

57. The Three Modes system of classification is not without its own difficulties, particularly since Zeami is not entirely consistent in his use of these terms. Sometimes they seem to be actual role names, but they can also be areas in which the actor is to train himself or broader styles or modes for the approach to an individual role. (See Kitagawa, "Monomane"; I am indebted to Karen Brazell for drawing my attention to this article.)

CHAPTER THREE

1. FSKD, p. 58.
2. FSKD, pp. 21-22.
3. The articles of apparel he mentions are still in use today. His actual words for these clothes are *kamuri-nōshi* and *eboshi-kariginu*, the former being the hat and robe of a Heian courtier in formal dress, the latter their informal counterparts. The kamuri, eboshi, and kariginu are frequently worn by shite playing old

men. For instance, the nochijite in *Oimatsu* wears *uikamuri* and *awase kariginu*; the shite in *Saigyōzakura* wears *kazaori eboshi* and *hitoe kariginu*. The *nōshi* is worn only in the Kanze school today, and rarely even there. The nochijite in *Tōru* and *Genjō* may appear in nōshi but more commonly wear kariginu. (Miyake Noboru, "Nō no funsō," in *Nōgaku zensho*, 4: 134.)

4. *Nikyoku santai ningyōzu*, pp. 124-25. The text was originally written in 1421, but the 1441 text is the oldest extant manuscript; it is in the hand of Konparu Zenchiku.

5. *Kakyō*, p. 86.

6. The old man appears to be wearing eboshi and kariginu.

7. *Sandō*, p. 136.

8. *Hachijōbon kadensho*, a noh treatise probably written in the latter part of the Tenshō era (1573-92), refers repeatedly to instrumental shōdan for characters' entrances. It seems to reflect a still earlier practice. (See especially book 4, in Hayashiya, pp. 557-84.)

9. Perhaps this would have been so obvious to Zeami's original readers—exclusively actors intimately connected with the artistic tradition of Kannami and Zeami—that he did not bother to mention the various shōdan. At any rate, his remarks in *Shūdōsho* (p. 239) clearly demonstrate that the kyōgen actor was expected to function as aikyōgen between the acts of a noh and to deliver a katari, or narrative, explaining various details of the story.

10. *Ibid.*, p. 286.

11. In *Hōjōgawa* the shite sets loose a fish from a bucket he carries. This simple action gave the play its original title—the hōjōe Zeami mentions is a religious gathering for the purpose of releasing captured animals—but it also attracted so much attention that the play could no longer be considered completely straightforward. Zeami says the play contains a twist (*kyoku*), and the character he uses in this context is illuminating. Kyoku as written seems to mean an interesting twist; compare the use of the same character in the expression *kyoku ga nashi*, "uninteresting," or again, the same character, this time pronounced *kuse*, in the expression *kusemono*. In the Edo period kusemono came to mean scoundrel, but earlier it meant an interesting or eccentric person. The shōdan name kuse is also written with this character, and I would conjecture that in this case, too, it means "interesting and unusual"; this, because the rhythm is congruent but more irregular than the standard congruent song in tadautai. The meaning of Zeami's expression *"nao shi hire ari"* in connection with *Aioi* (*Takasago*) is not entirely clear, but it apparently follows from the mention of fish in the reference to *Hōjōgawa*. The problem is *shi*, which may go with *nao* as an intensifier or with *hire* to form *shibire*, meaning "tail fins." A possibility no Japanese scholar seems to mention is that *shi* and *hire* may be taken together as *shibire* with the meaning "numbness." This reading is perhaps unlikely, but not altogether impossible when one recalls that *Takasago* proceeds less smoothly than *Yumi Yawata* because of its greater density of image and allusion.

12. *Go ongyoku no jōjō*, p. 200. The waka quoted is KKS 356, by the priest Sosei. The saying attributed to Prince Shōtoku is spurious, and its exact meaning is not clear (see Kōsai, *Zoku Zeami*, pp. 180-85).

13. Judging from extant records of Muromachi and Momoyama performances in Nose, pp. 1260-99, 1308, *Takasago*, with 87 recorded performances, is far and away the most popular of all noh. *Yumi Yawata*, probably because of its straightforward formality, was also performed a great deal, but it has only 44 re-

corded performances, barely over half the total for *Takasago*. Nose's Muromachi and Momoyama records cover the period 1429-1602, and though they are not absolutely comprehensive, they do provide reliable data concerning general trends.

14. The text I use for the translation of *Takasago* is the oldest reliable and complete text. It dates from 1713, but is reputed to be an exact copy of the handwritten text of Kanze Kojirō Nobumitsu (1435-1516). This is the text used in YK, 1: 219-25. I have also made frequent reference to the text in Koyama et al., 1: 53-65. Vocal notation is taken from *Kanzeryū* 1, pp. 6-17. I have frequently referred to a recorded performance of *Takasago* included in *Nō*, vol. 1 (Japan Victor SJ3005).

15. The last half of the 8-beat line would normally take the following configuration:

5	6	7	8
• a a	a	a a	•

But since there are only 4 syllables of text available and since the song ends with a strong cadence (its final syllable coming on the final beat), the syllables *sa* and *shi* both gain an extra half-beat:

1	2	3	4	5	6	7	8
hi mo yu ku –	– su e zo	• hi sa –	shi – ki	– •			

16. The modern schools add *Kiushiu Higo no kuni*, "the province of Higo in Kyushu," before *Aso no miya*, and instead of *michisugara no meisho* read *mata yoki tsuide nareba, Banshiu Takasago no ura o mo* "(journey there) and since this is a good opportunity, (see) the coast of Takasago in the province of Harima."

17. Interestingly enough, in the period in question, there was a shrine priest at Aso of this name (Itō, "Yōkyoku," p. 111).

18. YK, 2: 7.

19. In modern performance, there is a break after the first full 7-5 line. The last two syllables before the break are half a beat longer than usual, temporarily slowing the movement begun with *tabigoromo*. The break is called an *uchikiri*, after the name of the drum pattern played there. In this case, the uchikiri pattern is preceded by another pattern called *jōryaku*. After this break, however, the same 12-syllable line is repeated, and the movement, briefly arrested, takes up again all the stronger.

20. YK, 1: 200, suggests an allusion in line 13 to a travel poem by Fujiwara Ieyoshi (*Shokushūishū* 719): "Tabibito no / Koromo no seki no / Harubaru to / Miyako hedatete / Ikuka kinuran" (All the way to Koromonoseki, / The Barrier of Cloaks, / In traveling clothes— / How many days have come and gone / Since I left the capital behind?).

21. Zeami's holograph text of *Naniwa* is written out in this way. Such an ordering is called *kaiko no shiki* and was preceded by an auspicious song, sung by the waki (sometimes called the *kaikonin*). The practice continued on special occasions through the Edo period, but is now obsolete (ZZ, 462 n. 69).

22. For instance, the Shimogakari Hōshō school of waki acting specifies (Koyama et al., 1: 54): "Isogisōrō hodo ni, Banshū Takasago no ura ni tsukite sōrō. Hito kitatte, matsu no iware o tazunyōzuru nite sōrō" (In our hurry, we have arrived on the coast of Takasago in the province of Harima. When someone comes

by I will ask about the pine tree). The wakitsure then says, "Shikaru byō sōro" (Yes, please do). It seems likely that a similar tsukizerifu was delivered in Zeami's day as well. The handwritten manuscript of *Eguchi* contains such an announcement, as does the oldest reliable text of *Tōru*.

23. In harmony with this, the 1st dan shows more speed and simplicity than this one, which opens with a musically highly inflected issei at a slow pace.

24. *Senzaishū* 397.

25. Here I borrow the translation of *honkadori* in Brower and Miner, p. 506, although the technique used is not strictly speaking honkadori, if only because that technique belongs to waka and not to noh. The term seems nonetheless appropriate because, as in honkadori, this passage echoes "the words . . . of a well-known earlier poem in such a way that recognizable elements are incorporated into a new meaning, but one in which the meaning of the earlier poem also enters."

26. It is not surprising, considering the importance of these words, that the old name, *Aioi*—Zeami's own name for the play—has been replaced by *Takasago*.

27. Though the tsure joins the shite for part of this song, I have chosen to translate the passage in the first-person singular because she is little more than an appendage to the shite and has no distinctly articulated character of her own.

28. They also suggest the possibility of an allusion to a poem in Ietaka's poetic collection, *Minishū* (*Zoku kokkataikan* 14527): "Takasago no / Matsu no negura ya / Orenuran / Yuki no yo tsuru no / Ura ni naku naru" (I hear the crane / Crying from the coast of Tsuru / Through the snowy night. / Has its nest been crushed / In the branches of the pine of Takasago?). Additionally, they point out that the white snow is to be taken as white hair on the old shite's head. (YK, 1: 220, 442.)

29. Compare the kana preface to *Kokinshū*: "It is in poetry that [human beings] give expression to the meditations of their hearts in terms of the sights appearing before their eyes and the sounds coming to their ears" (translation of Brower and Miner, p. 3).

30. These variants may be innovations that were added in the Edo period for variety's sake, but it seems more likely that they are remnants of an older performance practice, because there is no such variant in the newest school of noh, the Kita (see Miyake Noboru, *Nō no enshutsu*, p. 45). The variants are identified as *Hachidan no mai* in the Kanze school, *Shin no kata* in the Konparu and Kongō schools, and *Tsukurimono dashi* in the Hōshō school.

31. The Iki pine, according to legend, grew from a branch that Empress Jingū stuck into the sand on the occasion of her military expedition to Korea. It is found in Fukuoka city in Kyushu.

32. Suminoe is the archaic reading of the characters that in the 9th and 10th centuries came to be pronounced Sumiyoshi.

33. He is probably also referring to KKS 906: "Sumiyoshi no / Kishi no hime-matsu / Hito naraba / Ikuyo ka heshi to / Towamashi mono o" (If the pretty pine / On Sumiyoshi beach were human, / Then I could inquire, / How many generations / It has spent there). This poem, however, is not mentioned in *Takasago*, and does not seem to throw any new light on the play's honzetsu.

34. The meaning of *aioi* as two trees growing from the same stump is also possible, but here seems to fit less immediately than the meanings discussed above. Yabuta, p. 12, believes that *aioi no matsu* originally meant "the pine that grew on the beach at Ae" (or, more correctly, Afë).

35. *Kokinwakashū no kikigaki*, quoted in Itō, "Yōkyoku," p. 114.

36. This is clear in the Kanze school's kotsuzumi drum score, which directs one

to play at *jo no kurai* ("jo level") from "Takasago Suminoe no" through the end of the mondō, then at ha level from the beginning of the kakeai through the shite's line *miyo o agamuru* (line 90), and finally at kyū level through the end of the kakeai. (*Kanze Shinkurō*, 1: 6-7.) I know of no recordings of *Takasago* with a Kanze-school kotsuzumi player. The recording mentioned in note 14 has a Kō school drummer, and his playing does not clearly show this particular jo-ha-kyū progression.

37. The Kanze and Kongō schools read *kokon* here in their modern texts and thus obscure the reference to *Kokinshū*.

38. The pun on Sumiyoshi requires that the pines of Sumiyoshi be chosen as a symbol of *Kokinshū*, even though, as Kōsai, *Nōyō*, p. 209, points out, there is not a single poem about the Takasago pine in *Man'yōshū*, so it might have been more logical for Takasago to represent *Kokinshū*, and Sumiyoshi *Man'yōshū*.

39. *Mohe zhiguan* (J. *Maka shikan*) was recorded by Guan Ding (560-632) from the instructions of Zhi I (538-97). I am indebted to Professor Shuen-fu Lin for the observation that *wakō dōjin* has its locus classicus in the Taoist classic *Dao De Jing* (*Tao Te Ching*).

40. Miyake Noboru in his otherwise very helpful chapter on *Takasago* reveals a Shinto-nationalistic prejudice when he says, "Throughout the play, there is not the slightest taint of Buddhism, and it forever remains in a mood of overflowing auspiciousness" (*Nō no enshutsu*, p. 26).

41. This effect is still more pronounced in the modern Kanze and Hōshō schools: the final seven-syllable line is divided between the shite (first three syllables) and the waki (last four syllables). In the Hōshō school the shite sings the first three syllables alone, but the waki joins in for the last four.

42. There is instead a pause of three beats and the last syllable of *medetakarikere* takes a melodic cadential inflection.

43. "Enkyokushū," in Niima et al., p. 60. All this is standard material for waki noh, and very similar allusions and quotations are to be found in Zeami's *Oimatsu* (in the shidai), *Yōrō* (in the shidai and the last sashi), and *Hōjōgawa* (in the shite's first ageuta), as well as in *Kinsatsu* (in the shidai in the Kanze, Hōshō, and Kongō schools) and other plays ascribed to Kannami.

44. Kawaguchi and Shida, p. 70. Fumitoki was the grandson of the illustrious poet Sugawara Michizane.

45. Some sources say that the pine's flowers bloom once in 100 years.

46. Translation from Brower and Miner, p. 3.

47. *Wakan rōeishū* 157, in Kawaguchi and Shida. The couplet was taken from a seven-character quatrain (*jueju*) in *Ruijū kudaisho*.

48. The ideas expressed are not actually Chōnō's, but Zeami attributes them to him. In a note to *Shūgyoku tokka* he states (p. 191): "Chōnō says, 'A springtime grove rustling in the eastern wind and autumn insects crying in the northern dew are both forms of poetry.' Thus the voices of sentient and nonsentient are all chanting poetry. This is the propitious response to the realization of the *jo*, *ha*, and *kyū*. The way plants and trees come into flower and fruit when they have received the blessings of rain and dewdrops also illustrates *jo-ha-kyū*. One finds it even in the voice of the wind and the sound of water." An 18th-century commentary on noh, *Yōkyoku shūyōshū*, attributes similar comments to Chōnō, quoting a work entitled *Chōnō shiki* (Chōnō's Personal Record), but the work is no longer extant and seems likely to have been wrongly attributed in the first place (YK, 1: 443 n. 125).

49. In *Shūgyoku tokka*, pp. 190-91, for instance, where we find this passage:

Question: In all arts and vocations, one hears the word "realization" [*jōju*]. Is this to be taken superficially, or is there a more profound meaning to it, and what is the reason for this?
Answer: "Realization" means to become complete, so in this art, it indicates the arousal of interest. This realization corresponds to *jo-ha-kyū*. The reason for this is that in becoming complete, things fall into place. Without this falling into place, the minds of spectators do not realize full appreciation. The moment that the acting is realized is the moment when one's interest is piqued. The proper progression through *jo-ha-kyū* brings about this realization.
Upon careful consideration, it becomes apparent that all phenomena in the universe, positive and negative, great and small, sentient and nonsentient, are each equipped for *jo-ha-kyū*. Even the chirping of birds and the crying of insects—the way each cries forth with its own particular truth—this is *jo-ha-kyū*. (This is precisely the realization of no-rank and no-mind.) Consequently, these have the power to create both interest and pathos. If there were no "realization" in these, there could be neither interest nor pathos.

This work is recorded as having been transmitted to Konparu Zenchiku in Shōchō 1 (1428), at least five years after *Takasago* must have been written.
50. *Shi ji* (Classic of History), "Qin Shi Huang ben ji" (Biography of Qin Shi Huang), quoted in YK, 1: 217 n. 21.
51. In modern performances this is obscured by the fact that the lines are sung in tsuyogin, and the pitches jō and chū, which were distinct in Zeami's day, are now the same. But the notation, as we have seen, preserves the distinction.
52. FSKD, p. 47.
53. "Matsu no ha no chiriusezu shite, masaki no kazura nagaku tsutawari" (The needles of the pine never fall leaving the tree entirely bare, the laurel vine spreads its tendrils a long way).
54. Lines 163-64 give a slight variation of the first half of a poem from *Taiheiki*, vol. 14: "Kusa mo ki mo/ Waga ōkimi no/ Kuni nareba/ Izuku ka oni no/ Sumika naru beki" (Since even grass and trees/ Are in our great lord's sway/ Where indeed/ Could any demon/ Find a home?). The variant form *tsuchi mo ki mo* is found in many other plays as well.
55. (*Machimōsan to*) *iu/yūnami ni*, "Saying (we will await you)/evening waves," is a very common kakekotoba, and (*kimi ga yo ni*) *sumi/Sumiyoshi*, though not particularly familiar from other contexts, has already appeared in the mondō of dan 3 (line 74).
56. For example, MYS 36: *Yasumishishi/Waga ōkimi no* (He who pacified the realm,/Our great lord's).
57. Aikyōgen part of the Shimogakari Hōshō school, quoted in Koyama et al., 1: 61-63.
58. Since the text for the ai was not stabilized until relatively late in the Edo period, none of this can confidently be attributed to the artistry of Zeami. In any event, the existence of an aikyōgen part at this point causes some theoretical problems for the present study. There must have been some sort of interlude here for a costume change, but in his discussion of the construction of a noh play, Zeami makes no mention of it. How, then, is the aikyōgen to be seen in the five-dan structure of the typical play? Does it have its own jo-ha-kyū? Because we have no help from Zeami on these questions, they must be left to some other study.

59. Where, for superstitious reasons, the *ideshio*, "seaward surf," is changed to *irijio*, "landward surf."

60. *Ise monogatari*, episode 117. The first poem is preceded by lines reading, "Long ago, His Majesty made a journey to Suminoe." Then, after the poem, we have this line: "The god appeared [and said] . . . ," which is followed by the second poem. It is uncertain whether the first poem is intended to be the Emperor's composition or that of one of his retinue. The word *himematsu* seems originally to have meant a pretty seedling pine, but in this context, such a reading is inappropriate. The first poem also appears as KKS 905, where the reading for Sumiyoshi is given as "Suminoe." The second poem is SKKS 1857, and in the Takabon text, *shiranami* is changed to *shirazu ya*, conforming more nearly to Zeami's reading and possibly indicating the source from which he got the poem. None of the extant texts of *Ise monogatari* has *shirazu ya*, but it appears in both of the poetic treatises of Fujiwara no Kiyosuke (1104-77)—*Ōgishō* and *Fukuro sōshi*.

61. *Nō* (1970), p. 116.

62. The 1713 text follows the Kanze and Hōshō schools' reading *arawareideshi kamimatsu no*, "has appeared the sacred pine's," but I have translated the jōnoei as it appears in the other three schools' texts in accordance with the opinion of Yokomichi and Omote, who conjecture that this is the original form (YK, 1: 444 n. 129). Actually there is a variation even among these schools. The Kita and Kongō read *Sumiyoshi no*, whereas the Konparu reads *Suminoe no*. Yokomichi treats this textual problem in some detail in his article "*Takasago* no hanashi," in *Nōgeki shōyō*, pp. 97-115.

63. *Shokukokinshū* 731.

64. Yokomichi, "Zeami no nō," in Kōsai, *Nōyō*, p. 290.

65. Yokomichi's speculation that the nochijite of *Takasago* was originally an old god, if true, would make it necessary to modify this argument. In that case, the original dance would seem more likely to have been something like the SHINNO-JONOMAI, as in *Oimatsu*, *Hōjōgawa*, or *Saigyōzakura*. This issue is discussed more fully later.

66. Part of it (lines 213-17) is commonly used as a *tsukeshūgen*, a song to end full performances of noh.

67. This return to the natural world after a supernatural encounter is characteristic of Zeami's works, most notably *Yashima* and the latter half of *Matsukaze*, but also quite evident in *Tadanori*, *Izutsu*, and *Taema*.

68. From the kakeai of dan 3. Text from Sanari, 6: 3225-27.

69. For example, compare *Yumi Yawata*, "Yotsu no umi nami shizuka naru toki nare ya" (It is a time of peace upon the waves of the four seas), and *Takasago*, lines 96-97. Or *Yumi Yawata*, the sageuta of dan 2, "Kami to kimi to no michi sugu ni ayumi o hakobu kono yama no" (The paths of prince and god run straight, and straight I carry my steps up this mountain), and *Takasago*, lines 205-6.

70. In modern practice the nochijite's appearance is preceded by a rather ill-placed narrative and dance by the kyōgen.

71. Text from YK, 1: 318-23, which is based on a text copied by Shinomura Nagaharu in 1589.

72. A quite irregular variant of *Tsurayukishū* 9: "Kakikumori / Ayame mo shiranu / Ōzora ni / Ari to hoshi oba / Omōbeshi ya wa" (In the great expanse of sky / Now obscured / By roiling clouds, / How was I to know / If there were stars?).

73. In the earlier *Ongyoku kuden* he quotes extensively from the play, classing it between the shūgen piece *Ashibikiyama* and the play *Sekidera Komachi*, which he says is a play of poignant nostalgia, or bōoku. (The meaning of bōoku is dis-

puted, but it seems to indicate something between nostalgia and obsession with the past, as discussed in Chap. 2.) According to zz, p. 97, *Tōru*, too, is to be classed as bōoku in *Ongyoku kuden*, although it is not specifically designated as such.

74. Yokomichi, "Zeami no nō," in Kōsai, *Nōyō*, p. 291, and yk, 1: 219; Mikata, in *Nō* (1970), p. 117. Mikata also points to Zeami's designation of the nochijite as "a male god." The original Japanese is *nantai* (lit., "male role"), and although young is not explicit in the word, Mikata thinks it is implied. The word does to some degree seem to distinguish the role from the standard old man's role in the Aged Mode. In the context of the passage, however, nantai is used to contrast with *tennyo*, "heavenly maiden," and it seems quite possible that Zeami is referring to the distinction of gender alone.

75. Some of the disparities between the model and the variations deserve mention. For example, *Takasago* is exactly the same as *Yumi Yawata* until dan 5, where it has a jōnoei before the issei and no noriji after it. *Oimatsu* is somewhat less like the norm in that it lacks both the sashi and the noriji before the dance of dan 5 and replaces the rongi that follows the dance with two noriji separated by an unspecified shōdan. The dance itself is not the fast KAMIMAI of both *Yumi Yawata* and *Takasago*, but the extremely slow and stately SHINNOJONOMAI. Furthermore, dan 4 lacks both kuri and rongi, and dan 3 leaves out the kakeai and replaces the aguta with a formally less distinct uta. *Yōrō* differs yet more from the model: after the sashi of dan 4, where one expects a kuse, one finds instead the sequence sageuta-ageuta-sageuta. Dan 5 is also somewhat different from *Yumi Yawata*'s, and it is preceded by an exchange between the kyōgen and waki quite unlike anything in the other basic plays in the Aged Mode. In *Tōru*, as well, dan 4 differs considerably from the model, and for the first time in the comparison, so does dan 1. Dan 5, on the other hand, is more like that of *Yumi Yawata* than the corresponding sections of both *Oimatsu* and *Yōrō*. *Aridōshi* is a one-act play, and is balanced in a different way from all the other plays under consideration, but it also contains the greatest number of unidentified shōdan, as well as certain shōdan that do not appear anywhere in the other plays (e.g., *notto*, ASHIRAIDASHI, and TACHIMAWARI).

76. Note, for instance, the movement in a majority of dan from unmetered noncongruent passages to metered congruent passages or even the fact that the majority of dan open with instrumental pieces. This latter continuity cannot be traced back to Zeami with certainty for lack of information on the instrumentation and instrumental pieces of his time. Nevertheless, for reasons explained in this chapter, I think there was some kind of instrumental piece at the beginning of the first, second, and fifth dan even in Zeami's day. Furthermore, the instrumental accompaniment of the kuri is of such a striking and flamboyant nature that it imposes itself on the viewer in much the same way as the purely instrumental pieces at the beginning of those dan. I would argue that this kuri is dan 4's counterpart to the SHINNOSHIDAI, SHINNOISSEI, and DEHA of dan 1, 2, and 5.

77. Bernstein, *Unanswered Question*, pp. 93-97.

78. YK, 1: 213. There is neither a kuri nor a rongi in dan 4. The uta of dan 3 is shorter and not so regular as the "standard" ageuta one finds in *Yumi Yawata*.

79. Yashima, "Sakuhin," p. 6. A number of scholars mention Ennen no furyū as one of the direct precursors of Muromachi sarugaku: Kitagawa, *Kannami*, pp. 155-58; Ueki Yukinobu, "Sarugaku nō no keisei," in *Nō* (1970), pp. 23-29; O'Neill, *Early Nō*, pp. 7, 68-100 *passim*. The use of ōnori has been associated by Yo-

komichi, among others, with the furyū and the representation of nonhuman characters. On the other hand, the rongi that replaces it at the end of such plays as *Takasago* and *Yumi Yawata* is considered a more "human" shōdan (Kōsai, *Nōyō*, p. 292). This may account for the relative paucity of ōnori passages in Zeami's Aged Mode plays.

80. *Wakan rōeishū* 56, in Kawaguchi and Shida.

81. YK, 1: 226.

82. In modern performance the shite of *Aridōshi* enters to the accompaniment of an ASHIRAIDASHI. This is a different sort of piece from the SHINNOISSEI and ISSEI of the other plays, and it is sometimes performed by the ōtsuzumi and ko-tsuzumi players alone, depending on which school the flute player belongs to. The use of an ASHIRAIDASHI here indicates a connection between this play and *Kinsatsu* and *Kuzu*.

83. The jōnoei is a short shōdan in einori sung at a high pitch and taking a waka as its text. Given the poetic content of such a shōdan and its highly inflected melody, one might logically expect it to heighten the lyricism of the dan in which it appears. This is probably the case in certain other plays where the jōnoei is used (e.g., *Kiyotsune*, *Yorimasa*, and *Ashikari*), but here the content, although it is a waka, is not particularly lyrical, and the shōdan itself blends so well with the following issei that one would be very unlikely to discriminate the jōnoei as a separate shōdan during a performance.

Syntactically, *Sumiyoshi no* of the jōnoei in *Takasago* leads directly to the *haru nare ya* of the issei. (It should be recalled that *Sumiyoshi no* is the reading of the Kita and Kongō schools. Konparu has *Suminoe no*, and the other schools *Kamimatsu no*.) Furthermore, there is a melodic link between the two shōdan at (*nami-*) *ma yori* and (*te ni*) *miteri*, where identical melodies are sung to the accompaniment of identical patterns on the three drums.

The *issei that follows immediately is somewhat irregular, whereas the corresponding issei in *Yumi Yawata* is perfectly regular. Metrically, *Takasago*'s *issei breaks down to lines of the following syllable count: 5, 7-5, 7-5, 8-6, 8-5, 7-7, 6-6. *Yumi Yawata*'s issei, on the other hand, runs 5, 7-5, 7-7, and is followed immediately by a noriji. It seems possible that the lack of a noriji in a similar place in *Takasago* is made up for by the last verses of the *issei. In this regard it will be helpful to compare the last lines of *Takasago*'s *issei with those of *Yumi Yawata*'s noriji. The former has a syllable count of 7-7, 6-6, the latter of 7-7, 7-6. Compare *Yōrō*, 8-8, 7-5, 7-6; *Shiga*, 7-5, 7-6; *Naniwa*, 7-7, 9-5; *Awaji*, 8-8, 7-7; and *Shironushi*, 7-5, 8-8, 5. There is considerable metrical flexibility in ōnori passages, and it seems quite possible to me, although I find no confirmation in Japanese sources, that *Takasago*'s *issei may originally have been a standard issei and a noriji.

84. According to Yokomichi (in Kōsai, *Nōyō*, p. 290), the last words of the ageha are irregular, although I fail to see the irregularity myself. He also points to melodic irregularities in the beginning of dan 5, and remarks that part of the final rongi approaches chūnori rhythm. I find one line that does so, 214:

1	2	3	4	5	6	7	8
ma – n	za i	ra ku	ni wa	i	no chi	o no –	bu •

85. It might also be noted that although the source of the play, the *Kokinshū* preface, is without parallel in terms of correctness and orthodoxy, the particular passage chosen by Zeami is somewhat ambiguous. He took advantage of this am-

biguity, as we saw above, and this liberty may account in part for the play's perceived eccentricity.

86. See, for example, the second issei in *Tōru*.

87. It is quite possible that Zeami's first exposure to these techniques came in his renga training, but the techniques themselves are not unique to renga. They are central to the tradition of waka poetics, especially in the editorial policies by which the imperial anthologies of waka were organized.

88. YK, 1: 227.

89. There are various textual problems in this song (see YK, 1: 444 n. 130). Unlike the sashi in *Takasago*, this one does not contain kakekotoba or jokotoba, but relies instead on an extended group of engo.

90. Wen Ting-yun, "Shang shan zao xing" (An Early Walk on Mount Shang). The last two lines of the poem are quoted in "Kanginshū," p. 209, in Niima et al., p. 174.

91. The shite's first sashi in *Tōru* is built in a similar way, but plays in the Aged Mode, the majority of which are waki noh, are less lyrical than those in the Woman's and Martial Modes, and this is probably the reason that renga-like progression is not conspicuous in the shite's first sashi in *Yumi Yawata*, *Oimatsu*, and *Hōjōgawa*.

92. For a good example, see the issei from *Oimatsu* in YK, 1: 215.

93. I follow the Konparu, Kongō, and Kita schools, which use *shōhaku*, "pine and birch," in line 3 instead of the Hōshō and Kanze schools' *shōkaku*, "pine tower." Note that the even-numbered lines all end with the syllables *ari*, which is pronounced *nari* in lines 2 and 4 because of the final *n* in the preceding word.

94. *Kaen no rintō* (line 6) is particularly difficult to interpret (see YK, 1: 443 n. 121).

95. YK, 1: 319.

96. Quoted in YK, 1: 319.

97. In dan 4 of *Yōrō*, there is an overabundance of allusion, which, had it been more successfully manipulated, might have served in this way. But in the absence of any overall unifying narrative context, it falls to the level of mere ornament and loses most of its significance, thus weakening the play considerably.

98. It is interesting to note that the issei of *Oimatsu* also contains an allusive variation, in this case on KKS 1081. The shite's first song in *Aridōshi*, although it is not an issei but instead a sashi, contains an allusion to two of the eight titles of the famous "Xiao Xiang bajing" (Eight Views of Xiao Xiang). Similarly, the issei of *Yōrō* and *Yumi Yawata* arouse suspicions that waka are being quoted or alluded to, although none have been identified.

99. This is not the place to attempt a systematic critique of attributions to Kannami, but the problem can be illustrated by observing that Kitagawa Tadahiko, for instance, identifies four plays "with absolute certainty" as the literary creations of Kannami: *Furu*, *Komachi* (*Sotoba Komachi*), *Jinen Koji*, and *Shii no Shōshō* (*Kayoi Komachi*). Yet Omote even questions, fairly convincingly, the attribution of *Furu*. (See Kitagawa, *Kannami*, p. 112; and Omote, *Nōgakushi*, pp. 499-500.)

100. *Go on* quotes from the waki's sashi and ageuta in *Kinsatsu* under the title *Fushimi*. The note "composed by my deceased father" is attached, so at least the music for the sashi and the ageuta can be attributed to Kannami. The lyrics cannot be definitely attributed to him, but, as Yokomichi says, "There is the possibility that he also wrote the words" (YK, 1: 43). The *Fushimi* referred to was, perhaps, an independent piece that became attached to *Kinsatsu* after the fact, but

considering the content of the kakeai following the notto in the piece, it seems likely that the whole play was at one time called *Fushimi*. The attribution to Kannami is, unfortunately, very tentative, but the play can be useful in this investigation as an example of an old play in the Aged Mode even if it is not entirely the work of Kannami.

101. Text from YK, 1: 43-48, which is based on an old but undated manuscript from the Tenri library.

102. YK, 1: 45.

103. There are passages with characteristics similar to monozukushi in other Zeami plays as well; *Takasago*'s final rongi with its bugaku titles is only one example. But again verbal interest is always subordinated to theme and structure.

104. Yet another type of wordplay that Kannami seems to be fond of, and that I do not find frequently in Zeami's Aged Mode noh, is the *tōin*, or head rhyme. There is an example in *Kinsatsu*: "Sugu naru beki ka Sugawara ya" (in the ageuta of dan 1), where *sug* of the first phrase rhymes with *sug* of the second. Yokomichi and Omote note other examples in their remarks on *Kinsatsu*, but they do not mention this device in the notes to the Zeami plays under examination. Zenchiku also often had recourse to head rhymes.

105. YK, 1: 45.

106. *Jika denshō* attributes *Ema* to a writer named Kongō, perhaps the same man Zeami mentions in *Sarugaku dangi* (p. 298). *Sakahoko* and *Himuro* seem to have been written by Miyamasu, a younger contemporary of Zeami's who is known for several of the vendetta plays based on *Soga monogatari*. *Mekari* and *Chikubushima* have been attributed to Konparu Zenchiku, and although the sources of this attribution are not any too reliable, it is probably not a great mistake to assume that the plays originated with the Konparu troupe of Yamato sarugaku.

107. *Ema* is probably unique in the modern repertory, and its performance varies widely from school to school. In some versions the shite of the final dan first dances a CHŪNOMAI and then a tsure in a male role dances a KAMIMAI while a tsure in a female role simultaneously dances a KAGURA. It is very unlikely that this reflects the original form of the play.

108. For example, *Momijigari* (Gathering Maple Leaves), *Tsuchigumo* (The Ground Spider), *Ryōko* (The Dragon and the Tiger), *Rashōmon* (Rashōmon Gate), and *Nomori* (Guardian of the Fields).

109. FSKD, p. 25.

110. The *kogaki* (i.e., variant performance style) of *Yōrō* called "Suiha no den," performed in the Kanze school, adds a nochitsure to the play. This character dances a TENNYONOMAI. The shite still dances a KAMIMAI, but it is modified to have a greater variety in tempo and a somewhat different melody. Similarly, in the kogaki of *Oimatsu* known as "Kōbaidono," a nochitsure precedes the shite onto the stage and dances either a TENNYONOMAI or a SHINNOJONOMAI. The shite dances an IROE. This kogaki is performed in the Hōshō, Kita, and Kongō schools, and a very similar kogaki known as "Kaeshidome no den" is danced in the Kanze school. Some have conjectured that these kogaki are reflections of the way the plays were originally done. This is certainly possible (and would explain certain inconsistencies in the structure of *Yōrō* in particular), but it also seems possible that these variant styles were created later to assimilate the plays to the non-Kanze form.

111. On the contrary, in the historical long run the non-Kanze style seems to have had more success than Zeami's waki noh in the Aged Mode. True enough,

there are many waki plays of the Aged Mode that follow very closely in both form and theme the pattern established by *Takasago* and *Yumi Yawata*; *Hōjōgawa*, *Awaji*, *Shironushi*, *Shiga*, and *Hakurakuten* are among those that remain in the modern repertory. Nevertheless, the writers of the late-15th and 16th centuries seem to have preferred the non-Kanze style. It is not surprising to find this trend among the Konparu-school writers of plays such as *Arashiyama* and *Tōbōsaku*. But even the later Kanze-school writers seem to have enjoyed more success with the non-Kanze-style plays in the Aged Mode than with the Kanze style. Thus Nobumitsu wrote such plays as *Kusenoto*, and Nagatoshi *Enoshima*, *Ōyashiro*, and *Rinzō*. There are, moreover, several plays now categorized not as waki noh, but as miscellaneous or demon plays, that more or less follow the pattern of the non-Kanze play in the Aged Mode. *Kuzu* and *Kasuga Ryūjin* are two examples.

CHAPTER FOUR

1. *Sandō*, p. 142.

2. There are several *Komachi* plays: *Sotoba Komachi*, *Kayoi Komachi*, *Sekidera Komachi*, *Ōmu Gomachi*, and *Sōshiarai Komachi*. But when Zeami himself quotes the play he calls *Komachi* (*Dangi*, p. 287), the lines are from the shite's ageuta in *Sotoba Komachi*.

3. *Sandō*, pp. 137-38. The old poem is GSIS 82: "Ume ga ka o/sakura no hana ni/niowasete/yanagi ga eda ni/sakaseteshi gana."

4. Omote, ZZ, p. 126, tentatively identifies the costume depicted as a *maiginu* and *ōkuchibakama* topped off by an eboshi. The maiginu is a light, loose-fitting kimono worn over the rest of a costume, particularly during dance sequences. The ōkuchi or ōkuchibakama is a pair of large stiffened trousers characteristically worn by upper-class women in noh, also sometimes worn by male characters. There are several types of headgear known as eboshi.

5. *Nikyoku santai ningyōzu*, p. 126. The specific meaning of the first passage is difficult to pin down. "The most important thing in dramatic representation is this," for instance, can be interpreted to mean "making sensibility the basis of one's acting and rejecting strength is the most important thing to remember while performing in the Woman's Mode," but it might as easily mean "the Woman's Mode is the most important in all dramatic representation." It seems fairly clear that the Woman's Mode is to be considered the basis of yūgen.

6. The last line of Zeami's remarks on the Aged Mode from *Sandō* (p. 137) thus has some bearing here: "The congratulatory play in the Woman's Mode also takes the same five-dan configuration." Strictly speaking, however, there are only two congratulatory plays in the Woman's Mode that are readily attributable to Zeami—*Unoha* and *Fujisan*. Both do indeed follow the five-dan configuration, but the shōdan sequences in their 4th dan are so different from those of *Takasago* and *Yumi Yawata* that this piece of information, too, seems to lead nowhere. Zeami's words for "congratulatory play in the Woman's Mode" are *nyotai no shūgen*. Omote glosses this as "congratulatory noh in which the shite is a goddess," and the four plays mentioned seem to fill these qualifications. Zeami specifically identifies only one of them, however, as a shūgen play, *Fujisan* (*Go on*, p. 208). On the contrary, he classifies *Hakozaki* and *Ukon* as yūkyoku (*Go on* and *Go ongyoku no jōjō*, pp. 201, 209). He does not classify *Unoha*. The term *nyotai kami nō*, "god noh in the Woman's Mode," seems to connote shūgen ("congratulations") as a matter of course, and I suspect that the *Go on* classifications of shūgen and yūkyoku are not

mutually exclusive. But until further research clarifies this matter, it remains open to question.

7. *Dangi*, p. 286.

8. Though *Michimori* then presents something of a problem, because it does not seem formally orthodox. I shall return to this problem in Chap. 5.

9. My primary text is from YK, 1: 274-79, which is based on a text dating from Tenshō 18 (1590). For vocal musical notation, I have referred to the present Kanze text, *Kanzeryū* 1, pp. 1173-83, as well as various historical texts. I have also made frequent reference to Koyama et al., 1: 271-79. The recording of *Izutsu* in *Nō*, vol. 1, Japan Victor SJ3005, has been of great help.

10. This shidai is normally sung first by the shite, and then repeated softly in a low register by the chorus in the technique known as *jitori*. The only exception is the abbreviated performance, when the following sashi and sageuta are omitted and the shidai is sung only once, by the shite.

11. The moon is then specifically identified as *shinnyo no tsuki*, "the moon of genuine thusness," and its salvific function becomes explicit.

12. *Aki no yo* may perhaps also be taken as "a tiresome world," to be reflected in *yo no naka*, "this world," of line 28. *Fuke* in *fukesugite* provides an example of the penetration of Shinkokin diction into noh. When the word was used by Fujiwara no Teika (1162-1241) in a famous poem (SKKS 420), his more conservative contemporaries pronounced it "Zen nonsense." (Kamo no Chōmei refers to this criticism in his *Mumyōshō*; see Hisamitsu and Nishio, p. 86.) By Zeami's time, however, this was not unusual diction. It nonetheless fits well into the fluid, sometimes synaesthetic language of noh.

13. KKS 870, a poem that the late-9th-century poet Furu no Imamichi wrote when Isonokami no Nanmitsu was awarded a court promotion even though he had long absented himself from court to live in the village of Isonokami: "Hi no hikari / Yabu shi wakaneba / Isonokami / Furinishi sato ni / Hana mo sakikeri" (Since the sunlight, / In its shining, / Makes no discrimination, / It falls upon the old village of Isonokami / And flowers burst into bloom).

14. YK, 1: 277, has *kokoro tokete*, "heart/mind melts," in line 96. I have chosen to follow the Kanze reading *togete* because it seems to make much better sense and because such a reading seems quite reasonable given the ambiguity in historical notation of voiced and unvoiced consonants.

15. Modern textual study reveals that *tsutsu izutsu* is a variant reading for the more common *tsutsu izu no*. The meaning remains the same.

16. *Ise monogatari*, pp. 126-27.

17. YK, 1: 278 n. 14.

18. Text from Sanari, 6: 3400-3410.

19. *Ise monogatari*, Episode 24, second poem: "Azusa yumi / Mayumi tsuki-yumi / Toshi o hete / Waga seshi ga goto / Uruwashi mise yo" (Treat her lovingly / As I have these many years, / And take her in your arms, / Like a fine catalpa bow, / Or like a bow of the spindletree). This poem is open to several interpretations. The first two lines (of the Japanese; the word order in the translation is reversed) serve as a jo for *toshi*, "year," by association with *tsuki*, "month," in *tsuki-yumi*, "spindletree bow." What significance the enumeration of types of bows has beyond this is open to question; perhaps the poet intends to compare a woman to a bow, because of the graceful curving shapes of both, or because a man takes both into his hands.

20. *Ise monogatari*, Episode 4; KKS 747: "Tsuki ya aranu / Haru ya mukashi no /

Haru naranu / Waga mi hitotsu wa / Moto no mi ni shite" (That is not the moon, / Nor is this / The spring of years gone by. / I alone remain / As I was before).

21. The kotsuzumi plays a unique pattern here, starting the line with *tsuzuke*, the natural companion to the tsuzuke pattern in the ōtsuzumi part. But the pattern is broken off with the last three beats of the measure, and the kotsuzumi player merely strikes the drum with the syllable *o* of *omokage*, then lapses into silence.

22. The phrase *iro nōte nioi nokorite* is Tsurayuki's criticism of Narihira's poetic style quoted directly from the *Kokinshū* preface.

23. *Jōwa 5:2:10 haiden rinji matsuri shidai no koto*, quoted in Nose, pp. 356-59.

24. The poem "Tsutsu izutsu" itself embraces both the innocent childhood of the two lovers and their erotic awakening at the well curb when Aritsune's daughter was 19.

25. There are numerous superficial differences. The SHINNOSHIDAI and SHIN-NOISSEI are used almost exclusively for waki noh, and would be inappropriate here, so *Izutsu* begins more quietly, with a NANORIBUE, etc. The *uta* of dan 1 is less formally distinct than *Takasago*'s ageuta, but performs more or less the same function. Dan 3 of *Izutsu*, proceeding as it does from a mondō directly to the chorus's ageuta, may at first seem quite different from the corresponding section of *Takasago*, but actually the only significant difference is in length. The end of *Izutsu*'s mondō is tapered in just the same way as *Takasago*'s kakeai, and again, the two dan function in basically the same way.

26. *Dangi*, p. 288. Zeami calls Amaterasu "Amateru" and Yamato Takeru "Yamato Dake."

27. This is one of the demands of formal convention for ageuta and rongi, and is not a particularly artful use of the device.

28. Similar effects are achieved at the end of *Sekidera Komachi* (probably by Zeami) between the two noriji before the final uta (YK, 2: 295), and at the end of *Matsukaze* (in the part of the play Zeami claims to have written), just before the CHŪNOMAI (YK, 1: 64-65).

29. Yashima, "Zeami"; Nishino, especially p. 46.

30. *Genkō shakusho*, Episode 28, quoted in Sanari, 4: 1840.

31. Text from Sanari, 4: 1839-55, which is based on an unspecified Kanze manuscript. For a translation of the play, along with a translation of part of Kobayashi Hideo's provocative essay on it, see Rimer, "Taema."

32. The way this dance is introduced suggests that it was originally a TENNYO-NOMAI ("Dance of the Heavenly Maiden"), the dance for which the Ōmi actor Dōami was so famous. Its appearance in a Zeami play is evidence of Dōami's influence on Zeami's style. (See Takemoto, pp. 119-21.)

33. This line is quoted in *Busshin hōyō*, according to Sanari, 4: 1842.

34. There are several minor differences early on in the plays. None begins with the SHINNOSHIDAI, for instance. This is because that particular instrumental piece is reserved for standard waki noh. This difference, however, probably grew up with performance practice during the centuries after Zeami's death and is not relevant to the present study.

35. The uta is, like *Yumi Yawata*'s ageuta, a song in tadautai style. It lacks the orthodox melodic configuration of the ageuta, however, and is in this sense less formal.

36. Text from Nogami and Tanaka, pp. 91-96, which is based on the early Edo period printed edition of noh texts known as the *Kurumaya bon*.

37. My characterization of the HANOMAI here as an extra dance may be histor-ically inaccurate. It is likely that dan 5 of *Unoha* represents an earlier step in the evolution of the mugen play, which contained several dances in the final dan. From this viewpoint, it is not that *Unoha* has an extra dance, but that *Yumi Yawata*, *Izutsu*, and the rest lack dances that would normally have been included. (See Takemoto, pp. 150-56.)

38. Thus, one finds the following conversation between a so-called mad woman and a ferryman in the play *Sumidagawa* (YK, 1: 38):

s   Nō nō, ware o mo fune ni nosete tamawaresōrae,
w   Okoto wa izuku yori izuku e kudaru hito zo,
s   Kore wa miyako yori hito o tazunete kudaru mono nite sōrō,
w   Miyako no hito to ii, kyōjin to ii,
    Omoshirō kurūte miseyo,
    Kurūte misezu wa kono fune ni wa nosemajii zo to yo.

s   Excuse me, you over there. Please let me ride across in your boat too.
w   Where are you coming from and where are you going?
s   I have come from the capital, and I am on a journey in search of a
      certain person.
w   Capital dweller or crazy woman, whichever. . . . Anyway, do some-
      thing crazy for me. If you don't, I won't let you ride in my boat.

39. FSKD, p. 23.

40. Text from YK, 1: 340-47, which is based on a 1544 text copied by Shimo-mura Nagaharu.

41. To this list can be added the religious ecstasy scene in *Kashiwazaki*, the shite's expression of intense resentment in *Kayoi Komachi*, the distracted plea of the shite in *Hyakuman*, and the shite's intoxication in *Tōboku*. All these scenes are written as noriji.

42. Other Zeami genzai plays about disoriented sensibilities follow more or less the same pattern. See, for instance, *Hanagatami* or *Sakuragawa* (there is a re-cent translation of the latter by Robert Huey).

43. Text from YK, 1: 285, based on a 1589 text copied by Shimomura Naga-haru.

44. See Omote, *Nōgakushi*, pp. 501-2.

45. *Sotoba Komachi* and *Yoshino Shizuka* are both in the Woman's Mode, and both are probably by Kannami, but they are genzai noh. *Kayoi Komachi* is also by Kan-nami and is a mugen noh; however, despite its title, it is not a Woman's Mode play but a demon play, originally called *Shii no Shōshō*. A translation of *Motomezuka* by Barry Jackman can be found in Keene, pp. 35-50. Omote now questions the at-tribution of *Motomezuka* to Kannami (lecture, "Nō to utai," Jan. 5, 1985, Ōtsuki Noh Theater, Osaka).

46. MYS 1801-3, 1809-11; *Yamato monogatari*, p. 147.

47. The *Yamato monogatari* ending varies considerably from this one: the suit-ors both die in an attempt to rescue the maiden, not in a duel.

48. Respectively, SHIDAI, shidai, nanori, ageuta, tsukizerifu; ISSEI, issei, sashi, sageuta, ageuta; and mondō, kakeai, sageuta, ageuta.

49. The rongi form lends itself quite well to catalogues of various kinds, and this may have originally been one of the shōdan's functions. See the *kizukushi* ("catalogue of trees") of the rongi in *Kinsatsu*, the *konomizukushi* ("catalogue of

fruits and nuts") of the rongi in *Kayoi Komachi*, the *urazukushi* ("catalogue of coasts") of the rongi in *Matsukaze* (originally from the old play *Tōei*), and the *kasazukushi* ("catalogue of head coverings") of the rongi in *Ashikari*.

50. There is a hint of this kind of description in the kakeai of the last act of *Higaki*, but it is subordinated to the description of age versus youth.

51. *Furu*, which may be partially attributable to Kannami, is also a mugen noh in two acts, and it too provides some evidence that Kannami played a part in the development of the mugen noh (Omote, *Nōgakushi*, p. 502).

52. For the *Matsukaze* sashi, see YK, 1: 59, or Koyama et al., 1: 364. Notice, for example, the string of associations from *ie*, "house," to *sato*, "village," to *kayoiji*, "road," to *tomo*, "friend"; or again *utakata*, "bubble," to *shiokumi*, "scooping up brine," to *ama no sode*, "fisher's sleeve," to *hosanu*, "not to dry." For contrasting translations, both of them by Royall Tyler, see Keene, pp. 17-34, and Tyler, pp. 88-103.

53. These attributions are based on *Jika denshō*, *Nōhon sakusha chūmon*, and *Kayō sakushakō*, on which see Chap. 2, n. 7, above.

54. YK, 2: 54. Yokomichi is speaking with direct reference to *Tamakazura*, but the comment applies to other plays as well.

55. Text from YK, 2: 46-53, which is based on a copy made by Konparu Zenpō (1454-1532). YK, 3: 53, and Koyama et al., 1: 313, both interpret *tsutana ya* of line 11 as "unlucky" or "ill-destined," and although the word can mean this, I think it is more appropriate in the context to interpret it as "pitiful" or "wretched to look at" (modern Japanese *misuborashii*).

56. Kanze, *Kokoro yori kokoro*, pp. 122-23.

57. Itō, "Zeami," argues against attributing the play to Zeami.

58. YK, 2: 438 n. 98.

59. There are many other plays traditionally attributed to Zeami, but not acknowledged as such in his treatises, that might be examined in the way I have looked at *Nonomiya*. Two that come immediately to mind are *Yūgao* and *Kakitsubata*.

60. ZZ, p. 574.

61. YK, 2: 49-51.

62. *Izutsu* is, to be sure, a special case even among Zeami's plays, but similar techniques are used in *Higaki* and *Tadanori*, to name only two examples.

63. YK, 2: 35.

CHAPTER FIVE

1. *Dangi*, p. 291.

2. FSKD, pp. 24-25.

3. Mikata Ken, "Nō no enshutsu," in *Nō* (1970), p. 125.

4. *Sandō*, pp. 138-39. Although plays of four or six dan can be found in the Aged and Woman's Modes as well, Zeami makes explicit mention of these configurations only in discussing the Martial Mode.

5. In some schools *Atsumori*'s CHŪNOMAI becomes an OTOKOMAI.

6. *Nikyoku santai ningyōzu*, p. 127. There are several stumbling blocks in the interpretation of this passage, largely because Zeami wrote it in an idiosyncratic pseudo-Chinese. I have relied primarily on Omote's interpretation, but have also made reference to Konishi, *Zeamishū*, p. 160. The phrasing is similar to that in the brief articles on posture in the plays in the other modes quoted in Chaps. 3

and 4, although some of the verbal resemblances have been lost in translation. A particularly important example is the phrase that I translate as "make strength the basis of your acting and infuse your movements with subtlety." The original reads *chikara o tai ni shite, kokoro o kudaku* (lit., "make strength the basis and pulverize the mind"). Compare, from the notes on the Woman's Mode, *kokoro o tai ni shite, chikara o sutsuru* (lit., "make the mind the basis and abandon strength"), which I render "make your sensibility the basis of your acting and reject any show of strength."

7. *Dangi*, p. 286.

8. But *Michimori* was not written by Zeami and is therefore not appropriate as an example of his style. Furthermore, as I indicated in n. 8 to Chap. 4, the characterization of that play as "straightforward" is rather confusing.

9. Text from YK, 1: 241-48, based on the *Komiyayama Motomasa shikigobon*, which is undated but seems to have been written between 1558 and 1592 (YK, 2: 20). I have also made reference to the texts in Koyama et al., 1: 157-68, and Sanari, 4: 1903-20. The text for the vocal music I have found in *Kanzeryū* 1, pp. 585-98. To my knowledge, there are no commercial recordings of *Tadanori*.

10. In modern performance the waki and his companions make their entrance to the music of a SHIDAI and the shōdan sequence carries on through a tsukizerifu. The text used by the Shimogakari Hōshō school (in Koyama et al., 1: 159) reads as follows:

w   Yōyō isogisōrō hodo ni kore wa haya Tsu no kuni Suma no ura to ka ya mōshisōrō. Mata kore naru isobe ni hitoki no hana no miete sōro. Uketamawarioyobitaru wakaki no sakura nite mo ya sōrōran. Tachiyori nagamebaya to omoisōro.

wt   Mottomo nite sōro.

w   Well now, since we have hurried on our journey, this must already be the coast of Suma in the Province of Tsu. And here upon the shore stands a tree in full bloom. I guess this must be the young cherry tree we heard about. I would like to go closer and look at it.

wt   By all means.

Although the old text used for the translation does not have such a shōdan, some conventional passage may well have been delivered after the ageuta.

11. Note how the poet is first identified as Shunzei, using the Sino-Japanese reading, then as Toshinari, using the native pronunciation for the same characters. The Sino-Japanese reading for a name such as this implies respect for the man's poetic accomplishments; the native reading is a more ordinary way of identifying him. It is significant in the original Japanese that the waki introduces himself first as a member of the household of Shunzei (the poet), only later admitting that Toshinari (the man) is dead.

12. Naniwa was well known for its reeds, which were immortalized in numerous waka from *Kokinshū* on. There may even be an allusion here to a poem by Saigyō (SKKS 625), although the commentators do not mention it:"Tsu no kuni no/Naniwa no haru wa/Yume nare ya/Ashi no kareba ni/Kaze wataru nari" (Spring in Naniwa in Tsu/Must have been a dream./Now I hear only/The passing wind/Rustling over dry dead reeds).

13. Purists might quarrel with Zeami's terminology here. He might better have used the term *wabi*, because the loneliness he speaks of is strongly colored by a feeling of poverty not usually associated with the lyric melancholy of *sabi*. This is

one of many places where Zeami uses the terminology of classical poetics to his own ends without necessarily taking its origins into careful consideration. He does not seem to have considered the distinction between sabi and wabi particularly important here; he uses words related to both terms in lines 35, 37, and 40 to describe a single overall aesthetic sensibility.

14. KKS 962. Here Zeami is following his own advice from *Fūshikaden* (FSKD, p. 47): "When writing about a famous place or a historical site, one should use Chinese and Japanese poems about the place—familiar poems—in the more concentrated parts of the play."

15. The word *gyakuen* in line 44 has a rather complicated history, as Omote and Yokomichi point out (YK, 1: 429 n. 28). I follow their interpretation into the modern Japanese *gūzen tōrikakatta teido no karisome no en de wa aru ga*, translating "although it is but chance that brings me." This may seem somewhat inconsistent with the line "Whenever I come back here," but I believe the inconsistency is a part of the original Japanese text, designed to add to the uncanniness of the old man, actually a ghost. He comes down to the Suma coast by much more than mere chance, and the kind of inconsistency we find in his speech is one of the clues that he is not simply an old woodcutter.

16. YK, 2: 241.

17. For example, SKKS 130 by Nijō-in Sanuki: "Yama takami / Mine no arashi ni / Chiru hana no / Tsuki ni amagiru / Akegata no sora" (As dawn breaks through the sky / Cherry petals hide the moon / Falling in the high mountains, / Blown down / By the gale off mountain peaks).

18. The allusion appears elsewhere in the poetry of the day (e.g., the renga sequence in *Anegakōji Imashinmei hyakuin renga*, link 38). See the headnote in Kaneko, p. 132. For a translation, see Hare, "Linked Verse." The "Suma" chapter of *Genji* makes condescending reference to something the peasants gather for firewood called *yamashiba* (see Seidensticker, p. 240).

19. Seidensticker, p. 243.

20. Compare KKS 95, by the priest Sosei:"Iza kyō wa / Haru no yamabe ni / Majirinan / Kurenaba nage no / Hana no kage ka wa" (Today let us go off / Into the springtime hills. / If darkness overtakes us, / How about the shelter / Of the delicate, falling blossoms . . . ?).

21. A case could be made that the waki's question is intended to remind the shite of Tadanori's poem. But this gives the waki more credit than he deserves, I think. He seems to be consistently characterized as deficient in poetic sensibility and rather shallow. In my view, Zeami sets up Tadanori's devotion to the way of poetry as an ideal, and means the waki's shallowness to stand in contrast to that devotion. The contrast is maintained throughout the play, and in its final lines I see a comment to the waki that he reconsider his abandonment of poetry.

22. Sanari, 4: 1912-14. Sanari uses the old text of the Ōkura school. This ai-kyōgen part contains a strange inconsistency with the rest of the play: it mentions an old cherry tree, whereas line 72 speaks of a young cherry.

23. The Kongō, Konparu, and Kita schools' replacement, an ageuta, reads as follows:

Ageuta

w/WT Sode o katashiku kusamakura,
Sode o katashiku kusamakura,
Yumeji mo sazo na iru tsuki no,
Ato mienu Isoyama no,

Yoru no hana ni tabine shite,
Kokoro mo tomo ni fukeyuku ya,
Arashi hageshiki keshiki kana,
Arashi hageshiki keshiki kana.

Ageuta
w/wt I spread out my sleeves and pillow my head in the grass,
I spread out my sleeves and pillow my head in the grass,
And set forth on the path to dreams.
The moon too travels west, to set,
And hides behind the coastal mountains,
While I sleep beneath the blossoms clad in darkness.
Age overtakes my mind as night grows late,
And the gale seems to blow with ever growing force.
And the gale seems to blow with ever growing force.

24. I am reminded of a poem by Minamoto Kaneaki, *Kin'yōshu* 288: "Awaji-shima / Kayō chidori no / Naku koe ni / Ikuyo nezamenu / Suma no sekimori" (How many nights / Has the guard at Suma Barrier / Wakened to the cry / Of plovers / Flying to and from Awaji?).

25. *Senzaishū* 66: "Sasanami ya / Shiga no miyako o / Arenishi o, / Mukashi Nagara no / Yamazakura kana" (At Shiga / Lapped by gentle waves / The ancient capital is gone to ruin. / But on Mount Nagara, / The mountain cherry blooms as long ago). *Nagara* is a kakekotoba; it can mean "as [long ago]" and is also the proper name of a mountain.

26. Brower and Miner, p. 234, mentions other cases along with Tadanori's.

27. Tadanori's pride in his poetry can be compared with Yorimasa's in the play by that name.

28. The poem is included in the *Bo Shi wen ji* and can also be found in *Kanshi taikan*, 4: 1727.

29. Kami, pp. 4-5.

30. YK, 2: 26.

31. Notice again the principle of dan symmetry operative here: the dan ends with a tadautai shōdan. This principle seems to have precedence over Zeami's suggestion to end plays in the Martial Mode with chūnoriji.

32. The line may allude to *Gosenshū* 445 (anonymous): "Kaminazuki / Furimi furazumi / Sadame naki, / Shigure zo fuyu no / Hajime narikeru" (The tenth month, / When they come and go / So unpredictably, / Ah, yes, I see, these rains / Must mark the fall of winter).

33. *Senzaishū* 122.

34. Music of the *biwa*, a kind of Japanese lute, also plays an important part in the short play *Tsunemasa*.

35. Text from YK, 1: 233-40, which is based on a 1713 text reputed to be an exact copy of a text written by Kanze Kojirō Nobumitsu.

36. Text from YK, 2: 265-74, which is based on a 1554 text written by Kanze Kojirō Motoyori. No quotations of or allusions to Chinese poems have been identified, but the frequent *kowaki kotoba*, difficult (Chinese) words such as *hatō*, *gyoō*, *seigan*, *shōsui*, and *sochiku*, strongly suggest that there is an allusion behind this sashi. If there is not, and the shite and the tsure are supposed to be making this up as they fish, then my point is made all the stronger.

37. In *Kanehira*, too, the maejite complains about his wearying life, and when questioned by the waki, reveals considerable historical and religious knowledge.

38. Text from YK, 1: 257, based on *Motomori shikigobon dōsō bon*. Motomori is Kanze Motomori, 9th head of the Kanze troupe (1535-77).

39. The first few dan of *Kiyotsune* are rather like a genzai noh, which may partially account for the waki's position in them.

40. Kami, p. 6.

41. *Mansai jugō nikki*, 11 v Ōei 21 (1414), quoted in Kōsai, *Nōyō*, p. 277.

42. *Ibid.*, p. 278.

43. The TACHIMAWARI is done only in the Kanze school. The Kita and Kongō schools have a KAKERI here, and the Hōshō and Konparu schools do not use an instrumental dance at all.

44. Text from YK, 1: 265-73, which is based on a text copied by Kanze Motomori in 1566.

45. *Dangi*, p. 288.

46. YK, 1: 249.

47. Text from YK, 1: 249-56, which is based on a text copied by Kanze Motoyori in 1554.

48. Yokomichi calls *Kasa Sotoba* "a play with the strong coloring of the original *shura* style" (YK, 2: 257).

49. In a fascinating but largely conjectural article, Nishino suggests that *Tomonaga* and *Tomoakira*, as well as certain defunct plays, may be the work of Motomasa or Motoyoshi.

50. *Dangi*, p. 287.

51. Just after the KAKERI there is a kakeai in which the deaths of Tadanori and Tsunemasa are mentioned. It is easy to imagine that this shōdan was originally much longer, giving detailed accounts of their deaths, and that it was followed by a still longer, more detailed account of Michimori's death.

52. Nishi, "Sakuhin," p. 6. But I fail to see how *Michimori* is any more straightforward in its treatment of its original source than other plays in the Martial Mode.

53. Sanari, 4: 1438.

54. According to the performance records in Nose, pp. 1300-1315, *Sanemori* and *Yashima* were among the most popular plays in the repertory.

55. "Zadankai 'Zeami no nō'" in Kōsai, *Nōyō*, p. 312.

CONCLUSION

1. FSKD, p. 42.

2. FSKD, p. 20.

3. FSKD, p. 42.

4. For example, in *Nikyoku santai ningyōzu*, pp. 123-24.

5. *Seigan Koji* may be an exception (see Omote, *Nōgakushi*, p. 499).

6. *Jinen Koji* was written by Kannami. The other three plays are traditionally attributed to Zeami, but strictly speaking, he is referring to characters, not plays, when he uses these names in *Sandō* (pp. 136, 139).

7. *Nikyoku santai ningyōzu*, pp. 123-24.

8. *Sandō*, p. 138. The entire passage is quoted in Chap. 4, pp. 131-32.

9. *Kakyō*, p. 102.

10. *Sandō*, p. 140.

11. "[An actor] who can't do anything but the demon role well is an actor who doesn't understand the flower. For this reason, the young actor's demon is com-

pletely uninteresting even though it seems well performed. He who can't do anything but the demon role well cannot really be said to understand what it is that makes the demon role interesting." This insight comes as early as the second section of *Fūshikaden* (p. 26). It is further developed in the seventh section and becomes more influential in later treatises. Here we may be able to see some of the legacy of classical poetics, specifically, Teika's concentration on poetic training within a limited aesthetic range that for the most part avoided the so-called demon-quelling style. (See Brower and Miner, pp. 246-48.)

12. Yamazaki Masakazu explores *riken no ken* and its broader implications in his article "Henshin no bigaku."

13. *Yūgaku shūdō fūken*, pp. 166-67.   14. Waley, p. 88.

15. *Dangi*, p. 274.   16. *Go ongyoku no jōjō*, p. 197.

17. *Dangi*, p. 276.   18. *Dangi*, p. 285.

19. From a letter to Zenchiku, zz, pp. 318-19.

20. In *Fūshikaden*, monogurui by old nuns, old women, and old priests are explicitly rejected. The old man in *Tokusa* is not a priest, but his role is still extremely unorthodox, especially in the context of the Aged Mode.

21. Konishi, "New Approaches."

22. The origin of this kind of noh is a thorny problem, but even if we cannot be certain that Zeami invented the form, we can confidently say that he brought it to its maturity. Zeami's waki noh (as opposed to those of the Konparu style) were probably among the first mugen plays. However, early plays such as the original *Unrin'in* and *Motomezuka* may predate Zeami's waki plays, casting doubt on the theory that Zeami created the form. Omote (*Nōgakushi*, pp. 499-502) argues persuasively that both *Furu* and *Eguchi*, traditionally attributed to Kannami, were actually written by Zeami. But he goes on to suggest that these two plays are the only evidence suggesting that the mugen noh (he actually says "*mugen nō keitai no nō*") were created before Zeami. Here he seems uncharacteristically hasty. He fails to mention *Motomezuka* and *Kayoi Komachi* (both of which may be by Kannami), as well as other mugen plays such as *Unrin'in* that seem to have been contemporary with, if not earlier than, Zeami's works. Does he perhaps mean "formally orthodox mugen noh" when he says *mugen nō* keitai *no nō*?

23. Actually, the noh of Kannami and his contemporaries are not so clearly centered on the shite. One often finds in them a tendency toward dramatic conflict, which, if further developed, might have made noh much more like the drama of the West. Indeed, as we have seen, in *Aridōshi* Zeami made uncharacteristically heavy use of dramatic conflict and gave the waki a role equal to that of the shite or of even greater weight. He called such a style archaic, however, and avoided it elsewhere.

24. YK, 1: 159. The first few lines of this passage are unmetered, and Yokomichi and Omote have gone so far as to separate them from the rest of the sashi, calling them a nanorizashi. This is useful in their excellent analysis of the structure of noh, but tends to obscure the fact that the sashi was in fact a nanori in early noh.

25. See YK, 1: 167-68.

26. zz, p. 212: Konishi, *Zeamishū*, p. 372.

27. YK, 1: 304. It is interesting to note that the play *Nomori*, cast in the "anti-style" of the *rikidōfū no oni*, or the demon of violent movement, has a nanorizashi, a sashi of self-introduction, as in the older plays, instead of a lyric sashi like the ones mentioned above.

28. See YK, 2: 319, 36, and 62, respectively.

29. See YK, 2: 144.

30. *Go on* explicitly attributes only the music to Kannami but there is a good chance that he wrote the text as well.

31. Kannami's version of the play was called *Saga monogurui* or *Saga no dainen-butsu no onna monogurui no nō*. There is no firm evidence that he wrote the play, but it is recorded as one of his most successful plays in performance (*Dangi*, p. 264).

32. *Jigoku no kusemai* was written by a certain Yamamoto with music by Naami (*Go on*, pp. 225-26).

33. I refer here to the plays by Kannami and the "old noh" (i.e., *kosaku* noh) included in the first volume of *Yōkyokushū*. The only exception is *Funabashi*, but it was heavily revised by Zeami from an old dengaku play, and the blending of conflicting strains in its mondō-kakeai sequence may well be his work.

34. There is an apposite comment in *Shūgyoku tokka*, p. 194. Zeami says there that no one has ever seen a real demon. The implication seems to be that "real demons" do not exist, and that therefore one best utilizes the notion of a demon by reflecting it in a human consciousness.

35. FSKD, p. 37.

Glossary

The following is a glossary for frequently used technical terms, in both Japanese and English. For convenience I have included references to text passages for those readers who want further information than is contained here; the Index can also be used for access to the plays mentioned and for terms used infrequently in the text or the Notes. All italicized words within a description that are not defined have their own entries. The major roles in the noh play are defined in the Introduction, pp. 2-3.

Aged Mode (*rōtai*), see under Three Modes.

Ageha. A one- or two-line solo passage centering on the upper register, usually sung by the shite at the beginning of the third part of a *kuse*.

Ageuta. Tadautai shōdan beginning in the upper register and ending in the lower, usually written in two sections. The most typical metrical pattern used is 5, 7-5, 7-5, . . . , 7-5; the last line and the first full 7-5 line are often repeated. *Ageuta* are among the most common *shōdan* in noh and fulfill a variety of functions. Among the special types of *ageuta* are the *michiyuki* and the *machiutai*.

Ai. Interlude in a noh play during which the shite leaves the stage for a costume change while the aikyōgen comes on stage, usually to deliver a narrative explaining the story behind the play.

Aishō, see under Five Sounds.

Allusive variation (*honkadori*). A rhetorical technique. The words, or sometimes the more abstract situation or expressive attitudes of a well-known older poem (*honka*), are echoed in a new poem. The new poem gains in depth and richness by elaborating or deepening some portion of the meaning of the older poem, and the situation of the older poem is given a new relevance in the new poem. Allusive variation differs from simple allusion in that more than the mere reuse of earlier materials is involved; the evocation of an earlier experience is essential to the new poem. The technique is most commonly associated with classical poetry, particularly that of the age of *Shinkokinshū*, but is applicable as well to noh, as in, for instance, the use of "Tsutsu izutsu" in *Izutsu*.

ASHIRAIDASHI. Simple entrance music, usually for the shite.

CHŪNOMAI. The most common dance (*mai*) in noh. Usually done by female characters, but sometimes by animal or plant spirits or even by the young warrior Atsumori (in certain schools). There are versions played on all three drums and flute, and versions for only *kotsuzumi*, *ōtsuzumi*, and flute.

Chūnori. The least common of three possible configurations of *congruent song* in noh. *Chūnori* allots two syllables of text to one beat of the music (see text Fig. 3). *Chūnori* is also called *shuranori* because one of the most common places it is used is near the end of a play depicting the sufferings of a *shura*, either in battle or in hell. This is one of the most dynamic rhythmic patterns in noh, but it is rarely found in extended passages. Usually it is mixed to some degree with lines of *hiranori* rhythm.

Chūnoriji. A *shōdan* in *chūnori*. *Chūnoriji* are frequently used at the end of plays in the Martial Mode.

Congruent song (*hyōshi au*). One of two major divisions of song style in noh. Congruent song is delivered in a specific rhythmic configuration whereby each syllable of the text corresponds to a specific beat or part of a beat in the music. For the three types of congruent song, see *chūnori*, *hiranori*, and *ōnori*; and text Fig. 3. Cf. *Noncongruent song.*

Dan. "Section." Zeami states that the standard play is to be constructed from five *dan*: The first is the beginning, the second, third, and fourth the development, and the fifth the conclusion (see *jo-ha-kyū*). In the typical noh play the first dan contains the waki's self-introduction, the second the appearance of the shite, the third a conversation between the two, the fourth a narrative by the shite, and the fifth a dance or mimetic performance by the shite. (Note: The word *dan* is used in a somewhat different manner by Yokomichi in *Yōkyokushū*.)

DEHA. Rhythmic entrance music for nonhuman characters, usually after the *ai*. Performed on all three drums and the flute.

Dengaku. A medieval performing art that had significant influence on the development of noh. Originating in agricultural rituals and festivities among the peasants, *dengaku* split into two strains sometime in the Heian period, one retaining its rustic amateur character, the other becoming more professionalized. *Dengaku* (as well as *sarugaku*) at one time consisted of dramatic performances as well as spectacles we might associate with the circus in the West, juggling, acrobatics, and the like. By Zeami's time highly skilled and well-patronized guilds (*za*) of *dengaku* actors were performing around the capital. The actors Kiami and Zōami in particular earned Zeami's respect.

Einori. One of two major classes of *shōdan* in noncongruent song. *Einori shōdan* are used primarily for the delivery of waka or Chinese poetry. They are generally sung either during a character's entrance onto the stage or immediately preceding dances. They are melodically highly inflected, or melismatic (see text Fig. 2) and are most commonly distinguished from one another by the general pitch at which they are sung. Two common types are the *genoei* and the *jōnoei*.

Engo. A rhetorical technique. The use of word association to create relations between parts of a poem or, in noh, parts of a song, independently of a standard discursive narrative. Often a word appearing in one part of a poem adds an additional meaning to one appearing in another part so that a new set of associations or images emerges to complement the most obviously apparent meaning of the poem.

Five Sounds (*Go on*). One of the typologies Zeami uses in discussing noh. The Five Sounds represent five different types of music to be found in noh. Of primary importance in its own right and as a foundation for the others is *shūgen*, the music of congratulations or auspiciousness. *Shūgen* has ritualistic significance and provides the basic emotional tenor for the *waki noh*. It is music of an uncomplicated, felicitous nature, and it is supposed to work a kind of sympathetic magic: in praising wise rule, it furthers the ends of that rule; in honoring the gods, it gains their favor; and in entertaining the patron, it assures the economic well-being of the acting troupe. For these reasons, it is seen as an underlying component of the other types of music. *Yūkyoku* ("elegant music") is the second type of music. It contains an element of grace or elegance not obvious in simple *shūgen* and has somewhat subtler musical effects. *Renbo* ("romantic longing") is the third type of music, and *aishō* ("mourning") the fourth. The emotional tenor of each is apparent from its title. The connection to *shūgen* is not made very clear by Zeami. The fifth type of music is called *rangyoku* ("consummate music"). It is not identified with a specific type of emotion, but is wholly determined by the performer. Only a virtuoso is capable of performing *rangyoku*, and when he does so, he can mix elements of the other types of music—even seemingly contradictory elements—at will, for a performance of ineffable profundity and power. Zeami did not fully articulate the Five Sounds until he wrote *Go ongyoku no jōjō* and *Go on* in 1430. Even then, one sometimes finds inconsistent usages of the terminology. This has led to difficulty in understanding the theory fully, and modern scholars are still uncertain about many aspects of it.

Geizukushi. A medley of diverse artistic performances in close succession. A common exhibition of the shite's talents in plays by Kannami and early playwrights. In *Jinen Koji*, for instance, the shite successively dances a CHŪNOMAI, recites a *kusemai*, delivers a *katari*, and performs another dance (KAKKO).

Genoei. Einori *shōdan* centering on the lower register; characteristically used for the delivery of a poem (*waka*).

Genzai noh. Plays in which the shite portrays a living human being. Zeami seems to have had less interest in *genzai noh* than his father and other playwrights.

Go on, see Five Sounds.

Ha, see *jo-ha-kyū.*

Hana. "Flower." One of Zeami's favorite metaphors. "The flower" is what lies behind a successful performance, the actor's power to charm and emotionally move his audience. In *Fūshikaden* several different types of "flower" are identified: the transient flower of simple novelty, the eternal flower of long training and deep understanding, the flower of secrecy, etc. In Zeami's early theory, when the metaphor is used most often, it seems to have particularly strong visual associations.

HANOMAI. A short dance often done in sequence with a JONOMAI.

Hashigakari. A bridge visible to the audience, extending from the greenroom to the back, right-hand (audience's left) corner of the stage, over which major characters make their entrances and exits.

Hataraki. A type of vigorous, usually mimetic exercise used in place of a dance in plays of a martial or demonic character. The modern instrumental *shōdan* HATARAKI is a descendant of Zeami's *hataraki*, but is probably narrower in scope and more specific than his.

HAYAMAI (also called BANSHIKI HAYAMAI). An elegant dance (*mai*) done by characters associated with the imperial court or women who have attained enlightenment. Performed on all three drums and flute.

Hiranori. The most common of three configurations of *congruent song* in the noh. Although it probably originated in a medieval song form called *sōga*, it is today unique to noh. In *hiranori* twelve syllables of text are matched to sixteen half-beats of music and certain half-beats are left without a syllable (see text Fig. 3). *Hiranori* is most commonly used for standard 7-5 verse texts (*tadautai*), but it is also used for special effect with irregular texts. The precise distribution of syllables around the odd beats of *hiranori* passages varies according to the school of acting and the historical period, but the distribution around even beats has remained stable, allowing us to reconstruct an approximation of historical *hiranori*. (See p. 268, above.)

Honkadori, see Allusive variation.

Honzetsu. A term borrowed from classical poetics. The *honzetsu* is the source or situation around which a poem or noh play is created. For Zeami, it was important to find a source—he sometimes says "seed"—that allowed the incorporation of dance and song into the play. The *honzetsu* need not be a story as such; it can consist merely of the traditional associations of a famous place or the lyric overtones of a well-known literary situation.

ISSEI. Rhythmic entrance music, usually for the shite. Performed on *kotsuzumi*, *ōtsuzumi*, and flute.

Issei. Einori shōdan centering on the higher register often used at the beginning of a *dan* or before a dance. The typical *issei* takes the following metrical pattern: 5-7-5/7-5; in some cases a second verse of 5-7/5-7 (called the *ninoku*) is added.

Jo, jokotoba, or *joshi.* "Preface words"; "preface." A rhetorical technique. One phrase is used to introduce another through a metaphorical or imagistic linking, often achieved through wordplay in the second phrase. The relationship between the first phrase and the second need not make any discursive sense, but may merely call up a clever image. The technique is commonly used in early Japanese poetry. In noh it is used to create nondiscursive strings of associated thoughts or images. The *jokotoba* is similar to the *makurakotoba*, except that it is presumably unique at each appearance and has no fixed number of syllables.

Jo-ha-kyū. Terms borrowed from *gagaku* (court music), where they apply to specific movements in a given piece. In noh *jo, ha,* and *kyū* take on a more comprehensive meaning and indicate the full process of a play. *Jo,* literally "preface," means the opening of the process, and it is generally characterized as smooth and even. *Ha* means "break" and indicates a change in tone from the *jo* as well as the main body of development of the play's theme. *Kyū* means "fast" and is taken as "fast finale," the climax of a play. Zeami came to see *jo-ha-kyū* as a universal organizational principle for all things existing in time, and he applied the term not only to the play as a whole, but to *shōdan* and even individual syllables of a text. See Chap. 2, n. 49.

Jōnoei. Einori shōdan centering on the higher register and characteristically used for the delivery of a poem (*waka*).

JONOMAI. A very common slow and elegant dance (*mai*) done by female shite. Some JONOMAI are performed on all three drums and flute, others omit the *taiko*.

Kakeai. Sashinori shōdan in the form of a dialogue. The text is for the most part in verse meter.

Kakekotoba. "Pivot-word." A rhetorical technique. In the most characteristic form of *kakekotoba*, one series of sounds is understood to mean two different things depending on whether it is read with the words preceding it or the words following it. For examples, see the text analyses of *Takasago, Izutsu*, etc.

KAKERI. A brief circling of the stage done by warriors and *monogurui* characters at moments of great emotion or tension. Performed on *kotsuzumi, ōtsuzumi,* and flute.

KAMIMAI. A fast, very rhythmic dance (*mai*) done by gods in *waki noh*. Performed on all three drums and flute.

Katari. *Kotoba shōdan* of some length aiming at strong narrative interest. Within the play proper a *katari* can be delivered by the shite or the waki, but the kyōgen actor often also delivers a *katari* during the *ai*. Sometimes the last part of the *katari* is delivered in *sashinori*.

Kiri. *Tadautai shōdan* with a strong sense of rhythm but little melodic inflection used to end plays.

Kiribyōshi, see under *Ōnori*.

Kogaki. Literally "small writing" or "subtitle," from its notation next to a play title in smaller characters on a written program. *Kogaki* are conventionally sanctioned variant performance styles that can be applied to certain plays. In the Tokugawa period, when the acting conventions of noh were strictly codified, it became desirable to retain some latitude of variation in the performance of certain plays. These variations were themselves institutionalized as *kogaki*, and they specified certain allowable changes in performance style, ranging all the way from the insertion of extra *shōdan* or the reversal of waki and shite roles to minute and almost indiscernible changes in costuming, properties, or stage business. Most *kogaki* are probably Tokugawa innovations (some may originally have been "mistakes" that proved dramatically effective). Others seem to preserve aspects of archaic or regional performance styles that were eliminated from the more standard performing style specified by Tokugawa authorities.

KOINONETORI. Entrance music for the shite in variant and particularly important performances of *Kiyotsune*. Performed by solo flute.

Kongin. One of three possible melodic styles for the vocal music of noh. *Kongin* freely mixes the two more basic styles, *yowagin* and *tsuyogin*. It is not common but is found occasionally in plays in the Martial Mode.

Kotoba. A form of declamation used in noh. It has neither fixed rhythm nor recognizable melody, but only a general pattern of inflection in which the first part of a phrase is delivered more or less in a level pitch and the second half in a swelling phrase with a sharp jump at the beginning and a return to the original level at the end of the phrase. Distinctions are made in the degree of the swell and the amount of time it takes to reach its highest pitch according to the type of character being represented. (See text Fig. 1.) Spoken *shōdan* are most common in earlier parts of a play; a typical example is the waki's *nanori*, or self-introduction. But certain highly artful *kotoba shōdan*—*katari*—appear in high points of plays, particularly in the Martial Mode. The *shōdan* delivered by kyōgen actors in noh plays are in *kotoba*.

Kotsuzumi. The smaller and far more sensitive of two hourglass-shaped drums used in noh. The *kotsuzumi* is held by the left hand near the right shoulder and beaten with the fingers of the right hand. Its many varying sounds provide color to the instrumental music of noh. Cf. *Ōtsuzumi*.

Kowaki kotoba. "Hard or stiff words." Difficult language, usually Chinese compounds, that cannot be readily understood aurally. Zeami cautions against their excessive use.

Kudoki. *Sashinori shōdan* centering on the lower register and usually used for the expression of laments or painful feelings. *Kudoki* are often preceded by *kuri*-like *shōdan*.

Kuri. Short melismatic *sashinori shōdan* centering on the higher register and frequently rising to *kuri* pitch, the highest standard level used in noh chanting.

In modern performances the *kuri* is often a sort of introductory *shōdan* for the aural high point of the play. It is most often sung by the chorus.

Kurui. *Kusemaiutai shōdan* usually used for texts relating to the aesthetically attractive derangement of the *monogurui* plays.

Kuse. The most common *kusemaiutai shōdan*, often the aural high point of a play. It usually consists of three sections. The chorus sings the first two in low and middle register, the shite (or sometimes another actor) then sings the first lines of the third in the higher register (see *ageha*), whereupon the chorus takes over again, also in the higher register, after which the song is brought to a conclusion in the lower register. *Kuse* delivered while the shite sits still at the middle of the stage are termed *iguse* ("sitting *kuse*"), as opposed to *maiguse* ("dancing *kuse*"), delivered while the shite dances. The *kuse* was adopted into the noh by Kannami from a separate performing art known as Kusemai. In Zeami's day suites built around a *kuse*, consisting of the *shōdan* sequence *shidai-issei-kuri-sashi-kuse-shidai*, were frequently performed as chamber pieces quite apart from full performances of noh. Few of these remain in the modern repertory, but one can find remnants of them, for example, in the play *Hyaku-man*. In this book I term these suites *kusemai* (with a lower-case "k" to distinguish them from the performing art).

Kusemai, *kusemai*, see under *Kuse*.

Kusemaiutai. The less common of two classes of *hiranori shōdan*. The texts of *kusemaiutai shōdan* are marked by a large number of irregular verses (i.e., verses not in 7-5 meter). When they are set to *hiranori* rhythm, the result is a kind of syncopation that provides strong rhythmic interest. *Kusemaiutai shōdan* are therefore frequently found in the aural high point of a play. The most common *kusemaiutai shōdan* is the *kuse*. An example of *kusemaiutai* from the play *Hagoromo* is discussed in Chap. 2, p. 256.

Kyū, see *Jo-ha-kyū*.

Machiutai. An *ageuta* sung by the waki at the end of the *ai*.

Mai. A dance of a primarily abstract nature accompanied solely by instrumentalists and generally performed during the last act or last part of a play. *Mai* such as the CHŪNOMAI and JONOMAI are among the mainstays of noh dancing today and are structured both musically and balletically somewhat like the "theme and variation" form in Western classical music. That is to say, a basic musical or dance configuration is outlined during the first section (*dan*) of the dance, and subsequent sections consist of variations and elaborations on that configuration. Zeami himself mentions both *mai* and *hataraki*, but it is uncertain to what degree those dances resemble the ones that go by those names today.

Makurakotoba. "Pillow word." A rhetorical device. Rather like the Homeric epithet, consisting of a five-syllable phrase conventionally associated with a specific word or set of words. The *makurakotoba* is usually placed directly in front of the word with which it is associated, and usually functions imagistically or for a heightened tone. The golden age of the *makurakotoba* was the age of *Man'yōshū*, and its use declined, both in frequency and in quality thereafter. In noh it is found most characteristically in older, less sophisticated plays.

Martial Mode (*guntai*), see under Three Modes.

Michiyuki. An *ageuta* describing a journey, usually sung at the end of the first *dan* by the waki (and wakitsure).

Mondō. *Kotoba shōdan* in the form of a dialogue, occasionally including isolated lines of *sashinori*.

Monogurui. Literally "a mad person." The *monogurui* is frequently the shite in *gen-*

zai noh. Indeed almost all of the *genzai noh* Zeami wrote are *monogurui* plays. The "madness" such characters exhibit is not of a violent, loud, or psychotic nature. Rather it takes the form of a heightened or somehow deranged sensibility caused usually by longing, grief, or sadness. The typical *monogurui* does not rage and foam at the mouth and curse, but instead shows a hypersensitivity to natural beauty, poetic charms, and the like; and his, or more frequently, her madness provides a kind of entertainment for bystanders. There are also *monogurui* whose "madness" is the result of possession by supernatural beings; these are most common in pre-Zeami plays.

Monomane. Dramatic imitation. Originally the mainstay of Yamato *sarugaku*, *monomane* at one time probably meant the careful and rather naturalistic depiction of a character on stage. Even in his first use of the term, Zeami limits the degree to which certain kinds of characters can be depicted, concentrating on the imitation of elegant upper-class people. In his mature theory *monomane* is consistently subordinated to *yūgen*.

Monozukushi. A catalogue or inventory of members of a class, trees, types of flower, mountains, chapters from *Genji monogatari*, or whatever. Examples of *monozukushi* can be found at least as early as mid-Heian in, for example, Sei Shōnagon's *Makura no sōshi* (Pillow Book). By Kannami's time the *monozukushi* seems to have become primarily a clever sort of amusement for common people in popular songs. In early (i.e. pre-Zeami) noh *monozukushi* are used for verbal interest in *shōdan* such as the *rongi*, and they often bear only the most tenuous relationship to the supposed thematic material of the play. A good example is the *konomizukushi*, "the catalogue of fruits and nuts" in Kannami's *Kayoi Komachi*. See also the "catalogue of trees" in *Kinsatsu* quoted in Chap. 3, pp. 123-24.

Mugen noh. "Phantasmal noh" or "Noh of dreams and apparitions." Plays in which the shite is a being from another dimension of existence, either a god, demon, faerie, or plant spirit or the ghost of a human being. In many *mugen* plays the waki is explicitly said to have gone to sleep, and the second act is a presentation of his dream, thus the "dreams and apparitions" in the word. This thematic element had such influence on the structure of *mugen* plays, however, that plays taking a certain formal configuration may be said to be *mugen noh* even if no explicit mention of dreams and apparitions is made. The majority of Zeami's plays are *mugen noh*. Some scholars consider *waki noh* (in which the shite is a god) a separate category, but in this study, I have considered *waki noh* a subset of *mugen noh*.

Nanori. *Kotoba shōdan* in which a character introduces himself.

NANORIBUE. A noh flute solo played for the entrance of the waki in certain plays.

NARAINOISSEI. A special variant of the ISSEI used for the entry of the shite in a few very highly revered plays. Performed on the *kotsuzumi*, *ōtsuzumi*, and flute.

NARAINOSHIDAI. A special variant of the SHIDAI used for the entry of a character (usually the waki) in a play of particular weight and dignity. Performed on the *kotsuzumi*, *ōtsuzumi*, and flute.

Nōkan. The flute used in noh, which evolved from the *ryūteki* flute of court music, but was altered to produce a highly idiosyncratic scale and set of overtones.

Noncongruent Song (*hyōshi awazu*). One of two major divisions of song style in noh. *Noncongruent song* is delivered with a specific melodic configuration, but without a specific one-to-one relationship between syllables of the text and beats or parts of beats in the music. Cf. *Congruent song*.

Noriji. *Ōnori shōdan* generally used for the appearance of characters from another dimension of existence or, in Zeami's plays, for characters in highly charged states of emotional derangement.

Notto. Solo *sashinori shōdan* written in imitation of a Shinto prayer (*norito*) and usually delivered by a character playing a Shinto priest or shrine attendant.

Ōnori. (Known to Zeami as *kiribyōshi*.) One of three possible configurations of *congruent song* in noh. *Ōnori* allots one syllable of text to one beat in the music with occasional variations and syncopations (see text Fig. 3). *Ōnori shōdan* are used most frequently during the appearance of characters from another dimension of existence—gods, demons, and other supernatural spirits. Zeami, however, uses *ōnori* for the depiction of emotional disorder and intensity. (See Chap. 4, pp. 169-71.) *Ōnori* rhythm is, in modern performance, close to the purely instrumental rhythm used in dances, and frequently provides a bridge between vocal and instrumental sections of a play.

OTOKOMAI. A swift *mai* usually performed by young male shite in *genzai* plays, but also used in some schools' versions of *Atsumori*. Performed on *kotsuzumi*, *ōtsuzumi*, and flute.

Ōtsuzumi (also called *ōkawa*). The larger of two hourglass-shaped drums used in noh. The *ōtsuzumi* is held on the left knee and struck with the right hand. It has a limited range of sounds, but performs a very important role in the rhythm of noh music. Cf. *kotsuzumi*.

RAIJO. Bright exit music for the maejite and entrance music for the aikyōgen. Performed on all three drums and flute.

Rangyoku, see under Five Sounds.

Renbo, see under Five Sounds.

Renga. Linked verse. An extremely popular type of poetry and poetic entertainment from the fourteenth to the eighteenth century. Practitioners gathered together, and one composed a 5-7-5 verse. Someone else then added lines of his own with 7-7-syllable count. A third person capped the 7-7 lines with 5-7-5, and so on for a series of usually 50 or 100 links. *Renga* began as a light entertainment for poets more seriously involved with *waka*, but by Zeami's time *renga* was taken very seriously in its own right and was composed by a wide range of the social classes. The composition of serious *renga* (*ushin renga*) was an extremely complex art with a formidable body of rules and conventions behind it. *Mushin*, less serious or "comic" *renga*, was bound by fewer constraints. Both types of *renga* had an influence on the development of writing for the noh theater, and some influence may have gone in the other direction as well.

Rongi. Tadautai shōdan written as a dialogue between two characters or one or more characters and the chorus. The last part is sung by the chorus.

Sageuta. Short *tadautai shōdan* centering on the middle and lower registers. Sometimes independent, but usually precedes an *ageuta* or *rongi*.

Saku. In Zeami's terms, "the structure." The second of three stages of composition as outlined by Zeami in *Sandō*. *Saku* means the arrangement of *dan* and *shōdan* sequences, which is to take place before the actual writing of the text.

SANDANNOMAI. A form of CHŪNOMAI danced in three sections.

Sarugaku. The artistic predecessor of noh. *Sarugaku* had its origins in temple and shrine entertainments following the rituals during holy days and festivals. In its earliest form it consisted of acrobatics and other circus-like entertainments as well as rudimentary dramatic performances. By Zeami's time there were numerous different regional styles of *sarugaku*. The most important for his career were Yamato *sarugaku* (his own tradition) and Ōmi *sarugaku*.

Sashi. Very common *sashinori shōdan* centering on the higher register. Often used for the delivery of lyric monologues and other texts of which the meaning is particularly important. Zeami calls these *shōdan sashigoto*.

Sashinori. One of two major classes of *shōdan* in *noncongruent song*. *Sashinori shōdan* are delivered with little melodic inflection in a manner somewhat reminiscent of recitative in opera (see text Fig. 2). Because they have neither a strong underlying rhythm nor a melismatic melody, they are among the most readily intelligible *shōdan* in noh and are used when it is particularly important that the audience grasp the precise meaning of the text.

SHIDAI. Common entrance music for the waki or the shite. Played on *kotsuzumi*, *ōtsuzumi*, and flute.

Shidai. Short *tadautai shōdan* used as an introduction to a play, a full *kusemai*, etc. Most frequently composed of a 7-5 line that is repeated and followed by a 7-4 line.

SHINNOISSEI. Majestic entrance music for disguised gods. Performed on the *kotsuzumi*, *ōtsuzumi*, and flute.

SHINNOJONOMAI. An extremely formal slow dance (*mai*) done by aged male gods or elegant female gods mostly in *waki noh*. Performed on all three drums and flute.

SHINNOSHIDAI. Stately entrance music for the waki generally in *waki noh* plays. Performed on *kotsuzumi*, *ōtsuzumi*, and flute.

Sho. In Zeami's terms, "the writing." The writing of the words of a text and the setting of music to that text. The third stage in the composition of a noh play as outlined in *Sandō*.

Shōdan. "Small *dan*." A term coined by Yokomichi Mario to designate the individual songs and spoken passages of which a noh play is composed.

Shu. In Zeami's terms, "the seed." The character or situation around which a noh play is written, the choice of which is the first stage in the composition of a play as outlined by Zeami in *Sandō*.

Shūgen, see under Five Sounds.

Shura. From the Sanskrit, *asura*, "titan." A class of beings whose karma entails constant engagement in battle. Originally superhuman beings with enormous powers. The *shura* in noh plays are more usually the ghosts of famous warriors who appear on stage to relive their past battles or to enact the torments they suffer in hell.

Shuranori, see *Chūnori*.

Sōga. A popular medieval song form that influenced the texts and music of noh.

TACHIMAWARI. Instrumental music, often used to accompany battles. There are numerous variations, some including *taiko*, some omitting it.

Tadautai. The more common of two classes of *hiranori shōdan* used to set standard 7-5 verse texts. *Tadautai shōdan* contain little if any syncopation and are very common in *noh*. The term is Zeami's and does not enjoy wide currency nowadays.

Taiko. A hat-box-shaped drum with two heads played with drumsticks. The *taiko* is only used in certain plays in which the shite has supernatural attributes, and even then, it is only used in the latter part (usually the fifth *dan*) of the play.

TENNYONOMAI, see *Mai*.

Three Modes (*santai*). Three basic approaches to the depiction of characters on the noh stage and the kinds of plays appropriate for such depiction. Sometimes the Three Modes are identifiable as three basic roles in noh, those of the old man, the woman, and the warrior. The idea of the mode, however, is usually broader than this, and indicates an approach to the general tenor of a dramatic portrayal. Zeami frequently refers to the Three Modes as guideposts in the training of an actor. The Aged Mode (*rōtai*) is closely associated with *waki noh* plays, and decorum and formal orthodoxy are major concerns. The Woman's Mode (*nyotai*) of course takes a woman as central character, but a wide range of specific roles is subsumed under this rubric. The Martial Mode (*guntai*) is narrower in range, but is the basis on which demonic roles are to be developed (if they are developed at all). Certain roles fall between the modes; for instance, the role of an old woman partakes of both the Aged Mode and the Woman's Mode, and the role of a mad woman may be tinged with the Martial Mode.

Tsukizerifu. Short *kotoba shōdan* announcing the arrival of a party at a particular place. Often follows the *michiyuki.*

Tsuyogin. One of three possible melodic styles for the vocal music of noh. *Tsuyogin,* the most dynamic and forceful of the styles, has a rather narrow pitch range and a powerful vibrato. See Chap. 2, p. 59.

Tsuzumi, see *Kotsuzumi*; *Ōtsuzumi.*

Two Arts (*nikyoku*). Song and dance, the first task of the child actor and the continuing basis for *yūgen* in any actor's performance.

Uta. Tadautai shōdan not melodically distinctive enough to qualify as an *ageuta* or a *sageuta.*

Waka. Classical Japanese poetic form of 31 syllables arranged 5-7-5-7-7. Also, an *einori shōdan* used directly before or after a dance. (In the text, the *shōdan* is italicized.) The text of a *waka shōdan* consists of a waka or part of one.

Waki noh. "Noh at the side." Congratulatory and formally very orthodox noh plays that appear after ("at the side") of the ritual piece *Shikisanban* (which opens traditional full performances of noh). Zeami says *waki noh* should be straightforward, not too subtle, and have decorous or correct sources (*honzetsu*). Most *waki noh* are of the Aged Mode (see Three Modes) and take an old god as shite, though some are cast in the Woman's Mode. Originally there was probably a relatively close connection between certain *waki noh* (especially of the old Konparu tradition) and the demon noh, but in Zeami's works this connection is all but completely gone.

Woman's Mode (*nyotai*), see under Three Modes.

Yowagin. One of three possible melodic styles for the vocal music of noh. *Yowagin* is the most lyrical and perhaps the best reflection of chanting in Zeami's day. See Chap. 2, p. 59.

Yūgen. An aesthetic ideal originating in Buddhist metaphysics designating the mysterious and dark, a profundity not apparent on the surface. In the poetics of the *Shinkokin* period, *yūgen* means "mystery and depth," and indicates a kind of veiled, deep, melancholy beauty, full of unstated overtones and richness. In his earliest references to it, Zeami identifies *yūgen* as the primary aesthetic aim of the troupes of Ōmi *sarugaku*. He seems to mean by the term an elegant, romantic, feminine, and, in large degree, visual beauty. He also finds *yūgen* in the beauty of a pretty child on stage. *Yūgen* came to occupy a central position in Zeami's treatises from the 1420's on, perhaps an indication of the influence of Ōmi *sarugaku* on his style, and it is seen as an especially important tool for the actor.

Yūkyoku, see under Five Sounds.

Annotated Bibliography

The following list contains all the works cited in this book. However, I have only annotated certain particularly useful and relevant volumes, all of which are in Japanese. Those volumes are marked with asterisks. All Japanese works are published in Tokyo unless otherwise noted. Many of the most useful articles in the field have later appeared in collections of essays on noh. In these cases I have generally omitted citing the original article, listing instead the collection in which it appears, which seems more likely to be available in Western libraries.

Bernstein, Leonard. *The Unanswered Question: Six Talks at Harvard.* Cambridge, Mass., 1976.

Bethe, Monica, and Karen Brazell. *Nō as Performance: An Analysis of the Kuse Scene from Yamamba.* Cornell University East Asia Papers, no. 16 (1978).

Brower, Robert H. *Fujiwara Teika's Hundred Poem Sequence of the Shōji Era.* 1977.

Brower, Robert H., and Earl Miner. *Japanese Court Poetry.* Stanford, Calif., 1961.

Flindt, Willi, and Frank Hoff. "The Life Structure of Noh," *Concerned Theater Japan,* 2 (June 1973): 16-41. Also published separately by Hinoki Shoten, 1973.

Fukuda Hideichi. "Zeami to Yoshimoto," *Geinōshi kenkyū,* 10 (July 1965): 46-50.

*Furutani Chishin, ed. *Yōkyoku zenshū.* 2 vols. 1911. Vol. 1 contains Kanze versions of the then current repertory. Vol. 2 is useful as a source for some 200 plays long since dropped from the repertory.

*Gotō Hajime, Matsuda Tamotsu, and Nishi Isshō, eds. *Chūsei geinō shiryōshū.* 1979. Texts for the study of medieval drama. Of particular relevance are the printed versions of four of Zeami's autograph texts of noh, *Eguchi no nō, Kashiwazaki, Morihisa,* and *Unrin'in.* The *Genna uzukibon* texts of the same plays are included for comparative purposes, as are the modern texts of *Kashiwazaki* and *Unrin'in.* Explanatory notes about noh treatises, historical and rural performance, and noh libretti follow the collection of texts. Some caution is necessary in studying the historical texts because of mistranscriptions.

Hachijōbon kadensho. Kodai chūsei geijutsuron, in *Nihon shisō taikei,* vol. 23. 1973.

*Haga Yaichi and Sasaki Nobutsuna, eds. *Kōchū yōkyoku sōsho.* 3 vols. 1914. A useful source for plays that were actively in the repertory until the early decades of the twentieth century, but have since been dropped.

Hagiwara Izumi. "Nō ni itaru tsuzumi no hensen," 2 parts, *Kanze,* 46.8 (Aug. 1979): 23-31; 46.9 (Sept. 1979): 27-32.

Hare, Thomas. "Linked Verse at Imashinmei Shrine: *Anegakōji Imashinmei Hyakuin,* 1447," *Monumenta Nipponica,* 34.2 (Summer 1979): 169-208.

*Hayakawa Junzaburō. *Enkyoku jūshichi chō, Yōkyoku sue hyakuban.* 1912. A source for obscure plays.

Hayashiya Tatsusaburō, ed. *Kodai chūsei geijutsuronshū*, in *Nihon shisō taikei*, vol. 23. 1973.
Hisamatsu Sen'ichi and Nishio Minoru, eds. *Karonshū, Nōgakuronshū*, in *Nihon koten bungaku taikei*, vol. 65. 1973.
Hisamatsu Sen'ichi, Yamazaki Toshio, and Gotō Shigeo, eds. *Shinkokin wakashū*, in *Nihon koten bungaku taikei*, vol. 28. 1958.
Huey, Robert, tr. "*Sakuragawa*," *Monumenta Nipponica*, 38.3 (Autumn 1983): 295-312.
Ijichi Tetsuo. "Zeami to Nijō Yoshimoto to renga to sarugaku," *Kanze*, 34.10 (Oct. 1967): 3-7.
Imaizumi Hideo, "'Kanze Kojirō gazō no san' no issetsu o megutte," *Nihon rekishi*, 330 (Nov. 1975): 53-68.
Imoto Nōichi and Kidō Saizō, eds. *Rengaronshū, Haironshū*, in *Nihon koten bungaku taikei*, vol. 66. 1961.
Ise monogatari, in *Nihon koten bungaku taikei*, vol. 9. 1957.
Itō Masayoshi. "Yōkyoku *Takasago* zakkō," *Bunrin*, 6 (Mar. 1972): 111-25.
————. "Zeami no kōseiron, sakushiron kara mita *Nonomiya, Teika*," in *Nō: kenkyū to hyōron*, pp. 17-22. 1972.
*Itō Masayoshi and Omote Akira, eds. *Fūshikaden, eiin sanshu*. 1978. Photographic reproductions of historical texts of the *Fūshikaden*, including Book 6, "Kashu," in Zeami's autograph. Brief explanatory notes and a short bibliography of texts and modern Japanese translations of the *Fūshikaden*.
Kami Hiroshi. "Sakuhin kenkyū: *Tadanori*," *Kanze*, 43.3 (Mar. 1976): 4-5.
Kaneko Kinjirō. *Renga haikai shū*, in *Nihon koten bungaku zenshū*, vol. 32. 1974.
*Kanze Hisao. *Kokoro yori kokoro ni tsutauru hana*. 1979. A collection of essays by the late, very talented and wide-ranging actor. Most of the pieces discuss theoretical concerns in Zeami's works from Kanze's practical perspective. Also included is his illuminating comparison of *Izutsu* and *Nonomiya*, "Yakusha to sakuhin," first published in *Tessen*, 265 (Dec. 1978): 5-10.
Kanze Shinkurō ryū tetsuke. 15 vols. 1974-80.
Kanzeryū yōkyoku hyakubanshū, Taiseiban ed. 1973. Texts for the more frequently performed half of the current noh repertory of the Kanze school. Vocal notation in the traditional style, small sketches illustrating high points in each play, and limited information on costuming, staging, and variant performances (*kogaki*) are also included. Similar volumes exist for the other schools of acting, but they are somewhat more difficult to locate, and the musical notation is sometimes a bit less exact.
Kanzeryū yōkyoku zoku hyakubanshū, Taiseiban ed. 1973. A complement to the previous volume with identical format, this contains the rest of the current Kanze repertory.
Kawaguchi Hisao and Shida Nobuyoshi, eds. *Wakan rōeishū, Ryōjin hishō*, in *Nihon koten bungaku taikei*, vol. 73, p. 70. 1965.
Kawase Kazuma, ed. *Tōchū Zeami nijūsambushū*. 1945.
————. *Zeami jihitsu denshoshū*. 1943.
Keene, Donald, ed. *Twenty Plays of the Nō Theatre*. Records of Civilization: Sources and Studies, no. 85. New York, 1970.
*Kitagawa Tadahiko. *Kannami no geiryū*. Miyai sensho books, no. 4. 1978. A collection of mostly previously published journal articles. Kitagawa compares the styles of Kannami, Zeami, Miyamasu, and other playwrights, and argues cogently that Zeami's style in the noh was in many respects a departure from the mainline tradition of his father. He demonstrates similarities between

Kannami and lesser known playwrights such as Miyamasu and Nobumitsu. Also includes articles on the development of *mugen* noh, *Sanemori*, and other medieval literary and performing arts and noh, and an index of play titles.

————. "*Monomane no jōjō kara santai ron e,*" *Bungaku,* 51.7 (July 1983): 47-56.

*————. *Zeami.* Chūkō shinsho books, no. 292. 1972. In this volume Kitagawa discusses literary style and noh theory to some degree, but seems at his best in his very interesting and readable biographical sketch of Zeami. Includes a chronology of Zeami's life and times and a bibliography of major sources, but, unfortunately, no index.

*Kobayashi Shizuo. *Yōkyoku sakusha no kenkyū.* 1974. Originally published in 1942. A pioneering study of the lives of Kannami, Zeami, Konparu Zenchiku, Konparu Zenpō, Kanze Kojirō Nobumitsu, Kanze Yajirō Nagatoshi, and Miyamasu, frequently citing contemporary documents (in *kanbun*). Also includes articles on attribution and style, but they are somewhat impressionistic. An intelligent discussion of the usefulness of the Tokugawa lists of attribution is appended.

*————. *Zeami.* Rev. ed. 1958. A study of Zeami, extremely useful for its biographical information (much of which is included in the previous entry, but is here translated from straight *kanbun* into classical Japanese, i.e., *kakikudashi*). Kobayashi's discussions of Zeami's dramatic treatises and the attribution of plays to him are also careful, if somewhat dated now. Includes a chronology of Zeami's life and a list of his treatises with certain textual information.

*Konishi Jin'ichi. "New Approaches to the Study of the *Nō* Drama," *Tōkyō Kyōiku Daigaku Bungakubu Kiyō,* 5 (1960): 1-31.

*————. *Nōgakuron kenkyū.* Hanawa sensho books, no. 10. 1961. An extremely valuable study of the development of Zeami's dramatic theory and its relation to medieval poetics, Buddhism, and Chinese poetic theory. Konishi's survey of Zeami's thought provides the only attempt at a comprehensive view of Zeami's theoretical corpus available today. At once accessible and rigorous, the book is full of insights reflecting the author's familiarity with both the Eastern and the Western intellectual tradition.

————. *Sōgi.* 1971.

*————, ed. and tr. *Zeamishū,* in *Nihon no shisō,* vol. 8. 1970. A text and modern Japanese translation of all of Zeami's treatises and letters except the *Sarugaku dangi.* Annotations are rather limited, but the modern Japanese translation is very helpful, and the introductory essay provides a good survey of the development of Zeami's dramaturgy. Includes a chronology and bibliography.

*Kōsai Tsutomu. *Nōyō shinkō: Zeami ni terasu.* 1972. As is true of the other three books by Kōsai listed below, this volume is a collection of numerous, usually very brief essays and observations on noh, mostly related in some way to Zeami. This volume contains somewhat more detailed studies of the plays *Ataka, Dōjōji, Sakuragawa,* and *Sanemori.* Also contains the record of an extremely interesting round-table discussion among many of the foremost modern scholars of noh, including Konishi Jin'ichi, Kōsai Tsutomu, Omote Akira, and Yokomichi Mario. There is an index of play titles.

*————. *Zeami shinkō.* 1962. The first of Kōsai's collections of essays on Zeami, this volume contains his important study of the Fuganji temple register in which Zeami's name is mentioned, and three articles relating to Zeami's religious affiliation. Also includes numerous brief notes on difficult vocabulary items from Zeami's treatises.

*————. *Zeshi sankyū.* 1979. A large collection, posthumously published, of brief

notes on vocabulary items from the treatises. Particularly useful is the section on technical terms from noh that appear in the 1603 Japanese-Portuguese dictionary published by the Jesuits (*Nippo jisho*).

*————. *Zoku Zeami shinkō*. 1970. More brief articles relating to Zeami and vocabulary items in his treatises.

*Koyama Hiroshi, Satō Kikuo, and Satō Ken'ichirō, eds. *Yōkyokushū*, vols. 1 and 2, in *Nihon koten bungaku zenshū*, vols. 33 and 34. 1973, 1975. A handsomely produced and carefully selected collection of important noh plays, with informative notes and a modern Japanese translation accompanying each text. Though not as scholarly as the collection edited by Yokomichi and Omote (see below), these volumes have a broader selection of plays, more information on variant performance styles (*kogaki*), and both color and black-and-white photographs. Some of the more representative *aikyōgen* texts are included as well. Vol. 2 contains a very useful glossary of technical terms and an index of all the plays in the collection.

Kubo Fumio. "Kannami shoden ni tsuite no shinken: Iga kara hakken sareta atarashii Kanze keizu ni tsuite," *Kanze*, 24.11 (Nov. 1957): 22-27.

————. "'Kanze-Fukuda keizu' o meguru shomondai," *Kokugo to kokubungaku*, 434 (May 1960): 57-65.

Matisoff, Susan. "Images of Exile and Pilgrimage: Zeami's *Kintōsho*," *Monumenta Nipponica*, 34.4 (Winter 1979): 449-65.

————. "*Kintōsho*: Zeami's Song of Exile," *Monumenta Nipponica*, 32.4 (Winter 1979): 441-58.

Matsuda Tamotsu. *Zeami to nō no tankyū*. 1972.

Matsushita Daisaburō and Watanabe Fumio, eds. *Kokka taikan*. 2 vols. 1942.

Miyake Kōichi. *Fushi no seikai*. Rev. ed. 1977.

————. *Hyōshi seikai*. 1977.

*————. *Utaigeiko no kihonjishiki*. 1975. An intelligent and practically oriented introduction to the vocal music of noh designed for amateur chanters. Miyake Kōichi's other two volumes are more detailed examinations of the rhythm and melody of noh.

*Miyake Noboru. *Nō no enshutsu*. 1948. A very informative introduction to the overall performance of noh with detailed studies of *Bashō, Dōjōji, Eguchi, Funa Benkei, Kagekiyo, Sotoba Komachi, Takasago,* and *Tamura*. Has a short, not terribly well-organized glossary of technical terms.

Morisue Yoshiaki, "Tōgen Zuisen no *Shikishō* ni miru Zeami," in *Nihon bungaku kenkyū shiryō sōsho*, vol. 45: *Yōkyoku, Kyōgen*, pp. 41-46. 1981. Originally published in *Kanze*, 37.2 (Feb. 1970).

Nearman, Mark, tr. and ed. "*Kakyō*," 3 parts, *Monumenta Nipponica*, 37.3 (Autumn 1982): 333-74; 37.4 (Winter 1982): 461-96; 38.1 (Spring 1983): 51-71.

————. "*Kyakuraika*, Zeami's Final Legacy for the Master Actor," *Monumenta Nipponica*, 35.2 (Summer 1980): 153-97.

————. "Zeami's *Kyūi*: A Pedagogical Guide for Teachers of Acting," *Monumenta Nipponica*, 33.3 (Autumn 1978): 299-332.

Nihon koten bungaku taikei, ed. Takagi Ichinosuke et al. 102 vols. 1957-68.

*Niima Shin'ichi, Shida Nobuyoshi, and Asano Kenji, eds. *Chūsei kinsei kayōshū*, in *Nihon koten bungaku taikei*, vol. 44. 1959. Contains *Kanginshū* and *Enkyokushū*.

Nishi Isshō. "Nō no tenkai to seiji," *Kokubungaku*, 23.7 (June 1978): 106-12.

————. "Sakuhin kenkyū: *Michimori*," *Kanze*, 37.7 (July 1970): 3-9.

————. Zeami kenkyū. 1976. Various articles on Zeami's life and relationship to Yoshimitsu, Yoshimochi, and Yoshinori, as well as an examination of *Unrin'in* in its older and newer versions. Includes extensive bibliographical lists and a chronology for Zeami.

Nishino Haruo. "Zeami bannen no nō," *Bungaku,* 39.5 (May 1971): 37-48.

*Nō. Bessatsu Taiyō books, no. 25. 1978. A magnificent collection of photographs and drawings relating to noh with essays ranging from the succinct and scholarly to the impressionistic. The photographs, which cover the history of noh from the fifteenth century on, include not only shots of modern performances, masks, and costuming, but also reproductions of historical documents and prints. Glossaries and explanatory articles serve the needs of scholars as well as those who are encountering noh for the first time.

*Nō: chūsei geinō no kaika, in *Nihon no koten geinō,* vol. 3. 1970. Articles by various scholars on the history, performance practice, and social context of noh. Among the more interesting are Kanze Hisao's "Zeami," an actor's perspective on Zeami's plays, and Mikata Ken's "Nō no enshutsu," concerning especially the *waki noh.*

Nō kyōgen men, in *Nihon no bijutsu,* vol. 108. 1975.

*Nōgaku zensho. 7 vols. 2d rev. ed. 1979-80. A collection of volumes on noh that is almost encyclopedic in its scope. Originally published in 1942-44, the work was revised in 1952-58 and revised again in 1979-80. The first edition remains the center of the enterprise and contains all the important articles in the collection. Some are rather dated, but a large proportion remain relevant to noh studies today. The revised edition was abridged and some of the more important articles in the original were inexplicably omitted. The new revised edition has restored the original contents and added corrections and various appendixes of considerable interest and usefulness. The contents of each volume are outlined below.

Vol. 1: *The Thought and Art of Noh.* Articles relating noh to other Japanese cultural and intellectual fields such as poetics and Buddhism. Appendix: a list and brief discussion of Zeami's and Zenchiku's treatises.

Vol. 2: *The History of Noh.* Articles on the development of noh, covering such subjects as its precursors in the performing arts, patronage, and subsequent influence. Appendixes: genealogies of noh acting families, a noh chronology.

Vol. 3: *The Literature of Noh.* Articles on the structure, authorship, and literary materials in noh. Appendixes: lists of traditional commentaries on plays, new noh plays, translations of noh into Western languages.

Vol. 4: *The Staging of Noh.* Articles on stages and staging, music, dance, etc. Appendixes: lists of variant performance styles (*kogaki*), names of masks.

Vol. 5: *Noh and Kyōgen.* Articles on the companion art, *kyōgen.* Appendixes: lists of *aikyōgen* narratives, new *kyōgen,* translations of *kyōgen* into Western languages.

Vol. 6: *The Appreciation of Noh and Kyōgen.* Articles on the various aesthetic aspects of noh, its visual beauty, its poetic qualities, the acoustics and lighting of the noh stage, etc. Appendixes: lists of the current noh and *kyōgen* repertory, a bibliography for noh, a glossary of technical terms.

Vol. 7: *The Performance of Noh.* Articles discussing various practical aspects of performance from the actors' viewpoint by famous noh and *kyōgen* actors of (mostly) the previous generation. Appendixes: lists of schools of acting, noh stages in Japan, artistic memoirs.

*Nogami Toyoichirō and Tanaka Mitsuru, eds. *Yōkyokushū*, vols. 1-3, in *Nihon koten zenshū*, vol. 72. 1949. A broader selection of noh plays than either Koyama et al. or Yokomichi and Omote. Limited notes.

Nonomura Kaizō. "Zeami fūshi no shikkyaku," *Bungaku* 4.4 (April 1936): 57-71.

*———, ed. *Nihon meicho zenshū: Yōkyoku sanbyaku gojūban shū.* 1927. A useful collection comprising the current repertory and about 100 of the more important plays that have been dropped from it.

*Nose Asaji. *Nōgaku genryūkō.* 1938. A meticulously detailed documentary history of noh covering its precursors (*sarugaku* and *dengaku*) and companion art forms. Careful quotation of an enormous number of documents bearing primarily on the external development of noh, where it was performed, who performed it, who patronized it, which plays were performed, etc. Somewhat disappointing to readers looking for commentary and insight into the aesthetic qualities of individual plays. Appendixes: documented performances of noh between 1429 and 1602, lists of attributions, and Nose's own attributions, now rather dated. Indexed.

Omote Akira. "Ichijō Takegahana kanjin sarugaku," *Tessen*, 250 (Jan. 1977): 4-6.

*———. *Nōgakushi shinkō.* 1979. The first volume of a projected series of Omote's writings on noh. Contains numerous careful studies of Tokugawa noh and *kyōgen* treatises and texts, articles on the *Fūshikaden* and the *Sarugaku dangi*, and Omote's very important article on the attribution of plays to Zeami, "Zeami sakunō kō." Indexed.

———. "Yoshimoto shōsoku kotoba ni tsuite, Tōdōriwa, 59," *Tessen*, 162 (Sept. 1968): 5-7.

———. "Zeami no shōgai o meguru shomondai," *Bungaku*, 31.1 (Jan. 1963): 13-24.

*Omote Akira and Katō Shūichi, eds. *Zeami, Zenchiku*, in *Nihon shisō taikei*, vol. 24. 1974. The most complete edition of Zeami's treatises. Omote's careful philological research has resulted in an extremely useful and reliable volume. The headnotes are technical and sometimes rather difficult. The supplementary notes are indispensable and packed with insights into the relationship among various treatises and plays. The treatises by Zenchiku are not annotated, so their usefulness is limited. Omote's essay on the life and accomplishments of Zeami is far more comprehensive than its brevity would lead one to expect, and is accompanied by a succinct analysis of the textual history of each of Zeami's treatises. There is also a brief note on Zenchiku's eight treatises and a discussion of the textual history of each. Katō has contributed an essay entitled "Zeami's Strategy of Battle, His Theory of Noh."

O'Neill, P. G. *Early Nō Drama: Its Background, Character and Development, 1300-1450.* London, 1958.

———. "The Letters of Zeami: One Received from Jūni Gon-no-kami and Two Sent to Zenchiku," *Nōgaku kenkyū* (Nōgaku kenkyūjo, Hosei University), 5 (1979-80).

———. "The Year of Zeami's Birth: A New Interpretation of *Museki isshi*," *Monumenta Nipponica*, 34.2 (Summer 1979): 231-38.

Rimer, Thomas, tr. "*Taema*," *Monumenta Nipponica*, 25.3-4 (Autumn-Winter 1970): 431-45.

Rimer, Thomas, and Yamazaki Masakazu, trs. *On the Art of the Nō Drama: The Major Treatises of Zeami.* Princeton, N.J., 1984.

Saeki Umetomo, ed. *Kokin wakashū*, in *Nihon koten bungaku taikei*, vol. 8. 1958.

Saku Misao, ed. *Kanshi taikan.* 8 vols. 1943.

*Sanari Kentarō, ed. *Yōkyoku taikan.* 7 vols. 1931-39. Text, annotation, and modern Japanese translation for the plays in the current repertory. A supplementary volume discusses and illustrates various aspects of performance.

Seidensticker, Edward, tr. *The Tale of Genji.* New York, 1976.

*Takemoto Mikio. "*Tennyo no mai* no kenkyū," *Nōgaku kenkyū* (Nōgaku kenkyūjo kiyō), 4 (1978): 93-158. A technically difficult but highly intelligent study of the old *tennyo no mai* dance and its influence on noh dancing, with fascinating insights into the role played by Ōmi *sarugaku* in early noh.

Taketori monogatari, in *Nihon koten bungaku taikei,* vol. 9. 1957.

Tamba Akira. *La Structure musicale du nô, théâtre traditionnel japonais.* Paris, 1974. Translated by Patricia Matore as *The Musical Structure of Nō.* Tokyo, 1983.

*Tanaka Mitsuru, ed. *Mikan yōkyokushū.* 31 vols. Koten bunko, 1963-80. A source of many plays not in the current repertory and unavailable elsewhere.

*Toita Michizō. *Kannami to Zeami.* Iwanami shinsho books, no. 719. 1977. A study of Kannami and Zeami from the perspective of the economic and social structure of Muromachi Japan.

———. "Uguisu." *Kanze,* 33.8 (Aug. 1968): 4-7.

Tyler, Royall. *Pining Wind: A Cycle of Nō Plays.* Cornell University East Asia Papers, no. 17 (1978).

Usui Nobuyoshi. *Ashikaga Yoshimitsu.* 1960.

Waley, Arthur, tr. *The Analects of Confucius.* New York, 1966.

Yabuta Kaichirō. *Nōgaku fudoki: nōgaku no rekishi chiriteki kenkyū.* 1972.

Yamato monogatari, in *Nihon koten bungaku taikei,* vol. 9. 1957.

Yamazaki Masakazu. "Henshin no bigaku: Zeami no geijutsuron," in *Nihon no meicho,* vol. 10: *Zeami,* pp. 7-72. 1975. Translated by Susan Matisoff as "The Aesthetics of Transformation: Zeami's Dramatic Theories," *Journal of Japanese Studies,* 7.2 (1981): 215-57.

Yashima Masaharu. "Sakuhin kenkyū: *Yumi Yawata,*" *Kanze,* 45.1 (Jan. 1978): 6-10.

———. "Zeami saibannen no sakufū," *Kokubungaku kenkyū,* 44 (Mar. 1971): 55-64.

Yasuda, Kenneth. "A Prototypical *Nō* Wig Play: *Izutsu,*" *Harvard Journal of Asiatic Studies,* 40 (1980): 399-464.

———. "The Structure of *Hagoromo,* a Nō Play," *Harvard Journal of Asiatic Studies,* 33 (1973): 5-89.

*Yokomichi Mario. *Nōgeki shōyō.* 1984. A collection of Yokomichi's articles spanning some thirty years and ranging from discussions of textual problems to notes on performance practice and the modern social context of noh and *kyōgen.* Index.

*Yokomichi Mario and Omote Akira, eds. *Yōkyokushū,* vols. 1 and 2, in *Nihon koten bungaku taikei,* vols. 40 and 41. 1960, 1963. A collection of important noh plays arranged according to author. Vol. 1 contains plays by Kannami, Zeami, and Motomasa as well as twelve "old plays." Vol. 2 contains plays by Zenchiku, Miyamasu, Nobumitsu, Nagatoshi, and Zenpō; plays contemporary with Zeami; and other important plays. The standards for attribution are relatively strict. The text for each play reflects the oldest reliable manuscript, and notes are included indicating significant textual variations between this manuscript and other modern versions. Each play is divided into *dan* and *shōdan* in accordance with Yokomichi's analysis of noh structure, and in an essay (which is continued across the two volumes) he carefully introduces his analytical method and its significance for performance. The headnotes and supplementary notes for each play are of uniformly high quality, and the brief introductory page before each play summarizes useful information on attribution, structure, textual history, and the play's individual characteristics. The second volume contains a catalogue and cross-references to common *shōdan* (pp. 24-32) and appendixes on costuming and conventions of pronunciation in noh performance. An indispensable set.

Yoshida Tōgo. *Nōgaku koten: Zeami jūrokubushū.* 1909.

Index

In the entries for individual shōdan, pages on which examples of the shōdan appear are italicized. Purely instrumental shōdan are listed in small caps, as in the text proper. All table mentions of shōdan are indexed.

Index

Library of Congress Cataloging-in-Publication Data

Hare, Thomas Blenman, 1952-
  Zeami's style.

  Bibliography: p.
  Includes index.
  1. Zeami, 1363-1443—Criticism and interpretation.
2. Nō plays—History and criticism. 3. Nō.   I. Title.
PL792.S4Z72   1985   895.6´22   85-17345
ISBN 0-8047-1290-5 (cl.)
ISBN 0-8047-2677-9 (pbk.)

This book is printed on acid-free paper.